Language and Minority Rights

LANGUAGE IN SOCIAL LIFE SERIES

Series Editor: Professor Christopher N Candlin
Chair Professor of Applied Linguistics
Department of English
Centre for English Language Education & Communication Research
City University of Hong Kong, Hong Kong

For a complete list of books in this series see pages *v* and *vi*

Language and Minority Rights

Ethnicity, Nationalism and the Politics of Language

Stephen May

Longman

An imprint of **Pearson Education**

Harlow, England · London · New York · Reading, Massachusetts · San Francisco · Toronto · Don Mills, Ontario · Sydney
Tokyo · Singapore · Hong Kong · Seoul · Taipei · Cape Town · Madrid · Mexico City · Amsterdam · Munich · Paris · Milan

Pearson Education Limited
Edinburgh Gate
Harlow
Essex CM20 2JE
England

and Associated Companies throughout the world

Visit us on the World Wide Web at:
www.pearsoneduc.com

First published 2001

© Pearson Education Limited 2001

The right of Stephen May to be identified as author of this work has been asserted by him in accordance with the Copyright, Designs and Patents Act 1988.

ISBN 0–582–40455–X PPR

British Library Cataloguing-in-Publication Data

A catalogue record for this book is available from the British Library

Library of Congress Cataloging-in-Publication Data

May, Stephen, 1962–
   Language and minority rights : ethnicity, nationalism, and the politics of language / Stephen May.
     p. cm. — (Language in social life series)
  Includes bibliographical references and index.
  ISBN 0–582–40455–X (pbk.)
    1. Linguistic minorities—Civil rights. 2. Language policy. 3. Ethnicity.
  4. Nationalism. 5. Language and education. 6. Language and culture. I. Series.
  P119.315.M39 2001
  306.44′9—dc21   00–052009

Set in 10/12pt Janson Text by 35
Produced by Pearson Education Malaysia Sdn Bhd
Printed in Malaysia, LSP

LANGUAGE IN SOCIAL LIFE SERIES

Series Editor: Professor Christopher N Candlin
Chair Professor of Applied Linguistics
Department of English
Centre for English Language Education & Communication Research
City University of Hong Kong, Hong Kong

To Janet, Ella and Gracie
E toru ngā taku ipo

. . . those who seek to defend a threatened [language] . . . are obliged to wage a total struggle.

(Bourdieu, 1991: 57)

The language of the conqueror in the mouth of the conquered is ever the language of the slave.

(Tacitus)

Contents

Preface

This book is about language but it is not a 'language' book, or at least not in a narrow disciplinary sense. Rather, it is avowedly interdisciplinary. It encompasses debates in the sociology of language, ethnicity and nationalism, sociolinguistics, social and political theory, education, law and history. The principal advantage of interdisciplinary work is the opportunity it provides to draw together a wide range of disciplinary debates (often at variance with each other) on a particular topic – in this case, the contentious question of language and minority rights. In so doing, different disciplinary verities can be critically assessed and, where necessary, challenged and reformulated. The challenges of interdisciplinary work are, at least in my experience, twofold. The first is that it simply takes much longer to get to grips with all the material in question than it might otherwise. Thus, this particular project began life in 1994 and, apart from an 18-month hiatus in 1998–1999, has preoccupied much of my time and energy since. But it also simply could not have been written at all had it not been for my own (almost wholly fortuitous) interdisciplinary background in sociolinguistics, education and sociology. The second challenge is actually to present something informed and worthwhile at the end of it all, rather than something superficial or, at worst, simply misinformed. I leave the reader to judge how well I have done here, but do take full responsibility for any oversimplification and/or misrepresentation that may occur in the following pages.

And while I am offering caveats, here are a few more. First, it will soon become apparent to the reader, if it is not so already, that I am personally committed both to the extension of minority-language rights and, concomitantly, to a greater recognition of cultural and linguistic plurality within modern nation-states. This in turn is a consequence of my long and active involvement in issues of multicultural and bilingual education over the years, beginning as a teacher and then teacher educator in Aotearoa / New Zealand. On this basis, some critics might suggest that my argument is a 'moralistic' one rather than a form of 'disinterested' academic enquiry (see, for example, J. Edwards, 1985: 144). I do not accept this critique or the distinction on which it is based. *All* positions that are taken on language and minority rights – academic or otherwise – involve a moral dimension, reflecting the particular values and ideologies of their exponents (cf. Woolard, 1998; Blommaert, 1999b). Ideology is not the sole preserve of minority-language proponents, although it is often painted as such. Seen in this light, the equation of academic disinterestedness with scepticism towards, and/or criticism of, minority languages may be seen for what it is – an ideological move in the wider politics of language, nothing more. Indeed, as I will argue, such a move may simply act to reinforce the hegemony of dominant ethnic groups, and the languages they speak, within modern nation-states.

Second, and more broadly, this position is consonant with debates in critical theory on the *situatedness* of any academic enquiry. As I have argued elsewhere (May, 1994a, 1997a), all research is value-laden and, as such, a researcher *must* begin from a theoretical position of some description, whether this is articulated or not in the ensuing study. Accordingly, it is better to state one's position at the start than to cloak it in the guise of apparent neutrality. Not only that, critical social research, of which the following forms a part, is not content with the interpretive concern of 'describing' a social setting 'as it really is', since this assumes an objective, 'commonsense' reality where none exists. Rather, this 'reality' should be viewed as a social and cultural *construction*, linked to wider power relations, which privileges some, and disadvantages other participants. As we shall see, the discourses of language and minority rights are prime sites where such power relations are articulated and outworked.

On a more technical note, since much of what follows is also concerned with the particular roles and functions of minority languages within modern nation-states, and the questions of their status, use and value, I have deliberately chosen not to follow the usual publishing procedure of italicising non-English words and phrases. This is not to imply their subsumption within English. Rather, it aims to act as a visual metaphor for a central tenet of my account – that the *normalisation* of minority languages within the public domain is a legitimate and defensible sociological, political and linguistic activity.

Finally, some thanks are due. I am grateful to the Colin McCahon Trust and the Robert McDougall Art Gallery for granting copyright and reproduction rights, respectively, for the Colin McCahon painting, *Light falling through a dark landscape (A)* (1972) that graces the front cover. McCahon (1919–1987) is the most celebrated modern painter of my native country, Aotearoa / New Zealand (see Brown, 1984; Wood, 1997), and I was particularly drawn to this painting because its metaphorical sense of hope against great odds captures so well the key concerns and themes of this book.

I would also like to thank the wide range of colleagues, many of whom I also count as friends, who have contributed either directly or indirectly over

This is a fine example of a rich, innovative and pluralistic interpretation of minority language rights and needs the world over, attending to national minority, indigenous and immigrant groups. Stephen May recognizes the true complexity of social identity and seeks to foster governmental arrangements that are equally varied and fair, both for the minorities and the states involved. His is a truly admirable example of scholarship and dedication, one that more scholars, students, writers and officials everywhere should emulate. With this book, cultural democracy arguments take a real step ahead. Bravo!

Professor Joshua A. Fishman, Stanford University and Yeshiva University

Language and Minority Rights is a book of international significance – Stephen May's most important contribution yet to current debates on the languages of the world and their survival. In a comprehensive, wide-ranging, interdisciplinary style, he provides much depth of analysis, originality in treatment and a hugely international understanding of current issues with respect to cultural and linguistic pluralism. The book is an excellent example of how interdisciplinarity raises the level of understanding and debate and the result is a vigorous and sophisticated defence of group-based rights for minority languages in the modern world. The book deserves to be in every college library and will become essential reading on many courses in sociolinguistics, the sociology of language, education, ethnicity, language planning and language rights. This is a top-rank, major contribution to international literature on the languages of the world.

Professor Colin Baker, University of Wales at Bangor

Language and Minority Rights is a new comprehensive analysis of ethnicity, nationalism, the politics of language and language planning. Designed as an interdisciplinary source-book, it covers a wide range of issues central to the major concerns of the study of language politics, policy and planning. Indeed, no fundamental issue of current interest has been omitted. Critical discussion of research methods, a balanced input of sociological and linguistic literature and an impressive bibliography make *Language and Minority Rights* an essential source for sociologists, anthropologists, ethnolinguists, contact linguists and scholars in political science and language policy. Furthermore, the book is written in a fluent and accessible style, with invaluable material based on recent references in the field guiding the reader through well structured and well defined chapters. I recommend that it should be purchased by all scholars involved in the fast developing interdisciplinary discourse on the implementation of language politics and, more broadly, by anyone interested in the future of languages in Europe and beyond.

Professor Peter Nelde, Katholieke Universiteit, Brussel

Introduction

This book attempts the unenviable and increasingly unfashionable task of defending the ongoing relevance and importance of minority languages in the modern world. This task is unenviable because so many of these languages are currently in rapid decline. Of the estimated 6000 languages spoken in the world today (Krauss, 1992; Grimes, 1996), it is predicted on present trends that between 20 per cent and 50 per cent will 'die' by the end of the twenty-first century (Krauss, 1992, 1995). Obviously, language death, or the extinction of a language, occurs when the last speaker of that language dies. But, in effect, once a language ceases to be spoken by a *community* of speakers, it has effectively already perished (see Baker and Prys Jones, 1998: 150). Language decline and language death always occur in bilingual or multilingual contexts, in which a 'majority' language – that is, a language with greater political power, privilege and social prestige – comes to replace the range and functions of a 'minority' language.[1] The inevitable result of this process is that speakers of the minority language 'shift' over time to speaking the majority language.

The process of language shift described here usually involves three broad stages. The first stage sees increasing pressure on minority-language speakers to speak the majority language, particularly in formal language domains; a state of affairs described in sociolinguistics as 'diglossia'. This stage is often precipitated and facilitated by the introduction of education in the majority language. It leads to the eventual decrease in the functions of the minority language, with the public or official functions of that language being the first to be replaced by the majority language. The second stage sees a period of bilingualism, in which both languages continue to be spoken concurrently. However, this stage is usually characterised by a decreasing number of minority-language speakers, especially among the younger generation, along with a decrease in the fluency of speakers as the minority language is spoken less, and employed in fewer and fewer language domains. The third and final stage – which may occur over the course of two or three generations, and sometimes less – sees the replacement of the minority language with the majority language. The minority language may be 'remembered' by a residual group of language speakers, but it is no longer spoken as a wider language of communication (Baker and Prys Jones, 1998).

A well-known alternative formulation of this process, which also usefully charts a minority language's private and public functions in relation to the nation-state (see below), is found in Joshua Fishman's 'Graded Intergenerational Disruption Scale' (see 1991: 81–121). In this eight-point scale, Stage 1 is seen as the most secure position for a minority language (with the proviso that intergenerational family transmission continues to occur; see Chapter 4) while Stage 8 is seen as the least secure. The various stages may be paraphrased as:

Stage 1: some use of the minority language (henceforth ML) in higher level educational, occupational, governmental and media realms

Stage 2: ML used in lower governmental and media spheres

Stage 3: use of the ML in the work sphere, involving (informal) interaction between ML and other language speakers

Stage 4: ML use as medium of instruction in education

Stage 5: informal maintenance of literacy in the home, school and community

Stage 6: intergenerational family transmission of the ML

Stage 7: while the ML continues to be spoken, most speakers of the ML are beyond childbearing age

Stage 8: remaining speakers of a ML are old and usually vestigial users

Of course, such language loss and language shift have always occurred – languages have risen and fallen, become obsolete, died, or adapted to changing circumstances in order to survive, throughout the course of human history. But what is qualitatively (and quantitatively) different as we enter the twenty first century is the unprecedented scale of this process of decline and loss – some commentators have even described it as a form of 'linguistic genocide' (Day, 1985; Skutnabb-Kangas, 2000). Such claims may seem overwrought and/or alarmist but they are supported by hard data. For example, a survey by the US Summer Institute of Linguistics, published in 1999, found that there were 51 languages with only one speaker left, 500 languages with fewer than 100 speakers, 1500 languages with fewer than a 1000 speakers, and more than 3000 languages with fewer than 10,000 speakers. The survey went on to reveal that as many as 5000 of the world's 6000 languages were spoken by fewer than 100,000 speakers. It concluded, even more starkly, that 96 per cent of the world's languages were spoken by only four per cent of its people (Crystal, 1999a, b). These figures graphically reinforce an earlier suggestion made by Michael Krauss (1992, 1995) that, in addition to the 50 per cent of languages that may die within the next century, a further 40 per cent of languages are 'threatened' or 'endangered'. Given the processes of language shift and decline outlined above, and the current parlous state of many minority languages, it is not hard to see why. Even majority languages are no longer immune to such processes, not least because of the rise of English as a global language (Crystal, 1997a, b; see Chapter 6). Thus, if Krauss is to be believed, as few as 600 languages (10 per cent) will survive in the longer term – perhaps, he suggests, even as few as 300.

Language loss: a question of biology or power?

Given the scale of language loss that is projected here, comparisons are increasingly made between endangered languages and endangered animal and plant species. As Steven Pinker observes, 'the wide-scale extinction of languages [currently underway] is reminiscent of the current (though less severe) wide-scale extinction of plant or animal species' (1995: 259). Likewise, James Crawford argues that each 'fall[s] victim to predators, changing environments, or more successful competitors', each is encroached upon by 'modern cultures abetted by new technologies' and each is threatened by 'destruction of lands and livelihoods; the spread of consumerism and other Western values . . .' (1994: 5). Conversely, some commentators have observed that when biodiversity is high, so too are cultural and linguistic diversity (see Harmon, 1995; Maffi, 2000).

The use of biological, evolutionary metaphors to describe the plight of many of today's minority languages seems particularly apposite, not least because such metaphors highlight the scale and seriousness of the potential loss of such languages to the world. But biological metaphors also contribute, ironically, to the equanimity with which potential language loss on such a scale is usually greeted. And this brings me to the second obstacle that one faces in the task of defending and promoting minority languages, its unfashionableness. In effect, biological metaphors reinforce, by implication, a widely held view that language loss is an inevitable part of the cycle of social and linguistic evolution. Thus, one could view the loss or death of a language as simply a failure on its part, or its speakers, to compete adequately in the modern world where, of course, only the fittest languages can (and should) survive. This form of linguistic social Darwinism is widely articulated by majority-language speakers – conveniently secure in their own linguistic and cultural heritage – but it is by no means limited to them. Many minority-language speakers likewise see their social, cultural and economic advancement, or evolution, in the guise of a majority language.

But in another more important sense, biological metaphors obscure the wider social and political factors at work in language loss. Language loss is not only, perhaps not even primarily, a linguistic issue – it has much more to do with power, prejudice, (unequal) competition and, in many cases, overt discrimination and subordination. As Noam Chomsky asserts: 'Questions of language are basically questions of power' (1979: 191). Thus, it should come as no surprise that the vast majority of today's threatened languages are spoken by socially and politically marginalised and/or subordinated national-minority and ethnic groups. I will distinguish analytically between these various minority groups later in this Introduction (see Chapter 2 for an extended discussion). Suffice it to say at this point that these groups have been variously estimated at between 5000 and 8000 (Stavenhagen, 1992) and include within them the 250–300 million members of the world's indigenous peoples (Tully, 1995; Davis, 1999), perhaps the most marginalised of all people groups. As Crawford (1994) notes, language death seldom occurs in communities of wealth and privilege, but rather to the dispossessed and disempowered. Moreover, linguistic dislocation for a particular community of speakers seldom, if ever, occurs in isolation from sociocultural and socio-economic dislocation as well (Fishman, 1995a). The loss of a minority language almost always forms part of a wider process of social, cultural and political displacement.

Situating languages, and language loss, within the wider context of social and political power leads to a further recognition: that biological metaphors understate, or simply ignore, the historical, social and political *constructedness* of languages (Hamel, 1997a, b). If languages, and the status attached to them, are the product of wider historical, social and political forces, we can discount the process of 'natural selection' that a biological account would seem to imply. There is nothing 'natural' about the status and prestige attributed to particular majority languages and, conversely, the stigma that is often attached to minority languages, or to dialects.[2] Indeed, this is clearly illustrated by the fact that the same language may be regarded as both a majority *and* a minority language, depending on the context. Thus Spanish is a majority language in Spain and many Latin American states, but a minority language in the USA (cf. Chapters 6 and 7). Even the term 'language' itself indicates this process of construction, since what actually constitutes a language, as opposed to a dialect for example, remains controversial (see Mühlhäusler, 1996; Romaine, 2000). Certainly, we cannot always distinguish easily between a language and a dialect on *linguistic* grounds, since some languages are mutually intelligible, while some dialects of the same language are not. The example often employed here is that of Norwegian, since it was regarded as a dialect of Danish until the end of Danish rule 1814. But it was only with the advent of Norwegian independence from Sweden in 1905 that Norwegian actually acquired the status of a separate language, albeit one that has since remained mutually intelligible with both Danish and Swedish. Contemporary examples can be seen in the former Czechoslovakia, with the emergence in the early 1990s of distinct Czech and Slovak varieties in place of a previously common language. While in the former Yugoslavia, we are currently seeing the (re)development of separate Serbian and Croatian language varieties in place of Serbo-Croat (see Chapter 4).

What these latter examples clearly demonstrate is that languages are 'created' out of the politics of state-making, not – as we often assume – the other way around (Billig, 1995). Independence for Norway and the break-up of the former Czechoslovakia and Yugoslavia have precipitated linguistic change, creating separate languages where previously none existed. These examples highlight, in turn, the centrality of the nation-state to the processes of language formation and validation, the significance of which I will examine more fully in the next section.[3] The pivotal role of the nation-state here in determining what is and what is not a language might also help to explain the scale of the projected language loss discussed earlier. One only has to look at the number of nation-states in the world today, at approximately 200, and the perhaps 300 or so languages that are projected to survive long term, to make the connection. That many of these languages are already recognised as either national or regional languages, or are currently spoken by groups who wish them to become so, serves only to strengthen this connection further (see Gellner, 1983: 43–50). Such is the narrow concentration of 'officially recognised' languages that around 120 nation-states have actually adopted either English, French, Spanish or Arabic as their official language, while another 50 have a local language as the language of the state (Colin Williams, 1996). In addition, Mackey (1991) notes that there are 45 languages that are accorded regional status. In short, currently less than 1.5 per cent of the world's languages are recognised officially by nation-states.

Nation-states, nationalism and nation-state congruence

Why then are nation-states, and the ideology of nationalism that underpins them, so central to the question of minority-language loss? The first and obvious response to this question is that we continue to live in the era of the nation-state. The nation-state remains the bedrock of the political world order, exercising internal political and legal jurisdiction over its citizens, and claiming external rights to sovereignty and self-government in the present interstate system. There are obvious advantages to the nation-state that help to explain its ongoing ascendancy. It liberates individuals from the tyranny of narrow communities, guarantees their personal autonomy, equality and common citizenship, and provides the basis for a collectively shared way of life (Parekh, 1995a). Or at least it does so in theory. As such, it is often viewed as the apogee of modernity and progress – representing in clear political terms the triumph of universalism over particularism.

The 'triumph' of universalism with respect to language is evidenced by the replacement over time of a wide variety of language varieties spoken within a nation-state's borders with one 'common' national language (sometimes, albeit rarely, a number of national languages). This process usually involves the *legitimation* and *institutionalisation* of the chosen national language. Legitimation is understood to mean here the formal recognition accorded to the language by the nation-state – usually, by the constitutional and/or legislative benediction of official status. Institutionalisation refers to the process by which the language comes to be accepted, or 'taken for granted', in a wide range of social, cultural and linguistic domains or contexts, both formal and informal. Both elements achieve a central requirement of the modern nation-state – that all its citizens adopt a common language and culture for use in the civic or public realm. At the same time, the chosen 'national' language comes to be associated with modernity and progress, while the remaining minority languages become associated with tradition and obsolescence.

The requirement of speaking a common language is unique to nation-states, and a relatively recent historical phenomenon. It is unique because previous forms of political organisation did not require this degree of linguistic uniformity. For example, empires were quite happy for the most part to leave unmolested the plethora of cultures and languages subsumed within them – as long as taxes were paid, all was well. The Greek and Roman Empires are obvious examples here, while 'New World' examples include the Aztec and Inca Empires of Central and South America respectively. More recent historical examples include the Austro-Hungarian Empire's overtly multilingual policy. But perhaps the clearest example is that of the Ottoman Empire, which actually established a formal system of 'millets' (nations) in order to accommodate the cultural and linguistic diversity of peoples within its borders (see Dorian, 1998).

It is historically recent because nation-states are themselves the product of the nationalisms of the last few centuries, beginning most notably with the French Revolution (see Chapter 2). Specifically, the emphasis on cultural and linguistic homogeneity associated with the rise of political nationalism is predicated on the notion of 'nation-state congruence'. Nation-state congruence holds that the boundaries of political and national identity should coincide. The view here is that people who are citizens of a particular state should also, ideally, be members of the same national collectivity. Ernest Gellner's definition of nationalism as a 'theory of political legitimacy which requires that ethnic boundaries should not cut across political ones' (1983: 1) clearly illustrates this standpoint.

The inevitable consequence of this political imperative is the establishment of an ethnically exclusive and culturally and linguistically homogeneous nation-state – a realm from which minority languages and cultures are effectively banished. Indeed, this is the 'ideal' model to which most nation-states (and nationalist movements) still aspire – albeit, as we shall see, in the face of a far more complex (and contested) multiethnic and multilinguistic reality. As Nancy Dorian summarises it: 'it is the concept of the nation-state coupled with its official standard language . . . that has in modern times posed the keenest threat to both the identities and the languages of small [minority] communities' (1998: 18). Florian Coulmas observes, even more succinctly, that 'the nation-state as it has evolved since the French Revolution is the natural enemy of minorities' (1998: 67).

And this brings me to the second response to the question of the inter-relationship between the nation-state and language loss. Despite the nation-state's current ascendancy, and its related normalisation and valorisation, it has in recent years come under increasing pressure – both from above and below. From above, the inexorable rise of globalisation, along with the burgeoning influence of multinational corporations and supranational political organisations, have required modern nation-states to reevaluate the limits of their own political and economic sovereignty. From below, minority groups are increasingly exerting the right either to form their own nation-states – as seen in various secessionist and irredentist movements around the world – or for greater representation within *existing* nation-state structures. It is this last development, and its implications for the social, cultural and political organisation of nation-states, which are most pertinent to the issue of minority-language loss and displacement. In effect, minority groups are increasingly beginning to question and contest the principles and effects of nation-state congruence, not least because of the long historical proscription of minority languages and cultures that has usually attended it. In the process, national identity, its parameters, and its constituent elements, have been opened up for debate – particularly with respect to questions of bilingualism and multiculturalism (see Chapter 3).

Nationalism, ethnicity and language

The significance of the nation-state, and political nationalism, to the issues of language loss and language rights raises another important question. Why has so little actually been written on the interrelationship between nationalism and language, since it is clear that this interrelationship is crucial to a fuller understanding of the processes at work here? The reason for this absence, it seems to me, can be explained largely by the hermetic nature of academic boundaries. Put simply, sociolinguists and social and political theorists have seldom engaged directly with each other's arguments in the complex and contested domains of language and nationalism, or in the related areas of ethnicity and identity politics. This lack of engagement, or dialogue, is compounded by the often radically different perspectives on the language–identity link adopted in these different academic fields of enquiry.

Thus, there is within sociolinguistics and the sociology of language a longstanding and extensive literature on issues pertaining to language loss and language shift. However, with the notable exceptions of Jan Blommaert (1996, 1999c; see also Blommaert and Verschueren, 1992, 1998), John Edwards (1985, 1994), Joshua Fishman (1989 a, b, c, 1999) and Sue Wright (1999, 2000), very little effort has been made to frame discussion of these issues within the wider contexts of ethnicity and nationalism. This is unfortunate, not least because sociological commentators, unlike sociolinguists, have generally been loath to apportion a prominent role to language in the explanation of minority ethnic and national identity claims. In this respect, the general orthodoxy among theorists of ethnicity and nationalism, at least until recently, has been that there is no necessary relation between particular cultural attributes, such as language, and particular (group) identities. Language is but one cultural marker among many and not even a particularly important one at that (see Chapter 1), or at least so it seems. This position immediately problematises the intrinsic link between language and identity that is normally presupposed in many sociolinguistic discussions of language loss.

Similarly, there is now a burgeoning literature on the topic of linguistic human rights (see Tollefson, 1991; Phillipson, 1992; Skutnabb-Kangas and Phillipson, 1995; Hamel, 1997c; Kontra et al., 1999; Phillipson, 2000; Skutnabb-Kangas, 1998, 2000). This literature highlights effectively and well the wider political and social processes underlying minority language loss and advocates, in response, that minority languages, and their speakers, should be accorded at least some of the protections and institutional support that majority languages already enjoy. These arguments are also echoed in much of the academic legal discourse that has developed in recent years with respect to minority-group rights (see Capotorti, 1979; Thornberry, 1991a, b; de Varennes, 1996a, b). However, both these sets of literature seldom engage directly with the problematic questions, much discussed in social and political theory, of what actually constitutes a 'group' and, given the complexities involved in defining groups (see below), whether any rights (linguistic or otherwise) can actually be attributed to them.

The principal problem here is that advocates of linguistic human rights tend to assume the identity of linguistic minority groups as given, the collective aims of linguistic minority groups as uniform, and the notion of collective rights as unproblematic. Thus Skutnabb-Kangas and Phillipson (1995) argue that the notion of linguistic human rights is reflected at the level of linguistic communities by the *collective* rights of peoples to maintain their ethnolinguistic identity and difference from the dominant society and its language. I agree with this in principle, but the way the argument is formulated assumes that the linguistic community in question is easily definable in the first place – or, rather, that all members of this group are (or will want to be) principally identified and identifiable by their language. And yet this simply cannot be assumed, not least because of the processes of language shift and loss, discussed earlier, which may already have led many group members to abandon the minority language in question and/or any identification they may have had with it. This, in turn, highlights the essentially contested nature of 'collective' aims. Even if some level of collective consensus is reached about language, or indeed any other aspect of group life – and this in itself is no easy task – there will always be individuals who will choose to dissent from these conclusions (Bentahila and Davies, 1993; J. Edwards, 1985, 1994). This common disjuncture between 'individual' and 'collective' aims immediately problematises the legitimacy of *any* claim to a group-based minority-language right, whatever its social and political merits.

So, if advocates of linguistic human rights are ever to carry the day, they must address more adequately the complexities – and, at times, contradictions – that surround debates on individual and collective identities, and their associated rights' claims. As a first step, the question of the link between language and identity needs to be critically examined, not just assumed. Second, the contingent nature of linguistic identity – as one of many (sometimes) competing identities available to the minority language speaker – needs to be acknowledged and accommodated. And third, the legitimacy of any group-based claim to rights needs to be defended in relation to a political system of nation-states and a political ideology of liberalism that are both predicated on the notion of *individual* citizenship rights.

Overview

It is with all these various questions in mind that I will attempt in this book a theoretical and practical defence of minority languages in the modern world. In Chapter 1, I highlight the pejorative perception of ethnicity – and, by extension, ethnic-minority groups, and the languages they speak – apparent in much academic and political discourse. This is primarily a result of the unfavourable juxtaposition of ethnicity with the nation-state – the one associated with primitivism and particularism, the other associated with modernity and universalism. From this, I explore in detail the various academic debates on ethnicity and, in particular, the broad polarisation between 'primordial' and 'situational' perspectives that marks the field. The former ascribes to ethnicity an enduring, intrinsic character that is associated with, and determined by, particular objective cultural characteristics – the 'cultural stuff' of ethnicity such as language, ancestry and history. The latter rejects this position as essentialist[4] and argues instead for the social and political constructedness of ethnicity, its fluidity and malleability, and its instrumental mobilisation to particular political ends. A situational account of ethnicity also specifically rejects any significant or even any particular link between ethnicity and language.

I tend largely to concur with a situational view of ethnicity. On this basis, I argue that language *is* a contingent marker of ethnic identity and that adopting any other position involves, inevitably, an essentialised view of the language–identity link. However, I believe that constructivist accounts of ethnicity have, at the same time, understated the collective purchase of ethnicity, and its often close links to particular, historically associated languages. Thus, a situational view of ethnicity cannot account adequately for the often prominent role that historically associated languages play in the identity claims and the political mobilisation of many minority movements in the world today (see Weinstein, 1983, 1990; Blommaert, 1996; Laitin, 1998; Safran, 1992, 1999). In theory, language may well be just one of many markers of identity. In practice, it is often much more than that.

In order to explain these apparent contradictions, I argue that the primordial/situational dichotomy of ethnicity is in the end unhelpful and unnecessary and that one can, and should, combine elements of the two (cf. R. Jenkins, 1994, 1997; Smaje, 1997; Fenton, 1999). Thus, ethnicity needs to be viewed *both* as constructed and contingent, *and* as a social, political and cultural form of life. In this sense, ethnic identities are not simply representations of some inner psychological state, nor even particular ideologies about the world (Billig, 1995). Rather, they are social, cultural and political *forms of life* – material ways of being in the modern world. To this end, I employ Bourdieu's (1977, 1990 a, b) notion of 'habitus' and Anthony Smith's (1986, 1991, 1995a) notion of 'ethnie' as useful means to theorise this position. In so doing, I also draw on related debates on the significance (and limits) of postmodernist conceptions of hybridity, syncretism and 'new ethnicities'.

I take much the same stance in Chapter 2, where I examine parallel debates on nationalism and the construction (and constructedness) of nation-states. Debates on nationalism, like those on ethnicity, have tended to polarise around essentialist and constructivist accounts. The former position, most often articulated by nationalists themselves, views nations as 'perennial', as if they have always existed in one form or other. In its most extreme form, it also equates nations directly with ethnocultural communities that are, in turn, defined by fixed cultural characteristics – particularly, but not exclusively, a common language. The latter position, which most academic commentators on nationalism have adopted, points to the formation of nation-states as a specific product of eighteenth- and nineteenth-century nationalisms and the related processes of industrialisation and modernisation (see, especially, Gellner, 1983; Hobsbawm, 1990; Anderson, 1991). This 'modernist' view thus attempts to debunk the central claim of many nationalist movements in the modern world – that the right to nationhood is based principally on *preexisting* ties of ethnicity. Rather, it stresses the contingent nature of national identities. National identities, like any other, are created out of particular sociohistorical conditions, are variable in salience depending on context, are subject to change, and are always out-worked in a complex interrelationship with other forms of social relations and identity.

Again, I tend to concur broadly with modernist accounts of nationalism. Be that as it may, the key problem with such accounts is their inability to explain away the *ongoing* influence of ethnicity and nationalism in the modern world (cf. Hutchinson, 1994; A. Smith, 1986, 1995a, b, 1998). After all, if modernism has now largely been achieved, and the nation-state is its apogee, so too should ethnic and national movements have atrophied. And yet this is clearly not the case. Thus, I suggest again that a middle position may be a more helpful way forward here – one that acknowledges not only the 'legal-political' dimensions of nationalism but also the 'cultural-historical' (A. Smith, 1995a). This avoids the modernist mistake of valorising the former over the latter – that is, perceiving the end product of nationalism, the nation-state, as principally a political rather than an ethnocultural/ethnolinguistic community (when in fact it is both). This in turn arises from the modernist concern to disavow *any* link between ethnicity and nationalism (see, for example, Hobsbawm, 1990). As we shall see, however, such a position conflates the nation and the state (Guibernau, 1996, 1999). In so doing, it fails to explore adequately the differential power relations that underlie the representation of the language and culture of the dominant ethnie, or majority ethnic group, *as that* of the *civic* culture of the nation-state (cf. Kymlicka, 1989, 1995a; Billig, 1995). The result is the marginalisation of a range of sociological minorities within modern nation-states whose languages and cultures are consigned to the private sphere.

The claims of minorities for greater representation within existing nation-states – particularly with respect to their languages and cultures – are explored further in Chapter 3 in relation to political theory. Here, I examine the prominent debate concerning the respective merits of individual and group-differentiated rights, as represented by the proponents of orthodox liberalism and multiculturalism, respectively (see also May, 1999a, 2001). Much of the debate, as perhaps one might expect, favours the former over the latter. Individual rights, which are associated with citizenship and the apparent neutrality of the civic realm, are valorised for their universalism, their protection of fundamental liberal freedoms, and their strict impar-tiality. Group-differentiated rights are viewed far more sceptically, often hostilely, by liberal commentators. They are most often associated with par-ticularism and the potential illiberality that may result – some would argue, *always* results – when one apportions rights differently between groups (see, for example, Rorty, 1991; Schlesinger, 1992; Waldron, 1993, 1995). My own position, following Iris Young (1990, 1993, 1997), Will Kymlicka (1989, 1995a, b) and Charles Taylor (1994), is that group-differentiated rights are defensible as long as they retain within them the protection of individual liberties. Of course, combining the two is not always easy. Nonetheless, I argue that such an alternative is necessary because the present articulation of individual rights within political liberalism implicitly, and at times explicitly, supports the hegemony[5] of the dominant ethnie within nation-states, along with the languages they speak.

The literature on group-differentiated rights is also useful in helping to distinguish between differing levels of group-based rights available to particular minority groups. Following Will Kymlicka (1995a), such groups can be described variously as national, ethnic and other social/cultural minorities. National minorities, including indigenous peoples, comprise those groups who retain a historical association with a particular territory but who have been subject to conquest, colonisation and/or confederation in that territory. Ethnic minorities comprise those individuals and groups who have migrated to another country, and have subsequently settled there. Other social and cultural minorities include 'new social movements' such as gays, women and the disabled. To each of these groupings, Kymlicka accords particular group-based rights: 'self government', 'polyethnic' and 'special representation' rights, respectively (although groups may well have access to more than one set of rights, depending on their circumstances). Self-government rights acknowledge that the nation-state is not the sole preserve of the majority (national) group and that legitimate national minorities have the right to equivalent inclusion and representation in the civic realm. Polyethnic rights are intended to help ethnic (and/or religious) minority groups to continue to express their cultural, linguistic and religious heritage, principally in the private domain, without it hampering their success within the economic and political institutions of the dominant national society. Finally, special-representation rights are a response to some systemic disadvantage in the political process that limits a particular group's view from being effectively represented. In line with Kymlicka's general argument, I will suggest that with respect to language, national minorities have access to qualitatively greater rights than other minority groups. However, this does not presuppose that the latter have no basis for greater linguistic rights; quite the reverse, in fact, as I proceed to demonstrate in Chapters 4 and 5.

The arguments outlined thus far help to unravel the complex dynamics that link nationalism, language and identity, and their equally complex (and contested) political articulation in the form of individual and group-based rights. Having thus addressed these questions and controversies directly, I return in Chapter 4 to questions of language loss and language shift, and the social, political and linguistic processes underlying them. Drawing principally upon sociolinguistic and sociology of language literature, I explore the link between particular languages and particular ethnic and/or national identities. In line with my previous discussions on ethnicity and nationalism, I argue here that a historically associated language is not a necessary marker of such identities, not least because of the growing prevalence of 'minority language shift' (Fishman, 1991). The loss of Irish and its replacement by

English in Ireland, provides an apposite example which I discuss at some length. However, I also critique the view held by some sociolinguists that particular languages are peripheral to one's identity, and the related implication that minority-language shift is an inevitable, voluntary and beneficial process for minority groups (cf. J. Edwards, 1985, 1994). Rather than being about 'modernisation', as it is often constructed, this process is more often about differential power relations than anything else. Bourdieu's (1982, 1991) notions of 'cultural capital', 'linguistic capital', 'symbolic violence' and 'misrecognition' provide an explanatory framework for this discussion – particularly with regard to the differential status and value accorded to majority and minority languages. The ascendancy of the former is principally achieved by their legitimation and institutionalisation within nation-states (Nelde et al., 1996) and the subsequent marginalisation of a wide range of other language varieties within the nation-state. I illustrate this process via a discussion of the development of French as the national language of France.

Chapter 5 explores the specific links between education and minority-language policy. Since education has often played a key role historically in facilitating, and at times enforcing, the transition to a majority 'national' language, one can assume that it might also be used effectively to promote a minority language. That said, it is also acknowledged that education cannot by itself effect language change, or reverse language shift (Fishman, 1991). Following Churchill (1986), various approaches to minority-language policy are examined here, ranging from the complete disavowal of minority languages to their formal inclusion within all significant institutional and language domains of the nation-state. In examining the variety of educational approaches adopted towards minorities in modern nation-states, this chapter also develops further the idea, first introduced in Chapter 3, that differing language rights can be accorded to minority groups. Drawing on Kloss's (1971, 1977) distinction between promotion-oriented rights and tolerance-oriented rights, I argue that only national-minority groups can claim the automatic right to formal representation of their language in the public domain, and to state-supported minority-language education – a promotion-oriented right, in effect. However, in my view, ethnic-minority groups have, at the very least, the right to preserve their language in the private, non-governmental sphere of national life. These latter tolerance-oriented rights may be narrowly or broadly defined, but they may include at their broadest, and where numbers warrant, some form of active state support, again most notably within the realm of education.

Having set out the broad theoretical parameters of the debates around minority languages, and their place in the modern world, I turn in the remainder of the book to specific case examples. In Chapter 6, I discuss briefly the current ascendancy, or hegemony, of English as the current world language. I then compare and contrast two quite different responses to this English-language hegemony within the North American context. The first is the 'English Only Movement' in the USA, which advocates that English should be made the official language of the US, and that all other languages should be limited to the private domain. The second is Québec's regional language policy, a policy that formally promotes French, and concomitantly delimits English, in the public domain. While both policies appear, at first sight, to be restrictive, I argue that only the former is illiberal since it constitutes a deliberate attempt to marginalise minority languages in the USA and to *penalise* minority-language speakers (cf. Crawford, 1989, 1992a; Dicker, 1996). In contrast, the aims of the latter are to effect the maintenance of a minority language (within Canada). As such, I argue that while Québec's language laws remain extremely controversial, they may not *necessarily* be illiberal (cf. Taylor, 1994; Coulombe, 1995).

Chapter 7 extends this latter position by examining the development of two prominent national-minority language policies in Europe – one in Catalonia, an autonomous region of the Spanish state, and the other in Wales, a constituent nation of the British state. Both policies are regarded as having been largely 'successful' in protecting and promoting their respective national-minority languages (Catalan and Welsh) within a public domain dominated by a majority national language (Castilian Spanish and English). The large degree of general support that now obtains towards such policies is in itself a remarkable achievement, given the long historical derogation and proscription of both Catalan and Welsh in their respective contexts. However, both examples also demonstrate clearly the ongoing contested (and contentious) nature of minority language policy development in modern nation-states. In Catalonia, controversy continues to attend the development and implementation of the (1998) Catalan Linguistic Policy Act (Hoffmann, 1999; see also Strubell, 1998). In Wales, recent attempts to promote bilingualism in the public sector, a central aim of the (1993) Welsh Language Act, have also been a focus of some controversy (May, 2000). In both instances, I argue that the long-term success of these minority-language policies rests on gaining a sufficient degree of support from majority-language speakers – what Grin (1995) terms 'tolerability'. Much has already been achieved to this end. However, the pejorative views of minority languages held by many majority-language speakers (as well as some minority-language speakers) remain pervasive and ongoing. Similarly, the intrinsic association of majority languages with modernity and progress, and of minority languages with tradition and obsolescence, remain equally hard to break.

Chapter 8 explores these same issues with respect to the claims of indigenous peoples for greater cultural and linguistic rights and recognition. Indigenous peoples present us with easily the starkest example of the cultural and linguistic genocide that I referred to at the beginning of this Introduction. In the process of colonisation, indigenous peoples have been consistently, often violently, dispossessed of their cultures, languages and lands, not to mention their very lives. The chapter focuses first on recent developments in national and international law that aim to gain a measure of justice and restitution for indigenous peoples from those who colonised them. Particularly in the last 20 or so years, indigenous peoples, and the political movements associated with them, have mounted a sustained assault on the established nation-state system by arguing for greater self-determination or autonomy within that system. In so doing, they have highlighted the limits of democracy and the colonial underpinnings of nation-state formation. They have also consistently brought to our attention the ongoing processes of imperialism and disadvantage to which they have been subjected in the name of both.

The central claim of indigenous movements – represented most clearly in the (1993) United Nations Draft Declaration on the Rights of Indigenous Peoples – is that they are 'peoples'. This, in turn, entails associated rights of self-determination in international law, including the active protection and promotion of indigenous languages and cultures within nation-states (Hastings, 1988; de Varennes, 1996b; May, 1997b, 1999c). This view has gained considerable credence in recent times, not least because of the effective advocacy of indigenous peoples themselves. However, like the national language policies described in Chapter 7, such a 'differentialist' view of group-based rights continues to be controversial and contested. The subsequent formal UN ratification process of the 1993 Draft Declaration, for example, is still ongoing at this time, with many established nation-states continuing to resist the extension of the notion of self-determination, and associated cultural and linguistic rights, to indigenous peoples.

These developments, and the debates and controversies that surround them, are also evident at national levels. Thus, by way of example, the remainder of the chapter briefly discusses recent developments in Norway, Canada and Australia towards greater indigenous self-determination, and the inevitable opposition and controversy attendant upon such developments. I then proceed to examine in detail the case of the indigenous Māori of Aotearoa / New Zealand.[6] The nascent reformulation of Aotearoa / New Zealand as a bicultural and bilingual nation-state in recent times is a direct result of Māori claims to greater self-determination. As in other contexts, these claims remain controversial and contested, and their long-term success thus also remains uncertain. Nonetheless, developments towards greater Māori autonomy have been most evident to date in the arenas of language and education. The result has been a significant revitalising of the Māori language and culture – principally, although by no mean exclusively, via Māori language education (cf. May, 1997b, 1999c).

By way of conclusion, Chapter 9 reiterates my position that minority-language rights are both sociologically and politically defensible in the modern world. Such a position also necessarily entails major social and political (not to mention theoretical) consequences. The most significant of these is the need to radically rethink, or *reimagine*, the traditional organisation of nation-states since it is this 'philosophical matrix of the nation-state' (Churchill,

1996), more than anything else, which most threatens the ongoing survival of minority languages. The first step in such a process is to deconstruct the orthodoxy that ascribes 'majority' or 'minority' status to particular languages, valorising the former and stigmatising the latter. This must be recognised for what it is – a social and political process, deeply imbued in power relations, and arising out of the political nationalism of the last few centuries. As such, it is neither inevitable, nor inviolate. Similarly, the apparently inexorable association of majority (national) languages with modernity and progress – and, conversely, of minority languages with tradition and obsolescence – is a product of the same historical, social and political forces, and needs to be interrogated accordingly.[7] When seen in this light, the continued stigmatisation and peripheralisation of minority languages in the modern world of nation-states can be effectively challenged and contested (see also Skutnabb-Kangas, 1998, 2000).

Second, the process of rethinking the nation-state in relation to minority languages must involve, to my mind, the legitimation and institutionalisation of the languages of national-minority groups in the civic realm of the nation-state. If national-minority languages are legitimated and institutionalised in this way, most often via a proactive minority-language policy, they have the opportunity to assume at least some of the status and range of majority 'national' languages. In so doing, national-minority languages can break out of the private familial domain and 'invade' the public or civic realm (while bearing in mind Fishman's (1991) caveat that the latter cannot act as a substitute for the former). This is crucial to the long-term survival of any minority language, since languages that are not accorded at least some degree of formal status or role in the public realm are the ones most likely to become marginalised and/or endangered in the longer (and sometimes shorter) term. History, if nothing else, teaches us this all too clearly.

But this is not all. A third key requirement for rethinking the linguistic orthodoxy of the nation-state is the *active* protection of all other minority languages – at the very least in the private domain, and where numbers warrant, in the public domain as well. This additional 'move' equates broadly with more radical forms of multiculturalism. It is crucial to establishing a genuinely more plural conception of the nation-state, not least because it guards against the propensity of many nation-states to 'play' the claims of different minority groups off against one another. Thus, some nation-states have formally recognised the cultural and linguistic rights of national-minority groups (Switzerland and Belgium for example), but have been loath to adopt a multiculturalist approach towards their migrant groups. Other nation-states have advocated the latter as official ideology (Australia and Canada, for example) but have generally been far less willing to recognise the claims of their national-minority groups, most notably their indigenous peoples. In short, unless the two approaches are combined, inequality is simply perpetuated at other levels and in other forms.

Prospects for change

So where does this leave us? While continuing to uphold the importance of citizenship and individual rights, it is my contention that a greater accommodation of minority languages and cultures within the nation-state provides a more just representation of the (at times differing) interests of all its citizens. Such a position inevitably entails an acceptance of the legitimacy of some form of group-based rights in modern liberal democracies. Establishing group-based rights with respect to language – as with differentiated group-based rights more generally – remains a fraught, contested and contentious process. If one is to avoid a return to the reified and essentialised group rights' models of the past, it requires a continuing acknowledgement of the ongoing interspersion of groups, the complex interconnections between ethnic and national identities and other forms of identity, and their varied (and variable) cultural and linguistic expression. However, group-based minority-language rights also recognise a central point too often overlooked in modern liberal democracies – that these language and identity processes can continue to be negotiated from *within* rather than determined from *without*. Or, to put it another way, the complex processes of language and identity can be negotiated on one's own terms (both individually and collectively), rather than the terms set by others, as has so often been the case historically for minority groups.

More pragmatically, the accommodation of minority-language rights may become a political necessity, given the growing discontent with existing nation-state structures evident among minorities today. And this highlights a more general point. If the increasing demands of minority groups for greater cultural and linguistic representation within the nation-state are not met, they may lead, in turn, to secessionist pressures and the potential fragmentation of the nation-state. Given the likely consequences of such fragmentation, and the hardening of ethnic and national boundaries that normally ensues, we should avoid this wherever we can. The recent spectres of Rwanda and the former Yugoslavia are sufficient reasons alone for doing so.

However, there is also a positive dimension to this. If nation-states are reimagined in more plural and inclusive ways, there is potential for the recognition of not only greater political democracy but greater *ethnocultural* and *ethnolinguistic* democracy as well (Fishman, 1991, 1995b; May, 1999e). Thus, far from undermining democratic principles – a common assumption among opponents of minority rights – the accommodation of cultural and linguistic group-based rights may well *extend* them. Indeed, my argument throughout this book is that ethnic and national conflicts are most often precipitated when nation-states *ignore* demands for greater cultural and linguistic democracy, not – as is commonly assumed – when they accommodate them (see also Parekh, 2000). Given the increasingly parlous state of the world's minority languages and the increasing fractiousness of modern social and political life, these questions, and their potential resolution, take on an even greater urgency.

Notes

1 While the distinction between 'majority' and 'minority' languages, as with majority and minority groups, tends to draw attention to numerical size, its more important reference is to differences in power, rights and privileges (see Tollefson, 1991; Nelde et al., 1996; May, 1997b; Skutnabb-Kangas, 2000). That said, the distinction between majority and minority languages needs to be treated with some caution since the dichotomy inevitably under-states the complex *situatedness* of particular language varieties with respect to power relations (Coulmas, 1998; Pennycook, 1998a). Nonetheless, I use the distinction here, and throughout this account, as a broad description of the clearly observable historical and contemporary trends which have led to the marginalisation and subjugation of so many 'minority' languages and the concomitant valorisation of 'majority' languages. A comparable approach is found in Grillo's (1989) distinction between 'dominant' and 'subordinated' languages.

2 As we shall see in Chapter 4, the process of stigmatising minority languages often involves their equation with or, more accurately, relegation to, dialects – i.e., a view that they are not 'really' languages.

3 For an extended discussion of the composition of the modern nation-state, and its historical antecedents in the political nationalism of the eighteenth and nineteenth centuries, see Chapter 2.

4 Essentialism is taken to mean here the process by which particular groups come to be described in terms of fundamental, immutable characteristics. In so doing, the relational and fluid aspects of identity formation are ignored and the group itself comes to be seen as autonomous and separate, impervi-ous to context and to processes of internal as well as external differentiation (Werbner, 1997b).

5 Following Gramsci (1971), hegemony is taken to mean here the diffusion and popularisation of a particular view of the world – that of the dominant group – as if it was representative of all other groups. In other words, so effective and widespread is the promotion and promulgation of a particular (dominant) point of view, that even those who may not initially share such a view come to accept it and *internalise* it as normative, as simply the com-monsensical 'way of seeing things'.

6 Aotearoa (the land of the long/white cloud) is the original Māori name for New Zealand.

7 Tove Skutnabb-Kangas provides a comparable analysis in her discussion of the three-part process of 'glorifying' the majority language, 'stigmatising' the minority language, and subsequently 'rationalising' this unequal rela-tionship as 'beneficial' to minority-language speakers (see 1998: 17–18).

1

The denunciation of ethnicity

In order to begin to understand why minority languages are held in such low esteem in the modern world, we need first to examine related debates on ethnicity. This is a crucial first step because the 'ideology of contempt' (Grillo, 1989) exhibited so consistently towards minority languages has more to do with the (minority) ethnicities with which they are historically associated, than with the languages themselves. Indeed, criticisms of minority languages almost always occur within a wider critique and/or dismissal of the particular ethnic affiliations of their speakers. If, as Grillo suggests, 'subordinated languages are despised languages' (1989: 174), then inevitably so too are those who speak them. Indeed, languages, in the end, only reflect the status of their speakers (Dorian, 1998). I will thus begin this chapter by charting briefly the long-held pejorative perception of ethnicity in much academic and popular commentary.

The predominantly negative view of ethnicity in academic and popular discourses arises from its unfavourable juxtaposition with the nation-state. For example, it is almost de rigueur now in academic discourse to view ethnicity as socially and politically constructed; an essentially anti-modern and regressive phenomenon that is mobilised instrumentally by particular groups to achieve certain (self-interested) political ends. Concomitantly, the 'cultural stuff' of ethnicity – that is the particular ancestry, culture, and language of the group(s) in question – is regarded as largely fictive. Indeed, many academic commentators view ethnicity as simply a convenient construction of an ethnic group's *supposed* distinctiveness that is employed *retrospectively* to engender 'ethnic solidarity' as a basis for social and political action.

Popular commentary reflects a similarly sceptical bias towards ethnicity, albeit of a somewhat different kind. Fuelled by lurid media reports of the immolation attending yet another 'ethnic conflict', the wider public locate in ethnicity the principal cause of many of today's social and political problems. Places such as Rwanda, Burundi, Sri Lanka, Northern Ireland and the former

Yugoslavia – to name just a few recent examples – suggest starkly the destructive and unproductive nature of ethnicity and ethnic mobilisation. Indeed, since the end of the Cold War, the most common sources of political violence in the world have been ascribed to these so-called 'ethnic conflicts' (Gurr, 1993). Such developments are closely related, in turn, to the proliferation of a variety of 'ethnonational movements' – movements based on ethnic affiliation which aim to establish a national state of their own and which may, but do not always, resort to violence to achieve their ends. The Tamil Tigers in Sri Lanka, the separatist ETA movement (Euzkadi 'ta Askatasuna) in the Basque Country, the Parti Québécois in the Canadian province of Québec, Plaid Cymru (the Welsh Nationalist party) in Wales, and the IRA Republican movement in Northern Ireland can all be cited as examples here. In addition, there are minority groups who, while not necessarily wanting to establish a state of their own, want greater recognition and representation within existing nation-states and agitate, sometimes violently, to this end. Most notable here, perhaps, are indigenous people groups such as the Māori of Aotearoa / New Zealand, the Aboriginal peoples of Australia, Sámi (Lapps), Inuit (Eskimos) and Native Americans.

Suffice it to say, that while these various developments present us with qualitatively different examples of ethnic-minority affiliation and mobilisation (see Chapter 2), they are widely held to be negative phenomena. This is so *even when* such groups may be seen to have legitimate and supportable claims. How (and why) has this negative perception of ethnicity come to hold such sway? I will attempt to answer this question in what follows by focusing in particular on the historical development of academic discourse in this area.

Academic denunciations of ethnicity

The widespread dismissal of the legitimacy and value of ethnicity as a form of social and political identification has been juxtaposed historically against the valorisation of *national* identity and the modern nation-state from which it springs. Nation-states are something to which we can legitimately give our allegiance it seems, but ethnic groups are not. Nation-states are embracing and cohesive whereas ethnic groups are exclusive and divisive. Nation-states represent modernity while ethnic groups simply represent a harping, misinformed and misguided nostalgia. Or so the story goes. Moreover, it is a story long told and with an impressive academic pedigree. In the nineteenth century, the British liberal John Stuart Mill argued in *Representative Government*: 'Free institutions are next to impossible in a country made up of different nationalities. Among a people without fellow-feeling, *especially if they read and speak different languages*, the united public opinion, necessary to the working of representative government, cannot exist' (1972: 361; my emphasis). Mill proceeds to elaborate on why he deems alternative ethnic affiliations (and their languages) to be so counterproductive to the political organisation of the nation-state. In so doing, he invokes a clear cultural hierarchy between different groups, arguing that smaller nationalities – the equivalent of 'ethnic minorities' in modern political parlance – should be assimilated into the nation-state *via* its 'national' culture and language; that is, the culture and language of the dominant (national) group:

> Experience proves it is possible for one nationality to merge and be absorbed in another: and when it was originally an inferior and more backward portion of the human race the absorption is greatly to its advantage. Nobody can suppose that it is not beneficial to a Breton, or a Basque of French Navarre, to be brought into the current of the ideas and feelings of a highly civilised and cultivated people – to be a member of the French nationality, admitted on equal terms to all the privileges of French citizenship . . . *than to sulk on his own rocks, the half-savage relic of past times*, revolving in his own mental orbit, without participation or interest in the general movement of the world. The same remark applies to the Welshman or the Scottish Highlander as members of the British nation [sic].[1]
>
> (1972: 395; my emphasis)

Likewise, the French nationalist and historian, Michelet – a near contemporary of Mill – was to conclude of the French Revolution that: 'this sacrifice of the diverse interior nationalities to the great nationality which comprises them undoubtedly strengthened the latter . . . It was at the moment when France *suppressed* within herself the divergent French countries that she proclaimed her high and original revelations' (1946: 286; my emphasis). In this view then, a homogeneous national identity – reflected in the culture and language of the dominant 'national' group – should supersede and subsume alternative ethnic and/or national identities and their associated cultures and languages. As we shall see in Chapter 3, many modern liberals continue to hold to this position. However, the merits of the dominant group's culture and language tend to be emphasised less overtly in contemporary commentary (although the cultural and linguistic hierarchies underpinning such assumptions remain). Rather, the argument is usually couched in terms of a defence of two ostensibly key liberal democratic principles – universal political citizenship, and the recognition of individual, as opposed to collective, rights. These two principles are seen as sufficient in themselves to repudiate the claims of other ethnic groups for greater social recognition in the public or civic realm of the nation-state – the private realm is seen as less problematic – and for associated cultural and linguistic recognition/representation. But more on this later.[2]

As for Marxist commentary on the legitimacy of ethnicity as a basis for social and political mobilisation, Marx and Engels were themselves to adopt a remarkably similar position to that of their contemporary liberal commentators. In discussing the position of ethnic minorities, Marx and Engels drew on Hegel's distinction between nation and state – equating the 'nation' directly with the modern nation-state and 'nationality' with ethnic groups, or ethnocultural communities, which lacked a state of their own (Nimni, 1995). On this basis, Engels could observe:

> There is no country in Europe which does not have in some corner or other one or several fragments of peoples, the remnants of a former population that was suppressed and held in bondage by the nation [nation-state] which later became the main vehicle for historical development. These relics of nations [ethnic groups], mercilessly trampled down by the passage of history, as Hegel expressed it, *this ethnic trash* always become fanatical standard bearers of counter-revolution and remain so until their complete extirpation or loss of their national character, just as their whole existence in general is itself a protest against a great historical revolution. Such in Scotland are the Gaels . . . Such in France are the Bretons . . . Such in Spain are the Basques . . .
>
> (Marx and Engels, 1976a: 234–235; my emphasis)

The position of Marx and Engels vis-à-vis ethnic minorities arises from their somewhat contradictory views on nationalism. On the one hand, Marx and Engels argued, as one might expect, that the working classes were the motor of history. In *The Communist Manifesto*, Marx observes: 'The working men have no country . . . National differences and antagonisms between peoples are daily more and more vanishing' (Marx and Engels, 1976b: 65). On the other hand, Marx and Engels also endorsed the nationalist causes of 'historic' nations where these were seen to facilitate and expedite the proletarian revolution. Thus Marx observes, again in *The Communist Manifesto*, that the struggle of the proletariat with the bourgeoisie is 'at first a national struggle' and that 'the proletariat of each country must, of course, first of all settle matters with its own bourgeoisie' (1976b: 60). In neither instance, however, were the claims of 'non-historic' nations or 'historyless peoples' (geschichtslosen Völker) recognised – that is, ethnic and/or national groups which lacked the 'historical vitality' to consolidate a national state of their own. As Nimni concludes in his lucid discussion of this question, 'Marx and Engels were, to put it mildly, impatient with and intolerant of ethnic minorities' (1995: 68; see also Guibernau, 1996: 13–21). In this regard, they were, like their liberal contemporaries Mill and Michelet, very much a product of their times. Indeed, Hobsbawm (1990) argues that it is 'sheer anachronism' to criticise them for holding such views since they were shared by nearly all nineteenth-century political theorists on both the right and the left.

And yet, having said this, Hobsbawm's views are not too dissimilar to his nineteenth-century counterparts. For example, Hobsbawm contrasts a positive unifying nineteenth-century nationalism – modelled on the French Revolution and located in the political formation of nation-states – with a negative and divisive twentieth-century variant, largely centred on ethnocultural and linguistic differences (ethnonationalisms, in effect). This is clearly comparable with the distinction drawn by Marx and Engels between 'historic' and 'non-historic' nations, and the transitory and regressive nature attributed to the latter. Other Marxist commentators have been less sceptical about the legitimacy of ethnicity and ethnic mobilisation (see Hechter, 1975; Wallerstein, 1979, 1983, 1991; Nairn, 1981; Hroch, 1985; Balibar, 1991), although such commentators continue to vary widely in the degree to which they regard capitalism as *determining* the construction of ethnic relations. Strongly class-determinist theories of ethnicity seek to reduce ethnic categories to the exigencies of more encompassing (class-based) experiences. Weaker versions attempt a more open-ended examination of the interconnections between ethnic and class mobilisation(s). However, in both cases, Marxist analyses of ethnicity continue to be predicated principally on the preeminent influence of capitalism and on the subsequent subsumption of ethnic and national relations within class relations. Thus, Marxist perspectives on ethnicity have considerable difficulty in accounting for the *specificity* of ethnic form and meaning in the circumstances of their mobilisation (Smaje, 1997; see below). More problematically still, they cannot account for the fact that it is often ethnic identity, rather than class, that is the principal catalyst of such mobilisation in the first place.

The academic rehabilitation of ethnicity?

More recently, postmodernists have developed what might be seen as a counterargument to this broadly articulated modernist position on ethnicity. Postmodernists argue that the rise of globalisation[3] – the next stage of the modernisation process – has significantly undermined previous forms of identification and political mobilisation. In this view, modern nation-states are finding it more difficult to impose a uniform national identity in the increasingly global economy and culture of today's world. Consequently, a new decentred and 'hybridised' politics of identities is emerging (Harvey, 1989; Jamieson, 1991; S. Hall, 1992a, b; Robertson, 1992; Bhabha, 1994; Featherstone, 1991, 1995). In the place of the previous certainties of nationhood and national identity, local, ethnic and gender identities have now become the principal sites of postmodern politics. As Stuart Hall observes, the result is the simultaneous rise of new 'global' *and* new 'local' identities and the consequent proliferation of supra- and subnational identities:

> Increasingly, the political landscapes of the modern world are fractured ... by competing and dislocating identifications ... National identities remain strong, especially with respect to such things as legal and citizenship rights, but local, regional, and community identities have become more significant. Above the level of the national culture, 'global' identifications begin to displace, and sometimes override, national ones.

(1992a: 280, 302)

Postmodernist analyses thus provide a space for the reemergence of ethnicity as a valid social and political form of identification and mobilisation. However, ethnicity in this context faces some stiff competition. The fragmented, dispersed and decentred individual of the postmodern world is supposedly able to choose from a bewildering range of identity styles and forms of political mobilisation, and ethnicity, it seems, is just one of them. As I will argue in this chapter, this position significantly understates the key role that ethnicity often assumes in the processes of identity formation and social and political mobilisation. Relatedly, postmodernists may also have underestimated the salience and resilience of 'national cultures' in which liberal and Marxist commentators have historically placed such store. Michael Billig cogently argues, for example, that national allegiances cannot simply be exchanged like 'last year's clothes'. As he asserts:

> There is a sense of 'as if' in some versions of the postmodern thesis. It is as if the nation-state has already withered away; as if people's national commitments have been flattened to the level of consumer choice; as if millions of children in the world's most powerful nation [the USA] do not daily salute one, and only one, style of flag; as if, at this moment around the globe, vast armies are not practising their battle manoeuvres beneath national colours.

(1995: 139)

And so we come to a point where – despite both consistent negative attribution, and confident predictions of its imminent demise, for over two centuries now – ethnicity continues to persist and prosper in the modern world. Many contemporary liberals are confounded and dismayed by the resilience of ethnic ties, and the increasing advocacy of ethnic-minority rights, within contemporary nation-states. Marxist commentators are similarly bemused by the emergent and ongoing claims of ethnonational movements in postindustrialist societies; a feature which the achievements of modernisation (and class-based politics) should have rendered obsolete. Likewise, postmodernists, while they rightly highlight the contingent and multiple aspects of identity formation, cannot explain adequately why ethnicity (and nationality) should so often 'trump' the competition. The salience of ethnicity may well vary from context to context and, as we shall see, its interrelationship with nationalism and national identity, and with other forms of social relations and social identity, may be complex, overlapping and at times contradictory. Nonetheless, ethnicity cannot be as easily discounted as we have been led to believe.

Moreover, the rejection of ethnicity as a valid form of social and political action is in itself problematic. As I will argue, if ethnicity has survived and prospered – despite, it seems, insuperable odds – this suggests that it has at least *some* basis in social reality (see also R. Jenkins, 1997; Fenton, 1999; Levine, 1999). Ethnicity cannot *simply* be a convenient and largely fictive construction, although such elements are clearly apparent within it. The 'cultural stuff' of ethnicity – ancestry, culture and (for our purposes) language – *does matter* to a significant number of people. Likewise, ethnicity has meaning not only at the level of social and political *mobilisation* but also as a principal form of individual and collective social *identity*. In short, and whether we like it or not, ethnicity continues to have a special claim on the individual and collective allegiances of many people in the world today and we need to understand why this should still be so.

Ethnicity and modernity

So what exactly is ethnicity and what are the key sociological questions which surround it? Before examining these questions in detail, I want to flag a central theme which should already be apparent from my discussion thus far and which pervades much of what will follow – that is, ethnicity's complex and ambiguous relationship to modernity. There is a dualistic tension in much of the academic debate about ethnicity which posits 'ethnic groups', ironically, as at once both a modernist creation – defined socially and politically by their *partial* incorporation into the modern nation-state – and as essentially *anti-modern*. The former is signalled by the usual collocation of 'ethnic' and 'minority'. Indeed, most of the discourse concerning ethnicity still tends to concern itself primarily with subnational units, or minorities of some kind or another (Chapman et al., 1989). The latter is suggested by the unflattering comparison of ethnic (minority) groups as atavistic and regressive in contrast to the modernity of the nation-state; a position that is particularly evident in nineteenth-century academic commentary, as we have seen, but is not exclusive to it. Thus, while these ethnic-minority groups may argue that their apparently distinct ethnicity predates their (incomplete) incorporation within the modern nation-state, ethnicity is generally viewed here as a *construction* of modernity – a by-product, in effect, of the political, cultural and ideational processes of nation-state formation – rather than an antecedent to it. Yet, at the same time, ethnic claims for social and political recognition are rejected on the basis that they fail to reach or reflect appropriate standards of modernity!

As I will argue in Chapter 2, both these assertions are problematic and have much to do with the primacy ascribed to political nationalism(s), and to its institutional embodiment in the modern 'nation-state', over the last two centuries. At this stage, however, it is enough to point out that this central dualism can be traced through much of the academic (as well as social and political) commentary on ethnicity.

Terminology

Not only that, it is also evident in the very terminology used, and the various attempts over the years to define both 'ethnicity' and 'ethnic group'. The first use of the term 'ethnicity' was attributed by Glazer and Moynihan (1975) to the American sociologist David Riesman in 1953, although other commentators suggest an earlier genesis in the 1940s (Sollors, 1989; Fishman, 1989a, 1997). Despite its apparent recency, however, ethnicity actually derives from the Greek word 'ethnos', meaning people or tribe. The equivalent term for ethnos in English – 'ethnic' – was used from the mid fourteenth century to the mid nineteenth century to describe someone as heathen or pagan (R. Williams, 1976).[4] This etymological association was subsequently to fit well with the pejorative construction of ethnic groups in relation to the nation-state. The related collocation of 'ethnic' and 'minority' is also reflective of this positioning since it assumes that majority groups are somehow not 'ethnic'; that they simply represent modernity, or the modern (civilised) way of life. However, as I will argue, *all* groups – both minority and majority ones – incorporate an ethnic dimension and the failure of the latter to recognise or acknowledge this has more to do with differential power relations between groups than with anything else.

Subsequent discussions of the term 'ethnicity' in the social sciences continue to reflect these ambiguities and tensions. Isajiw (1980), for example, found in a review of 65 studies of ethnicity, that 52 gave *no* explicit definition of the concept. If a particular view of ethnicity was assumed in these studies, it tended to accord de facto with the 'cultural stuff' of ethnicity – ancestry, culture and language. This position is reflected in its broadest terms by Glazer and Moynihan's much-cited assertion that ethnicity is 'the character or quality of an ethnic group' (1975: 1). More recently, however, a contrasting view of ethnicity as *subjective* and *situational* has come to the fore; a position which has much to do with Barth's (1969a) elaboration of ethnic *boundaries* and which is characterised by Eriksen's counterdescription of ethnicity as 'essentially an aspect of relationship, not a property of a group' (1993: 12).

These seemingly contradictory aspects of ethnicity are encapsulated within Max Weber's definition of the associated term 'ethnic group'. Weber argues that ethnic groups are 'those human groups that entertain a subjective belief in their common descent because of similarities of physical type or of customs or of both, or because of memories of colonisation and migration' (1961: 389). This definition highlights how ancestral, cultural, and at times racialised traits are commonly associated with particular ethnic groups, both by members of the groups themselves and by others. However, along with these traits, Weber also specifically emphasises the subjective nature of ethnic-group membership – the *belief* in 'their' common descent. For Weber, objective characteristics such as language and particular cultural practices do not in themselves constitute an ethnic group; they simply facilitate that group's formation. Rather, he stresses that it is the political community which engenders such sentiments of likeness, although ethnic bonds, once created, contribute in an ongoing way to the solidarity of the group (Guibernau, 1996). In other words, Weber seems to be suggesting that belief in ancestry and shared culture and language is a *consequence* rather than a *cause* of collective political action, acting in turn as a means of defining group membership, eligibility and access (R. Jenkins, 1997). As Richard Jenkins concludes of Weber's formulation: 'From this point of view, ethnic groups are what people believe or think them to be: cultural [and linguistic] differences mark "group-ness", they do not cause it (or indelibly characterise) it; ethnic identification arises out of and within interaction between groups' (1997: 11).

Polarities and their like

Max Weber's formulation is an early attempt to highlight, and where possible reconcile, the countervailing tensions between the objective and subjective aspects of ethnicity. Like most contemporary commentators (see below), it is clear that Weber tends to favour the latter over the former, adopting in the end a more constructionist approach to ethnic-identity formation. Nonetheless, Weber is able to hold the two in tension in a way that many who have come after him have not. Thus, much subsequent debate within sociology and anthropology has tended to a more dichotomous approach where ethnic identity has been viewed as *either* the product of objective cultural (and linguistic) characteristics *or* (much more commonly) the result of a malleable, fluid, and at times fictive process of identity construction. Accordingly, such analysis has largely been framed within and by the following kinds of polarities. Is ethnicity a premodern or a modern phenomenon? Is it an intrinsic attribute of human identity or a social construction that is mobilised to achieve certain political ends? Can it be defined by particular objective cultural attributes or is it subjectively maintained by shifting relational boundaries that allow groups to distinguish themselves one from another? Does it only apply to minority groups or does it encompass majority groups as well? Is ethnicity primarily material or symbolic, political or cultural, voluntary or involuntary, individual or collective? These dichotomies overlap in many instances and may be summarised as follows:

Ethnicity as:
- premodern or modern
- primordial or situational
- intrinsic or instrumental
- content or boundaries
- objective or subjective
- category or group
- involuntary or voluntary
- individual or collective
- material or symbolic
- minority or majority

In the remainder of this chapter, I aim to evaluate critically these debates on ethnicity and the various oppositions to which they give rise. In so doing, I will frame my analysis within the bifurcated approach that has been largely characteristic of these discussions until now – working, in particular, within the broad distinction commonly drawn between *primordial* and *situational* accounts of ethnicity. However, this should *not* be seen as an endorsement of this practice. I adopt it here simply as a useful heuristic device in order to compare and contrast the various positions adopted in these debates. My own argument is that such an approach is unhelpful. Adopting an oppositional stance, though a favourite pastime of social scientists, inevitably results in a partial view of the phenomena analysed. Self-evident as it may seem, the only sensible way forward is to endorse a middle ground – combining, where appropriate, salient elements of traditionally bifurcated positions. Thus, after presenting an overview of the relevant debates on ethnicity, including postmodernist conceptions, I will conclude the chapter by arguing that Bourdieu's concept of 'habitus' and Anthony Smith's notion of 'ethnie', in combination, provide us with the means of developing a more integrative – and, in the end, more adequate – account of ethnicity. Such an account will also help to explain not only the continuing influence of ethnicity in the modern world but also its complex interconnections with nationalism and national identity, the subject of the next chapter.

Ethnicity as primordial

One of the key reasons proffered for the enduring nature of ethnicity in the modern world is that it constitutes a primary aspect of human nature and human relations. This stance, which is broadly termed 'primordialism', is actually represented by a range of positions (A. Smith, 1995a). The extreme version, elaborated in the linguistic nationalism of the eighteenth-century 'German Romantics', Herder, Humboldt and Fichte, posits ethnic – and, by extension, national – identity as natural and immutable. Human beings are viewed, by nature, as belonging to fixed ethnic communities which are, in turn, defined by the constitutive elements of 'language, blood and soil' (see also Chapter 2). This particular ideology of primordialism naturalises ethnic groups and justifies ethnic chauvinism (R. Jenkins, 1997). A second stream of primordialism is represented by the sociobiology of Pierre van den Berghe (1979, 1995), who argues that ethnic groups are 'natural' because they are extensions of biological kin groups, selected on the grounds of genetic evolution (see A. Smith, 1998: 147–151 for a useful summary). The third and most plausible stream is associated most prominently with Geertz (1963, 1973), Isaacs (1975) and Shils (1957, 1980). Geertz, for example, in a much-cited passage, develops Shils' (1957) argument that the political actions of ethnic groups are often attributable, in the first instance, to primordial attachments. These primordial ties are regarded as a fundamental basis for collective action because they are rooted in our earliest socialisation, in kinship, and in the wider ties and solidarities built on and around kinship. As Geertz outlines:

> By a primordial attachment is meant one that stems from the 'givens' of existence, or more precisely ... the *assumed* givens of social existence: immediate contiguity and live connection mainly, but beyond them the givenness that stems from being born into a particular ... community, speaking a particular language ... and following particular social practices. These congruities of blood, speech, custom and so on, are seen to have an ineffable, and at times overpowering, coerciveness in and of themselves. One is bound to one's kinsman, one's neighbour ... as the result not merely of personal affection, tactical necessity, common interest or incurred moral obligation, but at least in great part by virtue of some unaccountable absolute import attributed to the very tie itself.
>
> (1973: 259; my emphasis)

On this basis, Geertz provides us with an explanation of why primordial attachments often trump what he describes as 'civil sentiments' – those sentiments and allegiances which arise from civic participation in the modern nation-state. This has often been construed in much subsequent academic commentary as an uncritical endorsement of a primordial view of ethnicity, although Geertz's position is more complex than this caricature suggests (see R. Jenkins, 1997; A. Smith, 1998; Fenton, 1999). Geertz is not arguing that ethnic ties or affiliations *are* primordial in any real sense – hence his deliberate qualification regarding 'the assumed givens of social existence'. Rather, he is arguing that people *perceive* these ties as primordial and thus as preeminent over other affiliative ties. Such a position then does not necessarily entail that ethnic groups are fixed and static, although ethnic groups are still equated in this conception with certain cultural characteristics – the 'congruities of blood, speech, custom and so on'.

Notwithstanding the more flexible accounts of Geertz et al., the primordialist position has been widely dismissed by many theorists of ethnicity (see Eller and Coughlan, 1993). A number of key objections have been raised in this regard. First, critics argue that while cultural attributes are often associated with ethnic distinctiveness, they do not constitute a *sufficient* explanation for ethnicity. To attempt to equate the two, in fact, amounts to cultural determinism. Nor does an emphasis on cultural characteristics explain adequately why some cultural attributes – language, for example – may be salient markers of ethnic identity in some instances but not in others. In effect, cultural differences do not always correspond to ethnic ones (see also my ensuing discussion of situational ethnicity). As Robert Thornton argues, an understanding of culture must thus involve more than 'simply a knowledge of differences, but rather an understanding of *how* and *why* differences in language, thought . . . and behaviours have come about' (1988: 25; my emphases). Second, and relatedly, cultural forms thus require a historical examination; as indeed do all aspects of ethnic-group formation (Mare, 1993; A. Smith, 1998). This is not something which a primordialist account can adequately provide. By situating the search for ethnicity within 'the assumed givens of social existence', the primordialist position conveniently explains both everything and nothing. It lacks, in effect, explanatory power and predictive value and is, at best, an ex post facto argument (Rothschild, 1981; Stack, 1986). As John Stack elaborates, the primordial approach 'fails to explain why ethnicity disappears [as an organising social category] during one historical period and reintensifies in another' (1986: 2). Third, and most tellingly perhaps, primordial accounts also underplay the multiplicity of social groups to which individuals may belong and the role of individual choice in selecting between and within them.

Situational ethnicity

This emphasis on individual choice is reflected in the alternative endorsement of a *situational* view of ethnicity, a view outlined most clearly in Barth's influential (1969b) *Ethnic Groups and Boundaries* (see also Moerman, 1965, 1974). Building on Weber's earlier formulation of ethnic groups (see above), Barth, in his introduction, argues that ethnicity is *not* some bundle of unchanging cultural traits which can simply be examined and enumerated in order to determine differences between ethnic groups. Indeed, the 'cultural stuff' of the group – language, culture, ancestry – is not even a key consideration for Barth. Rather, ethnic groups are situationally defined in relationship to their social interactions with other groups, and the boundaries established and maintained between them as a result of these interactions. As Barth asserts:

> ethnic categories provide an organisational vessel that may be given varying amounts and forms of content in different sociocultural systems . . . The critical focus of investigation from this point of view becomes the ethnic boundary that defines the group, not the cultural stuff that it encloses.

> (1969a: 14–15)

For Barth, ethnicity is about social relationships rather than specific cultural properties since 'we can assume no simple one-to-one relationship between ethnic units and cultural similarities or differences' (1969a: 14). Cultural attributes are not significant in themselves since any one of a range of cultural properties could be used to fill the 'organisational vessel' of a particular ethnicity. This may help to explain the diversity of cultural diacritica employed by ethnic groups in the world today to distinguish themselves from others. Instead, it is the *perceived* usefulness of these cultural attributes in maintaining ethnic boundaries which is central. Cultural attributes only become significant as markers of ethnic identity when a group deems them to be *necessary*, or socially effective, for such purposes. Thus, particular cultural attributes (such as a group's language) may vary in salience, may be constructed or reconstructed, and may even be discarded by an ethnic group, depending on the particular sociohistorical circumstances of their interactions with other groups, and the need to maintain effectively the boundaries between them. It is these ethnic boundaries which determine in the end who is and who is not a member of a particular ethnic group, as well as designating which ethnic categories are available for individual identification at any given time and place (Nagel, 1994). In short, shared culture in this model is best understood as generated in and by the processes of ethnic-boundary maintenance rather than the other way around (R. Jenkins, 1997).

Barth's emphasis on the relational, processual and negotiated aspects of ethnicity (Eriksen, 1993) also presupposes that the formation of ethnic identity is largely shaped by the group itself – that ethnic-identity formation is largely an *internal* process of ascription. This process will be in response to those on the other side of the ethnic boundary, and to changing circumstances, certainly. Likewise, the success of ethnic ascription will depend to a large extent on the reciprocity of other parties in recognising and accepting the distinctions involved. Nonetheless, Barth sees ethnicity as a product of *intra*group processes of negotiation rather than the direct result of outside forces. In short, an ethnic group is ultimately defined by its own members. As Barth clearly states, it 'makes no difference how dissimilar members may be in their overt behaviour – if they say they are A, in contrast to another category B . . . they declare their allegiance to the shared culture of A's' (1969a: 15).

Ethnicity as subjective

In adopting this position, Barth's account can be said to be a subjectivist one. It emphasises the role of individual agents, rather than social structure, as the primary force in the construction of ethnic identities. As such, it has been criticised for underplaying (or even ignoring) the social and cultural constraints facing actors in their ethnic choices (Worsley, 1984; Wallman, 1986; J. O'Brien, 1986; Fardon, 1987). As these critics argue, ethnogenesis, or the creation of new ethnicities, does not just happen. Identities are not – indeed, *cannot* – be freely chosen and to suggest otherwise is to adopt an ahistorical approach which reduces life to the level of 'a market, or cafeteria' (Worsley, 1984: 246).

While this criticism is a valid one, the answer probably lies somewhere in between both positions. As Eriksen astutely observes, 'ethnic identities are neither ascribed nor achieved: they are both. They are wedged between situational selection and imperatives imposed from without' (1993: 57). Joane Nagel likewise suggests that ethnic identity:

> is the result of a dialectical process involving internal and external opinions and processes, as well as the individual's self-identification and outsiders' ethnic designations – i.e., what *you* think your ethnicity is, versus what *they* think your ethnicity is . . . Ethnic boundaries, and thus identities, are constructed by both the individual and the group as well as by outside agents and organisations.
>
> (1994: 154–155)

In other words, ethnic groups are both internally and externally defined; distinguishing 'us' from 'them' is always a two-way process. Where the balance might lie between internal and external definitions of ethnicity, however, remains an open question. In any given instance it is a question of degree. The continuum that is possible here is perhaps best illustrated by the commonly drawn distinction between ethnic *categories* and ethnic *communities*. Anthony Smith (1991) argues that the former are identified by others as constituting separate cultural and historical groupings. However, they may have little self-awareness at the time that they form such separate collectivities. Ethnic categories, in short, are named, characterised and delineated principally by others (R. Jenkins, 1996, 1997). Ethnic communities, in contrast, define themselves, their name(s), their nature(s) and their boundaries, and are thus more akin to Barth's notion of an ethnic group. As Paul Brass describes it, an ethnic community 'has adopted one or more of its marks of cultural distinctness and [has] used them as symbols both to create internal cohesion and to differentiate itself from other ethnic groups' (1985: 17). Such communities are thus characterised by a sense of ethnic *solidarity* which, in turn, is usually mobilised via an insistence on certain social and political rights. These rights are said to derive from the specific 'group character' (Glazer and Moynihan, 1975) and often involve an association with a particular territory or homeland.[5] I will return to the notion of ethnic community in my later discussions of Anthony Smith's (1986, 1991, 1995a) use of the comparable French term 'ethnie'.

Ethnicity and 'race'

Discussion of the balance between internal and external ascription also allows us to explore the crucial distinction between ethnicity and 'race'. Michael Banton, for example, argues that this distinction can be made on the basis that 'membership in an ethnic group is usually voluntary; membership in a racial group is not' (1983: 10). In other words, ethnicity is internally defined, 'race' is externally ascribed. There are serious weaknesses with Banton's argument here – not least, the implicit assumption that racial groups are somehow real[6] – to which I will return. However, the distinction he draws is useful in highlighting the processes of ascription which have led to the stigmatising of certain groups on supposedly racial grounds and, from that, the establishment of social (and, in some cases, political) hierarchies between various groups.

This racialisation process has occurred in two principal ways. One has been via the imputation of biologically determined characteristics as a means of distinguishing between various groups. This process has been most prominently associated with the scientific racism of the nineteenth century (see Gould, 1981), although it continues to be represented in current academic discourse (see M. Kohn, 1995) and is still widely held at a popular 'commonsense' level (Omi and Winant, 1986; Miles, 1989, 1993).

A second, comparable process of ascribing essentialised cultural differences to groups has also become increasingly widespread. This has led to the rise of 'new racisms' which describe group differences principally in cultural and/or historical terms – ethnic terms, in effect – without specifically mentioning 'race' or overtly racial criteria (Barker, 1981; Wetherell and Potter, 1992; van Dijk, 1993; Small, 1994). New racisms, in this sense, can be described as a form of *ethnicism* which, as Avtar Brah describes it:

> defines the experience of racialised groups primarily in 'culturalist' terms: that is, it posits 'ethnic difference' as the primary modality around which social life is constituted and experienced . . . This means that a group identified as culturally different is assumed to be internally homogeneous . . . ethnicist discourses seek to impose stereotypic notions of common

cultural need upon heterogeneous groups with diverse social aspirations and interests.

(1992: 129)

Before proceeding further, however, a number of additional caveats need to be raised in relation to Banton's initial distinction between 'race' and ethnicity. First, the distinction considerably understates the reciprocal nature of group identification and categorisation discussed in the preceding sections. As Richard Jenkins (1994) argues, the definition of 'them' in terms of 'race' is likely to be an important aspect of our definition of 'us' (which may, in turn, incorporate a 'racial' dimension). Second, while many examples of ethnic categorisation do involve the imputation of essentialised notions of racial and/or cultural difference – and, from that, the positing of a hierarchy of group difference – many also do not. In this sense, racism in its various forms can be viewed as a particular subset – or, more accurately perhaps, specific subsets – of ethnic categorisation. However, they are not reducible one to the other. Ethnic categories *may* be essentialised in the same way as 'race' categories have been historically *but they need not be*. Nor are ethnic relations necessarily hierarchical, exploitative and conflictual in the same way that 'race relations' invariably are (Rex, 1973; R. Jenkins, 1997). Indeed, it has often been the case that the global impact of racism has overridden previously nonhierarchised ethnic categories (Balibar, 1991; Fenton, 1999). As such, it is simply wrong to conflate 'race' with ethnicity as some commentators are in the habit of doing (see, for example, Wallman, 1978, 1986; Anthias, 1992; Anthias and Yuval-Davis, 1992). Third, groups as well as being identified negatively by others, may actually seek to identify themselves in positive 'racial' terms; a feature which is notable in many forms of black nationalism and also within some indigenous peoples' movements. Finally, 'racial' and ethnic ascriptions both remain, in the end, comparable processes of social and cultural *construction*. As the development of 'new racisms' indicates, and as Richard Jenkins argues, 'it is emphatically not the case that the difference between ethnicity and "race" is a simple difference between the physical and the cultural, although it may be a difference between *purported* physical and cultural characteristics' (1994: 208; my emphasis; see also Goldberg, 1993). Paul Gilroy, in his discussion of 'race' and racism, similarly asserts:

Races are not . . . simple expressions of either biological or cultural sameness. They are imagined – socially and politically constructed . . . Dealing with these issues in their specificity and in their articulation with other [social] relations and practices constitutes a profound and urgent theoretical challenge. It requires a theory of racisms that does not depend on an essentialist theory of races themselves.

(1990: 264)

Much the same could be said for the broader concept of ethnicity. Acknowledging that ethnicity is a social and cultural construction allows us to explore its articulation with other social forces and the various, or multiple, manifestations which may result (including various racisms). In so doing, the way in which ethnicity is deliberately employed – or mobilised – in specific contexts becomes central, as do the particular ends pursued in the process of mobilisation. The mobilisation of ethnicity here can be summarised as 'the process by which a group organises along ethnic lines in pursuit of collective political ends' (Stack, 1986: 5). In order to examine this process more closely, we need to turn to discussions on the *instrumental* utility of ethnicity.

Instrumental ethnicity

Accepting a situational view of ethnicity invites an obvious corollary: if ethnicity is primarily an aspect of social relationships, then it can best be analysed through the various uses to which individuals and/or groups put it. Ethnicity can thus be regarded principally as a social and political *resource* and ethnic groups as specific *interest groups*, comparable to other groups that might mobilise on the basis of social class, or trade unionism, for example. This appears to be the consensus of most current commentators on ethnicity (see, for example, Cohen, 1974; Glazer and Moynihan, 1975; Rex and Mason, 1986; M. Nash, 1989; Roosens, 1989; Nagel, 1994). It is summarised, in its most trenchant form, by Peter Worsley: 'Cultural traits are not absolutes or simply intellectual categories, but are invoked to provide identities which legitimise claims to rights. They are strategies or weapons in competitions over scarce social goods' (1984: 249).

Such a view also presupposes the *fluidity* or *malleability* of ethnicity. In effect, the origin, content and form of ethnicity are all open to negotiation, reflecting the creative choices of individuals and groups as they define themselves and others in ethnic ways (Nagel, 1994). Such choices involve a wide range of possibilities. At one level, ethnic choices may be limited to what Gans (1979) has termed 'symbolic ethnicity'. This is common among many immigrant minority groups and, as Gans suggests, is 'characterised by a nostalgic allegiance to the culture of the immigrant generation, or that of the old country; a love for and pride in a tradition that can be felt without having to be incorporated in everyday behaviour' (1979: 9). In this regard, many hyphenated white identities in the United States (Italian Americans, Jewish Americans, etc.) continue to exhibit a 'symbolic ethnicity' even when previously demarcated ethnic boundaries within the white population (such as language, religion and endogamy) have atrophied over time (see Kivosto, 1989; Alba, 1990; Waters, 1990; Yinger, 1994). At the other end of the spectrum, ethnicity may be constituted as a (or the) principal form of social identity and political organisation – a context which is literally *saturated* by ethnicity (Fenton, 1999). As Steve Fenton argues, ethnicity becomes here a more or less dominant element of the framing of political power, its legitimation and exercise. This can be seen historically in Nazi Germany and apartheid South Africa, and currently in such places as Rwanda, Burundi and the former Yugoslavia. In addition, the recent immolation in the former Yugoslavia usefully demonstrates the varying *salience* of ethnicity over time with regard to social and political organisation. For example, from the time of the Second World War to the beginning of the major ethnic conflicts of the late 1980s, ethnicity had *not* been mobilised as a principal form of social and political delineation in the relations between Serbian, Muslim and Croatian groups in the area (see Bowman, 1994; Silber and Little, 1995; Glenny, 1996; Pavkovic, 1997; Rogel, 1998).

When viewed in this (instrumental) light, ethnic histories and ascriptions can be *adopted* and *adapted* by individuals and/or groups according to the particular social and political aims being pursued at the time. Eugeen Roosens (1989) provides one of the most pointed examples of this process at group level in his depiction of the Huron Indians of Québec. Roosens argues that the Huron developed – or rather reconstituted – their history as a Native American tribe in order to claim access to the political rights and rewards associated with 'indigenousness'. This 'invention of tradition' (Hobsbawm and Ranger, 1983) involved the establishment of a pan-Indian identity where before there was none. It also saw the development of a reified 'ethnic counterculture' (Roosens, 1989) in which the uniformly positive characteristics of Huron 'culture' were juxtaposed against the largely negative depictions of the colonial cultures which supplanted it. Of course, such reconstructions are not limited to indigenous peoples and, indeed, are a common characteristic of national as well as ethnic histories; a point which I will elaborate upon in the following chapter on nationalism and national identity. However, Roosens' principal argument – that the construction of ethnicity may comprise a largely fictive element in some instances – is a hard one to ignore (see also Sollors, 1989).

A comparable degree of scepticism is directed at individuals who decide to adopt or change a particular ethnic affiliation. As Roosens again observes, 'many people change their ethnic identity only if they can profit from doing so' (1989: 13; see also Steinberg, 1981: 256). In his ensuing discussion of ethnic-minority group members in the USA, Roosens elaborates on the particular utility of choosing to mobilise on the basis of an ethnic identity rather than, for example, on the basis of social class:

> It becomes more interesting to appear socially as a member of an ethnic group than as a specimen of a lower socioeconomic category. In a world where a reevaluation of 'oppressed' cultures is in vogue in many circles, this is a way of self-valorisation that cannot be achieved by considering

oneself, for example, a member of the working class or the lower middle class.

(1989: 13–14)

Similarly sceptical views have been expressed about the changing processes of ethnic ascription evident among the indigenous Māori of Aotearoa / New Zealand (Hanson, 1989; Mulgan, 1989; cf. Chapter 8). Suffice it to say at this point, that any notion of individual choice with regard to ethnicity is usually viewed pejoratively, particularly by majority-group members in any given society. This rejection of an apparent 'designer ethnicity' among minority groups occurs despite the fact that majority-group members may exhibit considerable latitude in their own ethnic choices and social identifications (Alba, 1990; Waters, 1990). Conversely, the latter may mobilise a composite 'white' identity to similar instrumental ends (Lieberson, 1985; Roediger, 1991; McLaren, 1995; Dyer, 1997; McLaren and Torres, 1999).

Mobilising particular identities will also depend, to a large extent, on the audience(s) being addressed. This may produce a pattern of 'ethnic layering' for different ethnic groups (Nagel, 1994). For example, Cornell (1988) discusses the various levels of ethnic identity available to Native Americans, including sub-tribal, tribal, regional and pan-Indian identities. A similar pattern is found for Māori in Aotearoa / New Zealand – ranging from whānau (extended family), through hapū (sub-tribe) and iwi (tribe), to a pan-Māori identity (R. Walker, 1990; see Chapter 8). A variety of situational levels of ethnic identification can also be found among African Americans (Waters, 1990), Hispanic Americans (F. Padilla, 1985), white Americans (Kivosto, 1989; Alba, 1990; Waters, 1990), British Asians (Anthias and Yuval-Davis, 1992; Modood, 1992, 1997) and African Caribbeans in Britain (Goulbourne, 1991a; Gilroy, 1987, 1993a).

Of course, the variety of ethnic identifications available to these – and, by implication, all other – ethnic groups should not surprise us. A situational view of ethnicity requires it. As Joane Nagel observes, a 'chosen ethnic identity is determined by the individual's perception of its meaning to different audiences, its salience in different social contexts, and its utility in different settings' (1994: 155). Relatedly, these various identities may overlap with, or crosscut, other social identities. For example, one may be a woman, a Muslim, a Bangladeshi, a Bengali speaker, an Asian, working class, a Londoner, English, an English speaker, and British, all at the same time. However, which of these identities predominate in any given circumstance, and how they interact with each other, will depend on the context, the audience, and the ongoing balance between the internal definition and external ascription of social identities, discussed earlier. This complex dialectic also suggests that there will be significant *intra*ethnic differences evident within any given ethnic group. The varying confluence of ethnicity, language, class, religion and gender will result in a full repertoire of social identifications and trajectories among individual members of a particular ethnic group. In this light, it also needs to be constantly borne in mind that ethnic, linguistic, class, religious and gender groups are themselves not solidary groups but have their own broad-based internal divisions. Paul Brass is thus surely right when he argues in relation to ethnicity and class (and one can add linguistic and other forms of identity here also):

> that the processes of ethnic – and class – identity formation and of inter-group relations always have a dual dimension, of interaction/competition with external groups and of an internal struggle for control of the group ... It [thus] becomes critical to have analytical categories that can be used to analyze both the internal conflicts and the external relations of the group and the points of intersection between the two.
>
> (1985: 33)

I will outline such analytical categories in my ensuing discussions of habitus and ethnie. However, before doing so, it is important to explore briefly where this complex, crosscutting conception of ethnic (and other) identities might eventually take us. For this, we need to turn to postmodernist concep-tions of identity, and particularly the notion of 'hybridity'.

Hybridity: the postmodernist politics of identity

The articulation of cultural hybridity – and related concepts such as mestisaje and creolisation – is a prominent feature of the work of British theorists Stuart Hall, Homi Bhabha and Paul Gilroy, among others. Hall's (1992a) discussion of 'new ethnicities', Bhabha's (1994) celebration of creolisation and subaltern voices from the margin, and Gilroy's (1993b) discussion of a Black Atlantic – a hybridised, diasporic black counterculture – all foreground the transgressive potential of cultural hybridity. Hybridity is viewed as being able to subvert categorical oppositions and essentialist ideological move-ments – particularly ethnicity and nationalism – and to provide, in so doing, a basis for cultural reflexivity and change (Werbner, 1997a). Out with the old singular, in with the new plurality – a plurality of cultures, knowledges, languages, and their continuous interspersion, where 'ethnic absolutism' has no place and 'where "race" will no longer be a meaningful device for the categorisation of human beings' (Gilroy, 1993b: 218).

Within the discourses of hybridity, and of postmodernism more broadly, the new social agents are plural – multiple agents forged and engaged in a vari-ety of struggles and social movements (Giroux, 1997). Conversely, hybridity theory is entirely opposed to universalism, traditionalism and any idea of ethnic or cultural (or linguistic) rootedness. In line with postmodernism's rejection of totalising metanarratives, exponents of hybridity emphasise the contingent, the complex and the contested aspects of identity formation. Multiple, shifting and, at times, nonsynchronous identi*ties* are the norm for individuals. Like situational accounts of ethnicity, this position highlights the social and historical constructedness of culture and its associated fluidity and malleability. It also posits contingent, local narratives – what Lyotard (1984) has described as 'petits récits' – in opposition to the totalising narratives of ethnicity and nationalism.

In short, postmodernist commentators reject any forms of 'rooted' identity based on ethnicity, nationality and (one must also assume) language. Rooted identities such as these are branded with the negative characteristics of essentialism, closure and conflict. Instead, postmodernist commentators such as Homi Bhabha (1994) argue that it is the 'inter' and 'in-between', the liminal 'third space' of translation, which carries the burden of the meaning(s) of culture in this postmodern, postcolonial world. Others have described this process as one of 'border crossing' (see Anzaldúa, 1987; Rosaldo, 1989; Giroux, 1992; di Leonardo, 1994). In the postmodern world we thus have access to a wide range of identities and an even wider range of their various permutations. Suffice it to say that in this brave new world any notion of historical continuity – ethnic, cultural or linguistic – is regarded as entirely unnecessary, if not irremediably passé.

Limits to the social construction of ethnicity

If this is the case, the argument for maintaining particular ethnic affiliations – and by extension, linguistic ones – comes into serious question. But before we dismiss such affiliations out of hand, we need first to examine critically the limitations of these various constructionist accounts of ethnicity. Can we be satisfied that ethnicity is a modern construction (an invention even), only incidentally related to culture, as 'situational' commentators would have it? Is it completely fluid and malleable – able to be mobilised at will, in virtually any form, by individuals and groups in their pursuit of social and political gain as 'instrumentalists' argue? And is the locus of identity now irretrievably in the 'gaps' rather than the substance as hybridity theorists now surmise? The answer to each of these questions is not entirely.

For all its persuasiveness, there is an obvious degree of overstatement in the situational view of ethnicity. If taken to its extreme, for example, all ethnic choices become possible; a position represented by the methodological individualism of rational-choice theory (see Banton, 1980, 1987; Hechter, 1986, 1987). Methodological individualism assumes that groups are 'constituted from individual behaviour and are subject to continual change as individuals respond to changes in their circumstances' (Banton, 1987: 140). In this view, social relations become a form of market relations with individuals making rational choices about their ethnic alignment(s) solely on the basis of the social and material gain it will bring them. As Michael Banton observes of this process, an individual will join in ethnic-group mobilisation 'only when he expects the benefits of his participation to exceed the costs' (1987: 136; see also Hechter et al., 1982). On this basis, it is argued that the ethnic options of individual actors can be predicted. However, serious limitations can be attributed to this analysis. The central premise that rationality equals self-interest is too narrow; one may also act rationally in someone else's – or a collective group's – interest. Likewise, such a position fails to address adequately the external constraints facing actors in their ethnic choices (see below). Given this, rational-choice theory presents us with a socially and economically reductive account of ethnicity (for a useful critique, see Figueroa, 1991).

Ethnicity may well be a social construction but it is clear that not everything will function equally well in the social legitimation of ethnic identities. Even avowed social constructionists, such as Eugeen Roosens, concede this point. As Roosens observes, 'Ethnic groups and their cultures are not merely a completely arbitrary construct: there is always a minimum of incontestable and noninterpretable facts necessary to win something from the opponent . . . The reality [of ethnicity] is very elastic but not totally arbitrary' (1989: 156; see also below). Thomas Eriksen puts it even more directly:

> If the agents themselves hold that a certain description of their culture is obviously false, it cannot provide them with a powerful ethnic identity. If a group's version of its cultural history is seriously contested by other groups . . . it may also be problematic to maintain the identity postulated by that account of history. So we cannot conclude that anything goes and that everything about ethnicity is deception and make-believe . . . rather, [ethnic] identities are ambiguous, and . . . this ambiguity is connected with a negotiable history and a negotiable cultural content.
>
> (1993: 73)

Negotiation is a key element here to the ongoing construction of ethnicity, but there are also limits to it. Individual and collective choices are circumscribed by the ethnic categories available at any given time and place. These categories are, in turn, socially and politically defined and have varying degrees of advantage or stigma attached to them (Nagel, 1994). Moreover, the range of choices available to particular individuals and groups varies widely. A white American may have a wide range of ethnic options from which to choose on the basis of their ancestry. An African American, in contrast, is confronted with essentially one ethnic choice – black; irrespective of any preferred ethnic (or, for that matter, other) alternatives they might wish to employ. As Nagel observes:

> the extent to which ethnicity can be freely constructed by individuals or groups is quite narrow when compulsory ethnic categories are imposed by others. Such limits on ethnic identification can be official or unofficial. In either case, externally enforced ethnic boundaries can be powerful determinants of both the content and meaning of particular ethnicities.

(1994: 156)

The above example also suggests that the different ethnic choices available to majority- and minority-group members are a product of *unequal* power relations in the wider society. In particular, it is the differing location(s) of particular ethnic groups within the nation-state that shapes and constrains the ethnic options available to them; a theme I will pursue more fully in the following chapters. Suffice it to say at this point, that when ethnicity is viewed solely as an instrumental resource these differences in power are not adequately addressed. Similarly, the power differentials *within* a particular ethnic group, and the broad-based divisions that may result, are also ignored (Brass, 1985; O. O'Brien, 1993).

Second, there are limits to the central instrumentalist notion that ethnic groups are simply one of many interest groups seeking resources in and from the nation-state. Such a view is problematic because it fails to answer the question of *why* ethnicity is so often chosen as a means of mobilisation over other possibilities. In attempting to answer this question we can leave aside the somewhat limited suggestion that ethnicity is more effective in attaining social and political goals. In some cases it may well be (see, for example, Roosens' comments above). In other instances, it clearly is not. After all, ethnic groups have been known to reproduce their ethnicity *even when* it reduces their chances of attaining prosperity and political power (Eriksen, 1993). Why is this? The reasons lie principally in the 'ineffable' cultural and symbolic attributes of ethnicity largely dismissed in instrumental accounts. Ethnic groups differ from other interest groups precisely in their particular concern with cultural attributes and symbols, language, kinship, and historical memory. These features are predicated principally on 'belonging' rather than 'accomplishment' (Kymlicka, 1995a; Margalit and Raz, 1995) and provide the basis not only for political action but also, crucially, for identity and meaning (Melucci, 1989; Guibernau, 1996; see also Chapters 3 and 4). They may well be socially constructed (or reconstructed) but their enduring influence cannot be explained on the basis of functionality alone. Ignoring the cultural matters that are important to ethnic groups is thus an analytical error since these are central to their distinction from other interest groups. Paul Brass argues to this end:

> Ethnic groups, by definition . . . are concerned not only with material in-
> terests but with symbolic interests. Moreover, no matter how old or new,
> 'genuine' or 'artificial', rich or superficial, the culture of a particular ethnic
> group may be, its culture and the definition of its boundaries are crucial
> matters that do not arise in the same way for other interest groups.
>
> (1985: 31)

The ongoing influence of culture, and cultural affiliations, are also not
adequately resolved by hybridity theory. For example, the heterogeneous,
hybrid and plural identities so enamoured of hybridity theorists are assumed
by them to be somehow unique to the (post)modern world, replacing the
homogeneous, bounded identities of the past (particularly ethnicity and nationalism). But this is simply wrong, or at the very least bad history. Cultural
mixture and adaptation have been features of all societies, in all historical
periods, as Lévi Strauss (1994) has rightly argued. Thus, the historicist model
adopted by hybridity theorists – of closed to open, absolutist to relativist,
static to dynamic – is simply implausible (R. Jenkins, 1997). It is also highly
modernist in its teleological view of 'progress'. And perhaps most ironically,
in assuming that heterogeneous identities have now replaced previously
bounded and homogeneous ones, hybridity theory ends up treating cultures
as complex wholes. This perpetuates an essentialist conception of culture
rather than subverting it (Friedman, 1997; Wicker, 1997). The juxtaposition
of purity/hybridity, authenticity/mixture – so central to hybridity theory –
is thus fundamentally misconceived. In the end, hybridity is meaningless
as a description of 'culture' because contrary to its stated intentions it actually museumises culture as 'a thing' (Werbner, 1997a; see also Caglar, 1997;
Modood, 1998a).

And if this were not enough, it is also abundantly clear that there is
considerable disparity between the intellectual celebration of hybridity (whatever its merits) and the reality of the postmodern world. This world *is*
increasingly one of fractured, and fracturing identities. But these identities
are generally *not* hybrid; just the opposite, in fact. As we shall see in the next
two chapters, nation-states are facing a plethora of ethnic, regional and
other social and cultural minority demands, many of which are couched in
singular, collectivist terms. The tendency to rootedness and to boundary
maintenance (often expressed via ethnicity) thus militates against ecumenism,
and these tendencies are generated and reinforced by the real fragmentation
occurring within and between nation-states in a global era (Friedman, 1997).
Given this, as Jonathan Friedman asserts, the valorisation of hybridisation is
largely self-referential and self-congratulatory:

> hybrids, and hybridisation theorists, are products of a group that self-
> identifies and/or identifies the world in such terms, not as a result of
> ethnographic understanding, but as an act of self-definition – indeed, of

self-essentialising – which becomes definition for others via the forces of socialisation inherent in the structures of power that such groups occupy: intellectuals close to the media; the media intelligentsia itself; in a sense, all those [and, one might add, *only* those] who can afford a cosmopolitan identity.

(1997: 81)

Ahmad (1995), in a similarly scathing critique, argues that articulations of hybridity fail to address adequately the social and political continuities and transformations that underpin individual and collective action in the real world. In that world, he argues, political agency is 'constituted not in flux or displacement but in given historical locations'. Moreover, it is sustained by a coherent 'sense of place, of belonging, of some stable commitment to one's class or gender or nation' (1995: 16, 14). In short, hybridity theory might sound like a good idea, but it is not in the end consonant with many people's individual and collective experiences. This disjuncture also holds true with social constructivist accounts of ethnicity more generally. After all, there is something strange going on when theorists proclaim that ethnicity is 'invented' and set out to 'decentre' it, while at the same time the news is full of ethnic cleansing and genocide (Levine, 1999). Consequently, we need to explain more adequately why ethnicity does seem to continue to mean something to so many people. Perhaps more importantly, we also need to be able to explain why when ethnicity matters, it can *really* matter (R. Jenkins, 1997).

Finding common ground – ethnicity as habitus

A useful first step to this end is to dispense with the dichotomous approach adopted to date in much of the primordialist/instrumentalist debate on ethnicity. Like so many dichotomies posited in the social sciences, it seems to have led us to a theoretical and practical impasse. Indeed, as Richard Jenkins has observed,

the debate about whether or not ethnicity is 'situational' or 'primordial' seems futile; it confuses the *ubiquity* of a social phenomenon such as ethnicity with 'naturalness', implying fixity, determinism and some kind of presocial power of causation.

(1994: 220; see also 1997: 47;
M. Nash, 1989: 124; A. Smith, 1998: 157)

Given this, I want to suggest that primordial and situational views do not form mutually exclusive conceptualisations of ethnicity but that each formulation represents a *partial* representation of the underlying social and cultural movements which they seek to describe. Following Jenkins, ethnicity can thus be viewed as both a cultural creation *and* a primary or first-order dimension of human experience: 'on the one hand, ubiquitous and, on the other, possessing a particular immediacy and compelling urgency in many social situations' (R. Jenkins, 1996: 72). As Jenkins argues, despite its limitations, the 'primordialist' position outlined by Geertz, Isaacs and Shils rightly highlights that ethnicity is something in which we actively participate, an integral aspect of ourselves, rooted in our earliest socialisation (see also Stack, 1986; Fenton, 1999). John Rex muses along similar lines that this may well explain 'why it is that, despite the very strong pressure in complex societies for groups to be formed on the basis of congruence of interest, many individuals do in fact stubbornly continue to unite with those with whom they have ties of ethnic sameness, even though such alliances might run contrary to patterns of group formation determined by shared interests' (1991: 11).

However, to take ethnicity seriously as a primary social sentiment in this way does not necessarily entail its reification as a set of fixed cultural properties. Stack (1986) argues, for example, that the primordialist position of Geertz, Shils and Isaacs has never denied the significant role of socioeconomic and political factors as intervening variables in the crystallisation of ethnicity. Nor, as I suggested earlier, has it conceptualised ethnicity as immutable and static (see, for example, Geertz, 1973: 258). We do not need to abandon the social constructionist consensus on ethnicity. Nor do we need to naturalise ethnicity as a sociobiological phenomenon as, for example, do van den Berghe (1979, 1995) and Kellas (1991). Ethnicity can still be viewed as socially constructed and fluid, *within certain limits* (see above). Likewise, its mobilisation by individuals and groups in the social and political domain, and within specific temporal and historical contexts, can be fully acknowledged and explored. In this sense, ethnicity can be viewed as both situational *and* pervasive (A. Smith, 1995a; Billig, 1995).

Similarly, acknowledging the constructedness of ethnicity does not necessarily foreclose the possibility that the 'cultural stuff' of ethnicity – including, for example, a historically associated language – may still have ongoing and significant influence and importance. As Richard Jenkins argues, a constructivist recognition of ethnicity as transactional and changeable does not mean that ethnicity is *always*, or *has* to be so, only that it *may* be. As he concludes, 'the recognition that ethnicity is neither static nor monolithic should not be taken to mean that it is definitively and perpetually in a state of flux' (1997: 51). In short, a sense of continuity does not preclude cultural and linguistic change and adaptation, *and vice versa*.

A way in which these apparent dualisms can be effectively incorporated and expressed is through Bourdieu's concept of habitus. Bourdieu's analysis of habitus is principally concerned with social class (see Bourdieu, 1984, 1990a, 1990b; Bourdieu and Passeron, 1990; Bourdieu and Wacquant, 1992).

However, since Bourdieu describes habitus as 'a system of dispositions common to all products of the same conditionings' (1990b: 59), the application of habitus to ethnicity and ethnic-identity formation is equally applicable (see Bentley, 1987; Smaje, 1997; Wicker, 1997; May, 1999a). For Bourdieu, habitus comprises all the social and cultural experiences that shape us as a person; his use of the term 'dispositions' is an attempt to capture fully this meaning. Specifically, there are four key aspects of habitus highlighted in Bourdieu's work which are useful to our discussion here: embodiment; agency; the interplay between past and present; and the interrelationship between collective and individual trajectories (see Reay, 1995a, b). I will look at each of these elements in turn.

First, habitus is not simply about ideology, attitude or perception, it is a *material* form of life which is 'embodied and turned into second nature' (Bourdieu, 1990a: 63). It is, in effect, an orientation to social action (Bourdieu, 1990b). Thus, via the concept of habitus, Bourdieu explores how members of a social group come to acquire, as a result of their socialisation, a set of *embodied* dispositions – or ways of viewing, and living in, the world. This set of dispositions – what Bourdieu would call 'bodily hexis' – operates most often at the level of the unconscious and the mundane and might comprise in the case of ethnicity such things as language use, dress, diet and customary practices (Smaje, 1997). The key point for Bourdieu is that habitus is both shaped by, *and also shapes*, the objective social and cultural conditions which surround it. As Roy Nash observes, the habitus is 'a system of durable dispositions inculcated by objective structural conditions, but since it is embodied the habitus gains a history and generates its [own] practices [over] time even when the objective conditions which give rise to it have disappeared' (1990: 433–434). Ethnic attitudes and practices, including language use, may thus be lived out implicitly as a result of historical and customary practice. As such, they may provide the parameters of social action for many. However, in the course of those very actions they may also begin to take on a life of their own (see below).[7]

Second, Bourdieu's notion of habitus is concerned to explore the interrelationship between agency and structure. While many have dismissed Bourdieu's position as structurally determinist (for a critique of this position, see Harker and May, 1993), his specific aim is actually to overcome the agency/structure dichotomy in sociological thought – 'to escape from structuralist objectivism without relapsing into subjectivism' (Bourdieu, 1990a: 61). Thus, Bourdieu argues that habitus does not *determine* individual behaviour. A range of choices, or strategic practices, is presented to individuals within the internalised framework of the habitus. Moreover, these practices, based on the intuitions of the practical sense, *orient* rather than strictly determine action. Choice is thus at the heart of habitus. However, not all choices are possible. As Bourdieu observes, 'habitus, like every "art of inventing" . . . makes it possible to produce an infinite number of practices that are relatively unpredictable (like the corresponding situations) but [which are] also limited in their diversity' (1990b: 55). These limits are set by the historically and socially situated conditions of the habitus' production; what Bourdieu terms both 'a conditioned and conditional freedom' (1990b: 55). As he elaborates,

> being the product of a particular class of objective regularities, the habitus tends to generate all the 'reasonable' and 'commonsense' behaviours (and only those) which are possible within the limits of these regularities, and which are likely to be positively sanctioned because they are objectively adjusted to the logic characteristic of the field, whose objective future they anticipate. At the same time . . . it tends to exclude all 'extravagances' ('not for the likes of us'), that is, all the behaviours that would be negatively sanctioned because they are incompatible with the objective conditions.

> (1990b: 55–56)

In short, improbable practices, or practices viewed as antithetical to the mores of a particular group, are rejected as unthinkable. Concomitantly, only a particular range of possible practices is considered, although this range of possibilities may evolve and change over time in relation to changing circumstances. Thus, Bourdieu posits that individuals and groups operate strategically *within the constraints* of a particular habitus, but also that they react to changing external conditions; economic, technological and political (Harker, 1984, 1990; Harker and May, 1993; May, 1999a).

This recursive position allows Bourdieu to argue that the habitus is both a product of our early socialisation, yet is also continually modified by individuals' experience of the outside world (Di Maggio, 1979). Within this complex interplay of past and present experience – the third key dimension highlighted here – habitus can be said to reflect the social and cultural position in which it was constructed, while also allowing for its transformation in current circumstances. However, the possibilities of action in most instances will tend to reproduce rather than transform the limits of possibility delineated by the social group. This is because habitus, as a product of history, ensures the active presence of past experiences which tend also to normalise particular cultural and linguistic practices, and their constancy over time (Harker and May, 1993). Nonetheless, this tendency towards reproduction of group mores and practices does not detract from the *potential* for transformation and change.

The fourth element of habitus – the interrelationship between individual action and group mores – also reflects this tension. In many instances, individual practices will conform to those of the group since, as Bourdieu argues, 'the practices of the members of the same group . . . are always more and better harmonised than the agents know or wish' (1990b: 59). Yet

Bourdieu also recognises the potential for divergence between individual and collective trajectories. In effect, habitus within, as well as between, social groups differs to the extent that the details of individuals' social trajectories diverge from one another (Reay, 1995a):

> The singular habitus of the members of the same [group] are united in a relation of homology, that is, of diversity within homogeneity reflecting the diversity within homogeneity characteristic of their social conditions of production. Each individual system of dispositions is a structural variant of the others, expressing the singularity of its position within the [group] and its trajectory.
>
> (Bourdieu, 1990b: 60)

There is, in all of this, a certain sense of vagueness and indeterminacy in Bourdieu's rendition of habitus, and debates about its efficacy in bridging the structure/agency divide remain ongoing (see R. Jenkins, 1992; Calhoun et al., 1993; Harker and May, 1993; R. Nash, 1999; D. Robbins, 1991, 2000). However, if the concept is employed as social *method* rather than as social *theory* – that is, as a way of thinking and a manner of asking questions, which is actually Bourdieu's preference (see Harker et al., 1990) – it can be usefully applied to a discussion of ethnicity. As Rob Gilbert summarises it, Bourdieu's approach 'suggests an explanation of the regularities of social practice [in this case, ethnicity] as structured by the relations between, on the one hand, an objective set of historically produced material conditions, and on the other, historically produced definitions of those conditions and predispositions to act in certain ways in any historical conjuncture' (1987: 40–41). In other words, ethnicity as socially constructed *and* as a material form of life is addressed by the concept of habitus. In so doing, the 'primordialist' mistake of assuming a realist definition of ethnicity is avoided without diminishing the *significance* of ethnicity and the processes of cultural and linguistic identification that may be associated with it (see also Smaje, 1997). As Bourdieu observes of social class, for example – and one can clearly add ethnicity here also:

> My work consists in saying that people are located in a social space, that they aren't just anywhere, in other words, interchangeable, as those people claim who deny the existence of 'social classes' [or ethnic groups], and that according to the position they occupy in this highly complex space, you can understand the logic of their practices and determine, inter alia, how they will classify themselves and others and, should the case arise, think of themselves as members of a 'class' [or ethnic group].
>
> (1990a: 50)

Similarly, the dichotomy between the 'ineffable' nature and the 'calculated' use of ethnicity is rendered negotiable by the concept of habitus. As Gilbert again observes:

> The notion of habitus, while recognising conscious intention, need not inflate it in explaining action, nor relegate the dynamic of social action to an ineffable consciousness. Further, the theory offers an explanation of human understanding and action which goes beyond individualism, but does not resort to abstract social forces, functionalist mechanisms or reified institutions as agents of social practice. Finally it allows us to see how ideologies through their symbols and representations [including, one assumes, language] are part of the objective presentation of the contexts of practice, the means for defining a situation, and the medium in which past and present practices are installed in the interpretive and generative operations of the habitus.
>
> (1987: 41)

Finally, habitus is also extremely pertinent to a discussion of ethnicity because it is employed by Bourdieu principally in order to explore inequalities in power between dominant and subordinate groups. As Bourdieu argues, the individual and collective habitus of the former is invariably constituted as *cultural capital* – that is, recognised as socially valuable – whereas the habitus of the latter is not. This has obvious parallels with the negative and commonly expressed views of ethnic-minority cultures and practices (including the speaking of a minority language) as regressive and 'premodern'. These views – which Lukes (1996) has aptly described as the product of 'ascriptive humiliation' – are expressed predominantly by majority-group members. However, they are also expressed by minority-group members themselves, usually as the end result of a process of negative internalisation. Bourdieu (1991) terms the process by which the latter is achieved as 'méconnaissance' or 'misrecognition' and its inevitably deleterious consequences as 'symbolic violence'. While I have already briefly addressed the historical antecedents of this pattern of negative ascription in the early part of the chapter, I will explore its social and political implications more fully in Chapters 3–5. At this point, it is sufficient to observe that the habitus of ethnic-minority individuals and groups tend to be specifically marginalised and devalued, both as a legitimate means of identity, and for their apparent lack of 'relevance' to the modern world.

Ethnies

If habitus provides us with a useful methodological framework for exploring ethnicity, Anthony Smith's notion of ethnie provides a consonant explanation of how the actual *particularities* of ethnicity and ethnic identity are *enacted* by individuals and groups. Smith's central argument – as in this account – is that the divide between primordialist and instrumentalist conceptions of ethnicity leads us into a theoretical cul-de-sac:

> By fixing attention mainly on the great dimensions and 'fault lines' of religion, customs, language and institutions, we run the risk of treating ethnicity as something primordial and fixed. By concentrating solely on the attitudes and sentiments and political movements of specific ethnie or ethnic fragments, we risk [seeing] ethnic phenomena . . . as wholly dependent 'tools' or 'boundary markers' of other social and economic forces.
>
> (1986: 211)

In order to avoid this dichotomy, Smith argues that any realistic account of ethnicity and ethnogenesis must 'reconstitute the notion of collective cultural identity itself in historical, subjective and symbolic terms' (1991: 25). As Smith elaborates, a conception of ethnic identity along these lines:

> refers not to *a uniformity of elements* over generations but to *a sense of continuity* on the part of successive generations of a given cultural unit of population, to shared memories . . . and to notions entertained by each generation about the collective destiny of that unit and its culture.
>
> (1991: 25; my emphases)

The parallels with habitus are obvious here. Particular sets of social networks are formed on the basis of believed or actual (ethnic) connectedness and are sustained, crucially, by a collective sense of continuity. Thus, ethnic groups in Smith's conception change more slowly than is often assumed by constructivist commentators of ethnicity and may express deeply held group values and meanings (Hutchinson, 1994). Nonetheless, an ethnic group may still rise or fall, subject to the vicissitudes of history. In this sense, Smith argues, such collectivities are doubly 'historical' since 'not only are historical memories essential to their continuance but each . . . is the product of specific historical forces and is therefore subject to historical change and dissolution' (1991: 20).

For Smith, the concept of ethnie, or ethnic community, best expresses the historical and symbolic processes highlighted here. Specifically, ethnies are said by Smith to comprise:

- a collective proper name
- a myth of common ancestry
- shared historical memories
- one or more differentiating elements of common culture

- an association with a specific homeland
- a sense of solidarity

As can be seen, most of these characteristics reflect a significant cultural and historical content and, except for aspects of a common culture, a strongly subjective component also. Given this, ethnies are not incompatible with a situational view of ethnicity (see A. Smith, 1998: 192). For example, in relation to the characteristic of common ancestry, Smith argues that it is 'myths of common ancestry, not any fact of ancestry (which is usually difficult to ascertain), that are crucial. It is fictive descent and putative ancestry that matters for the sense of ethnic identification' (1991: 22). Likewise, attachments to a specific territory or homeland may be most significant to ethnic identity for their mythical and subjective qualities; the 'sense of place' that they evoke. Even in relation to the more objective aspects of a common culture – language, religion and kinship, for example – it is the *diacritical significance* attached to these elements which makes them salient to ethnic identity, not the actual elements themselves (cf. Barth, 1969a). Finally, while Smith argues that these attributes are clearly characteristic of ethnic groups, they are also malleable and fluid. They may vary in their salience; singly and in relation to each other, within and between historical periods, and among individual group members and thus the group itself:

> As the subjective significance of each of these attributes waxes and wanes for the members of a community, so does the cohesion and self-awareness of that community's membership. As these several attributes come together and become more intense and salient, so does the sense of ethnic identity and, with it, of ethnic community. Conversely, as each of these attributes is attenuated and declines, so does the overall sense of ethnicity, and hence the ethnie itself would dissolve or be absorbed.

> (1991: 23)

Smith's notion of ethnie allows us then to see ethnic identification as a *dynamic* quality of group relations. More importantly perhaps, it provides us with an operational concept that encapsulates 'the central paradox of ethnicity: the coexistence of flux and durability, of an ever-changing individual and cultural expression within distinct social and cultural parameters' (A. Smith, 1991: 38). Interestingly, this position ends up actually being quite close to Barth's later (1989) formulation of 'streams of tradition' or 'universes of discourse' in which individual actors differentially participate but which possess a degree of stability over time (see also R. Jenkins, 1995). But an additional benefit of the concept of ethnie is that it allows us to explore effectively the close interrelationship between ethnic and national identities, the subject of the next chapter.

Notes

1 Britain is not a nation; it is a multinational state. For a fuller discussion of these distinctions, see Chapter 2.

2 There are important exceptions to this position within liberal ideology, as Will Kymlicka (1989, 1995a, b) highlights. I will return to this point, and its implications, in Chapter 3 when I discuss the question of the legitimacy of group-based minority rights within the modern nation-state.

3 Globalisation 'refers to those processes, operating on a global scale, which cut across national boundaries, integrating and connecting communities and organisations in new space–time combinations, making the world in reality and in experience more interconnected' (Hall, 1992a: 299).

4 As Fishman (1997) observes, this largely negative semantic association derives from the Biblical Hebrew distinction between goy and 'am, the former denoting an ungodly people and the latter a godly people. In the third century Greek translation of the Hebrew Bible (the Septuagint) the Greek word 'ethnos' was used for 'goy', hence its subsequent association with heathenism.

5 Handelman (1977) has proposed a more detailed continuum between ethnic categories and ethnic communities. Based on the principle of differing degrees of ethnic incorporation, he suggests two intermediary levels – the ethnic *network* and the ethnic *association*. An ethnic network 'suggests that people will regularly interact with one another in terms of an ethnic membership set' (1977: 269). An ethnic association involves the addition of some form of political organisation, enabling the collective interests of the ethnic group to be represented in the formal political sphere, usually in the form of a pressure group. Nonetheless, the broad distinction between ethnic categories and ethnic communities can still be said to apply.

6 This process of equating group differences on 'racial' grounds is now considered to be scientifically invalid (see, for example, Gould, 1981; Miles, 1989, 1993; Fenton, 1999); hence, the use of quotation marks around the term 'race'.

7 The material dimension of habitus outlined here is broadly consonant with Fishman's (1980) articulation of ethnicity as a matter of 'being', 'doing' and 'knowing'. I will explore in more depth Fishman's arguments about ethnicity, particularly with respect to language, in Chapter 4.

2

Nationalism and its discontents

Many of the academic arguments surrounding ethnicity have also been rehearsed at length in relation to national identity and nationalism. Indeed,
the field of nationalism studies reveals a very similar constructivist/essen-
tialist dichotomy, with modernist commentators on nationalism adopting
the former position, and primordialists adopting the latter (see below). Given
this, it is perhaps surprising that discussions of ethnicity and nationalism
have until recently been conducted largely in isolation from one another. As
Eriksen (1993) observes, the remarkable congruence between theories of
nationalism and national identity, and anthropological theories of ethnicity,
seems to have gone unrecognised, or at least unmarked, by many theorists
of nationalism (see, for example, Gellner, 1983; Hobsbawm, 1990; Anderson,
1991). This lack of cross-referral may well be attributable to the well-known
solidity of academic boundaries. However, it may also be due to the prevail-
ing modernist view among theorists of nationalism that ethnicity and
nationalism are separate phenomena. Hobsbawm argues, for example, that
nationalism and ethnicity are 'different, and indeed non-comparable, concepts' (1992: 4). Consequently, any connection between the two is seen as
more or less coincidental. By this, modernist commentators on nationalism
have attempted to debunk the central claim of many nationalist movements
in the modern world: that the right to nationhood is based principally on
preexisting ties of ethnicity. In its most extreme form, this latter position
equates nations directly with ethnocultural communities which are, in turn,
defined by fixed cultural characteristics – particularly, but not exclusively, a
common language. While this view is now largely limited to nationalist
proponents themselves, it also has some early currency in the academic
writings of the late-eighteenth-century 'German Romantics' Herder,
Humboldt and Fichte. However, like the debates on ethnicity in the previous
chapter, the common orthodoxy nowadays among theorists of nationalism
is to reject this position as essentialist and to argue for a more subjective,
situational, and socially constructed account of nationalism and nationhood.

I will explore these debates more fully in due course. However, before doing so, I want to foreshadow my own position. As in the previous chapter, my argument will be that the polarisation of primordial and modernist accounts has been unhelpful – resulting in limited and partial accounts of the phenomena of nationalism and nationhood which they seek to explain. Thus, after outlining the key tenets of the primordial/modernist debates, I will once again advocate an alternative position – one that combines salient elements of both extremes and, in so doing, returns ethnicity to the study of nationalism. This alternative can broadly be described as 'ethnicist' (Hutchinson, 1994) or 'ethno-symbolic' (A. Smith, 1998), although I prefer to use the former descriptor in what follows. Such a position has been perhaps most prominently associated with the long-standing work of Anthony Smith on nationalism and, in particular, his elaboration of the central concept of ethnie (see Chapter 1). An ethnicist perspective avoids the trap of essentialism associated with primordial accounts while still being able to explain the crucial interrelationship of ethnicity with nationalism and national identity, something modernist accounts have seen fit to ignore. As such, it provides an appropriate basis for the ensuing arguments in Chapters 3–5 in support of minority rights – both generally, and in particular relation to language and education. It is my view here that the historical denigration of ethnic-minority language(s) and culture(s) within modern nation-states, and their related exclusion from the public or civic realm, are fundamentally misguided. Moreover, for those groups that can claim to be national minorities (ethnies) in their own historic territory, such an approach can actually be said to be illegitimate (Kymlicka, 1995a; Guibernau, 1996, 1999).

The processes of denigration and exclusion to which minority groups have been subject stem from the long-standing pejorative views of ethnicity in both political and social-science commentary, discussed in Chapter 1. As I will argue in this and the next chapter, these views can be traced historically to an overemphasis on *political* nationalism and its institutional embodiment in the modern nation-state, and to the associated valorisation of civic over ethnic ties; the latter usually being invoked in support of liberal democracy. Such a position suits well the interests of majority (or dominant) ethnic groups in nation-states since it ends up representing their ethnic affiliations, particularly their language and cultural traditions, *as those of* the nation-state. In effect, the *ethnic* interests of the majority group are legitimated and naturalised as *civic* ones which, in turn, are equated directly with modernity. Concomitantly, the legitimate claims of minorities for similar recognition and inclusion in the public or civic realm are ignored, discounted and/or suppressed on the basis that they are merely 'ethnic'. At best, minority-group members may be able to continue to maintain their ethnic habitus in private, although the pressure to assimilate to the civic language and culture may remain intense. At worst, minority language(s) and culture(s) may be actively suppressed – a practice which remains an all too common feature of modern nation-state policy. The exclusion of Albanian from Kosovan schools, under the Serbian-controlled regime of the 1990s, is a recent prominent example of the state-sanctioned linguistic suppression of minority languages, not to mention also being a key catalyst in the subsequent bid for Kosovan independence from Serbia. The similar exclusion of Tibetan from schools in Chinese-controlled Tibet, and the more wide-ranging suppression of Kurdish in Turkey are just two of many ongoing examples of such policies.

Terminology

Before proceeding further, however, it behoves us once again to clarify our terms. Indeed, if it is not already clearly apparent, one of the principal difficulties in discussions of both ethnicity and nationalism has been the indeterminacy and confusion that have surrounded the meaning and use of key terms. As such, it is crucial at the start to define, and distinguish between, the following four central concepts: the 'nation', 'nationalism', the 'state' and the 'nation-state'. In due course, I will also examine the distinctions that can be drawn between 'political nationalism', 'cultural nationalism', the 'multinational state' and the 'polyethnic state', and will specify in detail how a variety of ethnic and national-minority groups are positioned in relation to all of the above.

Following Guibernau (1996), a 'nation' refers to a group of people who are conscious of forming a distinct community and who may be said to share:

- a historic territory, or homeland
- common historical memories
- a common culture
- a common (political) destiny and, relatedly,
- a desire for at least some degree of social and/or political self-determination

Thus, the 'nation' includes five key dimensions – psychological (consciousness of forming a group), territorial, historical, cultural and political. It is not identical to the notion of ethnie outlined in the previous chapter, but it may be regarded for the purposes of the following discussion as broadly comparable, or at least complementary.[1]

Following John Breuilly (1993) and Anthony Smith (1994), the ideology of nationalism can be broadly summarised as follows:

- the world is divided into nations, each with its own identity and destiny
- the nation is the sole source of political power, and the interests and values of the nation take priority over all other interests and values – loyalty to the nation is preeminent
- everyone must belong to a nation, if everyone is to be truly free

- to realise themselves, nations must be as politically independent as possible – political autonomy, or at least some degree of self-determination, are central tenets of nationalism
- to maintain peace and justice in the world, nations must be both sufficiently free and sufficiently secure to pursue their own (national) interests (see Breuilly, 1993: 2; A. Smith, 1994: 379)

Admittedly, it needs to be stressed here that the history of nationalism(s) is replete with numerous and wide variations. Accordingly, some commentators have despaired of finding, or even attempting, a universal definition of nationalism. John Hall, for example, makes the blunt assertion that 'no single, universal theory of nationalism is possible. As the historical record is diverse, so too must be our concepts' (1993: 1). Other commentators, while not endorsing this degree of relativism, argue that explanations of nationalism must at least take due account of the temporal and societal context (see, for example, Gellner, 1983; R. Jenkins, 1997; A. Smith 1995a, 1998). However, these caveats notwithstanding, there is sufficient consistency among nationalist proponents to present the above as the 'core doctrine' of nationalism, particularly as it has been mobilised historically and politically in the establishment of 'nation-states'.

Which brings us to the 'state' and the 'nation-state'. The 'state', following Max Weber, has been defined in western social science theory as an entity (a) with political sovereignty over a clearly designated territorial area, (b) with monopoly control of legitimate force and (c) consisting of citizens with terminal loyalty to it (Giddens, 1984; Oommen, 1994). The 'nation-state' – the raison d'être of so many historical and current nationalisms – is the confluence of the nation and the state. As Gellner asserts in his influential *Nations and Nationalism*, 'nationalism is *primarily* a political principle, which holds that the political and the national unit should be congruent' (1983: 1; my emphasis). In other words, the core tenet of what might be termed 'political nationalism' is the belief that 'the national state, identified with a national culture and committed to its protection, is the natural political unit' (Gellner, 1993: 409). It follows directly from this principle that all nations should aspire to be represented in and by a state of their own. Moreover, as Gellner's latter comment implies, once this coincidence of nation and state has occurred, the principal aim of the institutional nation-state is, recursively, to create (or recreate) and maintain a particular conception of nationhood and/or national identity. Thus, the Italian nationalist Massimo d'Azeglio could declare: 'We have made Italy, now we have to make Italians' (cited in Hobsbawm, 1990: 44). In so doing, the nation-state conflates the historical-cultural and the legal-political dimensions of nationhood in order to create a homogeneous national culture with which its members can identify and to which they will be committed. As we shall see, this is achieved principally through the establishment and promotion of a common language and civic culture, and via the agencies of the state – most notably, education.

The nation-state is thus a specifically modern phenomenon; the product, in effect, of the nationalism of the last two centuries. However, such is the pervasiveness of the nation-state in the modern world, and so unquestioned are the political principles upon which it is predicated, that it has come to be largely naturalised and taken for granted. So much so, in fact, that the 'nation-state' is often seen as synonymous with both 'society' and 'modernity'. With respect to the equation of the nation-state with society, Zygmunt Bauman observes of western social science generally, and of sociology in particular:

> Sociology, as it came of age in the bosom of Western civilisation and as we know of it today, is endemically national-based. It does not recognise a totality broader than a politically organised [nation-state]: the term 'society' . . . is, for all practical purposes, a name for an entity identical in size and composition with the nation-state.
>
> (1973: 42–43; see also Halle, 1962; Tilly, 1984)

Of the correspondence of modernity and the nation-state, Hobsbawm asserts that 'the basic characteristic of the modern nation and everything associated with it is its modernity' (1990: 14). These two tenets combine when nation-states – or, more specifically, those 'nations' whose culture is currently represented within and by a 'state' – are compared with nations without a corresponding state. As David McCrone observes in this regard, of the early development of *British* sociology:

> British sociology simply accepted that 'society' was coterminous with the British state, unitary and highly centralised, driven by social change in the political and cultural heartland of southern Britain [i.e., England]. If there was a particular sociology of the 'periphery' – in Wales, Ireland and Scotland – it had to do with analysing a 'traditional', pre-capitalist way of life. It was judged to be the task of the sociologist of these parts merely to chart its decline and ultimate incorporation into 'modern' society, or so it seemed.
>
> (1992: 5)

And so, by implication, we return once again to the pejorative distinction between 'ethnicity' and the modern 'nation-state', first discussed in Chapter 1. However, we can also now specifically include within the former category the sublimation of 'national minorities', or nations not currently represented by a state. Hroch (1985, 1998) has described these as 'smaller nations'. Guibernau (1999) has termed them more accurately, albeit prosaically, as 'nations without states', while Keating (1996, 1997) refers to them as 'stateless nations'. In order to explore further the origins, nature and validity of the particular construction on which this distinction is based, I want now to turn to a closer examination of nationalism and the various debates and controversies which have surrounded it.

Linguistic nationalism

For many nationalists, nations are perennial; they have always existed in one form or another. In this view, modern nations can trace their antecedents to the Middle Ages and, in some cases, to 'natlones' in antiquity. Relatedly, in a position that closely parallels the primordial conceptions of ethnicity, the enduring influence of nations, and nationhood, is explained by an ideology of preexisting kinship or ethnic ties.[2] From this, the nation is objectified via a range of 'national' characteristics – including language, history, and a variety of specific cultural practices. Both primordial ties and the weight of history are thus regularly invoked by nationalists in their assertions of (and for) nationhood. Indeed, it is this 'deep-seated sense of kinship which infuses the nation' (Connor, 1993) that nationalist leaders have so effectively employed in mobilising individual members of nations on behalf of nationalist causes.

This view of nations as objective, pre-given and fixed social entities has been principally expounded by nationalists themselves, although it was also to gain some early currency in academic commentary on nationalism. Friedrich Schleiermacher (1768–1834), for example, viewed the nation as 'a natural division of the human race, endowed by God with its own character' (cited in Kedourie, 1960: 58). However, it was the late-eighteenth-century triumvirate of Herder, Humboldt and Fichte – the 'German Romantics' as they have come to be known – who have been most closely associated with this position in the social sciences. Thus, Johann Gottfried Herder (1744–1803) argued, along very much the same lines, for the divine inspiration of the nation as a natural form of human organisation: 'a nation is as natural as a plant, as a family, only with more branches' (1969: 324). From this, Herder and Humboldt, and subsequently Fichte, were to advocate an 'organic' or 'linguistic' nationalism where culture – and particularly, language – were viewed as central to the essence or character (Volksgeist) of the nation. In this perspective, language came to be the *most* important distinguishing characteristic of nationhood – indeed, its very soul. The interrelationship between language and the soul or spirit of the nation is most clearly stated by Wilhelm von Humboldt (1767–1835): '[the nation's] language is its spirit and its spirit is its language' (see Cowan, 1963: 277). Or, as he observes elsewhere: 'From every language we can infer backwards to the national character' (Humboldt, 1988: 154). Indeed, Humboldt is credited as a result with the development of the twin theories of linguistic determinism and linguistic relativism – that language plays a significant role in determining culture, and that each language has a different way of 'looking at the world' (Clyne, 1997; see Chapter 4). As Kedourie observes of the German Romantics, language was seen as 'an outward sign of a group's particular identity and a significant means of ensuring its continuation' (1960: 71). Or, put another way, the continuing existence of a nation was inconceivable without its own language. Without a language, Herder argued, a Volk is an absurdity (Unding), a contradiction in terms (see Barnard, 1965: 57).

The culturalist and linguistic emphases of the German Romantics – emphasising 'language, blood and soil' as constitutive elements of the Volk – were established in direct opposition to the political nationalism of the French Revolution and its associated notions of equality and popular sovereignty. Indeed, the anti-French feeling of Herder, Humboldt and Fichte, and their general ethnocentrism, are prominent features of their writings. Fichte (1762–1814) is the most extreme in this regard. In his *Addresses to the German Nation* [1807], he argued that of all the 'Teutonic' peoples only the Germans retained their original language: 'the German speaks a language which has been alive ever since it first issued from the force of nature, whereas the other Teutonic races speak a language which has movement on the surface but is dead at the root' (1968: 58–59). On the basis of this anthropomorphic view of language, Fichte asserted that if German was superior to all other languages, then on Herder's principle of the centrality of language to nationhood, the German nation was also, by definition, superior to all others. Consequently, Fichte has been attributed with extrapolating Herder's (and Humboldt's) ideas about language distinctiveness into the wider sociocultural and political arena (Kedourie, 1960).[3] Thus, for Fichte, 'it is beyond doubt that, wherever a separate language can be found, there a separate nation exists, which has the right to take charge of its independent affairs and govern itself' (1968: 184). Kedourie succinctly summarises the logic of this process of extrapolation as follows: 'a group speaking the same language is known as a nation, and a nation ought to constitute a state' (1960: 68).

I will have much more to say about the interrelationship between language, ethnicity and nationalism in Chapter 4 and will outline there why language *can* be regarded as a significant marker of ethnic and national identity. Suffice it to say at this point, that the arguments of linguistic nationalism do little to give this view any kind of credibility, and rightly so. The view of nations as both natural and linguistically determined – or, as Richard Handler describes it, as 'bounded cultural objects' (1988: 27) – is both essentialist and determinist. As such, it holds little if any currency today, except perhaps among some nationalists. Certainly, it is widely dismissed by most commentators on nationalism, many of whom have instead opted for a modernist perspective. In this latter view, two principles are seen to be central to any sensible discussion of nations and nationalism:

1   Attempts to adduce a clearly definable set of 'national' criteria (such as language, for example) simply cannot account for all contexts and variants. Consequently, more subjective criteria are necessary to describe effectively the formation of nations and national identities.
2   Modern nations can be distinguished quite clearly from their historical antecedents; the link between the two is not necessarily continuous.

I will deal with each of these key tenets in turn.

The will to nationhood

As we have seen in our discussions on ethnicity, objectivist definitions exclude as much as they include; there are always variants and exceptions that do not fit easily into an established schema of objective criteria. Hans Kohn, for example, argues that nationalities 'come into existence only when certain objective bonds delimit a social group' (1961: 3). However, he also quickly concedes that these 'bonds' are not sufficient in themselves to provide an adequate definition of the nation. This 'subjectivist' view was first articulated in the nineteenth century – generally, in direct response and opposition to the tenets of cultural and linguistic nationalism outlined earlier. One of the most notable early proponents of this more subjectivist account of nationhood was Ernest Renan (1823–1892). In his lecture 'Qu'est ce qu'une nation?', delivered at the Sorbonne on 11 March 1882, he argued that various objective criteria – language, religion, material interest, geography and 'race' – were all insufficient delimiters of the nation. In relation to language, for example, and in direct contravention to Fichte, he states: 'Language may invite us to unite but it does not compel us to do so' (1990: 16). This leads him to conclude that the nation is, in essence, 'a soul, a spiritual principle' (1990: 19) that is not directly linked to any particular objective marker(s). Rather, two aspects constitute this principle for Renan, one of which lies in the past, one in the present:

> One is the possession in common of a rich legacy of memories; the other is present-day consent, the desire to live together, the will to perpetuate the value of the heritage that one has received in an undivided form. A nation is therefore a large-scale solidarity . . . It presupposes a past; it is summarised, however, in the present by a tangible fact, namely consent, the clearly expressed desire to continue a common life. A nation's existence is, if you will pardon the metaphor, a daily plebiscite . . .
>
> (1990: 19)

The *will* to nationhood both unifies historical memory – that history 'received in an undivided form' – and secures present-day consent. The former requires some serious forgetting, or sublimating, of countervailing and contradictory histories. As Renan famously observes, 'forgetting, I would even go so far as to say historical error, is a crucial factor in the creation of a nation' (1990: 11). The latter implies a continual renegotiation of the boundaries of consent – the desire to live together: 'the wish of nations is, all in all, the sole legitimate criterion, the one to which one must always return' (1990: 20). Both dimensions suggest our active participation in the *construction* of nationhood; that is, the construction of a particular 'discourse on society that *performs* the problem of totalising the people and unifying the national will' (Bhabha, 1994: 160–161).

Max Weber, in his essay on the structures of power, reaches some remarkably similar conclusions. Near the outset of his brief analysis of the nation, he states:

> If the concept of 'nation' can in any way be defined unambiguously, it certainly cannot be stated in terms of empirical qualities common to those who count as members of the nation. In the sense of those using the term at a given time, the concept undoubtedly means, above all, that one may exact from certain groups of men a specific sentiment of solidarity in the face of other groups. *Thus, the concept belongs in the sphere of values.* Yet, there is no agreement on how these groups should be delimited or about what concerted action should result from such solidarity.
>
> (1961: 172; my emphasis)

Weber's analysis, like Renan's, suggests the constructed nature of nationhood; its place 'in the sphere of values'. As a result, Weber goes on to explore, and discount, a number of commonly invoked prerequisites of nationhood. With regard to a common language, for example, he suggests that 'national solidarity among men speaking the same language may be just as well rejected as accepted' (1961: 173). Likewise, he dismisses the notion of 'ethnic solidarity' as a *sufficient* condition of nationhood, although he does concede that 'the idea of the "nation" is apt to include the notions of common descent and of an essential, *though frequently indefinite*, homogeneity' (1961: 173; my emphasis), a point to which I will return.

The conclusions drawn by Renan and Weber clearly emphasise the subjective over the objective in the development of nationhood; a central characteristic of modernist accounts. The will to nationhood, in Renan's evocative terms, is both a conscious choice and a particular construction of history and therefore cannot be equated directly with preexisting ethnic, cultural and/or linguistic communities. This position seems to be given credence by the many instances where the use of objective 'national' criteria is shown to be clearly inadequate as a predictor of nationhood and nationalism. With regard to ethnic affiliation, for example, Connor (1991) notes that modern

Greeks are not descended from their alleged ancestors, the ancient Hellenes, but from Slavs who first migrated to mainland Greece in the sixth century AD. Language and religion are also problematic as national indicators. Language may or may not be a key focus of national identity, as seen in the nationalist movements of Wales and Scotland respectively. Even where it is, as in Wales, it may not be so across the population as a whole (see Chapter 7). Likewise, religion differs in significance from one national context to another. For example, the Catholic/Protestant religious divide is a principal factor in nationalist struggles in Northern Ireland but not in Scotland.[4] More complicated still, objective characteristics such as religion and language may vary in salience both internally within a national group and across different historical periods. When the Belgium state was established in 1830, for instance, religious differences were far more important than linguistic ones. However, more recently, there has been far greater emphasis in Belgium on the linguistic differentiation between French and Flemish speakers (S. Lamy, 1986; Vos, 1993; Blommaert, 1996; Nelde, 1997). A similar trend is observable in Québec, where nationalist claims since the Quiet Revolution have focused increasingly on the French language at the expense of an earlier focus on Catholicism (Handler, 1988; Penrose, 1995; see Chapter 6).

In short, no single distinguishing feature fits all national contexts. As Anthony Smith observes, 'a national identity is fundamentally multidimensional; it can never be reduced to a single element' (1991: 14). The strident claims of linguistic nationalism can thus be safely dismissed since language, it seems, is only one of many characteristics which may (or may not) be salient at any given time and place. Where national symbols do achieve significance in particular national contexts, and/or in particular historical periods, it is principally because of their role in differentiating 'us' from 'them'. As Armstrong (1982) observes, objectified national characteristics act in this way as symbolic 'border guards'. These border guards are closely linked to specific cultural codes and function to identify people as members or nonmembers of the specific national collectivity. This is not too dissimilar a position to a situational account of ethnicity with its emphasis on ethnic boundaries (cf. Barth, 1969a, b).

The modern nation

The second, and related, tenet of the modernist position on nationalism is the argument that modern nations are just that – modern – and thus fundamentally distinct from previous forms of collective organisation. In short, modernists proclaim that nations – by which they actually invariably mean nation-*states* (see below) – are the product of the age of nationalism (see, for example, Kedourie, 1960; H. Kohn, 1961; Deutsch, 1966; Nairn, 1981; Gellner, 1983; Hobsbawm and Ranger, 1983; Giddens, 1984; Hobsbawm, 1990; Anderson, 1991; Breuilly, 1993). Moreover, it is argued that this age of nationalism arose out of the specific historical and social developments of modernisation and its concomitants – industrialisation, political democracy and universal literacy – in eighteenth- and nineteenth-century Europe. Prior to this, the feudal, dynastic and largely agrarian societies of the day had little notion of national sentiment – those feelings of collective 'national' belonging – that characterises the modern nation. In this view, to equate the modern nation with its ancient predecessors is to commit the sin of 'retrospective nationalism'. As Anthony Smith summarises it: 'according to the modernist perspective, nations and nationalism are not logically contingent; they are sociologically necessary only in the modern world' (1994: 377).

The important distinctions between premodern and modern nations highlighted by modernists can be summarised as follows. First, modern nations tend to be equated directly with their political representation in the nation-state. In other words, modern nations are seen as 'mass' nations, based on the notion of universal enfranchisement, and with the specific goal of administrative and political representation in the form of the nation-state (A. Smith, 1995a). In this, they are a product of postEnlightenment political rationalism and the ideology of nationalism, both of which emerged only in the eighteenth century. One only has to look to the nation-states which comprise the United Nations to confirm this since most did not exist, either in name or as an administrative unit, more than two centuries ago. Indeed, as Immanuel Wallerstein argues, there are actually very few nation-states which can trace a name and a continuous administrative entity in a particular geographical area to a period prior to 1450. Of some 200 contemporary nation-states, perhaps only France, Russia, Portugal, Denmark, Sweden, Switzerland, Morocco, Japan, China, Iran and Ethiopia can claim such a lineage. However, even these claims are somewhat problematic since it can still be argued that these states came into existence as modern sovereign nation-states only with the emergence of the present world system. A number of other modern nation-states such as Egypt, India and Greece have perhaps had a longer lineage but theirs has been discontinuous (see Wallerstein, 1991: 80–81).

Second, and relatedly, the term 'nation' in its modern sense embodies two interrelated meanings – the 'nation' as the people living *within* a nation-state and the 'nation' as *the* nation-state (Billig, 1995). Accordingly, the modern nation is viewed as both a 'historical culture-community' and a 'legal-political' one (A. Smith, 1995a), with the latter invariably taking precedence over the former. These two dimensions, and their coalescence in the institutionalised nation-state, are again products of the ideology of political nationalism. Thus, on the one hand, nationalism legitimates the construction of a particular sense of national identity for those historical culture-communities that are said to inhabit their own nation-state. This involves the exercise of *internal* political and legal jurisdiction over its citizens and the construction (or attempted construction) of a homogeneous national culture in which political and ethnic boundaries are seen to coincide (Gellner, 1983). On the other hand, political nationalism also includes the general principle that nations should, if at all possible, possess their own state. For already established nation-states, this latter principle involves the exercise of *external* rights to sovereignty and self-government in the present interstate system, along with the defence of these rights – by war if necessary. For those historical culture-communities that do not currently possess their own state, this principle is expressed via the many secessionist and irredentist nationalist movements in the world today.

Third, the link between the modern nation, and its institutional embodiment in the nation-state, is further predicated on the rise of a bureaucratic state organisation, a capitalist economy, and a 'high' literate and scientific culture; the latter based, usually, on a single and distinctive vernacular language. All of these are characteristic of modernisation (see below). In contrast, previous cultural communities tended to be localised, largely illiterate, and culturally and linguistically heterogeneous (Birch, 1989; Hutchinson, 1994).

In the modernist view then, nations (as represented in and by the nation-state) are the product of very specific social, economic and political circumstances. Their emergence as the primary social community in the modern era is directly related to the advent of modernisation and the concomitant rise of the state and the ideology of nationalism. This is an important qualification to Renan's and Weber's emphasis on the 'will to nationhood' discussed earlier. As Gellner (1964, 1983, 1997) argues, for example, the volitional aspect of nationhood is an important but insufficient identifier of the modern nation since other collectivities have also possessed this in various historical periods. In Gellner's view, the emergence of the modern nation is thus primarily associated with the structural changes brought about by modernisation.

Following from this, some modernist commentators – Hobsbawm (1990) and Balibar (1991) to name just two – argue that any attempt to present the nation as a natural and/or ancient form of human organisation must involve what we saw described in our discussion of ethnicity in Chapter 1 as 'the invention of tradition'. Like proponents of a situational view of ethnicity, such commentators view nations as, at best, socially constructed and, at worst, simply invented. That said, the degree to which, and fervour with which, this constructivist position is held varies considerably among modernist commentators on nationalism, as does the related disavowal of any link between nationhood and a preexisting ethnicity. With respect to the latter, some do acknowledge a connection between ethnicity and nationhood (see, for example, Gellner, 1983, 1997; Anderson, 1991), while others, such as Hobsbawm (1990), argue that the two phenomena are entirely unrelated. But, these differences notwithstanding, modernists *are* all agreed that nationhood is the *result* of political modernisation – expressed in nationalism and the construction of the nation-state – and not the result of preexisting ethnicity.

The modernists

The preceding discussion suggests that what is broadly termed the modernist position on nationalism is by no means undifferentiated. In particular, modernists differ over the historical timing of nationalism, and the nation-states to which it gave rise, and over the key influences which have surrounded the development of nationalism. In relation to the former, a range of starting points for nationalism is offered. Hans Kohn (1961) and Leah Greenfeld (1992) suggest the seventeenth-century British rebellion against the monarchy, Anderson (1991) the American Revolution, Best (1988) and Alter (1989) the French Revolution, and Kedourie (1960) and Breuilly (1993) the German response of Herder et al. to the political implications of the French Revolution. All are agreed, however, about the historical recency of nationalism[5] and its rapid and widespread development. As Best (1982) succinctly observes, by the beginning of the nineteenth century the world was full of it. In relation to the latter, modernist writers attribute a range of key influences to the rise of nationalism. Gellner (1964, 1983, 1997) has argued, for example, that the emergence of nationalism is predicated on the impact of industrialisation, Anderson (1991) on the role of print capitalism, and Giddens (1984), Breuilly (1993) and Brubaker (1996) on the development of the modern state.

It is not my intention here to explore in any depth the full range of modernist theories; there are numerous books already devoted to such a task (for some recent examples, see James, 1996; Calhoun, 1997; McCrone, 1998; A. Smith, 1998). However, it is my intention to examine in some detail two exemplars of this position – Ernest Gellner (1983) and Benedict Anderson (1991). These two theorists illustrate the modernist position writ large and their work on nationalism has been particularly prominent and influential. As we shall see, both theorists also place a prominent emphasis on the interconnections between nationalism, language and education, a concern which is central to this account and which will be explored more fully in the following chapters.

Gellner's theory of industrialisation

Gellner argues, in *Nations and Nationalism* (1983), that the rise of nationalism cannot simply be explained ideologically – that is, as the result of a contest of ideas – but must be rooted in the material changes brought about in Europe at the end of the eighteenth century by industrialisation. In this, his analysis is essentially functionalist, although it bears similarities to some Marxist perspectives on nationalism. The main difference here between Gellner's theory and most Marxist perspectives (see, for example, Nairn, 1981; Hroch, 1985; Hobsbawm, 1990) is that Gellner sees nationalism as the concomitant of industrialisation (in any form), whereas Marxist analyses link nationalism more specifically to capitalism.

For Gellner, nationalism developed within the context of the transition from traditional agrarian societies to modern industrial societies. In the former, literacy performed a specialised function and, along with occupational mobility, was limited to a small elite. Mass public education was unheard of. Political control was also largely decentralised and populations spoke a variety of languages and dialects. Localism in both speech form and cultural identification was the norm and, consequently, there was little, if any, emphasis on achieving a uniform state culture. As Gellner observes, 'what is virtually inconceivable within such a system is a serious and sustained drive for linguistic and cultural homogeneity . . . Both the will and the means [and, one might add, the *need*] for such an aspiration are conspicuously lacking' (1987: 15). Thus, prior to industrialisation, political forms of organisation required neither the demarcation of clear territorial boundaries nor the fostering of internal integration and homogeneity. Feudal elites, for example, controlled wide territories but exercised little centralised control. Empires, larger in scale again, demanded political loyalty (and taxes) from their diverse people groups but made little, if any, demands for cultural and linguistic homogeneity.

In contrast, the modern industrialised society – with its literate, mobile and occupationally specialised division of labour – required cultural and linguistic continuity and, where possible, cultural and linguistic homogeneity in order to function effectively. While work in premodern society had been predominantly manual, work in modern industrial society was now predominantly semantic (A. Smith, 1998). The latter also required its workers to be 'substitutable'. In effect, workers had to be able to cope with and move between the increasingly complex and differentiated roles created by the division of labour. What made the individual substitutable in this way was a significant degree of cultural and linguistic *standardisation*. Here the development of a standardised, context-free and unitary language becomes crucial, with this in turn facilitating and reflecting the development of a 'high' literate (and common) culture.

In his earlier 1964 account, *Thought and Change*, Gellner had placed greatest emphasis on the role of a unitary language as the cement of modern society – bringing together a wide range of people from different regions and backgrounds in developing urban centres. However, by the time of *Nations and Nationalism*, language, though still a factor, had come to be viewed as subsidiary to the role of mass education systems in establishing an effective common culture (see Laitin, 1998; O'Leary, 1998; A. Smith, 1998) – a process he describes as 'exo-socialisation'. For Gellner, mass education – established, maintained and monitored by the state – provided the literacy and 'technological competence' necessary for producing 'full' or 'effective' citizens in modern industrial societies.

The principle of 'one state, one culture' thus saw the state, via its education system, increasingly identified with a specific language and culture (Taylor, 1998). As Gellner asserts: 'whereas in the past the connection [between state and culture] was thin, fortuitous, varied, loose and often minimal . . . now it [became] unavoidable. That is what nationalism is all about' (1983: 38). The result was the emergence of the nation-state in which cultural and political boundaries were seen to conveniently converge. In Gellner's view, the rise of nationalism is thus inextricably linked to the *prior* development of a strong state culture *from which* a homogeneous nation could be shaped. As he observes:

> It is not the case that the 'age of nationalism' is a mere summation of the awakening and political self-assertion of this, that, or the other nation. Rather when general social conditions make for standardised, homogeneous, centrally sustained high cultures, pervading ethnic populations and not just elite minorities, a situation arises in which *well-defined educationally sanctioned and unified cultures* constitute very nearly the only kind of unity with which men willingly and often ardently identify. The cultures now seem to be the natural repositories of political legitimacy. Only *then* does it come to appear that any defiance of their boundaries by political units constitutes a scandal.
>
> (1983: 55; my emphasis in the first instance)

Gellner's analysis situates nationalism in the social, economic and political changes of the time while also linking nationalism specifically to the development of a literate, national 'high' culture. Nationalism has flourished, he suggests, because 'well-defined, educationally sanctioned and unified cultures' offer a path to modernity, a basis of political legitimacy, and a means of shared cultural and linguistic identity.

Anderson's 'imagined communities'

Benedict Anderson's likening of the modern nation to an 'imagined political community' evokes a similar conception. In his influential analysis, Anderson argues that all national communities are '*imagined* because the members of even the smallest nation will never know most of their fellow-members, meet them, or even hear of them, yet in the minds of each lives the image of their communion' (1991: 6). This is not to say that a sense of national consciousness or identity is *imaginary*. It is merely to suggest that the idea of a collective 'national' community, like all large-scale collectivities, has to be *specifically* and *consciously* cultivated since it involves conceiving of something that is beyond one's immediate day-to-day experience. As he outlines, 'my point of departure is that nationality, or, as one might prefer to put it in view of that word's multiple significations, nation-ness, as well as nationalism, are cultural artefacts of a particular kind' (1991: 4).

Anderson argues that the development of the modern nation 'conceived as a solid community moving steadily down (or up) history' (1991: 26) arose from the congruence of industrial capitalism and print technology in fifteenth- and sixteenth-century Europe. The convergence of capitalism and print technology at this time saw the rapid spread in print of previously localised vernacular languages, aided in part also by the Protestant drive to vernacularise scripture. These developments gave a new fixity to language and created unified fields of exchange and communication below Latin (the dominant administrative language of the day) and above the spoken vernaculars. They were also aided by the concurrent, albeit haphazard, elevation of vernaculars as languages of political administration. As a result, vernacular languages came to assume many of the administrative functions previously enjoyed only by Latin and rose to be 'languages-of-power'. As speakers of languages with widely different dialects became capable of comprehending one another, via print, they also came to recognise themselves as belonging to one particular language (and cultural) group among many. With the advent of modernisation and the increasing centralisation of state control, this was to lead, in turn, to an emerging sense of national consciousness. By this process, a *shared* sense of a particular nation's history – along with its associated language(s) and cultural symbols – began to be cultivated.

Anderson argues that this emerging national consciousness 'could arise historically only when substantial groups of people were in a position to think of themselves as living lives *parallel* to those of other substantial groups of people – if never meeting, yet certainly proceeding along the same trajectory' (1991: 188). In this way, a new kind of indirect relationship was formed in which the biographies of individuals, and the nation as a whole, could be joined in a common historical narrative (Calhoun, 1993a). We may all have our own personal histories but the claim to nationhood provides us with a collective sense of history:

- by linking us to past and future generations
- by situating us in the global context as a member of one nation among many
- by providing formal equivalence for us as one member among many of a specific nation

As I have already discussed, other modernist commentators (see, for example, Hobsbawm and Ranger, 1983; Hobsbawm, 1990; Balibar, 1991) would suggest at this point that the construction of such collective histories is fictive. In the British context, for example, this is said to be reflected in the invented traditions of Scottish tartans and highland culture (Trevor-Roper, 1983), in the nineteenth-century druidic inventions of the Welsh eisteddfodau (see Chapter 7), and even in the supposed centrality of the monarchy to conceptions of British identity (Cannadine, 1983; Colley, 1992). This 'inventionist' position, most trenchantly outlined by Hobsbawm (1990), has clear parallels with Roosens' (1989) account of the construction of Huron ethnicity outlined in Chapter 1. Anderson, however, is less concerned here with outlining a moral(ist) position on nationalism (a feature of much political and social-science commentary, dating from Lord Acton's critical account in 1862). He argues simply that *all* modern nations are imagined in this way. It is not so much the falsity/genuineness of nations which is thus in question but the *style* in which they are imagined. In this sense, Anderson adopts a position that is closer to earlier modernists such as Kedourie (1960), Deutsch (1966), Seton-Watson (1977) and Tilly (1975). These earlier commentators highlighted the fictive elements of nation formation. However, they also assumed that nations, once formed, were real communities of culture and power; a Durkheimian 'social fact', in effect (A. Smith, 1995b).

Like Gellner, then, Anderson asserts that the rise of nationalism has *effected* the construction of the modern nation as we know it in its nation-state form – an anonymous, socially differentiated and large-scale collectivity with its basis in the categorical relationships of equivalent individuals (see also Calhoun, 1993a, b). The sense of commonality that results has seen 'the "imagined community" . . . spread out to every conceivable contemporary society' (1991: 157). Nonetheless, the nation and nationality are, for all that, still cultural artefacts. Nationalism has produced nations (as nation-states) and national identity, not the other way around.

Limits of the modernist account

As with situational accounts of ethnicity, however, modernist conceptions of nationalism and national identity may be overstated. Modernists have been rightly sceptical of primordial accounts which attempt to 'naturalise' nationhood via a preexisting ethnicity and/or language and have also highlighted the apparent disjunctures between modern nation-states and earlier collectivities. However, on this basis, modernists cannot account for the ongoing *persistence* of nationalism in the modern world – particularly in situations where political modernisation has already been achieved. After all, the logic of the modernist argument is that as nationalism supersedes ethnicity, so should internationalism replace nationalism as the next stage of the modernisation process. Instead, neither has really occurred. The rise today of an increasing internationalisation appears *in conjunction with* nationalism rather than as a replacement for it (Robertson, 1992; see Chapter 1). Likewise, ethnicity continues to feature prominently in relationship to nationalism, as the increasing proliferation of 'ethnonationalisms' in the modern world highlights.

Part of this inability to predict the ongoing salience of ethnicity and nationalism, and their interconnections, can be explained by Anthony Smith's observation that, in rejecting primordial accounts entirely, modernist commentators on nationalism have confused individual and collective levels of ethnicity. As I argued in Chapter 1, we may, as individuals, demonstrate a considerable degree of latitude in our attachment to and choice of particular social and political identities. As such, ethnic choices and identifications may vary in their salience – both in themselves, and in relation to other social identities – at any given time and place. However, this view needs to be balanced by the recognition that 'at the collective as opposed to the individual level, ethnicity remains a powerful, explosive and durable force' (A. Smith, 1995a: 34).

Some modernists have countered here with an economic 'core–periphery' explanation – that ethnonationalism persists because modernisation proceeded unequally, leading to the uneven economic development of certain historical cultural and linguistic groups within particular nation-states and, thus, to the growth of ethnonationalist movements (see, for example, Deutsch, 1966; Wallerstein, 1979). An obvious example here is the 'internal colonialist' thesis advanced by Hechter (1975; see also Nairn, 1981). Hechter argued that uneven economic development in Britain led to a stratified 'cultural division of labour' in the 'Celtic fringe' of Wales, Ireland and Scotland which, in turn, could account for their respective nationalisms:

> To the extent that social stratification in the periphery is based on observable cultural differences, there exists the probability that the disadvantaged group will, in time, reactively assert its own culture as equal or superior to that of the relatively advantaged core. This may help it conceive of itself as a separate 'nation' and seek independence.
>
> (1975: 10)

However, the model of internal colonialism has since been widely contested. McCrone (1992, 1998), for example, points out that while the Scottish highlands, or Gaeltachd, may have been seen as a suitably appropriate example of the model, the 'culturally anglicised' and 'overdeveloped' lowlands of Scotland certainly were not. Likewise, in relation to Wales, internal colonialism considerably understates the centrality of south Wales to the rapid development and expansion of *British* industrialisation (Gwyn Williams, 1982, 1985). In Williams' view, the industrialised south of Wales was no mere satellite of an imperial economic core based in London, as Hechter would have it. Rather, the imperial core came to Wales. This can be demonstrated by the huge influx of migrants to the area in the late nineteenth century, and by the consequent reconstruction of local Welsh issues and concerns as British ones (Colin Williams, 1994; see Chapter 7).

If one looks more widely, the relatively prosperous Catalan, Basque and Québécois nationalist movements also illustrate the limits of the core–periphery approach. The Catalan national minority, for example, was politically and culturally oppressed under Franco's fascist regime until his death in 1975. However, the Catalan region itself has been historically one of the strongest economic regions in Spain. Thus, in 1980 Catalans comprised 16 per cent of the Spanish population but 20 per cent of GDP, while per capita income was 30 per cent above the Spanish average. Moreover, this long-standing economic and demographic power had, in the nineteenth century, formed the basis of the cosmopolitan and high-culture Catalan language movements Renaixença and Modernista (Miller and Miller, 1996; see Chapter 7).

In short, while adverse economic factors may play a significant part in some ethnonationalist movements, they are not a sufficient explanation for the ongoing prominence of such movements in the modern world. Moreover, economic considerations aside, a modernist conception still cannot answer the question of *why* ethnicity – as opposed to religion, regionalism or class, for example – is so often chosen as the principal focus of nationalist mobilisation. Nor can it explain why ethnonational claims persist, even when such claims may entrench, rather than ameliorate, socioeconomic and/or political disadvantage – i.e., when there appears to be no immediate (or even long-term) 'pay off' (see A. Smith, 1998: 63–69; cf. Chapter 1).

Ethnicist approaches to nationalism

For a more adequate explanation, we need to consider an approach which returns ethnicity and ethnic identity to the study of nationalism (see, for example, Fishman, 1989b; A. Smith, 1986, 1995a, 1998; Hutchinson, 1994; R. Jenkins, 1995, 1997). As Richard Jenkins argues:

> If the concept [of nationalism] is to retain its analytical value, the varieties of what we persist in calling 'nationalism' must also have something in common. Although not the only common thread – political membership conceived as citizenship might be another – ethnicity, personal and collective identity which draws upon a repertoire of perceived cultural differences, is the most ubiquitous and plausible . . .

> (1995: 369)

Ethnicist approaches accept many of the tenets of modernism – particularly the, at times, constructed nature of national identity. However, they also address three of the key weaknesses of the modernist thesis: its historicity, its conflation of the 'nation' and the 'nation-state', and its separation of political and ethnic nationalism(s) (see also Castells, 1997). I will deal with each of these key issues in turn.

Historical continuity

First, while ethnicist commentators acknowledge the distinctive characteristics of the modern nation, they also argue that the processes of nation formation need to be examined within and through a longer and more cyclical account of history. To this end, ethnicist commentators have attempted to distinguish national sentiment – understood here as those feelings of collective belonging to a nation – from the ideology and movement of nationalism itself. This is important because, as Anthony Smith (1994, 1998) argues, one can have nationalist movements and ideologies among a given population without any corresponding diffusion of national sentiment in that population. The reverse can also be found, and it is from this latter scenario that historians such as Seton-Watson (1977), Armstrong (1982), Hroch (1985), Colley (1992) and Greenfeld (1992) have convincingly argued that the emergence of national sentiment was evident some centuries before the development of nationalism itself.

This more cyclical historical approach does not necessarily entail a perennial view of nations (see A. Smith, 1998: 159–176). Rather, it attempts to situate nationalism within a wider theory of ethnic formation, emphasising *commonalities* as well as *differences* between the premodern and modern eras. As Anthony Smith argues, the rise of nationalism and the nation-state *has* been shaped by premodern ethnic identities (ethnies), whatever modernists might say, and thus can be situated within a larger cycle of ethnic resurgence and decline in history.[6] His position specifically links 'the consequences of modernity with an understanding of the continuing role played by cultural ties and ethnic identities which originated in premodern epochs' (1995a: 47). Richard Jenkins reiterates this view in his observation that 'nationalism is an aspect of the growth of . . . complex political units, based, to some degree, on notions of ethnic and cultural commonality (however much, *pace* Anderson, imagined)' (1995: 370).

Following this argument, the formation of modern nations is seen to involve the appropriation of some of the key attributes of preexisting ethnies. In the process, many extant memories, myths and symbols are assimilated, while additional ones are invented where necessary. Crucially, this view also allows us to extend the principle of nation formation beyond established nation-states to include those nations which are currently not represented by a corresponding state (see below), something not countenanced in modernist accounts. Thus, for example, the modern Breton nationalist movement draws heavily on the persistence of Breton traditions, myths, memories and symbols (including language) which have survived, in various forms, throughout the period of French domination since 1532. Likewise, Catalan nationalism – first instigated in 1880, revived in the 1930s, and again in the 1980s – draws on Catalonia's long maritime history and the attraction and prestige of the Catalan language and culture (Castells, 1997; see Chapter 7). Accordingly, the difference between modern nations and ethnies becomes a question of degree rather than kind. As Richard Jenkins observes, 'the boundary between "ethnicism" and "nationalism" . . . becomes indeterminate, lying somewhere along a continuum of change within historically evolving traditions or universes of discourses' (1995: 372).

In adopting a more evolutionary position, however, ethnicist commentators do not make the mistake of assuming a *causal* relationship between prior ethnies and the subsequent formation of modern nations. As Hutchinson observes, 'to do so without empirical examination is to make uncritical assumptions about continuities between premodern ethnic and modern national identities and to fall into the post hoc ergo propter hoc fallacy' (1994: 26; see also Fishman, 1989b: 111). Nonetheless, they hold that the distinction between modern nations and premodern ethnic communities has been too starkly drawn by modernists. Thus, a modernist account such as Gellner's can be criticised for its teleological overtones in emphasising a single and revolutionary transition from preindustrial to industrial society as an explanation for nationalism.[7] Gellner's difficulty here is that in many contexts nationalism predates industrialisation. In Serbia, Ireland, Mexico and Japan, to name just a few examples, there was no industrial development at the time that nationalism emerged in these contexts. One could even argue that nationalism was already a significant force before the onset of industrialisation in France and Germany (A. Smith, 1998). The role of mass education as an agent of nationalism may be similarly overstated, since nationalist movements again often predated the former (Hroch, 1985, 1993). Relatedly, the advent of industrialisation also at times significantly predated formal education, most notably Britain, where mass education was not established formally until 1870, some one hundred years after the advent of industrialisation there.

In ethnicist accounts, then, nationalism is viewed not only as a means to achieve modernity but also, crucially, as a means of (re)creating a sense of distinctive collective identity and autonomy (Hutchinson, 1994). The nation is not seen just as a *political* community represented by the nation-state. It is viewed also as an *ethnocultural* community that may or may not be so represented and yet which is still shaped by shared myths of origins, and a sense of common history and ways of life. Moreover, it is principally this latter dimension which endows its members with identity and purpose. In this sense, nationalism and national identity can be understood in relation to the notion of habitus, and to the related limits concerning the constructedness of ethnic identities discussed in Chapter 1. Bhikhu Parekh argues, for example, that national identity is a process of self-creation that does not occur in a historical vacuum. Rather,

> A [national] community *inherits* a specific way of life . . . which sets limits to how and how much it can change itself. The change is lasting and deep if it is grafted on the community's suitably reinterpreted deepest tendencies and does not go against the grain. A community's political [and cultural] identity then is neither unalterable and fixed, nor a voluntarist project to be executed as it pleases, but a matter of *slow* self-recreation within the limits set by its past.
>
> (1995b: 264; my emphases)[8]

Such a position shifts the focus away from the increasingly arid debates surrounding the historical and political legitimacy of nationalism. As Joshua Fishman has argued, in an essay first published in 1972, 'we must not ask if [nationalism] is "good", if it is "justified", if it is based on "valid arguments". Rather, we must ask "why does it occur, and when, and how can its obvious power be most productively channelled"?' (1989b: 104). These questions are crucial to unravelling the ongoing salience and alliance of ethnicity and nationalism in the modern world. By attending to the popular base and cultural framework of nationalism – an area which modernists have seen fit to ignore – ethnicist accounts provide us with a plausible explanation to these questions. After all, it is not chronological or factual history that is the key to the nation but *sentient* or *felt* history (Connor, 1993). As Craig Calhoun observes, 'ethnicity or cultural traditions are bases for nationalism when they effectively constitute historical memory, when they inculcate it as habitus . . . not when (or because) the historical origins they claim are accurate' (1993a: 222).

Uncoupling the nation-state

In so doing, an ethnicist approach also allows us to untangle the confluence of the historical-cultural and legal-political dimensions of nationhood as they have come to be represented in the institutionalised form of the nation-state. As I have already suggested, this has arisen from the central principle of political nationalism – nation-state congruence – which holds that the boundaries of political and national identity should coincide. The view here is that people who are citizens of a particular state should also, ideally, be members of the same national collectivity. Gellner's definition of nationalism as a 'theory of political legitimacy which requires that ethnic boundaries should not cut across political ones' (1983: 1) clearly illustrates this standpoint. The end result of nationalism, in this view, is the establishment of the ethnically exclusive and culturally homogeneous nation-state.

This attempt to make both state and national culture coextensive entities has resulted in the nation-state system as we know it today and continues to form the basis of many of the current nationalist claims for self-determination. And yet, interestingly, the earliest uses of the term 'nationalism' did not actually conflate the nation and the state in this way (Connor, 1978). However, by the nineteenth century, nationalist doctrine had come to hold that nation and state were coterminous; that every nation deserved a state. Not only this, an important corollary had also by then emerged – that each state should represent one nation. As Gellner describes it, nationalism holds that the nation and state 'were destined for each other; that either without the other is incomplete, and constitutes a tragedy' (1983: 6). Max Weber appears to reiterate this in his observation that 'a nation is a community which normally tends to produce a state of its own' (1961: 176). This crucial interlinking of the idea of nation and its political representation in the state is perhaps not too surprising. As Immanuel Wallerstein observes:

> Why should the establishment of any particular sovereign state within the interstate system create a corresponding 'nation', a 'people'? This is not really difficult to understand. The evidence is all around us. States in this system have problems of cohesion. Once recognised as sovereign, the states frequently find themselves subsequently threatened by both internal disintegration and external aggression. To the extent that 'national' sentiment develops, these threats are lessened. The governments in power have an interest in promoting this sentiment, as do all sorts of subgroups within the state . . . States furthermore have an interest in administrative uniformity that increases the efficacy of their policies. Nationalism is the expression, the promoter and the consequence of such state-level uniformities.
>
> (1991: 81–82)

Wallerstein argues, along with other modernist commentators, that nationalism arose *out of* the emergence of the modern state system: 'in almost every case statehood precede[s] nationhood' (1991: 81). Political expression in the form of the nation-state thus *legitimates* and *institutionalises* nationhood. However, a sense of national sentiment is also at the same time promoted by the agencies of the state – particularly education and the media – and this acts recursively to maintain the nation-state's internal cohesion. This, in turn, provides a basis on which to counter possible outside threats to its autonomy. The state's role is thus crucial in accomplishing the three recurrent goals of nationalism that I outlined at the beginning of this chapter – national identity, national unity and national autonomy (see A. Smith, 1994, 1998). The process of imbuing citizenship with 'national' sentiment also helps to explain for modernists why 'national' identities commonly 'trump' other personal or group identities (Calhoun, 1993a).

The principal difficulty with the formulation of nation-state congruence, however, is *its inability to accommodate and/or recognise the legitimate claims of nations without states, or national minorities.* This limitation has both a theoretical and a practical dimension. Theoretically, the conflation of the nation and the state assumes that the two concepts are reducible to each other when they clearly are not. Nations are often but *not always* represented in and by a [nation-]state. Or, to put it another way, *citizenship* does not always equate directly with *nationality.* Practically, and following from this, the 'nation-state' is actually a misnomer since its construction as ethnically exclusive and culturally homogeneous is directly contradicted by demographic and political realities.

In relation to the former, it is worth noting that Weber's earlier comment on the link between nation and state contains an important qualification: 'a nation . . . *normally tends* to produce a state of its own' (1961: 176; my emphasis). The qualification suggests a distinction between nation and state and Weber reiterates this distinction even more clearly elsewhere in his observation that a ' "nation" is . . . not identical with the "people of the state", that is, with the membership of a given polity' (1961: 172). In short, nation and state are not one and the same thing. As such, the 'nation' should be seen as a separate ideological and political construct from that of the 'nation-state' (Anthias and Yuval-Davis, 1992).

In relation to the latter, as even the most cursory examination of the world's nation-states should make clear, the happy coincidence of national and state loyalties, while the central aim of political nationalism, seldom actually occurs. Anthony Smith (1983) notes, for example, that even in Europe – where, arguably, the ideal of the nation-state is strongest – there were, at the time of his writing, 73 nations and only 24 states. Likewise, several nations can coexist within the boundaries of a particular state – Britain and India are obvious examples here. The Welsh nationalist Dafydd Elis Thomas is at pains to point out this distinction between nation and state in the British context:

> Britain is a state rather than a nation. The British state, imposed upon the English, Scottish, Welsh and part of the Irish peoples and then imposed world wide, is an inherently imperial and colonial concept at home and abroad. The British state cannot and should not be an object of affection, save for those who want to live in a form of authoritarian dependency.
>
> (cited in Gilroy, 1990: 263)

A comparison of the terms 'nationalism' and 'patriotism' may help to illustrate this distinction further. As Walker Connor argues, 'Nationalism, in correct usage, refers to an emotional attachment to one's people – one's ethnocultural group. It is therefore proper to speak of an English, Scottish, or Welsh nationalism, but not of 'British' nationalism, the latter being a manifestation of PATRIOTISM' (1993: 374; emphasis in original). On this argument, nationalism and patriotism will only coincide in 'true' nation-states; that is, in states where the population is ethnically homogeneous. However, Connor proceeds to point out that this is extremely rare since most states, by this definition, are not actually nation-states at all. For example, in 40 per cent of all states there are at least five or more statistically and/or politically significant ethnic groups, while in nearly one-third of all states (31 per cent) the largest national group is not even the majority (Connor, 1993; see also Nielsson, 1985). These groups comprise national and indigenous minorities such as Irish, Scots and Welsh in Britain, Hawaiians and Native Americans in the USA, Québécois and Aboriginal peoples / Native Canadians in Canada, Sámi in 'Sápmi' (which includes areas of Russia, Finland, Norway and Sweden), and Māori in Aotearoa / New Zealand. They also include a wide variety of immigrant groups. The result is that most states are *multinational* (comprising a number of national minorities) and/or *polyethnic* (comprising a range of immigrant groups). Indeed, most countries in the world have been historically, and remain today, a combination of the two (Kymlicka, 1995a). I will explore the distinctions between multinational and polyethnic states, and between national, indigenous and immigrant minorities, more fully in the final section of this chapter. But for now, we can surely agree with Anthias and Yuval-Davis that:

> Today there is virtually nowhere in the world in which . . . a pure nation-state exists, if it ever did, and therefore there are always settled residents (and usually citizens as well) who are not members of the dominant national collectivity in the society. The fact that there still exists this automatic assumption about the overlap between the boundaries of the state citizens and 'the nation', is one expression of the naturalising effect of the hegemony of one collectivity and its access to ideological apparatuses of both state and civil society. This constructs minorities into assumed deviants from the 'normal', and excludes them from important power resources.
>
> (1992: 21–22)

If, as these commentators suggest, the ethnically exclusive and culturally homogeneous 'nation-state' is a misnomer, how has it come to so dominate conceptions of nationalism and nationhood? This, in turn, leads us to another question. Even if we acknowledge the primacy of multinational and polyethnic states – and it is hard not to – why does the dominant ethnic group in these states so often continue to perceive the state as the political expression of *their* particular ethnic group (and, usually, theirs alone)? I will explore these questions more fully in the final section of this chapter. Before doing so, however, I want to turn to the final limitation of modernist conceptions of nationalism – which is closely related to much of the preceding discussion – that is, the dominance of statist (or political) nationalisms over what might be termed 'cultural nationalisms'.

Statist and cultural nationalisms

An inevitable corollary of the modernist rejection of ethnicity as a central variable in nation formation is, as we have seen, an overemphasis on the political and civic elements of nationalism at the expense of its cultural dimensions. In effect, this has involved the legitimation of the 'Staatsnation' over the 'Kulturnation'. The latter, accordingly, has often been relegated to an 'ethnic' rather than a 'national' concern, a move illustrated by the commonly invoked distinction between ethnicity and nationalism in the academic literature. Anthias and Yuval-Davis provide us with a representative example of this distinction:

> there is no inherent difference (although sometimes there is a difference in scale) between ethnic and national collectivities. What is specific to the nationalist project and discourse is the claim for a separate political representation for the collectivity. This often – but not always – takes the form of a claim for a separate state.
>
> (1992: 25)

However, in reality, the distinction drawn here between ethnicity and nationalism is not nearly so straightforward. As Craig Calhoun observes, in a somewhat more nuanced analysis:

> The relationship between nationalism and ethnicity is complex... Nationalism, in particular, remains the preeminent rhetoric for attempts to demarcate political communities, claim rights of self-determination and legitimate rule by reference to 'the people' of the country. Ethnic solidarities and identities are claimed most often when groups do not seek 'national' autonomy but rather a recognition internal to or cross-cutting national or state boundaries. The possibility of a closer link to nationalism is seldom altogether absent from such ethnic claims, however, and the two sorts of categorical identities are often invoked in similar ways.
>
> (1993a: 235)

Even this analysis though does not go far enough, since it continues to assume, unproblematically, nationalism's principal preoccupation with *political* and *civic* legitimation – externally via the principle of self-determination in the interstate system, and internally via the establishment of national citizenship. In this regard, the aspiration of nations for statehood may be overdrawn. While attaining statehood is often the central aim of nationalist movements, it may not always be, and nationalist movements may be content to pursue more limited political aims in relation to self-determination (see Chapters 7 and 8). Nationalist sentiments need not therefore be limited to the questions of state formation or secession; indeed, statehood need not even be the central issue at stake. The long-held emphasis on statist definitions of nationalism has thus tended to preclude the recognition of a much wider range of *cultural* nationalisms (Fishman, 1989b; Hutchinson, 1987, 1994). These cultural nationalisms are a recurring force in the modern world and, ironically perhaps, seem currently to affect most those western nations whose state power and boundaries have long been settled. Such nationalisms are concerned principally with what constitutes national *identity*, and with the moral regeneration of the national *community*, or 'way of life', rather than with state secession as such. Via this communitarian emphasis, cultural nationalisms attempt to reconstruct tradition (be it historical, cultural or linguistic) in order to meet more adequately the demands of modernity (Hutchinson, 1994). Indeed, this central emphasis of cultural nationalism on 'modernisation from within' counters the often invoked criticism that such movements are merely traditionalist and reactionary (see, for example, H. Kohn, 1961; Gellner, 1964, 1983; Schlesinger, 1992). They may well be, but they need not always be. I will explore these criticisms, and their inherent weaknesses, more fully in the following chapters.

Cultural nationalisms can thus be seen as contrapuntal to political nationalisms. They are often present when the aims of political secessionist nationalisms have been exhausted, or are simply no longer feasible or relevant (hence the prominence of cultural nationalisms in established western nation-states). Cultural nationalisms accordingly differ from political nationalisms in the nature and extent of their political organisation, comprising largely small-scale 'grass roots' movements which have as their principal foci specific historical, linguistic and educational concerns (Hutchinson, 1994).[9] That said, cultural nationalisms will always incorporate some political aims and, as such, may themselves develop into political nationalisms with their attendant claims to independent statehood – as seen, for example, in Québec in recent times (see Chapter 6). In effect, as Calhoun's previous comment suggests, both political and cultural emphases are likely to be present at any given time in nationalist movements, even if different weightings are ascribed to them. These weightings may also vary in salience over time. Nonetheless, cultural and political nationalism can be seen as distinct variants, with differing emphases and concerns.

Wales provides us with a clear example of cultural nationalism here. As Richard Jenkins (1991, 1995) argues, Wales has had a long history of political and economic incorporation into the British state; much more so than Scotland, for example, which has managed throughout to retain its own church, law and education system. Despite recent developments which have seen limited political and economic devolution extended to both Scotland and Wales (see May, 1999e), the degree of Welsh political incorporation into the British state remains considerable. Given this, Welsh nationalism has sought its legitimacy historically largely in 'cultural continuity' and collective memory (Colin Williams, 1994). This can be seen particularly in the promotion of Welsh culture, and its associated traditions, and in the particular importance placed on the Welsh language. As Richard Jenkins argues: 'In Wales, the defence and promotion of Welsh culture – symbolised most sharply by the Welsh language – [has been] the dominant item on the nationalist agenda, with some form of devolved self-government coming a poor second' (1991: 32). Indeed, given this historical tendency, the actual referendum for the approval of Welsh devolution, conducted in September 1997, was only just passed, again in contrast to Scotland, where the comparable referendum was strongly supported (May, 1999e). The history of Welsh nationalism thus clearly demonstrates that there are means other than state recognition by which national distinctiveness can be attained and maintained. Moreover, the move to greater regional autonomy in Britain, and elsewhere, does not necessarily fuel the fires of political nationalism at the expense of former culturalist emphases. In the European Union, for example, the increasing emphasis on regional autonomy has strengthened rather than weakened the tenets of some cultural nationalist movements there (Keating and Jones, 1995; D. Smith and Wright, 1999). Certainly, this is the case in both Wales and Catalonia, as we shall see in Chapter 7.

It is also the case, in a different political arena, for indigenous peoples' movements. In recent years, Sámi (Lapps) in Norway, Inuit (Eskimos) and Native Canadians in Canada, Māori in Aotearoa / New Zealand and, to a lesser extent, Aboriginal peoples and Torres Strait Islanders in Australia, have all been granted varying degrees of cultural, linguistic, educational and administrative autonomy, albeit in the face of considerable opposition. As I will discuss further in due course, these developments have been the direct result of indigenous advocacy, in national and international arenas, for greater autonomy *within* the nation-states which colonised them, rather than for secession as such (May, 1999c, d; see also Chapter 8).

The modernist mistake then has been to assume that cultural and political nationalisms are entirely separate phenomena – the former related only to 'ethnic' groups, the latter only to 'national' ones – rather than distinct variants of the same phenomenon. This dominance of statist or political forms of nationalism, and the consigning of cultural nationalism to the realms of 'mere ethnicity', can be traced back to the principle of nation-state congruence discussed in the preceding section. Nationalism is only nationalism (and therefore justifiable), it seems, when it is tied to the modernising state (Calhoun, 1993a). This is to miss an essential element of the power of nationalism, its protean or chameleon-like quality (A. Smith, 1995a; Brubaker, 1998). However, as Anthony Smith argues:

It is also crucially to misunderstand the relationship between culture and politics in nationalism. Nationalism cannot be reduced to the uniform principle that the cultural unit must be made congruent with the political unit. Not only does this omit a number of other vital nationalist tenets, it fails to grasp the fact that the development of any nationalism depends on bringing the cultural and moral regeneration of the community into a close relationship, if not harmony, with the political mobilisation and self-determination of its members.

(1995a: 13)

In short, the principal consequence of this approach has been to legitimate the 'legal-political' dimensions of nationhood over the 'cultural-historical'. For majority ethnic groups, the result has been relatively unproblematic since the latter dimension (their ethnic habitus, in effect) is seen to correspond directly with the former. In the process, their 'ethnic' ties are normalised and legitimated as 'civic' ones. For minority groups, however, their ethnic habitus is seen to be distinct from and oppositional to the legal-political interests of the nation-state. Accordingly, any claims which are made for some degree of ethnic autonomy vis-à-vis the nation-state, and/or greater civic representation within it, are viewed as inherently parochial and destabilising.

Dominant ethnies

The fundamentally different treatment of majority and minority ethnic groups within the nation-state is indicative of what Michael Billig (1995) describes as the 'projection' of nationalism onto 'others' and the 'naturalisation' of one's own. Billig describes the latter process as *banal* nationalism and he equates this, as I have, with contemporary 'civic' loyalties to nation-states. The naturalisation of such ties means that banal nationalism – that is, the nationalism of the dominant ethnie – 'not only ceases to be nationalism . . . it ceases to be a problem for investigation' (1995: 17). By this, the *hegemonic* construction of the nation-state is overlooked, or at the very least, is viewed as unproblematic. And yet, as Billig again observes:

The battle for nationhood is [specifically] a battle for hegemony, by which a part claims to speak for the whole nation and to represent the national essence . . . The triumph of a particular nationalism is seldom achieved without the defeat of alternative nationalisms and other ways of imagining peoplehood.

(1995: 27, 28)

Walker Connor (1993) uses the term 'Staatsvolk' to illustrate the process by which the dominant ethnic group comes to determine the 'national essence' of the nation-state. Staatsvolk describes a people who are culturally and politically preeminent in a state, even though (as we have seen) other groups may well be present in significant numbers. Connor suggests that, by their preeminence, the dominant group's culture and language come to be represented as the core or *national* culture and language. Minority groups, and their languages and cultures, consequently tend to be excluded from 'national' recognition. At the same time, minority groups are also variously encouraged and/or coerced by the dominant ethnie to assimilate to 'national' (i.e., dominant ethnie) norms. These countervailing pressures place minority groups in a double bind. If they resist, their attempts at maintaining a distinct identity are often labelled as a parochial and anti-national form of communalism. This is despite the fact that the dominant ethnie's advocacy of a 'universalistic' national consensus is simply a majoritarian version of the same process (Dench, 1986). If they acquiesce, and assimilate, minority groups may still face exclusion from the full benefits of a 'national' identity determined and delimited by the dominant ethnie (see below).

The ethnic hegemony which results sees a situation in which members of the Staatsvolk control knowledge/power, and thus the creation of sociocultural reality, through both their socioeconomic dominance and their control over the major institutions of the state (Bullivant, 1981). At the same time, many members of the Staatsvolk, or dominant ethnie, are often largely unaware of this process of ethnic hegemony. In the British context, for example, England, and particularly its southeast region, has long held dominance over the affairs of the British state (see, for example, Hechter, 1975; Nairn, 1981; N. Evans, 1989). A consequence of this dominance is that many English people use the terms 'English' and 'British' interchangeably – assuming implicitly that one amounts to the other, when in fact one describes a national affiliation and the other a state affiliation. This, of course, simply reminds the Welsh, Scots and other non-English peoples living in Britain that they live in a multinational state dominated by the English (Connor, 1993; Crick, 1989, 1995; Miles, 1996).

Most modernist accounts of nationalism accept this process of ethnic hegemony uncritically, assuming it to be the necessary price of modernisation. Gellner, for example, has argued that it was the requirements of a modern industrialised society that led to the perceived need for an homogeneous national culture in the first place, particularly in the form of a common language and culture. This was reflected in the 'one state, one culture' principle discussed earlier. As he states:

> the culture needs the state and the state *probably* needs the homogeneous cultural branding of its flock, in a situation in which it cannot rely on largely eroded sub-groups either to police its citizens, or to inspire them

with that minimum of moral zeal and social identification without which social life becomes very difficult . . .

(1983: 140; my emphasis)

The need for a 'minimum of moral zeal and social identification' is the basis on which a homogeneous national culture is advanced. Accordingly, any alternative form of ethnic and cultural identification is seen as *oppositional* to this overarching conception of national culture and, thus, undermining of social cohesion (see Chapter 3). Furthermore, since the nation-state represents in the modernist view the end point of the transition from tradition to modernity, alternative ethnic and cultural identifications are also, by definition, seen as regressive and premodern. As such, the nation-state appears as a new form of group life *at odds* with that of separate ethnic groups; these being, no doubt, the 'largely eroded sub-groups' to which Gellner refers (Rex, 1991). This position is not too dissimilar to the nineteenth-century views of Mill, Michelet and Engels on minority groups, outlined in Chapter 1. For Gellner, the best such groups can hope for – aside from assimilation or the (unlikely) prospect of secession – is to be represented in the modern nation-state 'in a token and cellophane-packaged form' (1983: 121; see also 1994: 108).

The construction of sociological minorities

To recapitulate, it has been my argument that modernist accounts of nationalism fail adequately to explain the ongoing link between ethnicity and nationalism in the modern world. This inadequacy is demonstrated in both the historical and cultural realms. In relation to the former, explaining the rise of nationalism via the transition to modernity in the eighteenth and nineteenth centuries leads to a teleological account of history which overemphasises the role of modernism and underplays, or ignores, the influence of preexisting ethnies. In relation to the latter, nation-state congruence leaves little or no room for minority ethnies to have their historical, cultural and linguistic concerns recognised by and expressed within appropriate state hierarchies. As Richard Jenkins concludes, both these dimensions are interconnected:

Historically, the [modernist] argument tends towards tautology: nationalism is what supersedes ethnicity, which is what precedes nationalism. Culturally, we are left with no authentic place within modern nation-states for ethnicity, other than an axiomatic homogeneity on the one hand, or an immigrant or peripheral presence on the other.

(1995: 372)

The result has seen the juxtaposition in today's nation-states of (modern) 'national' and (premodern) 'ethnic' identities and, relatedly, of *dominant ethnies* and a wide range of *sociological minorities*. The distinction drawn here between dominant ethnies and sociological minorities highlights two often overlooked features of national life. The first relates to its *heterogeneity* – a characteristic which, at the individual level, we may take for granted but at the level of the polity we tend to ignore. As I noted earlier, Max Weber highlights this disjuncture in his observation that the idea of the nation includes 'an essential, *though frequently indefinite*, homogeneity' (1961: 173; my emphasis). As he observes:

> If one believes that it is at all expedient to distinguish national sentiment as something homogeneous and specifically set apart . . . one must be clearly aware of the fact that sentiments of solidarity, very heterogeneous in both their nature and origin, are comprised within national sentiments.
>
> (1961: 179)

The second, and related, aspect is that if some 'sentiments of solidarity' take precedence over, and/or subsume, others in the construction of the nation-state, they must do so on the basis of a differential apportionment of status and value. As Billig succinctly comments, 'the aura of nationhood always operates within contexts of power' (1995: 4; see also S. Hall, 1992a). Given this, sociological minorities can be defined as groups which are a numerical minority in a given state *and* which are also politically nondominant (Minority Rights Group, 1997). Indeed, in this context, while the term 'minorities' tends to draw attention to numerical size, its more important reference is to groups with few rights and privileges (see Chapter 5). This is not to suggest that majority–minority relationships are fixed since, by definition, they are relative and relational and may differ from one context to the next (Eriksen, 1993; Young, 1993). Nonetheless, sociological minorities are usually characterised by a history of social, economic and political marginalisation and/or exploitation by dominant ethnies within given 'nation-states' (Hechter, 1975; Byram, 1986; Churchill, 1986; Dench, 1986; Thornberry, 1991a, b; Tollefson, 1991).[10]

In this final section, I want to outline briefly the key distinctions that can be drawn between various sociological minorities. In so doing, I will employ Eriksen's (1992, 1993) useful attempts at a typology along these lines. Given the inevitable limitations of typologies, I will also draw on a number of complementary categorisations where appropriate (see, for example, Churchill, 1986; Ogbu, 1987; Gibson and Ogbu, 1991; Kymlicka, 1995a; Fenton, 1999). However, this attempt at a more nuanced categorisation notwithstanding, the following distinctions should be seen primarily as useful heuristic devices rather than as definitive and/or exhaustive categories. It should also be borne in mind that these minority ethnies are no more homogeneous than any other grouping and will, accordingly, reflect significant *intra*group as well as *inter*group differences, along with a considerable degree of overlap (see Chapter 1).

Indigenous peoples

Indigenous peoples refer to aboriginal groups who are politically nondominant and who are not, or are only partially, integrated into the nation-state. They include such groups as Māori, Sámi, Australian Aboriginal peoples and Torres Strait Islanders, Native Americans, Hawaiians and Inuit. These groups are associated historically with a nonindustrial mode of production and a state-less political system (Minority Rights Group, 1997). The extreme disadvant-ages faced currently by many indigenous groups in modern nation-states are the result of colonisation and subsequent marginalisation within their own historic territories. Such historic processes have usually seen the expropri-ation of land, and the destruction, or near destruction, of their language(s) and traditional social, economic and political practices – not to mention the very groups themselves. In Australia, for example, British colonisers in the nineteenth century declared sovereignty on the basis that the land was terra nullius. In effect, Australian Aboriginal peoples were deemed to be so un-civilised as to be safely ignored. Indeed, as late as 1953, the Australian delegate to the United Nations Sub-Commission on the Prevention of Dis-crimination and the Protection of Minorities could state that 'there were no minority problems in Australia . . . There were, of course, the aborigines [sic], but they had no separate competing culture of their own' (cited in Kingsbury, 1989: 145).

Accordingly, the predominant concerns of indigenous peoples are for separate political and cultural recognition *within* the nation-state and, where possible, for political and economic redress for past injustices. In this regard, political pressure from indigenous peoples has led to a limited range of reparative legislation within nation-states in recent times, notably in Canada, Aotearoa / New Zealand, Australia, Brasil and Norway. Indigenous concerns have also been articulated at an international level by the World Council of Indigenous Peoples (WCIP) and the United Nations Working Group on Indigenous Populations (WGIP). The increasing influence of this broad movement has led, for example, to the development by the United Nations of a (1993) Draft Declaration on the Rights of Indigenous Peoples, although the final status of this document in international law remains a subject of some contention. In Chapter 8 I will explore in further detail these national and international developments with respect to indigenous peoples.

As Eriksen (1992, 1993) observes, however, the concept of 'indigenous peoples' is not an accurate analytical one since it excludes groups such as the Welsh, Catalans and Basques, who could also claim to be 'indigenous' but who do not share all the attributes ascribed to these groups as they have come to be defined. In this regard, Stacy Churchill's (1986) distinction between 'indigenous' and 'established' minorities is a useful addendum here. Churchill argues that 'established' and 'indigenous' minorities are both minority groups that have been long established in their native countries. However, where indigenous peoples are characterised by a 'traditional' culture which is often regarded as being at odds with that of the majority group, established minorities are characterised by a lifestyle similar to the remainder of the national society, although sometimes falling behind in rate of evolution. As such, established minorities are more likely to be able to lay claim to a right to conserve their identity and to back it with political might. This distinction is not entirely unproblematic. However, it does point to the overlap of established minorities with the next group in Eriksen's typology, 'proto-nations'.

Proto-nations

Proto-nations are most commonly associated with the growing number of secessionist and irredentist nationalisms in the world today that have come to be termed 'ethnonational movements'. As discussed previously, these comprise historical culture-communities which are territorially based and which do not currently possess their own nation-state – 'nations without states' in Guibernau's (1999) terms. Such groups are usually no more or less modern than other national groups and are fully differentiated along class and educational lines. Their numbers may be said currently to include Kurds, Palestinians, Southern Tamils, Tibetans, Basques and the Québécois, among others. The most commonly associated aim of ethnonational movements is to (re)claim statehood and to be recognised subsequently in the world interstate system. As such, their concerns more closely reflect political nationalisms (see above). However, there is also often a considerable degree of overlap within such movements between an overtly separatist political approach and one that favours more culturalist (and nonsecessionist) emphases. The distinctions between the Basque separatist ETA organisation and moderate Basque politicians, and the separatist Parti Québécois and other Francophone nationalist organisations in Québec, illustrate these differences.

Urban ethnic minorities

Unlike the preceding groups, which can be broadly classified as national-minority ethnies – that is, as previously self-governing and with a historic claim to a particular territory – urban ethnic minorities comprise immigrant groups which have settled in the country of destination. Usually such groups have come to be concentrated in urban areas, although this may not have been the case historically. Thus, Indian and Chinese minorities in Malaysia,

Fiji and Aotearoa / New Zealand were initially employed as predominantly agricultural migrant labour in the nineteenth century before subsequently settling in cities in the twentieth century. African Caribbeans in Britain provide a more recent example of direct migration to urban areas in the 1950s as part of a postwar British employment policy to fill low-skill, low-wage positions in the depleted labour market of the time.

While these ethnic-minority groups may retain elements of their culture, language and traditions – sometimes over the course of a number of generations – their general aim is to integrate into the host society and to be accepted as full members of it. As such, immigrant minority groups can be distinguished from national-minority ethnies since their ethnic and cultural distinctiveness is manifested primarily in the private domain and is not inconsistent with their institutional integration into the nation-state (Kymlicka, 1995a). This is not to suggest that such groups do not face racism, discrimination and exclusion within the host nation-state, nor that they may resist assimilation to the norms of the dominant ethnie. Quite the reverse in fact, since the so-called 'ethnic revival' that emerged in the 1960s has seen immigrant groups increasingly assert the right to express their ethnic particularities (see Chapter 3). However, such minorities do not usually seek separate and self-governing status within the nation-state, as is typically demanded by national minorities. Rather, they argue for a more plural and inclusive conception of national identity and culture which recognises their contribution to and influence on the historical and contemporary development of the host nation-state. In the process, the boundaries of nationhood – what it is that constitutes the national community – are opened up for debate. Of central concern in this debate are the questions of who is (and who is not) to be included in the national collectivity, and on what (and whose) terms are the criteria for inclusion to be based.

That said, there are a number of caveats that need to be addressed before proceeding further. First, these so-called 'ethnic minorities' may become national minorities over time if they settle together and acquire self-governing power in the interim (Kymlicka, 1995a). This is particularly evident in ex-colonial societies such as the USA, Canada, Australia and Aotearoa / New Zealand, where white settler groups have subsequently come to constitute the dominant ethnie(s) in the modern nation-state. Likewise, the one possible exception to the broad distinctions so far outlined is the example of African Americans in the USA. African Americans clearly do not fit either the national or immigrant category. They have no historic territorial claim to the Americas (unlike Native Americans) and their historical subjection through slavery clearly precludes voluntary immigration.

The apparently anomalous position of African Americans has led Steve Fenton (1999), who also uses Eriksen's typology as a useful starting point, to adopt the additional category of 'post-slavery minorities'. Another means of analysis is via John Ogbu's (1987) distinction between 'voluntary' (immigrant) and 'involuntary' (caste-like) minorities (see also Gibson and Ogbu, 1991). Adopting a predominantly culturalist approach, Ogbu argues that all minority groups are subject to racism and discrimination to some degree, as well as facing cultural and language discontinuities in relation to their integration in the nation-state. However, for voluntary minorities these discontinuities are seen as *primary cultural/linguistic differences*; that is, they existed prior to their immigration to the host country and are thus viewed as barriers to be overcome. As such, voluntary minorities are more likely to accommodate to the 'cultural model' of the majority group or dominant ethnie. In contrast, involuntary minorities – including in Ogbu's view, African Americans and indigenous people groups – are characterised by a history of exploitation and/or subjugation *within* a particular nation-state. Accordingly, involuntary minorities tend to develop a *secondary cultural system* in which cultural differences are viewed in light of that history, and in opposition to the majority group.

Cultural and language differences thus come to serve a boundary-maintenance function (see Chapter 4). They are seen as symbols of identity to be maintained rather than barriers to be overcome and may consequently develop into oppositional cultural (and political) nationalist movements. Such political nationalism has been represented among African Americans principally through the call for a separate black state. This was first supported in the 1930s, resurfaced again briefly in the 1960s in association with the 'Nation of Islam' movement, and again gained prominence in the 1990s under the current leader of the Nation of Islam, Louis Farrakhan. These developments notwithstanding, much of the political effort among African Americans – including the principal concerns of the civil rights movement – has centred on gaining full and equal rights and benefits for African Americans *as US citizens*. As such, the concerns of African Americans approximate more closely to immigrant minorities than national ones (Kymlicka, 1995a).

Ethnies in plural societies

Eriksen (1992, 1993) makes one final distinction based on ethnic groups within so-called 'plural societies'. Plural societies are most prominently associated with the work of Furnivall (1948) on Burma and M. G. Smith (1965) on the British West Indies. They have come to refer to ex-colonial societies, primarily Asian and Caribbean, with self-consciously culturally heterogeneous populations. The groups that make up these societies are divided internally by class and rank but are also clearly identifiable through ethnic and cultural differences. They are compelled to participate in uniform political and ethnic systems although one particular group will usually dominate. Ethnic relations are characterised consequently by intergroup competition. Secessionism is usually not an option since the groups involved have no external nation-state to which they realistically relate.

Having said this, the utility of the term 'plural society' has more recently been brought into question (see R. Jenkins, 1986, 1997; Eriksen, 1998). This is because plural societies are not the exception, as the above formulation suggests, but are actually the norm. As I have already discussed, most contemporary states can be regarded as plural or *polyethnic* in this way. In short, contemporary 'nation-states' increasingly comprise a variety of ethnic groups which are in competition for the resources of the state – a process I outlined more fully in my discussion of situational ethnicity in Chapter 1. The USA is perhaps the clearest example of a plural or polyethnic state in this regard. To complicate matters further, polyethnic states are often *multinational* ones as well. In other words, indigenous and national-minority groups are also present in many of the same states (the USA being no exception; see Chapter 3). However, what has tended to happen up until now is that both these types of minority group have been treated *in the same way* by the dominant ethnie. As a result, indigenous peoples and other national minorities have been denied their historical rights as ethnies and have been treated as merely one of a number of competing 'ethnic groups' laying claim to the nation-state's limited social, economic and political resources.

As I have argued, this elision has been the inevitable result of the exclusion of ethnicity from the realms of nationalism, which has, in turn, been predicated on the principle of nation-state congruence and the related separation of political and cultural nationalisms. It may also help to explain the continued spread of ethnonationalism(s) in the modern world. The voices of dissenting national minorities are increasingly questioning the pejorative distinction drawn between the (modern) 'national' identity of the dominant ethnie and their own supposedly (premodern) 'ethnic' identities. Not only this, they are also increasingly dissatisfied with the concomitant rejection by the former of their claims for greater civic recognition and inclusion within the nation-state. As Homi Bhabha argues, we are confronted with the nation-state 'split within itself, articulating the heterogeneity of its population . . . a liminal signifying space that is *internally* marked by the discourses of minorities, the heterogeneous histories of contending peoples, antagonistic authorities and tense locations of cultural difference' (1994: 148; emphasis in original).

Of course, such minority disenchantment is by no means a new phenomenon, nor is the state–minority relationship from which it springs. However, what I have argued here is that these developments include a growing number of indigenous and established national minorities who are less concerned with independent statehood – although it may inevitably spill over into this – than with challenging and changing the hegemonic construction of 'national' culture upon which nation-states have traditionally been based. As Colin Williams observes, 'it is clear that as many societies become increasingly multiethnic in composition the question of national congruence will have to be redefined and more appropriate answers given than those which are currently practised in many states' (1994: 12). What might be involved exactly in redefining or *rethinking* the nation-state to this end, particularly with respect to questions of language and education, is the focus of the next three chapters.

Notes

1   I will distinguish further between ethnies and nations later in this chapter where I discuss ethnicist accounts of nationalism.

2   It is important to note, however, that perennial accounts of nationhood do not necessarily entail a primordial conception as well (see A. Smith, 1998).

3   That said, the political objectives of Herder and Fichte did differ significantly. While Herder, as I have already suggested, was clearly not immune to anti-French sentiment, his general view of the direct links between language and 'national' communities led him to adopt a pluralist and egalitarian stance towards other ethnocultural/ethnolinguistic groups (see Fishman, 1989d: 570–571). This can be contrasted directly with Fichte's subsequent hierarchising of these same communities; principally via his application of Herder's views on language to the tenets of political nationalism.

4   I am not suggesting here that religious sectarianism is absent in Scotland (see, for example, McCrone, 1992), simply that, unlike Northern Ireland, it is not the *principal* factor in questions of Scottish nationalism and national identity.

5   The historical recency of nationalism is highlighted by the term 'nationalism' itself, which, as Connor (1978) points out, only gained a permanent place in dictionaries in the nineteenth century. Likewise, it was probably Lord Acton (1907) who first coined the term 'nationality' (J. Edwards, 1985).

6   Smith argues that there are two principal types of ethnie: *lateral*, which develop round a centralised state and are confined to a social and political elite; and *vertical*, which are usually subordinated status groups that are sustained by cultural and religious institutions and values that act to unify the population (see 1986: Ch. 4). In either case, however, the preexisting profile serves to shape the contours of the modern nation-state.

7   It should be noted, however, that Gellner never accepted this widely made criticism of his work. In response, he argued that his account was causal rather than teleological. The development, diffusion, and related discontents associated with industrial society, in his view, *caused* nationalism (see Gellner, 1996).

8   Parekh does not adopt an 'ethnicist' position in the way described here. Nonetheless, his description of national identity lends itself well to a comparison with habitus.

9   Anthony Smith has argued that the different historical and organisational trajectories of statist and cultural nationalisms relate to the distinction between lateral and vertical ethnies (see n. 6); a position that Hutchinson

in his formulation of cultural nationalism also implicitly accepts. However, I am inclined to agree with Richard Jenkins' (1995) conclusion that this perpetuates the 'ethnic' and 'civic' divide within nationalism and that, rather, all nationalisms should be regarded as in some sense 'ethnic'. If there is a more appropriate distinction to be drawn, then perhaps it is between those nationalisms which claim territory on the basis of putative ethnic commonality and those which attempt to construct ethnic commonality within an already occupied territory (see R. Jenkins, 1995: 387). The latter, in my view, are more often associated with cultural forms of nationalism.

10 Although see my previous provisos in relation to economistic accounts of the spread of ethnonationalisms.

3

Liberal theory, multiculturalism and minority rights

It has been my argument thus far that the construction of national and ethnic minorities, and their pejorative and marginalised status, are the result of what Stacy Churchill (1996) has termed the *philosophical matrix of the nation-state*. A philosophical matrix denotes 'a combination of ideas, not easy to separate or define, that embodies the expectations of society as to how it should function' (MacLachlan, 1988: x–xi). The philosophical matrix of the nation-state, rooted in the political nationalism of the eighteenth and nineteenth centuries, has been predicated on the confluence of nation and state and on the establishment (often retrospectively) of a common civic or 'national' language and culture.

Interestingly, it was Fichte who first advocated this linking of nation, state and language into an indissoluble whole. Fichte, as we have seen, incorporated Herder's views on language and culture within a statist account of nationalism (Hutchinson, 1994). This led to the development of the linear 'one language, one nation, one state' principle of linguistic or organic nationalism; a principle which has subsequently been widely discredited as essentialist and which has also been associated (pejoratively) with many contemporary ethnonationalisms. In contrast, political nationalism argued that it was the state that preceded and precipitated the rise of the nation, not the other way around. The key principle that followed from this can be summarised as 'one state, one nation, one language' and it has since come to represent the common orthodoxy in discussions of nationalism, not to mention the development of modern nation-states themselves. Indeed, as early as 1862, Lord Acton argued unequivocally on this basis for the superiority of political nationalism over linguistic nationalism:

> The State may in course of time produce a nationality . . . but that a nationality should constitute a State is contrary to the nature of modern civilisation . . . [Such a position is] in defiance of the modifying action of external causes, *of tradition and of existing rights*. It overrules the rights and

wishes of the inhabitants, absorbing their divergent interests in a fictitious unity, sacrifices their several inclinations and duties to the higher claim of nationality and crushes all natural rights and established liberties for the purpose of vindicating itself.

(1907: 288; my emphasis)

And yet political nationalism, and the modern nation-state with which it is associated, can be accused of these very same proclivities. The nation-state, as it has come to be constructed, *creates* sociological minorities by establishing a civic language and culture that is largely limited to, and representative of, the dominant ethnie or Staatsvolk. Minorities are, in turn, denied legitimate rights to their *existing* language and cultural traditions where these differ from those of the dominant ethnie. Political nationalism may thus have prided itself on the reversal of the linguistic nationalists' language-nation-state connection but it has left the *linearity* of the principle untouched. As such, what results is still ethnic and linguistic hegemony, albeit from a different direction. Moreover, the hegemonic construction of the nation-state is far less readily apparent than more 'overt' ethnonationalisms. Cloaked as it is in the apparently neutral representation of a modern 'national' language and culture, the legitimation and valorisation of the dominant ethnie's habitus often escapes notice or critical comment. As Billig observes, this 'banal nationalism' is simply 'overlooked, forgotten, even theoretically denied' (1995: 17), which perhaps helps to explain why dominant groups so seldom come to define themselves as 'ethnic'.

A further explanation of the uncritical acceptance of this elision of civic and ethnic ties rests with the key liberal democratic principles of universal political citizenship, and the related primacy of individual over collective rights. These principles have been regularly invoked over the last two centuries by liberal commentators in their dismissal of ethnicity as a valid form of collective social and political organisation and identity (cf. Chapter 1). Concomitantly, they have also been consistently employed in support of the present political organisation of the nation-state. In this chapter, I will examine the cogency of this orthodox liberal defence of the nation-state, and the key tenets on which it is based, and will argue that these accounts are framed within, and thus constrained by, the notion of nation-state congruence arising from political nationalism. If this assumption is dropped, the recognition of a more plural conception of the nation-state – based, at least to some degree, on group-differentiated rights – becomes a possibility. In this regard, it is my view that national minorities (including indigenous and established minorities) have rights to greater inclusion within the civic realm of the nation-state – that is, 'civil society' in Gramsci's (1971) sense[1] – than many currently enjoy. Moreover, these rights of inclusion are *distinct* from those of other ethnic minorities (see Chapter 2). Accordingly, I will concentrate in much of what follows on the particular rights of national minorities. However, I will return to the question of other ethnic-minority groups, and the wider implications of my own position with regard to them, in Chapters 5 and 9.

The pluralist dilemma

A central concern in current debates surrounding the organisation and legitimacy of modern nation-states has to do with what Brian Bullivant (1981) has termed 'the pluralist dilemma'. The pluralist dilemma, for Bullivant, is 'the problem of reconciling the diverse political claims of constituent groups and individuals in a pluralist society *with the claims of the nation-state as a whole*' (1981: x; my emphasis); what he elsewhere describes as the competing aims of 'civism' and 'pluralism'. Other commentators have suggested similar distinctions: 'roots' and 'options' (Rokkan and Urwin, 1983); 'state' and 'community' (A. Smith, 1981); and, drawing on de Saussure, 'parochialism' and 'intercourse' (J. Edwards, 1994). All these distinctions emphasise, like Bullivant's, the apparent polarities involved in the task of national integration; the difficulties of reconciling social cohesion on the one hand with, on the other, a recognition and incorporation of ethnic, linguistic and cultural diversity within the nation-state. In an earlier analysis, Schermerhorn has described these countervailing social and cultural forces as *centripetal* and *centrifugal* tendencies. As he observes:

> Centripetal tendencies refer both to cultural trends such as acceptance of common values, styles of life etc., as well as structural features like increased participation in a common set of groups, associations, and institutions . . . Conversely, centrifugal tendencies among subordinate groups are those that foster separation from the dominant group or from societal bonds in one way or another. Culturally this most frequently means retention and presentation of the group's distinctive tradition in spheres like language, religion, recreation etc.
>
> (1970: 81)

How then can the tensions arising from the pluralist dilemma best be resolved in the social and political arena? Two contrasting approaches have been adopted in response to this central question, which Gordon (1978, 1981) has described as 'liberal pluralism' and 'corporate pluralism'. Liberal pluralism is characterised by the absence, even prohibition, of any ethnic-, religious-, or national-minority group possessing separate standing before the law or government. Its central tenets can be traced back to the French Revolution and Rousseau's conception of the modern polity as comprising three inseparable features: freedom (nondomination), the absence of differentiated roles, and a very tight common purpose. On this view, the margin for recognising difference within the modern nation-state is very small (Taylor, 1994). In contrast, corporate pluralism – now more commonly known by the term 'multiculturalism' (see May, 1999a, 2001) – involves the recognition of minority groups as legally constituted entities, on the basis of which, and depending on their size and influence, economic, social and political awards are allocated. Glazer (1975) and Walzer (1992, 1994) draw similar distinctions between an approach based on 'nondiscrimination' – which involves, in Glazer's memorable phrase, the 'salutary neglect' of the state towards ethnic minorities – and a 'corporatist' (Walzer) or 'group rights' (Glazer) model.

It is clear, however, that for most liberal commentators the merits of liberal pluralism significantly outweigh those of a group-rights or multiculturalist approach. In effect, the answer to the pluralist dilemma has been consistently to favour civism over pluralism.[2] On this basis, the 'claims of the nation-state as a whole' – emphasising the apparently inextricable interconnections between social cohesion and national homogeneity – have invariably won the day over more pluralist conceptions of the nation-state where ethnic, linguistic and cultural differences *between different groups* are accorded some degree of formal recognition. This should perhaps not surprise us, since the former is situated squarely within the 'philosophical matrix of the nation-state' to which I referred earlier. Relatedly, liberal pluralism also accords closely with the long-standing pejorative distinction between *citizenship* and *ethnicity* – a distinction first illustrated in Chapter 1 by the likes of the nineteenth-century liberals Mill and Michelet, and the socialists Marx and Engels. In this light, it is perhaps worth observing that the consensus between liberal and Marxist commentators on the position of ethnic and national minorities within the nation-state has also been reflected in the subsequent construction of liberal-democratic and socialist states. As such, while I will concentrate in what follows on the political organisation of liberal democracies, it should be pointed out that socialist and other nondemocratic states have also tended to adopt a very similar position vis-à-vis national and ethnic minorities. In this latter regard, Churchill (1996: 268–269) and Kymlicka (1995a: 69–74) provide useful discussions of the history of the former Soviet Union with respect to its treatment of minorities.

The result of this broad consensus has been the construction in contemporary orthodox liberal accounts of a range of interrelated, and at times overlapping, polarities which are outlined below. In each, the former feature is associated (positively) with liberal pluralism while the latter is associated (negatively) with a corporatist approach:

- universal or particularist
- individual or collective
- autonomy or identity
- private or public
- informal or formal
- fluid or bounded
- dialogic or ghettoised
- changing or static
- modernity or tradition
- commonality or difference
- cohesion or fragmentation

In orthodox liberal accounts, individual and universal 'citizenship' rights are invariably constructed in opposition to collective and particularist 'ethnic' rights. As such, formal differentiation within the nation-state on the grounds of (ethnic) group association is rejected as inimical to the individualistic and meritocratic tenets of liberal democracy. Where countenanced at all, alternative ethnic affiliations should be restricted solely to the private domain since the formal recognition of collective (ethnic) identity is viewed as undermining personal and political autonomy, and fostering social and political fragmentation. As Will Kymlicka observes, 'the near-universal response by liberals has been one of active hostility to minority rights . . . schemes which single out minority cultures for special measures . . . appear irremediably unjust, a disguise for creating or maintaining . . . ethnic privilege' (1989: 4). Any deviation from the strict principles of universal political citizenship and individual rights is seen as the first step down the road to apartheid. Or so it seems.

In a similar vein to postmodernist commentators (see Chapter 1), many liberal critics also argue that any acknowledgement and accommodation of group-related differences must significantly understate the fluid and dialogic nature of inter- and intragroup relations (Goulbourne, 1991a, b; J. Edwards, 1985, 1994; Waldron, 1993, 1995). The resulting liberal consensus is well illustrated by Brian Bullivant:

> Certain common institutions essential for the well-being and smooth functioning of the nation-state as *a whole* must be maintained: common language, common political system, common economic market system and so on. Cultural pluralism can operate at the level of the *private*, rather than public, concerns such as use of ethnic [sic] language in the home . . . But, the idea that maintaining these aspects of ethnic life and encouraging the maintenance of ethnic groups almost in the sense of ethnic enclaves will assist their ability to cope with the political realities of the nation-state is manifestly absurd.
>
> (1981: 232; emphases in original)

Defending liberal democracy

This 'de-ethnicised' view of liberal democracy, and the various polarities which characterise it, are clearly evident in the work of three contemporary liberal commentators – John Porter, Arthur Schlesinger Jr and Harry Goulbourne. In what follows, I want to explore briefly their respective arguments. Before doing so, however, I should point out that Porter and Schlesinger tend towards the conservative end of the liberal continuum while Goulbourne's position is considerably further to the left. This raises an important point. The orthodox defence of liberal democracy, in the form of liberal pluralism, is advocated by commentators on both the left and right of the political spectrum – albeit for somewhat different reasons, as we shall see (cf. May, 1999a; Bonnett, 2000; Ch. 5). Nonetheless, the wide support that liberal pluralism garners reinforces the degree to which the political tenets of nation-state congruence underlying it have come to be taken as given.

The vertical mosaic

The late John Porter wrote extensively (1965, 1972, 1975) on pluralism in Canada, particularly in relation to the 'ethnic revival' of the 1960s and 1970s. In this regard, he was a strong advocate of liberal pluralism and a sharp critic of the corporatist model. As he observes, 'the organisation of society on the basis of rights or claims that derive from group membership is sharply opposed to the concept of a society based on citizenship, which has been such an important aspect in the development of modern societies' (1975: 297). From this, Porter argued that the maintenance of collective ethnicity in modern societies was regressive and historically naive. Moreover, it resulted in a form of ethnic stratification which, in combination with social class, reduced the social and economic mobility of individuals. Thus, in his influential study *The Vertical Mosaic* (1965), Porter argued that ethnicity was a principal factor in the formation and persistence of the social stratification system in Canada. In his view, this stratification process, or vertical mosaic, was initiated by the colonial contest between the British and French. When the French settlers lost this contest, they were accorded secondary status to their British counterparts. Subsequent immigrant groups were assigned an 'entrance status' which located them at various positions lower down the social hierarchy, while Native Canadian and Inuit occupied the lowest levels (see also Chapter 6).

Consequently, the stark choice facing Canadians, he asserted, was 'between ethnic stratification that results from ethnic diversity and the greater possibilities for equality that result from a reduction of ethnicity as a salient feature of modern society' (1972: 205; see also 1975: 288–304). Like many other liberals, Porter directly equated 'modern society' here with the homogeneous civic culture of the nation-state. On this basis, he advocated the *assimilation* of ethnic minorities into Canadian national life and rejected any form of multiculturalism which would perpetuate ethnic and/or cultural distinctiveness. This was clearly in the best interests of ethnic-minority groups, he believed, since in modern society:

> the emphasis was on *individual* achievement and in the context of a new nation with *universalistic* standards of judgement it meant forgetting ancestry and attempting to establish a society of equality where ethnic origin did not matter.
>
> (1975: 293; my emphases)

In advocating this position, Porter does allow for some recognition of minority languages. As he concedes, 'identification with and the use of their own language, particularly in school, may be important in providing opportunity for very low status groups' (1975: 302). However, he quickly proceeds to argue that 'such use of language is quite different from the goal of having ethnic communities become a permanent compensation for low status, or as psychic shelters in the urban-industrial world' (1975: 303). For Porter, it was only *citizenship* that could provide minority ethnic-group members with the individual social mobility and achievement necessary to make their way in the modern world. This, in turn, implied 'a commitment to the values of modernism and a movement away from the [minority] ethnic community with each succeeding generation' (1975: 302). The reason for this was obvious enough. Minority cultures were 'tradition bound' and 'less and less relevant for the post-industrial society' (1975: 303). As Porter concludes, ethnicity in the modern world is simply an anachronism: 'Many of the historic cultures are irrelevant to our futures. Opportunity will go to those individuals who are future oriented in an increasingly universalistic culture. Those oriented to the past are likely to lose out' (1975: 304).

The cult of ethnicity

More recently, these themes have been echoed in the often vituperative debates surrounding multiculturalism, bilingualism and 'Afrocentrism' in the United States, particularly in relation to education. Arthur Schlesinger's *The Disuniting of America* (1992) provides us with a representative example of the conservative critique of corporate pluralism here.[3] As his title suggests, Schlesinger, a noted liberal historian, has argued to much public acclaim against the 'disuniting' of America by the 'cult of ethnicity':

> A cult of ethnicity has arisen both among non-Anglo whites and among non-white minorities to denounce the idea of the melting pot, to challenge

the concept of 'one people', and to protect, promote, and perpetuate separate [ethnic] communities . . . The new ethnic gospel rejects the unifying
vision of individuals from all nations melted into a new race [sic]. Its
underlying philosophy is that America is not a nation of individuals at all
but a nation of groups, that ethnicity is the defining experience for most
Americans, that ethnic ties are permanent and indelible . . . The ethnic
interpretation, moreover, reverses the historic theory of America as one
people – the theory that has thus far managed to keep American society
whole.

(1992: 15–16)

For Schlesinger, this 'ethnic cheerleading' is preservationist rather than
transformative and results in a view of America which, instead of being 'composed of individuals making their own unhampered choices', is increasingly
'composed of groups more or less ineradicable in their ethnic character'.
The result is a 'multiethnic dogma [which] abandons historic purposes,
replacing assimilation by fragmentation, integration by separatism' (1992:
16–17). In the face of this assault, Schlesinger gloomily wonders: 'The national ideal had once been *e pluribus unum* [out of many, one]. Are we now to
belittle *unum* and glorify *pluribus*? Will the centre hold? Or will the melting
pot give way to the Tower of Babel?' (1991: 14; see also 1992: 18).

Schlesinger directs particular opprobrium here at the emergence among
African Americans of an 'Afrocentric' view of American (and world) history,
along with its formal promotion in schools under the rubric of multiculturalism. For Schlesinger, these developments are simply nationalist myth-
making, along the lines of Hobsbawm's (1990) 'invention of tradition', and
lead inevitably to cultural reification and essentialism. The rise of Afrocentrism may be understandable, he argues – given the consistent exclusion
of black voices in previous historical accounts – but it is still *bad* history,
albeit of a manifestly different kind from that which preceded it (see also S.
Howe, 1998). Moreover, the whole notion of using history as therapy, whose
principal function is to raise minority self-esteem, is misguided. After all, as
Schlesinger points out, 'the absence of historical role models seems [not] to
have handicapped two other groups in American society – Jewish Americans
and Asian Americans' (1992: 89).

In saying this, Schlesinger does acknowledge the effects of racism – both
historically and currently – on the African-American community, albeit within
an implicitly pathological frame of reference. As he observes, 'black Americans,
after generations of psychological and cultural evisceration, have every right
to seek affirmative action for their past . . . For blacks the American dream
has been pretty much a nightmare and, far more than white ethnics, *they
are driven by a desperate need to vindicate their own identity*' (1992: 60; my emphasis). However, in his view, Afrocentrism is not the answer to the problem
since it simply replaces one form of ethnic and/or cultural exclusiveness (and

exclusion) with another. Indeed, Schlesinger argues that the end game of this 'filiopietistic commemoration' (1992: 99) – or, more prosaically, the worship of ancestors – will actually confirm rather than reduce self-pity and self-ghettoisation among African Americans. Rather, he asserts:

> would it not be more appropriate for [ethnic-minority] students to be . . . encouraged to understand the American culture in which they are growing up and to prepare for an active role in shaping that culture? . . . As for self-esteem, is this really the product of ethnic role models and fantasies of a glorious past? Or does it not result from a belief in oneself that springs from achievement, from personal rather than [ethnic] pride?
>
> (1992: 90, 92)

Finally, Schlesinger extends his trenchant and apocalyptic critique to include an attack on bilingualism and the bilingual movement in the USA (see Chapter 6), along with its strong links to various Hispanic communities there.[4] Unlike Porter, who was at least prepared to countenance a limited role for minority languages, Schlesinger rejects out of hand the official recognition of minority languages – a position presaged by his previous allusion to the Tower of Babel:

> The separatist movement is by no means confined to the black community. Another salient expression is the bilingualism movement . . . In recent years the combination of the ethnicity cult with a *flood* of immigration from Spanish-speaking countries has given bilingualism new emphasis. The presumed purpose is transitional . . . Alas, bilingualism has not worked out as planned: rather the contrary . . . indications are that bilingual education retards rather than expedites the movement of Hispanic children *into the English-speaking world* and that it promotes segregation more than it does integration. Bilingualism shuts doors. It nourishes self-ghettoisation, and ghettoisation nourishes racial antagonism . . . using some language other than English *dooms* people to second class citizenship in American society.
>
> (1992: 107–108; my emphases)

I will revisit in greater depth the arguments about bilingualism, the role of English, and the particular preoccupation with Hispanic communities in Chapter 6, where I examine the key tenets of the 'English Only' movement in the USA. Suffice it to say at this point, that in attributing bilingualism with the same fractious and regressive characteristics as Afrocentrism, Schlesinger invokes, once again, the rhetoric of national cohesion. 'A common language is a *necessary* bond of national cohesion in so heterogeneous a nation as America . . . *institutionalised* bilingualism remains another source of the fragmentation of America, another threat to the dream of "one people"'

(1992: 109–110; my emphases; see also Hirsch, 1987). His parting comments echo this conclusion when he returns directly to the question of the pluralist dilemma: 'The question America confronts as a pluralistic society is how to vindicate cherished cultures and traditions without breaking the bonds of cohesion – common ideals, common political institutions, common language, common fate – that hold the republic together?' (1992: 138). His answer, by now, should come as no surprise: 'the bonds of social cohesion in our society are sufficiently fragile, or so it seems to me, that it makes no sense to strain them by encouraging and exalting cultural and linguistic apartheid. The American identity will never be fixed and final; it will always be in the making' (1992: 138). QED, or so it seems.

The communal option

The final example of liberal pluralism that I want to discuss is Harry Goulbourne's (1991a) account of the position of nonwhite ethnic minorities in post-imperial Britain. As I suggested earlier, Goulbourne's arguments are somewhat different in both tenor and substance to the previous two commentators, largely due to his long involvement with, and commitment to, antiracism in the British context. In particular, he clearly acknowledges that *majoritarian* conceptions of a common (national) culture and identity may be just as exclusive and exclusionary as those of ethnic-minority groups – more so, perhaps, since they tend to be implemented and maintained by the machinery of the state. This ethnic nationalism 'which in a very real sense *belongs* to the majority although it formally claims the loyalty of all' (1991a: 14; emphasis in original) stimulates, in turn, an 'ethnic' response within minority communities. In this regard, Goulbourne's account is far more aware of the cultural hegemony with which the 'common culture' argument of conservative apologists such as Porter and Schlesinger is imbued. Nonetheless, his conclusions can still be situated broadly within an orthodox liberal defence of the nation-state.

The reasons for this lie principally with his dismay – in line with other liberal commentators – about the growing 'assertion of difference' between various ethnic groups in Britain. As he observes of these developments:

> Whilst in the past *similarities* between groups of people formed the basis of unity or collective existence, the growing demand, or emphasis, today, is for communities to be bound together by the factors which establish *difference* from others ... This new nationalism demands ethnic *singularity* and ... often exhibits unnecessary intolerance and insistence on securing particularist rights, [even though] its righteousness and demands are generally couched in terms of strengthening democracy.
>
> (1991a: 12; emphases in original)

For Goulbourne, such emphases lead to what he describes as 'the communal option', by which he means 'the generalised encouragement, and the increasing desire, of many individuals to be a part of an identifiable group, and for each group not only *to exist entirely within its own confines* but also to ensure that individuals conform to the supposed norms of the group. This is rapidly becoming the British experience' (1991a: 13; emphasis in original). Indeed, in his view, the pursuit of the communal option is clearly evident in both 'cultural conservative' and 'new pluralist' (multicultural) conceptions of Britain. The former seeks to establish a narrow sense of Britishness which excludes nonwhite minorities from full participation in the national community (see, for example, Honeyford, 1988). As Goulbourne observes of this, 'while the membership of [nonwhite] minorities is accorded formal recognition, this recognition is constructed in such a manner that their legitimate presence and participation in Britain are nearly always questioned' (1991a: 2). The latter wishes to present as a desirable social good the image of Britain as characterised by a diverse range of ethnic, cultural and linguistic groups (see, for example, The Swann Report, DES, 1985). While clearly more sympathetic to the politics of the new pluralism, Goulbourne remains sharply critical of both positions, arguing for the abandonment of the harping nostalgia and exclusivism of cultural conservatism and the optimism and naivety of multiculturalism:

> Where the one wishes to maintain a pre-imperial, almost nativist, conception of the British community, the other would arrest the present imperfect, still emerging, moment and make that the ideal, preferred, social condition. The cultural conservative's position suggests that Britain's non-white population have made no contribution to the community in which they, in any event, ought not to belong. Multiculturalism holds out the prospect that the cultural differences between groups in Britain should not be respected only by social institutions; these differences should be publicly supported and maintained. Its pessimism lies in its underlying assumption that present differences between groups of people in Britain is a desirable long-term good for the nation [sic].
>
> (1991a: 31)

Goulbourne's solution is to argue for a reconceived multiculturalism which rejects 'defensive minority communalism' (1991a: 14) and is reconstituted within the tenets of liberal pluralism. This would involve firstly separating the claims of social justice for ethnic-minority groups from those of cultural preservation. Thus, instead of the current emphasis in much multiculturalism on *cultural* recognition, the *social* and *political* implications of equality and justice would come to dominate (see also Bullivant, 1981). Second, greater emphasis should be placed on commonality since the assumption that 'the social aggregate of . . . separate ethnic groups amounts to the whole and this whole is, or will, constitute the full expression of British society' (1991a: 236–37) is fundamentally misplaced. In his view, it is simply naive to think that different groups can live together peacefully without having anything in common; a position which echoes Furnivall's (1948) and M.G. Smith's (1965) discussions of ethnies in plural societies (see Chapter 2). Finally, Goulbourne returns to the merits of individualism as an answer to the pluralist dilemma: 'What is obviously required is a *will*, a *disposition*, on the part of most if not all groups to participate – not as groups but as individuals – in the construction of a common national community' (1991a: 241; emphasis in original). For this to occur, however, he does concede that much depends on the largesse of the dominant ethnie: 'Whilst the challenge for [this] social synergism . . . is likely to come from non-white minorities, it will largely be the willingness within the majority population to abandon its own communal response . . . which will determine success or failure' (1991a: 242).

Critiquing liberal democracy

Such is the current orthodoxy among liberals to the question of the pluralist dilemma. When in doubt, the historical and political imperatives of nation-state congruence should prevail, as should (for conservative commentators at least) the related prerogative of the dominant ethnie to determine civic culture. But how satisfactory is this broadly articulated position and what viable alternatives are there, if any? We can begin to unravel these questions by first highlighting some of the key inconsistencies that are evident in each of the preceding accounts.

John Porter's strong advocacy of assimilation, for example, was based on his long-held and principled commitment to egalitarianism. Unlike other conservative commentators, his arguments did not stem principally from a sense of nativism, racism, or exclusion towards ethnic minorities. Rather, his advocacy of assimilation was promoted specifically on behalf and for the benefit of ethnic-minority groups. In this sense, Porter represents the 'old' liberal position of the likes of Mill and Michelet. 'Ethnic' practices were seen as antediluvian and, it was assumed, would thus atrophy and eventually die in the face of modern (and modernist) civic culture. Consequently, the sooner ethnic groups were disabused of such 'traditional' practices (including the speaking of a minority language) the sooner they could contribute in and to the forward march of progress and civilisation. This march of progress was also, by implication, most clearly evident in the dominant ethnie. However, its actual representation was couched almost exclusively in terms of the more 'objective' notions of 'individual achievement' and 'universalistic standards of judgement', with the state assuming the role of neutral arbiter. From this, all individuals were to be treated as 'equal' members of the civic polity

– irrespective of their personal, social, religious and ethnic backgrounds – in order to 'establish a society of equality where ethnic origin did not matter' (1975: 293).

Porter's position is consistent here with an orthodox view of liberalism that addresses the person *only* as a political being with rights and duties attached to their status as *citizens*. Such a position does not countenance private identity, including a person's communal membership, as something warranting similar recognition. These latter dimensions are excluded from the public realm because their inevitable diversity would lead to the complicated business of the state mediating between different conceptions of 'the good life' (Rawls, 1971, 1985; Dworkin, 1978). On this basis, personal *autonomy* – based on the political rights attributable to citizenship – always takes precedence over personal (and collective) *identity* and the widely differing ways of life which constitute the latter. In effect, personal and political participation in liberal democracies, as it has come to be constructed, ends up denying group difference and posits all persons as interchangeable from a moral and political point of view (Young, 1993).

However, this strict separation of citizenship and identity in the modern polity understates, and at times disavows, the significance of wider communal affiliations, including ethnicity, to the construction of individual identity. As Michael Sandel (1982) observes, in a communitarian critique of liberalism, there is no such thing as the 'unencumbered self' – we are all, to some extent, *situated* within wider communities which shape and influence who we are.[5] Likewise, Charles Taylor argues that identity 'is who we are, "where we're coming from". As such, it is the background against which our tastes and desires and opinions and aspirations make sense' (1994: 33–34). These arguments have clear parallels with my discussion of habitus in Chapter 1. They also highlight the obvious point that certain goods such as language, culture and sovereignty cannot be experienced alone; they are, by definition, communally shared goods. A failure to account for these communal goods, however, has led to a view of rights within liberal democracy which is inherently individualistic and which cannot appreciate the pursuit of such goods other than derivatively (Van Dyke, 1977; Taylor, 1994; Coulombe, 1995). This approach can be regarded as even more problematic when one considers, for example, that indigenous and other nonwestern groups tend to place greater emphasis on shared communal values *as ends in themselves* than does the more individualistically oriented west (Corson, 1993, 1998; May, 1994a, 1999d; see Chapter 8).

In short, individualistic conceptions of the good life may preclude shared community values that are central to one's identity (Kymlicka, 1989, 1995a). Conversely, as Habermas has put it, 'a correctly understood theory of [citizenship] rights requires a politics of recognition that protects the individual in the life contexts in which his or her identity is formed' (1994: 113). As Habermas observes:

A 'liberal' version of the system of rights that fails to take this connection into account will necessarily misunderstand the universalism of basic rights as an abstract levelling of distinctions, a levelling of both cultural and social differences. To the contrary, these differences must be seen in increasingly context-sensitive ways if the system of rights is to be actualised democratically.

(1994: 116)

Criticism of the inherent individualism of orthodox liberalism is not limited to communitarian critiques, however. This is an important point since communitarian critiques have themselves been criticised for essentialising group identities (see Mouffe, 1993; Burtonwood, 1996; Ellison, 1997; Carter and Stokes, 1998). Thus, Will Kymlicka (1989) argues from a liberal perspective that the attempts of theorists such as Rawls (1971) and Dworkin (1978) to separate citizenship from communal identity actually still retain an implicit recognition of cultural membership as a primary good. The only reason they do not explicitly give it status as a grounds for differential rights claims, Kymlicka suggests, is because they accept uncritically the notion of the nation-state as politically and culturally coterminous (see Chapter 2). If this assumption is dropped, cultural membership has to be explicitly recognised as a possible source of injustice and/or inequality – a point which earlier theorists of liberalism, such as Hobhouse and Dewey, actually recognised. I discuss this latter point, and the significance of Kymlicka's wider contribution, more fully later in the chapter.

The dissociation of citizenship from individual identity, and the social and cultural context in which the latter is inevitably formed, highlights a related problem with orthodox liberal accounts such as Porter's – their inherent belief in the ethnic neutrality of the state. In other words, for orthodox liberals, the civic realm of the nation-state is a forum in which ethnicity does not (and *should* not) feature. However, as I have argued in the preceding chapters, ethnicity is *never* absent from the civic realm. Rather, the civic realm represents the particular (although not necessarily exclusive) *communal* interests and values of the dominant ethnie *as if* these values were held by all. In Charles Taylor's analysis, the 'supposedly neutral set of difference-blind principles [that constitute the liberal] politics of equal dignity is in fact a reflection of one hegemonic culture . . . [it is] a particularism masquerading as the universal' (1994: 43–44). In a similar vein, Iris Marion Young argues that if particular groups 'have greater economic, political or social power, their group related experiences, points of view, or cultural assumptions will tend to become the norm, biasing the standards or procedures of achievement and inclusion that govern social, political and economic institutions' (1993: 133).

This hegemonic process is clearly illustrated in Porter's direct equation of citizenship with modernity and the associated valorisation of homogeneity as simply the proper application of Reason (Goldberg, 1994). It is even more starkly apparent in Schlesinger's advocacy of a common American culture. In Schlesinger's account, the possibilities of heterogeneity are at least acknowledged by him, albeit somewhat grudgingly. However, his overall argument is unequivocal about homogeneity as the historically prevalent condition of social life and, as such, an ideal to be pursued and recaptured at all cost. This conclusion is encapsulated in his bald assertion of American history as 'the dream of one people' (1992: 110); a far from unproblematic assertion, as it turns out, since it can be accused of the very same features of 'bad history' and 'history as therapy' which he has levelled at Afrocentrism. As Robert Hughes, another liberal commentator, candidly concedes, America 'has always been a heterogeneous country and its cohesion, whatever cohesion it has, can only be based on mutual respect. There never was a core America in which everyone looked the same, spoke the same language, worshipped the same gods and believed the same things' (1993: 12; see also Chapter 6).

The idea of a homogeneous common culture is thus simply another variant of nationalist myth-making since, as we saw in Chapter 2, *all* nationalist histories are therapeutic to some extent and contain inevitable elisions and absences. The key question then becomes not so much the teaching of bad or therapeutic history but *whose* history one wants to teach. And this returns us once again to the central issue of hegemonic power relations. As Peter McLaren asserts of Schlesinger and other conservative critics in the USA:

> conservative attacks on multiculturalism as separatist and ethnocentric carry with them the erroneous assumption by White Anglo constituencies that North American society fundamentally constitutes social relations of uninterrupted accord. The liberal view is seen to underscore the idea that North American society is largely a forum of consensus with different minority viewpoints accretively added on. We are faced here with the politics of pluralism which largely ignores the workings of power and privilege.
>
> (1995: 126–127)

McLaren's analysis allows us to question the very notion of a commonly shared (American) culture and the supposedly unified and consensual history underpinning it. Common to whom, one might ask, and on whose terms? Who determines its central values and/or sets its parameters? Who is subsequently included and/or excluded from full participation in its 'benefits' and, crucially, *at what cost*? After all, those whose cultural and linguistic habitus are not reflected in the public realm are more likely to pay a far higher price for their subsequent participation in that realm. In contrast, those whose habitus are consonant with the civic culture and language – and, as such, are regarded as cultural and linguistic capital – have no such difficulties.

I will return to these questions more fully in the following chapter, but it is enough to point out here that Schlesinger does not address them. Like other conservative commentators, he assumes a homogeneous common culture as an historical and political given and, following from this, that the choice in the pluralist dilemma is one of either/or. National and ethnic minorities[6] must *either* give up their cultural and linguistic identities *or* prejudice both the social cohesion of the nation-state and the possibilities of their own individual social and economic success. As McLaren observes, this approach wants to assimilate such minorities 'to an unjust social order by arguing that every member of every ethnic group can reap the benefits of neocolonialist ideologies and corresponding social and economic practices. But a prerequisite of "joining the club" is to become denuded, [de-ethnicised] and culturally stripped' (1995: 122). Indeed, even those minority members who plead the conservative line – and who are, accordingly, much trumpeted as a result – generally do so from a position of personal ethnic and/or cultural dislocation (see Rodriguez, 1983, 1993). The result leaves little or no room for negotiation; little or no opportunity for changing 'the rules of the game'. And why is this? Because 'our' common bonds are too fragile, too easily dismembered or dismantled by the demands of particularism. One wonders what should be so fragile about western civilisation and, conversely, what is so radical about multiculturalism that this should be the case (Hughes, 1993)? But this, conservatives such as Schlesinger insist, is what is centrally at stake.

This brings us to a related inconsistency in conservative accounts of liberal pluralism, of which Schlesinger's polemic is an exemplar. On the one hand, Schlesinger derisively describes group-based affiliations as mere 'ethnic cheerleading' and argues that these are essentially preservationist rather than transformative. And yet, on the other hand, he ends up, as we have seen, invoking a majoritarian version of the same process – a *prior*, and *preeminent* civic or 'national' identity to which all should subscribe. While deploring the nationalistic jargon of Afrocentrism, Schlesinger thus asks us to make the same kind of nationalistic choice – to choose a homogeneous *national* identity over an *ethnic* one. It must be one or the other – a prior nationalism that trumps all other identities (Calhoun, 1993a).

Such a position considerably understates the possibilities of holding dual or multiple identities, except oppositionally. And yet it is clear that many of us can and do hold multiple and complementary identities – social, political, and linguistic – at one and the same time, albeit not always easily (see Chapter 1). Certainly, one can hold both a regional and a national identity without these necessarily being conflictual. Why then should this not also be the case for ethnic and national identities (Stepan, 1998; Taylor, 1998)? Likewise, the juggling of different linguistic identities is a familiar activity for many minority-language speakers, not least because they invariably have to operate in a majority language as well (see Chapter 4). Thus, Schlesinger's position is problematic simply because it does not represent the reality of everyday life for many of us. However, it is also problematic for our purposes because it allows no room for a dynamic and multifarious conception of nationhood. The end result is thus not too dissimilar to the preservationist and group-based conceptions that conservatives such as Schlesinger have purportedly set themselves against. As Sonia Nieto (1995) observes, the charge of ethnic cheerleading by conservatives may stem more from the fear that *their* ethnic cheerleading is being challenged than from any notion of wanting to retain a common national identity 'for the good of all'.

In this light, the racism underlying much of the conservative critique of cultural and linguistic pluralism also becomes more readily apparent, despite protestations to the contrary. For example, it is hard to imagine Schlesinger defending his view of bilingualism as self-ghettoisation in relation to speaking French or some other 'prestigious' language variety (Dicker, 1996, 2000); indeed, one might well expect the reverse to be the case. Rather, in directing his critique of bilingualism towards Hispanic communities in the USA, it is clear that the central issues for Schlesinger have more to do with 'race', immigration and class than with bilingualism per se (see also my discussion of the US 'English Only' movement in Chapter 6).

Moreover, the inevitable connections that are drawn by Schlesinger and other conservatives (see, for example, Honeyford, 1988; Wildavsky, 1992; Lind, 1995; Frost, 1997) between ethnic differentiation, conflict and fragmentation remain open to serious question. While conflict and fragmentation have undoubtedly occurred from ethnic differentiation, they need not always do so. Likewise, the national integration envisaged by conservatives has not always resulted in – indeed has seldom actually achieved – inclusion, consensus and cohesion for *all* ethnic groups within multinational and/or polyethnic states. (Nor, one might venture, would some necessarily want it to.) Rather, as Young asserts, 'when oppressed or disadvantaged social groups are different from the dominant groups, then an allegedly group-neutral assimilationist strategy of inclusion only tends to perpetuate inequality' (1993: 133).

These criticisms, however, cannot be levelled at Goulbourne's analysis. Unlike Schlesinger, he is aware of the hegemonic processes involved in the construction of civic culture – in this case, in relation to Britain – and the nativism, racism and exclusion which often attend it. Consequently, Goulbourne's analysis is far more even-handed – criticising the retreat into communal laagers of a majoritarian communalism on the one hand and a defensive minority communalism on the other. Both militate, in his view, against the formation of a new plurally defined British national community. That said, Goulbourne's argument is still principally concerned with a favourite theme of liberal commentators – the idea that a communitarian approach to rights in a liberal democracy necessarily essentialises and reifies ethnic groups.

For Goulbourne, this process arises from an unhealthy emphasis on ethnic differences at the expense of what may be shared in common. Moreover, the communal politics which are its source promote the misplaced notion that ethnic groups should exist 'almost entirely within [their] own confines' and, relatedly, that individuals should be required to 'conform to the supposed norms of the group' (1991a: 13). Goulbourne's response to these developments is rightly sceptical. An overemphasis on *inter*ethnic differentiation, he argues, clearly understates the traffic between cultures, the fluidity of individual ethnic identification(s), and the possibilities therein of significant *intra*ethnic differences, all of which may operate in combination with a variety of other social, cultural and political allegiances (see Chapter 1). Relatedly, the limiting of individual freedom in the face of supposedly fixed group norms can be regarded as patently illiberal. As he observes elsewhere, ascriptive group membership denies the separate existence of individuals, thus undermining 'much that has taken centuries of struggle to define and secure' (1991b: 225).

These are valid and serious criticisms that Goulbourne raises, and ones that are shared widely by other liberal theorists. In effect, communitarians are charged with operating a model of group membership which is at odds with the complexities of identity in the modern world (Burtonwood, 1996; see also Ellison, 1997). As Edward Said argues, 'no one today is purely one thing. Labels like Indian, or woman, or Muslim, or American are no more than starting points' (1994: 407). Likewise, Jeremy Waldron objects to the idea that our choices and self-identity are defined by our ethnicity and asserts, instead, the need for a 'cosmopolitan alternative'. As he dismissively observes, 'though we may drape ourselves in the distinctive costumes of our ethnic heritage and immure ourselves in an environment designed to minimise our sense of relation with the outside world, no honest account of our being will be complete without an account of our dependence on larger social and political structures that goes far beyond the particular community with which we pretend to identify' (1995: 104). On this view, people can pick and choose 'cultural fragments' from various ethnocultural sources, without feeling an allegiance to any one in particular. Thus, Waldron argues, an Irish American who eats Chinese food, reads Grimm's Fairy Tales to their child, and listens to Italian opera actually lives in a 'a kaleidoscope of cultures'. While Waldron concedes that we need cultural meanings of some kind, he argues that we do not need *specific* cultural frameworks: 'we need to understand our choices in the contexts in which they make sense, but we do not need any single context to structure our choices. To put it crudely, we need culture, but we do not need cultural integrity' (1995: 108; see also Hannerz, 1992).

However, these various criticisms also have their limitations. In Goulbourne's account, for example, there is still an implicit assumption throughout that the very recognition of ethnic differences is regressive, leading ultimately to the destruction of any sense of national commonality. Yet, at the same time, much of his analysis of postwar Britain demonstrates how a 'difference-blind' approach has specifically disadvantaged and marginalised nonwhite minorities. This has led, in some cases, to the denial of basic civil rights – as seen, for example, in Britain's increasingly repressive immigration laws (Goulbourne, 1991a: Ch. 5; Solomos, 1993; Solomos and Back, 1996). Given this, it is not enough for Goulbourne to lamely conclude that the merits of individualism will somehow provide the answer to a new plurally defined Britain where 'difference is merely secondary' (1991a: 242) and where justice and equality reign for all. One wonders how exactly? Goulbourne does not say, except to suggest vaguely, and somewhat hopefully, that it lies in the ability of ethnic-minority groups to initiate such change and, more crucially, in the willingness of the majority to accept it. However, the recent history of Britain's approach to nonwhite ethnic minorities, so clearly outlined by Goulbourne, would seem to make this particular scenario highly unlikely.

This apparent contradiction is also linked to Goulbourne's analysis of multiculturalism – or the 'new pluralism' as he refers to it – in which he highlights the Swann Report (DES, 1985) as an exemplar. Goulbourne is rightly critical here of the report's emphasis on cultural rather than social and political change (see also Troyna, 1993; May, 1994a, b), a limiting feature characteristic of much of the literature on multiculturalism. However, his own conclusions on liberal pluralism end up, somewhat ironically, very close to those of the Swann Report – a point which seems to escape him. In this regard, it is apparent that the report, while adopting the catch phrase 'diversity in unity', clearly favours the latter over the former. In so doing, it advocates an approach to cultural pluralism which 'enables all ethnic groups, both minority and majority, to participate fully in shaping society . . . *within a framework of commonly accepted values*, practices and procedures, whilst also allowing, and where necessary assisting the ethnic-minority communities in maintaining their distinct ethnic identities within this common framework' (1985: 5; my emphasis). In emphasising this 'framework of commonly accepted values', however, the Swann Report fails crucially to address the key questions of *which* values are agreed, how they are chosen, and who benefits most from the choice. In the end, then, Swann's conclusions are little different from Goulbourne's own ambivalent and somewhat contradictory position on the pluralist dilemma; it is 'cultural diversity *within* social unity' which matters most, although why this should be so, and how we get there, remain far from clear.

More broadly, the assertion that any group-based recognition of rights necessarily entails an essentialist construction of groups may well be overstated. In this sense, orthodox liberal critiques of communitarianism may be said to face similar limitations to the postmodernist arguments of hybridity theorists, discussed in Chapter 1, which they so strongly echo. As I will proceed to argue, a corporatist model of rights within liberal democracies may often result in, but does not necessarily entail, a reified and essentialised view of groups themselves (see also Werbner and Modood, 1997; May, 1999a, 2001). Nor, indeed, are essentialism and reification limited to communitarian approaches. We have already seen, for example, that such processes may just as easily result from the hegemonic construction of civic culture, as represented in and by the dominant ethnie. Moreover, in contrast to Waldron's position, a group-based approach may be able to accommodate a view of ethnic and cultural groups as dynamic and fluid while still retaining some sense of distinct cultural identity. In this regard, Margalit and Raz (1995) argue that people today may well participate in a wide range of different social and cultural activities but that this does not necessarily diminish their allegiance to an 'encompassing group' with which they most closely identify (see also Miller, 1995). And finally, an approach which acknowledges the importance of cultural membership to the allocation of rights within a liberal democracy need not necessarily conflict with and/or supersede the rights of individuals as citizens.

While far from easy, then, the two broad approaches of liberal and corporate pluralism may after all be, if not entirely reconcilable, at least not mutually exclusive. As Pierre Coulombe observes: 'No one (I hope) wants to live in a society which only protects our personal autonomy. Nor does anyone (I'm sure) want to be treated as an heteronomous being. The challenge, therefore, is to rethink a political community that springs from our self-image as self-authored, yet situated, citizens' (1995: 21). One might add here, of course, that we need to do this while, at the same time, avoiding the traps of reductionism and essentialism that have beset so many previous attempts at recognising some notion of group-related rights. This difficult balancing act can be found in the work of Iris Marion Young (1989, 1990, 1993) and Will Kymlicka (1989, 1995a, b).

Rethinking liberal democracy

Those theorists who have become increasingly disenchanted with the orthodox liberal position on minority rights, and the philosophical matrix of the nation-state which underpins it, have begun to ask a number of key questions in their quest for a viable alternative approach. Following Mallea (1989), these questions may be summarised as follows:

- How can the values of individualism and pluralism be pursued simultaneously?
- Does the existence of ethnic and cultural diversity necessarily result in reduced levels of social cohesion?
- Can any society that embraces a monistic view of culture be considered democratic?
- What form might consensual theories of government take in plural societies?

- How much decentralisation can political systems cope with in responding to the legitimate aspirations of national- and ethnic-minority groups?
- Does the concept of valid community lie in the extent to which it creates and maintains its own cultural norms?
- What levels of tolerance for contradiction and ambiguity can and should exist in plural societies?

Young and Kymlicka provide us with two of the most influential attempts at addressing these questions (see also Taylor, 1994) – attempts which, as we shall see, can usefully inform the issue of minority-language rights as well. It is not my intention here to examine each of the questions outlined above in specific detail. However, it will soon become apparent that their various themes resonate throughout the work of both Young and Kymlicka. In what follows, I will discuss Young's postmodernist 'politics of difference' perspective, which attempts to formulate an approach to rights within liberal democracies that is based on a recognition of group-related disadvantage and oppression, while at the same time recognising and accommodating the relational and fluid nature of group identities. Will Kymlicka's work is examined for its development of the importance of cultural membership within a liberal (as opposed to communitarian) theory of rights. His central distinction between national and ethnic minorities, and the premise of historical rights which underpins it, will also be explored in relation to my own arguments along these lines.

Differentiated citizenship

Iris Young is a prominent critic of the conservatism and uniformity inherent in the notion of equal citizenship in liberal democracies. Her principal theoretical focus has to do with the impact of this undifferentiated process on women as a disadvantaged social group. However, her work also has much broader application to a wide range of other minority groups, including, for the purposes of this discussion, national- and ethnic-minority groups. Young argues, in effect, that the process of treating everyone as abstract individuals, undifferentiated by ethnicity, sex, or class, actually reinforces the norms of the dominant group(s) within the nation-state at the expense of a wide variety of marginalised and/or oppressed groups. As she asserts:

> In a society where some groups are privileged while others are oppressed, insisting that as citizens persons should leave behind their particular affiliations and experiences to adopt a general point of view serves only to reinforce privilege; for the perspectives and interests of the privileged will tend to dominate this unified public, marginalising or silencing those of other groups.
>
> (1989: 257)

Instead, she advocates a form of 'differentiated citizenship' where group-representation rights are accorded to marginalised and oppressed groups within a single polity on the basis of their systemic disadvantage: 'the solution lies at least in part in providing institutionalised means for the explicit recognition and representation of oppressed groups' (1989: 258; see also 1990: 183–191). Her suggested list of those groups in the USA for which such recognition might be appropriate is extremely broad. It includes: 'women, blacks, Native Americans, Chicanos, Puerto Ricans and other Spanish-speaking Americans, Asian Americans, gay men, lesbians, working class people, poor people, old people and mentally and physically disabled people' (1989: 261). The inclusion of such diverse groupings is not without its problems, as I will discuss later in relation to Kymlicka's more focused position. However, Young's argument for a more heterogeneous conception of the nation-state is an important one. Various social, cultural and ethnic-minority groups have the right in her view to a differentiated place in the civic realm. This right, in turn, is based on the *mutual* recognition and valuing of their specificity and worth in the public domain (Young, 1993). The notion of social justice is central here to Young's argument:

> The primary moral ground for this heterogeneous public is to promote social justice in its policies. Besides guaranteeing civil and political rights, and guaranteeing that the basic needs of individuals will be met so that they can freely pursue their own goals, *a vision of social justice provides for some group related rights and policies*. These group institutions will adhere to a principle that social policy should attend to rather than be blind to group difference in awarding benefits or burdens, in order to remedy group based inequality or [to] meet group specific needs.
>
> (1993: 135–136; my emphasis)

Young is thus principally preoccupied with questions of justice and oppression, particularly as these affect a wide range of disadvantaged and/or oppressed groups within modern nation-states. In this respect, she is concerned both with the recognition of oppressed groups via political and institutional devices, and the recognition of cultural differences as a basic principle of equality and justice (see 1990: 174). However, in arguing for the recognition of group-based rights, she also meticulously tries to avoid the mistake of reifying groups. In fact, she specifically rejects the two common alternatives in addressing the pluralist dilemma – assimilation and separatism – for doing exactly this. Assimilation, she suggests, rightly champions individual freedom, equality and self-development. However, it wrongly assumes that *any* assertion of group identity and difference is, by definition, essentialist. Separatism may help establish cultural autonomy and political solidarity for oppressed groups and does challenge the hegemonic construction of the nation-state. However, it tends also to understate the historical *interrelations* between different groups – particularly, in modern mass, urban societies – and to simplify and freeze its own group identity in ways that fail to acknowledge intragroup differences. In this sense, Young can be seen to criticise both orthodox liberal and communitarian approaches to rights and identity. Her rejection of separatism – i.e., the key tenet of political nationalism – is also broadly consonant with a more culturalist conception of nationalism, as discussed in Chapter 2. Indeed, in more recent times she has argued for a relational concept of self-determination that closely accords with the key tenets of cultural nationalism (Young, forthcoming; cf. Chapter 8).

For Young, both assimilation and separatism end up reinforcing the notion of difference as 'Otherness'. In this view, each group has its own nature and shares no attributes with those defined as Other. In effect, difference as Otherness 'conceives social groups as mutually exclusive, categorically opposed' (1993: 126). Moreover, in a similar vein to the discussion of 'ascriptive humiliation' (Lukes, 1996), and 'misrecognition' and 'symbolic violence' (Bourdieu, 1991) in Chapter 1, Young argues that when this process of social relations occurs between a privileged group on the one hand, and a disadvantaged group on the other, the attribution of Otherness invariably takes on a pathological characteristic for the latter. As she asserts:

> while the privileged group is defined as active human subject, inferiorised social groups are objectified, substantialised, reduced to a nature or essence. Whereas the privileged groups are neutral, exhibit free, spontaneous and weighty subjectivity, the dominated groups are marked with an essence, imprisoned in a given set of possibilities . . . Using its own values, experience, and culture as [universal] standards, the dominant group measures the Others and finds them essentially lacking . . .
>
> (Young, 1993: 124–125)

More broadly, Young argues that this particular logic of identity essentialises and substantialises group natures, generates dichotomy at the expense of unity (even when it is couched in terms of the latter), and runs counter to the relational and fluid nature of inter- and intragroup relations. In a position which echoes Eriksen's observation that ethnicity is 'essentially an aspect of relationship, not a property of a group' (1993: 12; see Chapter 1), Young observes:

> Defining groups as Other actually denies or represses the heterogeneity of social difference, understood as variation and contextually experienced relations. It denies the difference among those who understand themselves as belonging to the same group; it reduces the members of the group to a set of common attributes . . . The practical realities of social life, especially but not only in modern, mass, economically interdependent societies, defy

the attempt to conceive and enforce group difference as exclusive opposition, there are always ambiguous persons who do not fit the categories . . . partial identities [that cut] across more encompassing group identities.

(1993: 127–128)

In contrast, Young argues that her conception of a differentiated approach to public policy is better able to recognise heterogeneity and the interspersion of groups. Such an approach does not posit a social group as having an essential nature composed of a set of attributes defining only that group, nor does it repress the interdependence of groups in order to construct a substantial conception of group identity. Rather,

a social group exists and is defined as a specific group only in social and interactive relation to others. Social group identities emerge from the encounter and interaction among people who experience some differences in their way of life and forms of association, even if they regard themselves as belonging to the same society . . . Group identity is not a set of objective facts, but the product of experienced meanings.

(1993: 130)

This position is closely parallel to the conclusions drawn about situational ethnicity in Chapter 1. It is also akin to Charles Taylor's (1994) emphasis on the *dialogical* nature of identity formation in his comparable discussion on 'the politics of recognition' (see also Honneth, 1995). The result is a conception of difference which allows for specificity, variation and heterogeneity *within* the nation-state, as well as a central acknowledgement of the unequal power relations within which such difference is invariably framed. The expression of group differences is encouraged but within common institutions and a shared commitment to a larger political order. Moreover, groups are understood 'as overlapping, as constituted in relation to one another and thus as shifting their attributes and needs in accordance with what relations are salient' (1993: 123–124). As Young concludes, 'different groups always potentially share some attributes, experiences, or goals . . . The characteristics that make one group specific and the borders that distinguish it from other groups are always *undecidable*' (1993: 130*)*. Accordingly, a relational and contextualised conception of difference within the plurally conceived nation-state helps make more apparent 'the necessity and possibility of togetherness in difference' (1993: 124).

Inevitably, there are problems with Young's account (for a useful overview and critique, see Fletcher, 1998). For example, her concern to equalise political influence for marginalised and oppressed groups within the nation-state necessarily entails a wide-ranging remit – too wide-ranging perhaps, since the conglomeration of such groups is potentially unending. Her own description of the diverse range of groups who might be included in her formulations bears this out. Kymlicka observes, for example, that this 'list of "oppressed groups" in the United States would seem to include 80 per cent of the population . . . In short, everyone but relatively well-off, relatively young, able-bodied, heterosexual white males' (1995a: 145). There is also a problem with bringing such disparate groups together on the singular basis of disadvantage and/or oppression. One can argue, for example, that the rights of Native Americans as an indigenous people in North America, or of Māori in Aotearoa / New Zealand – both of whom she includes in her discussions of group-differentiated citizenship (see 1990: 175–183; 1993: 143–147) – are quite distinct from those of a broad social group such as poor people. Focusing on disadvantage as the principal criterion for their inclusion thus obscures the *particular* demands of these national minorities for greater self-determination within the nation-state. Native Americans and Māori can claim greater access to and representation within the state not simply because they are marginalised groups (although they *are* marginalised), but because of their legitimate historical and territorial rights as ethnies. Relatedly, an emphasis on disadvantage implies only *temporary* representation until such time as the disadvantage has been redressed. This form of political affirmative action, in effect, is again clearly inadequate in addressing the long-term demands of national minorities for greater acknowledgement and representation in the civic realm (Kymlicka, 1995a; see below).

However, Young's failure to distinguish the rights of national minorities from other ethnic, cultural and social groups is not unusual in discussions of the pluralist dilemma. Indeed, this elision is also clearly apparent in the countervailing accounts of Porter, Schlesinger and Goulbourne. It is clear, for example, that each of these more orthodox liberal accounts is characterised by an almost exclusive preoccupation with *ethnic* or *immigrant* minorities – that is, urban ethnic minorities and ethnic groups in plural societies, as defined in Chapter 2. Accordingly, the arguments employed in defence of the nation-state gain much of their moral suasion from the implicit underlying belief that immigrant groups should have less claim to official recognition by the state than the national 'majority'. Apart from a few desultory references to Canadian Aboriginal peoples, Native Americans and the Celtic national minorities by Porter, Schlesinger and Goulbourne, respectively, none addresses, or even acknowledges, the question of national-minority rights. Thus, each fails to differentiate the claims of national minorities from those of other ethnic-minority groups. Indeed, even within the latter category, Schlesinger adopts an undifferentiated approach, as seen, for example, in his glib comparison between the social and educational trajectories of African Americans, and Jewish and Asian ethnic communities in the USA. Such a comparison is clearly both inadequate and inappropriate since it takes little, if any, account of class as a significant factor, or the voluntary/involuntary status of these groups (Ogbu 1987; see Chapter 2).

Multicultural citizenship

Will Kymlicka, in his various seminal discussions on multicultural citizenship, is one of the few theorists on either side of the pluralist dilemma debates to draw a clear distinction between the rights of national minorities (including indigenous peoples) and other minority ethnic, cultural and social groups (see also Walzer, 1982; Spinner, 1994; Taylor, 1994). As he observes of these discussions, most 'focus on the case of immigrants, and the accommodation of their ethnic . . . differences within the larger society. Less attention has been paid to the situation of indigenous peoples and other non-immigrant "national minorities" whose homeland has been incorporated into the boundaries of a larger state, through conquest, colonisation, or federation' (1995a: vii). On this basis, Kymlicka defines national minorities 'as distinct and *potentially self-governing* societies incorporated into a larger state' and ethnic-minority groups as 'immigrants who have left their national community to enter another society' (1995a: 19; my emphasis). The key distinction for Kymlicka is that national minorities, at the time of their incorporation, constituted an ongoing 'societal culture' – that is, 'a culture which provides its members with meaningful ways of life across the full range of human activities . . . [and] encompassing both public and private spheres' (1995a: 76). Ethnic minorities, in contrast, may well wish to maintain aspects of their cultural and linguistic identities within the host nation-state but this is principally in order to contribute to and modify the existing national culture rather than to recreate a separate societal culture of their own (see also Gurr, 1993: 15). Kymlicka's analysis here closely accords with my own discussion in Chapter 2 of the key distinctions between ethnic and national minorities and the related significance of cultural and political nationalisms. As I argued there, political nationalism is not the only determining feature of nationalist movements since such a view, while received wisdom for many, relegates national minorities which are not (yet) politically active to the status of mere 'ethnic groups'. Kymlicka's emphasis on incorporation into the nation-state, rather than on political mobilisation per se, provides a useful complement to my own argument. It allows for quiescent national minorities and highly mobilised immigrant groups without confusing the political status of the two.

In addition, both national and ethnic minorities in Kymlicka's formulation can be distinguished from 'new social movements' such as gays, women, and the disabled who have been marginalised within their own national society or ethnic group. Kymlicka thus provides us with a more nuanced analysis that allows for the possibility of attributing *differing* rights to various minority groups within the nation-state. In this regard, his position is a significant advance on much of the literature concerned with multiculturalism which has largely failed historically to make these kinds of distinctions. This, in turn, has led to the valid charge of cultural relativism levelled against multiculturalism by its critics on both the right and the left, not to mention the attendant difficulties that such cultural relativism inevitably entails (May, 1999a; see also Chapter 4). In what follows, I will concentrate principally on the specific concerns of indigenous and other national-minority groups, although I will also briefly address the specific rights attributable to ethnic-minority groups and new social movements. I will return, however, to the wider implications of the latter, and specific ways of addressing the problems of cultural relativism, in Chapter 9.

Meanwhile, as we saw in Chapter 2, the distinction between the respective positions of national and ethnic minorities in modern nation-states can be illustrated by the terms 'multinational' and 'polyethnic'. As Kymlicka observes of this, most states are actually a combination of both: 'obviously, a single country may be both multinational (as a result of the colonising, conquest, or confederation of national minorities) and polyethnic (as a result of individual and familial immigration)' (1995a: 17). However, most countries are also reluctant, more often than not, to acknowledge this combination in their public policy. Indeed, nation-states may well acknowledge neither, although this is rare, at least in liberal-democratic states. More usually, they may acknowledge one or the other. Thus, in the USA there is recognition of the country's polyethnicity – albeit, a grudging one among conservatives – but an unwillingness to distinguish and accept the rights of national minorities such as Native Americans, Hawaiians and Puerto Ricans. Likewise, Australia and Aotearoa / New Zealand have historically argued that they are settler colonies and hence have no national minorities; a position which ignores entirely the rights of Australian Aboriginal peoples and Māori, who were the subject of European colonisation. In Belgium and Switzerland, however, the reverse applies. The rights of national minorities have long been recognised but an accommodation of immigrants and a more polyethnic society has been less forthcoming. Recognising both dimensions, then, and the respective rights attendant upon them, is the central challenge for developing a more plurally conceived approach to public policy in modern nation-states.

Following from this, Kymlicka argues that in addition to the civil rights available to all individuals, three forms of group-specific rights should be recognised in liberal democracies: (1) self-government rights; (2) polyethnic rights; and (3) special-representation rights (see 1995a: 26–33). Self-government rights acknowledge that the nation-state is not the sole preserve of the majority (national) group and that legitimate national-minority ethnies have the right to equivalent inclusion and representation in the civic realm. Accordingly, national minorities should be provided with rights to their autonomy and self-determination within the nation-state, which, if necessary, could be extended to incorporate the possibilities of secession. Ostensibly, this right of minority national groups to self-determination is not inconsistent with international law. The (1945) United Nations Charter, for example, clearly states that 'all peoples have the right to self-determination'. However, the term 'peoples' is not defined by the UN and the injunction has tended to be interpreted only in relation to overseas colonies (the 'salt water thesis') rather than to national minorities, even though the latter may have been subjected to the same processes of colonisation. Self-determination has thus been limited *in practice* to existing states and attempts at broadening the principle to include national minorities have until recently met with limited success (Thornberry, 1991a; although see Chapter 8). Where national minorities have been recognised within existing nation-states, federalism has been the most common process of political accommodation that has been adopted. An obvious example here is the degree of autonomy given to the predominantly French-speaking Québec as part of a federal (and predominantly Anglophone) Canada (see Chapter 6). Self-government rights, then, typically involve the devolution of political power to members of a national minority who are usually, but not always, located in a particular historical territory. The key in providing for such rights is their *permanent* status. They are not seen as a temporary measure or remedy which may one day be revoked.

Polyethnic rights also challenge the hegemonic construction of the nation-state but for a different clientele and to different ends. Polyethnic rights are intended to help ethnic-minority groups to continue to express their cultural, linguistic and/or religious heritage, principally in the private domain, without it hampering their success within the economic and political institutions of the dominant national society. One might add here that these rights are also available so that an undue burden of cultural and linguistic loss and/or change is not placed upon such groups (see Chapter 4). Like self-government rights, polyethnic rights are thus also seen as permanent, since they seek to protect rather than eliminate cultural and linguistic differences. However, their principal purpose is to promote integration *into* the larger society (and to contribute to and modify that society as a result) rather than to foster self-governing status among such groups. In this regard, integration comes to be seen as a *reciprocal* process rather than a simple accommodation of ethnic-minority groups to the majoritarian national culture. It is a *revision* of integration rather than a *rejection* of it (see also Spinner, 1994; Spinner-Halev, 1999). Finally, special-representation rights, along the lines outlined earlier by Young, are a response to some systemic disadvantage in the political process which limits a particular group's view from being effectively represented. Special-representation rights aim to redress this disadvantage but do so principally on a temporary basis. Once the oppression and/or disadvantage has been eliminated, the rights no longer apply.

Taken together, these three kinds of rights can be regarded as distinct but not necessarily mutually exclusive. Indigenous peoples, for example, may demand special-representation rights on the basis of their disadvantage, *and* self-governing rights on the basis of their status as a national-minority ethnie.

However, the key point is that these claims need not go together. Thus, the disabled may claim special-representation rights but would not be able to claim either polyethnic or self-government rights. Likewise, an economically successful ethnic-minority group may seek polyethnic rights but would have no claim to special-representation or self-governing rights, and so on. Assuming the validity of such group-differentiated rights in the first place, however, does return us to the central questions surrounding the legitimacy of minority rights in liberal democracies and the difficulties involved in ascribing and/or determining particular group identities for the apportionment of such rights. Kymlicka's response to both these concerns is to defend minority rights on the basis of liberal theory rather than from a communitarian stance. In so doing, he manages to uphold the importance of individual citizenship rights while, at the same time, developing an understanding of the importance of cultural membership to such rights.

Kymlicka brings a range of arguments to bear in support of his position. First, he rejects the assumption that group-differentiated rights are 'collective' rights which, ipso facto, stand in opposition to 'individual' rights. Group-differentiated rights are not necessarily 'collective' in the sense that they privilege the group over the individual – they can in fact be accorded to individual members of a group, or to the group as a whole, or to a federal state/province within which the group forms a majority. For example, the group-differentiated right of Francophones in Canada to use French in federal courts is an *individual* right that may be exercised at any time. The right of Francophones to have their children educated in French-medium schools, outside of Québec, is an individual right also but one that is subject to the proviso 'where numbers warrant' (see Chapter 5). In contrast, indigenous land and fishing rights are usually exercised by the collective tribal group – as, for example, in the case of Native Americans in North America and Māori in Aotearoa / New Zealand. Finally, the right of the Québécois to preserve and promote their distinct culture in the province of Québec highlights how a minority group in a federal system may exercise group-differentiated rights in a territory where they form the majority, an example I will discuss in more depth in Chapter 6. In short, there is no simple relationship between group-differentiated rights accorded on the basis of cultural membership and their subsequent application. Thus, the common criticisms of 'collective rights' in the debates on the pluralist dilemma have little actual relevance to the question of group-differentiated rights. As Kymlicka concludes of the latter, 'most such rights are not about the primacy of communities over individuals. Rather, they are based on the idea that justice between groups requires that the members of different groups be accorded different rights' (1995a: 47).

Second, Kymlicka rejects the inevitable association of group-differentiated rights with illiberality. This is a particular concern of commentators on the left. We have already seen the issue raised directly in Goulbourne's work, for example. Feminist critics, concerned with the perpetuation of patriarchal practices within minority groups, have also raised objections to group-based rights on this basis (see, for example, Phillips, 1997; Yuval-Davis, 1997a; Okin 1998, 1999). Kymlicka addresses this problem by drawing a key distinction between what he terms 'internal restrictions' and 'external protections' (1995a: 35–44). Internal restrictions involve *intra*group relations where the ethnic or national-minority group seeks to restrict the individual liberty of its members on the basis of maintaining group solidarity. These rights are often associated with theocratic and patriarchal communities and, when excessive, may be regarded as illiberal. In contrast, external protections relate to *inter*group relations where an ethnic or national minority group seeks to protect its distinct identity by limiting the impact of the decisions of the larger society. External protections are thus intended to ensure that individual members are able to maintain a distinctive way of life *if they so choose* and are not prevented from doing so by the decisions of members outside of their community (see Kymlicka, 1995a: 204. n.11). This too has its dangers, although not in relation to individual oppression in this case but rather the possible unfairness that might result between groups. The ex-apartheid system in South Africa provides a clear example of the latter scenario. However, as Kymlicka argues, external protections need not result in injustice: 'Granting special representation rights, land claims, *or language rights* to a minority need not, and often does not, put it in a position to dominate other groups. On the contrary . . . such rights can be seen as putting the various groups on a more equal footing, by reducing the extent to which the smaller group is vulnerable to the larger' (1995a: 36–37; my emphasis).

Kymlicka argues that, on this basis, liberals can endorse certain external protections where they promote fairness between groups while still contesting internal restrictions which unduly limit the individual rights of members to question, revise, or reject traditional authorities and practices (see also Kymlicka, 1999a, b). In relation to the various group-differentiated rights outlined earlier, Kymlicka concludes that 'most demands for group-specific rights made by ethnic and national groups in Western democracies are for external protections' (1995a: 42). Even where internal restrictions are also present, these are usually seen as unavoidable by-products of external protections rather than as desirable ends in themselves. As we shall see in the ensuing chapters, this latter point has particular relevance to minority-language rights. However, like Kymlicka, I will argue that such language rights may nonetheless be regarded as a form of external protection.

Third, Kymlicka argues that a recognition of the importance of cultural membership to one's individual rights has historical precedent in both liberal theory and political practice. Indeed, the rigid separation of individual *autonomy* from individual and collective *identity* has only really occurred in liberal theory and practice since the Second World War. Prior to this, liberal commentators did not assume that the state should treat cultural membership as a purely private matter. On the contrary, 'liberals either endorsed the legal recognition of minority cultures, or rejected minority rights not because they rejected the idea of an official culture, but precisely because they believed there should only be *one* official culture' (1995a: 53–54). The latter position is clearly illustrated by the arguments of Mill discussed in Chapter 1. The former view is exemplified in the work of Hobhouse and Dewey in the early part of the twentieth century. They both argued, on the basis of the importance of cultural membership, that some accommodation should be made for the distinctive group-related rights of national minorities within the nation-state (Kymlicka, 1989). Hobhouse, for example, believed that if the claims of national minorities were satisfied by greater cultural equality, the distinctive problems of secession would not arise. In contrast, failure to address the legitimate rights of national minorities might actually hasten the break up of the nation-state rather than the reverse. On this view, individual citizenship rights were *insufficient* to the continued maintenance of the nation-state:

> The smaller nationality does not merely want equal rights with others. *It stands out for a certain life of its own* ... [To] find the place for national rights within the unity of the state, to give scope to national differences without destroying the organisation of a life which has somehow to be lived in common, is therefore the problem which the modern state has to solve if it is to maintain itself. It has not only to generalise the common rights of citizenship as applied to individuals, but to make room for diversity and give some scope to common sentiments *which in a measure conflict with each other*.
>
> (1928: 146–147; my emphases)

These concerns for the cultural protection of minorities were also reflected in political practices prior to the Second World War. In the nineteenth century, treaties were often employed for the protection of minority groups, initially on the basis of religion and later on the grounds of nationality (Thornberry, 1991a). These practices culminated in the general organisation of the League of Nations, established in the wake of the First World War. The League endorsed a range of bilateral treaties aimed at securing special political status for minority groups within Europe in what came to be known as the Minority Protection scheme.[7] This was to change significantly, however, with the advent of the Second World War and the associated excesses and abuses of the said scheme by the Nazi regime, whereby Hitler used a supposed concern for the rights of German minorities elsewhere in Europe as a catalyst for the war. As a result, there was a postwar shift in emphasis to establishing generic human rights, irrespective of group membership, through the establishment and subsequent activities of the United Nations and other supranational agencies such as the EU. In so doing, it was assumed that no additional rights need be attributed to the members of specific ethnic or national minorities (see also Chapter 5). As Claude has observed of these developments:

> The leading assumption has been that members of national minorities do not need, are not entitled to, or cannot be granted rights of special character. The doctrine of human rights has been put forward as a substitute for the concept of minority rights, with the strong implication that minorities whose members enjoy individual equality of treatment cannot legitimately demand facilities for the maintenance of their ethnic particularism.
>
> (1955: 211)

Consequently, all references to the rights of ethnic and national minorities were deleted from the (1948) United Nations Universal Declaration of Human Rights.[8] Relatedly, a widespread conviction began to emerge among liberals that minority-group rights were somehow incompatible with national and international peace and stability. However, as Kymlicka asserts, these assumptions are fundamentally misplaced. As we have seen, individual autonomy is inevitably dependent, at least to some extent, on one's cultural membership. Moreover, the failure of modern liberal theory and practice to acknowledge the specific rights of minorities has left them subject to the majoritarian decision-making processes of the nation-state. The result has been to render minorities 'vulnerable to significant injustice at the hands of the majority, and to exacerbate ethnocultural conflict' (1995a: 5), trends which the UN and other supranational bodies have only recently begun to address.

Fourth, Kymlicka argues that Waldron's 'cosmopolitan alternative', which disavows the importance of one's *particular* cultural membership, is significantly overstated. On this basis, Waldron rejects the codification of minority rights as a misplaced and misguided anachronism since most people now move easily between cultures and thus do not need, it seems, to be attached to just one. Concomitantly, there is no reason on this view why minority group members should not simply dispense with their cultural and linguistic backgrounds and adopt those of the dominant ethnie.

Waldron's view here is reminiscent of the advocates of situational ethnicity, discussed in Chapter 1, who emphasise the fluid and multiple nature of ethnic (and other group) identities and the varied instrumental ends to which these are put. Not surprisingly perhaps, criticisms of Waldron's position are also similar to those directed at the more extreme instrumentalist positions adopted by some advocates of situational ethnicity. People do clearly move between cultures – immigrants are an obvious example here – but cultural loss and/or subsumption is not nearly as easy and as unproblematic a process as Waldron suggests. Indeed, Margalit and Raz (1995) have argued that the transfer from one culture to another is often extremely difficult, even for voluntary migrants, not only because it is 'a very slow process indeed', but because of the importance of cultural membership to people's self-identity (see also Tamir, 1993; Taylor, 1994). This is even more so for national minorities who are often forced, in effect, to renounce the language and culture of their own 'societal' or 'encompassing' group for another's (see Chapter 4). As Margalit and Raz observe, this ignores the fact that:

> membership of such groups is of great importance to individual well-being, for it greatly affects one's opportunities, one's ability to engage in the relationships and pursuits marked by culture. Secondly . . . the prosperity of the culture is important to the well-being of its members . . . people's sense of their own identity is bound up with their sense of belonging to encompassing groups and . . . their self-respect is affected by the esteem in which these groups are held.
>
> (1995: 86–87; see also Taylor, 1994; Honneth, 1995)

In short, ethnic and national identities cannot simply be exchanged like last year's clothes, as we saw Michael Billig observe in Chapter 1. Moreover, if members of the dominant ethnie typically value their own cultural and linguistic membership, it is clearly unfair to prevent national minorities from continuing to value theirs'. As Kymlicka concludes, 'leaving one's culture, while possible, is best seen as renouncing something to which one is reasonably entitled' (1995a: 90). Relatedly, he argues:

> The freedom which liberals demand for individuals is not primarily the freedom to go beyond one's language and history, but rather the freedom to move within one's societal culture, to distance oneself from particular cultural roles, to choose which features of the culture are most worth developing, and which are without value.
>
> (1995a: 90–91)

Kymlicka's (and Margalit and Raz's) position closely accords with my own view of ethnicity as habitus, outlined in Chapter 1.[9] In addition, Kymlicka's last observation provides us with a rejoinder to a related criticism of Waldron's, that a defence of minority rights inevitably reinforces a homogenous conception of ethnic groups (see Waldron, 1995: 103–105). Waldron is particularly critical here of notions of cultural 'purity' and 'authenticity' which, he argues, are regularly employed by indigenous peoples and other national minorities in support of their claims to greater self-determination. These attempts at cultural delineation are manifestly artificial in his view and can only result in cultural stasis and isolationism. As such, liberals should regard them as anathema. However, as Kymlicka counters, the assertion of national-minority rights does not necessarily preclude the possibilities of cultural adaptation, change and interchange:

> there is no inherent connection between the desire to maintain a distinct societal culture and the desire for cultural isolation. In many cases, the aim of self-government is to enable smaller nations to interact with larger nations on a more equitable basis. It should be up to each culture to decide when and how they adopt the achievements of the larger world. It is one thing to learn from the larger world; it is another to be swamped by it, and self-government rights may be needed for smaller nations to control the direction and rate of change.
>
> (1995a: 103–104)

Indeed, the desire of national minorities to survive as a culturally distinct society is most often *not* based on some simplistic desire for cultural 'purity'. Defenders of minority rights (including minority language rights) are rarely seeking to preserve their 'authentic' culture if that means returning to cultural practices long past. If it were, it would soon meet widespread opposition from individual members. Rather, it is the right 'to maintain one's membership in a distinct culture, and to continue developing that culture in the same (impure) way that the members of majority cultures are able to develop theirs' (1995a: 105). Cultural and linguistic change, adaptation and interaction are entirely consistent with such a position. As Kymlicka argues elsewhere (1995b: 8–9), minority cultures wish to be both cosmopolitan and to embrace the cultural interchange that Waldron emphasises. However, this does not necessarily entail Waldron's own 'cosmopolitan alternative' which denies that people have any deep bond to their own historical cultural and linguistic communities. In similar vein, Kymlicka asserts that minority rights 'help to ensure that the members of minority cultures have access to a secure cultural structure *from which to make choices for themselves*, and thereby promote liberal equality' (1989: 192; my emphasis). On this view, national minorities continue to exercise their individual rights within their particular cultural and linguistic milieux and, of course, contextually, in relation to other cultural groups within a given nation-state (see Young, 1993). The crucial element, however, is that members of the national minority are themselves able to retain a significant degree of control over the process – something which until now has largely been the preserve of majority group members. The key issue thus becomes one of cultural and linguistic *autonomy* rather than one of retrenchment, isolationism or stasis.

Kymlicka's liberal defence of national-minority rights is a cogent one. In reconceptualising liberal theory – principally, by unshackling it from the 'philosophical matrix of the nation-state' within which it has come to be subsumed – he provides a powerful theoretical framework and intellectual justification for such rights. In so doing, he also comes closest to balancing what Hobhouse earlier highlighted as those 'common sentiments *which in a measure conflict with each other*' (1928: 146–147; my emphasis); namely, citizenship and (minority) ethnicity. This is not to say, however, that Kymlicka resolves the measure of conflict between such sentiments. Indeed, no account which deals with such issues could ever do so fully, nor indeed would it necessarily be helpful to do so, since the point in the end is that the various claims involved are *competing* ones (see also Chapter 9). As Homi Bhabha argues, 'the question of cultural difference faces us with a disposition of knowledges or a distribution of practices that exist beside each other, abseits designating a form of social contradiction and antagonism that has to be negotiated rather than sublated' (1994: 162). On this basis, what is required is a *negotiated* settlement that acknowledges difference, and accommodates it where it can, rather than a compromise that subsumes it and/or attempts to resolve all its contradictory aspects.

The inevitability of these ongoing tensions does mean though that Kymlicka has faced his own fair share of criticism. For example, communitarian critics such as Charles Taylor (1994) have argued that while Kymlicka's argument accounts for the cultural survival of existing groups who currently face pressure from majority cultural forces, it does not ensure their continued survival over generations, which, for such groups, is the central issue at stake. For the latter to occur, collective goals would in some circumstances have to be preferred to individual ones, a position that Kymlicka is reluctant to take. Indeed, for Kymlicka, the principal importance of cultural membership is that 'it allows for meaningful individual choices' (1989: 172). Thus, freedom of choice must be regarded as prior to the ties that bind us to community; in effect, community must remain commensurable with individual liberty (Coulombe, 1995). However, as Moore (1991) argues, there remains a certain contradiction in a position which claims that the value of autonomy is derived from its role in fostering community while also asserting that autonomy is the ultimate value on which that community is to be assessed (see also Tomasi, 1995). Relatedly, there is an ambiguity at times as to what actually constitutes a group for Kymlicka and, by extension, who might be eligible for the rights associated with such groups (Burtonwood, 1996). Kymlicka is rightly sceptical here of any notion of a group identity that is pregiven or fixed but articulates this less clearly than, say, Iris Marion Young. Accordingly, the problem of closure – the risk that institutionalised forms of group representation could block further development and change – is not completely obviated (Phillips, 1995), even if, as we have seen, cultural fluidity and change is clearly countenanced by Kymlicka.

Marrying a theory of rights to the complexities of political practice is a necessarily difficult and, at times, fraught process. Nonetheless, it remains my conviction that Kymlicka's arguments about rights, combined with Young's more nuanced conception of the fluidity and interfusion of groups, provide us with a powerful explanatory model for a legitimate defence of national-minority rights within liberal theory. And yet, proponents of minority rights within political theory have seldom actually addressed, except by implication, how such rights might be applied specifically to minority languages.[10] This link is the focus of the next chapter.

Notes

1   As Gramsci argues, in order to understand any nation-state as a whole, one must always distinguish between its 'state' or political and administrative structure, and its 'civil society'. The latter comprises, for example, its principal nonpolitical organisations, its religious and other beliefs, and its specific 'customs' or way of life. In making these distinctions, there are inevitably features that do not fit easily under either category. However, as Nairn summarises it: 'that is relatively unimportant. What matters is that they are distinguishable, and that the singular identity of a modern society depends upon the relationship between them' (1981: 131).

2   This is certainly the position of Gordon and Glazer in their respective analyses of the two approaches (see also Glazer, 1997), although Walzer adopts a more sympathetic stance towards pluralism, most notably through his (1994) attempt to distinguish between Liberalism 1 and Liberalism 2. Other examples of this rejection of a more pluralist perspective include the likes of Bullivant (1981), Dworkin (1978, 1983), Gleason (1984), Rawls (1971), Rorty (1991), J. Edwards (1985, 1994), and Waldron (1993), (1995).

3   For other examples of this broadly articulated position, see Bloom (1987), Hirsch (1987), Schlesinger (1991), Ravitch (1992), Hughes (1993), D'Souza (1991, 1995), Lind (1995) and Glazer (1997).

4   Hispanic communities in the USA are not a single category, as so often described in the literature. Rather they comprise a diverse range of groups, including Spanish-speaking national minorities (Puerto Ricans and Chicanos), various Spanish-speaking immigrants from Latin America, Cuban refugees, and illegal Mexican migrant workers (Kymlicka, 1995a: 15–17; see also Macías, 1979; Hernández-Chávez, 1995; Zentella, 1997).

5   Communitarians believe that we discover our ends embedded in a social context, rather than choosing them ex-nihilo. Their principal objection in this regard is thus to the idea of a self divorced from, or stripped of, the social features of identity (Coulombe, 1995).

6   The distinction here is mine, not Schlesinger's. Like most commentators, Schlesinger makes no distinction between national and ethnic minorities, assuming all minority groups to be the latter (see Chapter 2 and also below).

7   It must be said that the League of Nations did not initially encompass a formal concern for minority rights. Indeed, no provisions dealing with the

protection of minorities, nor for that matter human rights generally, were incorporated within its original remit. However, these omissions created significant controversy and led the League of Nations subsequently to adopt and oversee the Minority Protection scheme. It should also be pointed out here that the latter was as much concerned with providing a mechanism for the protection of individual rights, especially the right to equality, as with the specific concerns of national minorities. As such, the League of Nations' approach is not inconsistent with the more recent adoption of universal human rights (see de Varennes, 1996a: 26–27; see also below).

8   Article 2 of the Declaration states: 'Everyone is entitled to all the rights and freedoms set forth in this Declaration, without distinction of any kind, such as race [sic], colour, sex, religion, political or other opinion, national or social origin, property, birth or other status'. Consequently, minorities, as such, do not enjoy rights in the Declaration. Various attempts at including a recognition of minorities in the text were strongly opposed at the draft stages, the consensus being that 'the best solution of the problems of minorities was to encourage respect for human rights' (see Thornberry, 1991b: 11–12).

9   Margalit and Raz's (1995: 81–91) discussion of encompassing groups could easily be applied to the notion of ethnicity as habitus. At one point, for example, they observe: 'familiarity with a culture determines the boundaries of the imaginable. Sharing a culture, being part of it, determines the limits of the feasible' (1995: 86).

10   The few notable exceptions, at least to date, have been by French Canadian political theorists discussing the issue of Québec – see, for example, Coulombe (1995, 1999) and Réaume (1999). Of course, one might also add Charles Taylor's (1994) seminal contribution on the 'politics of recognition' here as well, although language forms only a part of his wider discussion, and tends also to be framed primarily in relation to Québec (see Chapter 6).

4

Language, identity and minority rights

Much of the debate surrounding the pluralist dilemma has been concerned with – some would say, consumed by – its implications for language and education within the nation-state. Conservative commentators such as Schlesinger (1992), for example, are quick to denounce bilingualism in the USA and to point out the supposedly pernicious influence of multicultural and bilingual education on the fabric of American society. Likewise, advocates of cultural and linguistic pluralism often invest education with the capacity to transform public policy – and, by implication, public attitudes – to their more pluralist ends. The Swann Report (DES, 1985) in Britain, with its prominent advocacy of multicultural (but not bilingual) education, provides an exemplar here.

This preoccupation with language and education should not surprise us, given their centrality to the formation and maintenance of modern nation-states (see Chapter 2). In effect, the battle for nationhood is most often a battle for linguistic and cultural hegemony. Consequently, education – and, crucially, the language(s) legitimated in and through education – play a key role in establishing and maintaining the subsequent cultural and linguistic shape of the nation-state. However, this is not a 'once and for all' process, as much as some conservative commentators would want it to be. In contrast, established nation-states in the western world are having to revisit these questions in the light of changing demographic patterns and, more significantly for our ends, the increasing disenchantment of national-minority groups with current cultural and linguistic hegemonies. In this chapter I want to explore the validity of these national-minority claims in specific relation to language and identity, along with the various issues to which this gives rise. In Chapter 5, I will examine more closely the role of education. However, in attempting to maintain some analytical distance between the two dimensions in what follows, I also acknowledge that it is often very difficult to separate them *in practice* when it comes to the pluralist dilemma.

Language and identity

In Chapter 1 we saw how language may be a salient marker of ethnic identity in one instance but not in another. While a specific language may well be identified as a significant cultural marker of a particular ethnic group, there is no inevitable correspondence between language and ethnicity. In effect, linguistic differences do not always correspond to ethnic ones – membership of an ethnic group does not necessarily entail association with a particular language, either for individual members or for the group itself. Likewise, more than one ethnic group can share the same language while continuing without difficulty to maintain their own distinct ethnic (and national) identities. Indeed, even where language *is* regarded as a central feature of ethnic identity, it is the *diacritical significance* attached to language which is considered crucial, not the actual language itself (cf. Barth, 1969a; see below). Moreover, languages, along with other cultural attributes, vary in their salience to ethnicity both within and between historical periods. Languages may come and languages may go, or so it seems. These themes were reiterated in Chapter 2 when we examined the tenets of linguistic nationalism à la Herder, Humboldt and Fichte. There we concluded, along with most modernist commentators, that the view of nations as both natural and linguistically determined was little more than sociological (and linguistic) nonsense. As Ernest Renan has argued, language may well be a factor in national identity but it is certainly not the only one, nor is it even essential: 'language may invite us to unite but it does not compel us to do so' (1990: 16).

Given this, one might be able to assume that language has little actual significance to, or bearing on, questions of ethnic and national identity. However, this would be to make a grave mistake, for a number of reasons. First, there is considerable evidence that while language may not be a *determining* feature of ethnic and national identity, it remains nonetheless a *significant* one in many instances. To say that language is not an inevitable feature of identity is not the same as saying it is unimportant, yet many commentators in (rightly) assuming the former position have also (wrongly) assumed the latter. As I will argue, language may not be intrinsically valuable in itself – it is not primordial – but it does have strong and felt associations with ethnic and national identity. As such, language cannot be relegated, as some commentators would have it, to a mere secondary or surface characteristic of ethnicity (see, for example, Glazer, 1975, 1983; Eastman, 1984; J. Edwards, 1984, 1985; Rodriguez, 1983, 1993).

Second, and relatedly, the *cultural* significance of language to ethnic and national identity may help to explain, at least in part, its *political* prominence in many ethnic and ethnonationalist movements (cf. Blommaert, 1996, 1999c). In this regard, the interconnections between the cultural and political dimensions of language become central, most obviously in the official status accorded to particular languages within the nation-state. As Manning Nash observes:

> Language seems straightforwardly a piece of culture. But on reflection it is clear that language is often a political fact, at least as much as it is a cultural one. It has been said that 'language is a dialect with an army and a navy'. And what official or recognised languages are in any given instance is often the result of politics and power interplays.
>
> (1989: 6)

The official status of language(s) to which Nash refers is a key dimension in many of the debates on the pluralist dilemma and concerns majority group members as much as it does minorities. We have already seen the salience of language (and language rights) to the dominant ethnie from Schlesinger's comments in the preceding chapter, and we will encounter this preoccupation with language, from all sides, again and again in what follows. However, Nash's comment also alludes to the fact that the official status ascribed to any one language is a somewhat arbitrary process – as much to do with political and social power relations as with anything else. This point has already been presaged by Gellner's (1983) and Anderson's (1991) accounts in Chapter 2 of the development of national languages (often retrospectively) within nation-states. And it brings me to the third reason for not underestimating the significance of language to ethnic and national identity. Language construction and/or reconstruction may well be a somewhat arbitrary process at times. Nonetheless, a certain linguistic arbitrariness does not, ipso facto, diminish the affective and/or political importance of the languages concerned for those who come to speak them. Indeed, if this were the case, it would be hard, if not impossible, to explain why particular national languages have such sociopolitical currency and meaning for their adherents; a currency which extends far beyond the reach of its solely 'linguistic' functions. In short, the legitimacy, or otherwise, of a language's provenance does not much matter. If a particular language comes to serve important cultural and/or political functions in the formation and maintenance of a particular ethnic or national identity, it *is* important. With this in mind, I want now to turn to a more detailed examination of each of the three key principles just outlined.

Identity in language

Towards the end of his influential account *Imagined Communities*, Benedict Anderson avers of language:

What the eye is to the lover – that particular, ordinary eye he or she is born with – language – whatever language history has made his or her mother tongue – is to the patriot. Through that language, encountered at mother's knee and parted only at the grave, pasts are restored, fellowships are imagined, and futures dreamed.

(1991: 154)

And yet Anderson is also the first to reject any suggestion of some kind of primordial status to language. It is always a mistake, he argues, to treat languages in the way that certain nationalist ideologues treat them – 'as *emblems* of nation-ness, like flags, costumes, folk dances and the rest'. Much the more important aspect of language is 'its capacity for generating imagined communities, building in effect *particular solidarities*' (1991: 133; emphases in original). The sociolinguist Monica Heller makes a similar point when she discusses the interrelationship between language and ethnic identity in a French immersion school in Toronto, Canada:

Language use is . . . involved in the formation of ethnic identity in two ways. First, it constrains access to participation in activities and to forma-tion of social relationships. *Thus at a basic level language use is central to the formation of group boundaries.* Second, as children spend more and more time together they share experience, and language is a central means of making sense out of that shared experience.

(1987: 199; my emphasis)

Language, as a communally shared good, serves an important boundary-marking function (Tabouret-Keller, 1997). In this sense, the boundary-marking function of language has clear parallels here with Armstrong's (1982) notion of 'symbolic border guards', discussed in Chapter 2. After all, being unable to speak a particular language places immediate restrictions on one's ability to communicate – and, by extension, identify – with those who speak that language and any ethnic and/or national identities with which it is associated. This process of demarcation may be more salient for minority groups since such groups are likely to be more conscious of the need for clear linguistic boundaries in relation to a surrounding dominant language and culture. The usefulness of linguistic demarcation may also thus help to explain why language often has a heightened sense of saliency in relation to identity when its role as only one of a number of cultural markers might suggest otherwise. Moreover, to the extent that language boundaries are employed as a demarcating feature of identity, then a decreasing emphasis on, or a blurring of, these boundaries would be regarded as a threat to a group's existence (Khleif, 1979).

Relatedly, where language is regarded as central to identity – or, as Smolicz (1979, 1993, 1995) terms it, where language is a 'core cultural value' – the *sharing* of that language may engender particular solidarities. Certainly, ethnic and nationalist movements have seen the potential this connection offers – often choosing language as a rallying point for the alternative histories, and associated cultural and political rights, that they wish to promote. In so doing, many such movements are simply reflecting long-held views of the language and identity link which are reflected in the language itself. The Welsh word 'iaith', for example, originally meant both language and community; the word for foreigner, 'anghyfiaith', means 'not of the same language'; while the word for a compatriot, 'cyfiaith', means 'of the same language'. Likewise, the Basque define their territory 'Euskalherria' on the basis of where 'Euskera', the Basque language, is spoken. Frequently invoked nationalist slogans also reflect the primacy given to the language and identity link: 'Sluagh gun chanain, sluagh gun anam' is Gaelic for 'A people without its language is a people without its soul', while 'Hep brezhoneg, breizh ebet' is Breton for 'without Breton there is no Brittany', and there are numerous other examples on which one could draw (see, for example, J. Edwards, 1994: 129; Fishman, 1997: 331–333).

From the above, it is clear that the link between language and identity encompasses both significant cultural and political dimensions. The former is demonstrated by the fact that one's individual and social identities, and their complex interconnections, are inevitably mediated in and through language. The latter is significant to the extent that languages come to be formally (and informally) associated with particular ethnic and national identities. These interconnections also help to explain why a 'detached' scientific view of the link between language and identity may fail to capture the degree to which language is *experienced* as vital by those who speak it. It may also significantly understate the role that language plays in social organisation and mobilisation (Fishman, 1997). In short, the 'shibboleth of language', as Toynbee (1953) coined it, still holds much sway. While the cultural and political dimensions of language and identity are inevitably closely intertwined, I want to look briefly in what follows at each of these aspects in turn.

Language and culture

It does not take much to demonstrate that language is a communally shared good since language, almost by definition, requires dialogue. What is harder to determine is whether one's *own* language is a good. Is a particular language significantly related to one's cultural identity or would any language suffice? This is a crucial question since, if the latter is proved, the case for specific language rights – that is, rights relating to the protection and promotion of specific languages – is dealt a perhaps terminal blow. However, even if the former tenet is accepted, one must be able to account for the historical, social and political *construction* of the language and identity link and its clear *variability*, both at the inter- and intragroup level. This is not an easy task by any means but the work of the prominent sociolinguist Joshua Fishman provides us with a useful place to start.

Fishman (1991) argues that language and ethnocultural identity are crucially linked in three key ways: indexically, symbolically and in a part–whole fashion. First, a language associated with a particular culture 'is, at any time during which that linkage is still intact, best able to name the artifacts and to formulate or express the interests, values and world-views of that culture' (1991: 20). This is the indexical link between language and culture. Such a link does not assume that a traditionally or historically associated language is a perfect isomorphic match with an attendant culture, nor that other languages might not be able to replace this traditional link in the longer term. However, in the *short* term (that is, at any particular point in time), 'no language but the one that has been most historically and intimately associated with a given culture is as well able to express the particular artifacts and concerns of that culture' (1991: 21). In other words, the traditionally associated language reflects and conveys its culture more felicitously and succinctly than other languages, *while that language-in-culture link remains generally intact*.

Fishman's position here reflects a weak version of what is known in linguistics as the Sapir-Whorf hypothesis. This theory – named after its proponents, Edward Sapir and Benjamin Whorf – was popular in the early part of the twentieth century and can be traced back, in turn, to Herder and Humboldt's views on language. Sapir's argument was that one's social and cultural experiences are organised by language and thus each language represents a particular worldview. His pupil Whorf extended this by arguing that thought is not independent of the language used because language carves up experience according to its particular grammatical structure, categories and types. Accordingly, the key implication of the Sapir-Whorf hypothesis is that people who speak different languages are likely to have somewhat different cultural outlooks on the basis that the particular structure of each language results in a culturally specific structuring of reality. Indeed, a strong version of the hypothesis attests that languages are *causal* vis-à-vis culturally specific behaviours; a view which is broadly comparable with that held by Herder et al. and which has since been widely rejected as linguistically determinist. However, a weak version of the thesis, as here, highlights the *influence* of language in shaping our *customary* ways of thinking and can be regarded as both reasonable and unsurprising (J. Edwards, 1994).[1] If identity is understood here in relation to habitus as 'the background against which our tastes and desires and opinions and aspirations make sense' (Taylor, 1994: 33–34), then a traditionally associated language would seem to have a significant part to play. Indeed, linguistic habitus, in Bourdieu's (1991) terms, is a subset of the dispositions which comprise the habitus: it is that set of dispositions acquired in the course of learning to speak in particular social and cultural contexts.

Language and culture are also linked symbolically; that is they come to stand for, or symbolically represent, the particular ethnic and/or national collectivities that speak them. Accordingly, the fortunes of languages are inexorably bound up with those of their speakers (J. Edwards, 1985, 1994; Dorian, 1998). Languages do not rise or fall simply on their own linguistic merits – indeed, it has long been accepted that all languages are potentially equivalent in linguistic terms. Rather, the social and political circumstances of those who speak a particular language will have a significant impact on the subsequent symbolic and communicative status attached to that language. This fact often escapes speakers of dominant national languages, and particularly speakers of English as the current world language, who take the 'natural' ascendency of these languages for granted. In contrast, the current international currency of a language like English has much more to do with the sociopolitical dominance of those nation-states, notably the USA, for which English is the accepted language of public discourse (Tollefson, 1991; Pennycook, 1994; Phillipson, 1992, 1998; see Chapter 6). Likewise, national languages reflect the greater sociopolitical status of their speakers in relation to minority languages and cultures within the nation-state.

The final aspect – the part–whole link – reflects the partial identity between a particular language and culture. Since so much of any culture is verbally constituted (its songs and prayers, its laws and proverbs, its history, philosophy and teachings), there are parts of every culture that are expressed, implemented and realised via the language with which that culture is most closely associated. Fishman argues that it is within this part–whole relationship that:

> child socialisation patterns come to be associated with a particular language, that cultural styles of interpersonal relations come to be associated with a particular language, that the ethical principles that undergird everyday life come to be associated with a particular language and that even material culture and aesthetic sensibilities come to be conventionally discussed and evaluated via figures of speech that are merely culturally (i.e. locally) rather than universally applicable.

(1991: 24)

Fishman's analysis highlights the cultural significance of language to identity. This does not imply, however, the reification of the latter or the assumption that such identity can be 'preserved' in some pure, unaltered state. Nor does it link particular languages inexorably with particular identities. Rather, a traditionally associated language is viewed as a significant *resource* to one's ethnic identity, both at the level of societal integration and social identification (see also Ruiz, 1984). While such a resource may ultimately be discarded (see below), it remains important until such a time as this occurs. As Fishman concludes, 'a preferred, historically associated mother tongue has a role in [the] process of individual and aggregative self-definition and self-realisation, not merely as a myth (i.e., as a verity whose objective truth is less important than its subjective truth) but also as a genuine identificational and motivational desideratum in the ethnocultural realm' (1991: 7).

Given this, the concern to repudiate language as a significant feature of identity may be overstated. However, be that as it may, Fishman's argument still needs to account for the exceptions it implicitly acknowledges but does not necessarily explain. How do we accommodate those individuals and groups for whom a particular language is clearly not an important feature of their identity? How do we explain language shift, which suggests that these associations, while important, are by no means irreplaceable? And how do we counter the charge that the language and identity link is largely arbitrary – a social and political construction along the well-rehearsed lines of the 'invention of tradition' argument? To answer these questions, we need to explore further the interconnections between the cultural and political dimensions of language and identity.

Language, culture and politics

The language and identity link cannot be understood in isolation from other factors of identity, nor from the specific political conditions in which it is situated. The relation between language and identity is thus *contingent* on both subjective factors and particular political circumstances (Coulombe, 1995). On this basis, it can be argued that the language we speak is crucial to our identity *to the degree to which we define ourselves by it*. This will obviously vary widely, both among individuals and within and between groups. As such, it may well be that some individuals and groups will regard a particular language as a largely superficial marker of their identities and have no great sense of loss in abandoning it. Immigrant ethnic minorities, for example, often adopt the language of the host country in which they reside, albeit usually over the course of two or three generations, on the basis of enhancing their integration and social mobility within that country. On this view, Carol Eastman has proffered the explanation that language use is merely a surface feature of ethnic identity and thus adopting another language would only affect the language use aspect of our ethnic identity, not the identity itself. As she asserts, 'there is no need to worry about preserving ethnic identity, so long as the only change being made is in what language we use' (1984: 275). Accordingly, immigrant ethnic groups may retain their original language as an 'associated' language – one that group members no longer use, or perhaps even know, but which continues to be a part of their heritage.

Such an association is clearly comparable with Gans' (1979) notion of symbolic ethnicity discussed in Chapter 1.

These arguments can be extrapolated to the relationship between language and national identity as well. Gellner, for example, has argued that 'changing one's language is not the heart-breaking or soul-destroying business which it is claimed to be in romantic nationalist literature' (1964: 165). Ireland is regularly invoked as an example here because, over the course of the last two centuries, English has come largely to supplant Irish Gaelic as the ethnic (and national) language. Irish may still be spoken by a minority in the Gaeltacht (the Irish-speaking heartland),[2] and it still retains official status as the 'first official language' of Ireland. However, the reality of Irish as a rapidly declining language has been clear for some considerable time now. For example, an extensive sociolinguistic research study conducted in the 1970s, entitled 'Committee on Irish Language Attitudes Research' (CILAR, 1975), found that less than three per cent of the overall population used Irish in any regular way. There was also little interest in the restoration of Irish, hostility to the compulsory aspects associated with learning Irish (see below), and significant pessimism about the continued maintenance of the Irish still in use at the time. Nonetheless, a symbolic valuing of Irish was still evident and, as such, was thought to continue to form part of Irish ethnic and national identity. As the CILAR observes: 'the average person would seem to place considerable value on the symbolic role of the Irish language in ethnic identification and as a cultural value in and of itself . . . [but this] seems to be qualified by a generally pessimistic view of the language's future *and a feeling of its inappropriateness in modern life*' (1975: 29; my emphasis). This conclusion accords with Ussher's more succinct, and certainly more cynical observation: 'the Irish of course like their Irish, but they like it *dead*' (1949: 107).

Two complementary explanations can be offered for this clear process of language shift in Ireland. One is that while language is often a 'core cultural value' for many ethnic and national groups, it is not so in relation to Irish identity. Thus, Smolicz, who has promoted this notion of core cultural values, argues that the core values of the Irish ethnic group are 'unquestioningly centred on the Catholic religion' (1979: 63) rather than on the Irish language itself, a process that has been intensified by the fact that English was adopted as the language of Irish Catholicism from the late eighteenth century onwards. As Smolicz concludes of these developments: 'Bereft of their ancestral tongue, it was in Catholicism that the Irish found the refuge and shield behind which they could retain their identity and awareness of their distinction from the conquering British Protestants' (1979: 64). This might well explain the ongoing decline of the Irish language, despite the adoption from the nineteenth century onward of informal, and subsequently formal, language policies aimed at mitigating this language loss (J. Edwards, 1985; Hindley, 1990; Ó Riagáin, 1997; see also below).

There is some merit in the 'core cultural value' explanation, although how the 'Irish ethnic group' is defined remains extremely problematic since intragroup differences are likely to be much more complex than such an analysis allows. In this regard, it is almost self-evident that different sections of the community, not to mention individuals, will have different relationships to their language(s) for a variety of political, social and/or religious reasons, thus significantly weakening the core-value explanation (Clyne, 1997). In light of this criticism, a more nuanced approach to core cultural values has since been attempted. While still holding that some cultures are more language-centred than others, Smolicz and Secombe (1988) differentiate four broad approaches to minority languages that are evident between and within ethnic-minority groups. These comprise: *negative evaluation* of the language; *indifference* – seeing no purpose in language maintenance and showing no interest in it; *general positive evaluation* – regarding the language as a vital element of ethnicity but not being prepared personally to learn it; *personal positive evaluation* – regarding the language as a core cultural value and putting this language commitment into practice (see also Clyne, 1990).

Even so, a more compelling explanation of language shift is likely to reside in the social and political processes which have seen the rise of English as the language of Ireland over the course of the last few centuries. These sociopolitical factors have linked English inextricably with modernisation, thus providing the language with increasing symbolic and communicative currency in Ireland. Given this, the sociopolitical milieu of Ireland merits closer examination since it illustrates, writ large, the difficulties facing minority languages and cultures in the modern world.

Language decline: the death of Irish?

Irish enjoyed its 'Golden Age' from the sixth to the ninth centuries, when it was spoken as a common vernacular, alongside Latin, not only in what we now know as Ireland but also in the coastal areas of both southern and northern Britain. Indeed, Irish was so highly regarded at this time that by the eighth century it had supplanted Latin as the principal literary and religious medium, while the reach of the Irish-speaking community had extended over almost the whole area of present-day Scotland. The dominance of Irish first began to be undermined though with the advent of the Norman invasions of the twelfth century. New towns were built by the Normans in Ireland, as elsewhere in Britain, and led to the introduction of a Norman French- and subsequently English-speaking bourgeoisie (Ó Murchú, 1988). Even so, this process, which continued until the sixteenth century, was a slow and limited one. Indeed, by the late fifteenth century, most Normans living outside of the Dublin area had actually come to be assimilated into the wider Irish language and culture. Irish thus continued to have a strong societal and regional base and remained the dominant language among all classes in the countryside. It also remained the primary language of communication in urban areas (although English was used for public affairs) in what appears to have been some form of Irish–English diglossia.[3]

From the sixteenth century, however, English began to make its irrevocable advance. Henry VIII issued proclamations discouraging Irish (see Crowley, 1996) and, more significantly, plantation schemes were initiated to replace Irish with English settlers (Ó Riagáin, 1996). The latter proved to be crucial – resulting, as one writer has observed, in the 'Gaelic world [dying] from the top down' (de Paor, 1985; cited in Ó Riagáin, 1997: 4). By 1800, English – or, at least, an Irish variant of it – was spoken regularly by half the population; crucially, the most powerful half. Irish speakers were increasingly limited to the poor and underdeveloped Gaeltacht while English speakers constituted the propertied rural and urban population. This language decline was compounded by the abandonment of Irish by the Catholic church, its formal exclusion from the English-language National School system established in 1831, and the impact of rural depopulation (by both death and emigration) from the Famines of the 1840s. These trends, which can be regarded as largely external, were also hastened by the apparent willingness of Irish speakers themselves to abandon the language. As John Edwards observes, 'the mass of Irish people were more or less active contributors to the spread of English' (1984: 285). As a result, by the mid nineteenth century, the percentage of the population who remained Irish-speaking had declined to just under 30 per cent. Despite various attempts to revive Irish from the mid nineteenth century on – exemplified most prominently in the activities of such nationalist-inspired language bodies as the Gaelic League (Conradh na Gaeilge), established in 1893 (see Tovey et al., 1989) – the decline of Irish continued into the twentieth century.

By the time the Irish Free State was established in 1922, the pattern of language decline appeared almost terminal. At most, only 10 per cent of the population now used Irish as their daily language and this group was almost exclusively situated in the Gaeltacht (Ó Ciosáin, 1988; Ó Riagáin, 1996). Broader language trends were equally bleak. Census figures in 1926 indicated that only 18 per cent could actually speak Irish and that very few of these were monoglot speakers (Ó Gadhra, 1988). Moreover, even this estimate would appear to have been overstated, since many of those returned as Irish speakers in the census were in older age groups and scattered across communities where Irish had ceased to be an everyday language (Ó Riagáin, 1997).

Given the parlous state of the language, a formal language policy was adopted by the newly independent Republic of Ireland with the specific aim of reversing this decline. Four main strategies were promoted here. In

English-speaking areas, Irish would be compulsorily taught to all children in schools by immersion methods. This, it was hoped, would produce an adult population with functional competence in Irish within a generation. The second strategy was to strengthen and extend the use of Irish in the Gaeltacht, principally via economic regional development policies. The third element required the ongoing use of Irish in the public sector – most significantly in the Irish Civil Service. The final element focused on measures to standardise and modernise the language itself (Ó Ciosáin, 1988; Ó Riagáin, 1997).

It soon became apparent, however, that education was deemed to be the key element in this language policy. In this sense, the language policy reflected the previous emphases of Conradh na Gaeilge (the Gaelic League) at the end of the nineteenth century. At that time, the League had successfully lobbied for Irish to be used as a language of instruction in schools where it remained the first language of most of its pupils, and for its inclusion as an ordinary school subject elsewhere. It had also actively promoted teacher training in Irish via the establishment of its own teacher-training colleges. This almost transcendental belief in the power of education to effect language change arose in turn from the belief that if the nineteenth-century education system had contributed to the demise of Irish via its advocacy of English, the reverse could also well apply. Indeed, such was the faith invested in schools that Timothy Corcoran, an educational advisor at the time of the establishment of the Irish language policy, could assert: 'the popular schools can give and can restore our native language. They can do it even without positive aid from home' (1925: 387; cited in J. Edwards, 1985: 56).

However, such optimism was to prove ill-founded, at least in the Irish case. While I will argue in the next chapter that education *is* a key component of any minority-language policy, the example of Ireland demonstrates that the aim of restoring communicative competence in a language cannot be achieved on the backs of schools alone (see also Fishman, 1991; J. Edwards, 1984, 1985, 1994; Colin Williams, 1994). This overemphasis on education in the Irish context was further compounded by a lack of suitable teachers of Irish and by the ambivalence – and at times, outright opposition – of many teachers towards the language restoration project. Accordingly, by the 1960s/1970s the bulk of educational effort had been restricted to teaching Irish in the primary (elementary) sector. Even here though, teacher-training colleges were no longer instructing their students in Irish, with the result that teachers of Irish were themselves not particularly competent. That said, the more recent development of Naíonraí – locally initiated Irish-immersion-speaking preschools, initially outside of the regular school system – represents something of a countertrend, growing in number from one in 1968 to 185 in 1988. The result has been the subsequent reemergence of Irish-medium schools to cater for Naíonraí graduates, most of which are situated outside of the Gaeltacht. There were 80 such schools in 1994, the bulk of which had been established since 1970 (Ó Riagáin, 1997). Once again though, their development cannot in itself be expected to redress the language loss previously outlined (Fishman, 1991; see Chapter 5).

Allied initiatives in the public sector have also met with limited success in Ireland. Support for Irish at the state level continues, with most official documents printed bilingually. The Bord na Gaeilge (Irish Language Board) was established in 1975 by the government to promote Irish in daily life and includes within its remit the provision of language advice and information, language courses and translation services. However, neither has had much impact on the actual language use of ordinary Irish people themselves. Moreover, as the CILAR (1975) sociolinguistic study found, and as more recent studies have confirmed (Ó Ciosáin, 1988; Ó Riagáin, 1988a), the compulsory dimensions associated with Irish – particularly, the Irish-language requirement for the Civil Service – engendered actual hostility towards the language. This hostility to the compulsory language requirement remained prominent until its eventual abandonment in 1974, and despite a generally favourable attitude to Irish and to bilingualism at the level of ethnic and cultural association.

Finally, even economic measures aimed at preserving some measure of Irish in the Gaeltacht have backfired. For example, efforts to discourage the emigration of Irish speakers from the Gaeltacht have included industrialisation projects aimed at improving employment prospects. However, rather than safeguarding and reinforcing the Irish-speaking communities, such projects have actually undermined them further by importing skilled and supervisory staff with no knowledge of Irish. Likewise, those Irish speakers who have been drawn back have, in the interim, acquired non-Irish-speaking partners, thus increasing the number of non-Irish-speaking households in the area (O'Cinneide et al., 1985). Consequently, the Irish-speaking communities in the Gaeltacht continue to decline. While they still account for 7.4 per cent of all Irish speakers and 45 per cent of all Irish-speaking families, they currently comprise only 2.3 per cent of Ireland's total population (Fishman, 1991).

The result is that 'Irish as a group seem not to have lost their national identity, but to have enshrined it in English' (J. Edwards, 1985: 62), a conclusion encapsulated in the title of Hindley's (1990) *The Death of the Irish Language*. Even those with a more optimistic view of Irish, such as Ó Riagáin, who argues that there has been 'some measure of revival', also concedes that it is 'of a scale that is continuously vulnerable to final submersion in the mainly English-speaking population' (1988b: 7). All of this would seem to indicate the futility – not to mention the naivety and misguidedness – of attempting to maintain minority languages in the face of modern social and political realities. But before consigning Irish – and, by extension, other minority languages – to what might seem to be their inevitable fate, let us examine more closely the constituent elements of the Irish case.

Language revival: flogging a dead horse?

Ireland is an instructive example of a minority-language policy that has met with limited success – indeed some go so far as to describe it as an archetypal failure. As such, it is often invoked as a cause célèbre by sceptics and opponents of minority-language rights. John Edwards, for example, employs the Irish case to argue that the concerted revival of such languages should not be attempted when this operates 'in the face of historical realities' (1985: 64). Language revival in these circumstances is inherently artificial and bound to fail. As he argues elsewhere:

> language shift reflects *sociopolitical change* and this, given the historical perspective, absolutely dwarfs efforts made on behalf of language alone. This is not to say . . . that language cannot serve a vital rallying purpose in nationalistic political movements, but it only does so when it retains some realistic degree of communicative function.
>
> (1984: 288; emphasis in original)

On this basis, it is a profound error to think of language decline as anything other than a symptom of widespread social confrontation between unequal forces (J. Edwards, 1994). If this is the case, the next question must surely be 'should we attempt to reverse language decline at all'? John Edwards and other like-minded commentators (see, for example, Coulmas, 1992; Bentahila and Davies, 1993) answer this question in the negative; endorsing, in effect, a form of linguistic social Darwinism. Such a conclusion may seem to many simple commonsense. However, it betrays a number of inherent contradictions that I want to explore further, not only in relation to the Irish case but also with respect to some of its wider implications.

To begin with, there are specific aspects of the Irish case that militated against successful language revival. For example, by the time that serious language-restoration attempts were promoted and implemented in the late nineteenth and early twentieth century, much of the language had already been lost to the majority of the population. Thus, while state support and a prominent role for education *are* important factors in language revival, as I will argue in the next chapter, they cannot be expected *by themselves* to reverse an already changed linguistic demography. Fishman (1991) makes exactly this point, in contradistinction to the Irish approach, when he asserts that intergenerational family transmission of any language is the key to its continued survival. While he argues that 'the family (and even the immediate community) *may not be enough* [to reverse language shift], particularly where outside pressures are both great and hostile . . . without this stage safely under . . . control the more advanced stages have nothing firm to build on' (1991: 94). In short, 'nothing can substitute for the rebuilding of a society at the level of . . . everyday, informal life' (1991: 112). Fishman develops this specific point further in his discussion of the Graded Intergenerational Disruption Scale (1991: 81–121; see p. 2 for its description). Stage 6 of this scale involves intergenerational family transmission and is thus ostensibly at the scale's lower, more 'basic' end. However, Fishman argues that many language-revitalisation movements tend to overlook this crucial stage in their rush to establish ostensibly more 'advanced' stages such as minority-language education (Stage 4). Invariably, he suggests, this proves counter-productive in the long term, as in the Irish case. This conclusion is reiterated from within the Irish context itself by Ó Gadhra's observation that 'the failure to recognise, for a very long time, the extremely low base from which we set out, has been one of the failures of the Irish revival effort' (1988: 254).

A related feature of the Irish case that merits discussion is the political context in which language restoration came to be situated. The well-known comment by the Irish nationalist Eamon de Valera clearly illustrates this context: 'If I had to make a choice between political freedom without the language [Irish], and the language without political freedom . . . I would choose the latter' (cited in J. Edwards, 1994: 129). De Valera's assertion highlights the prominent political prerogative underpinning the motivation to restore Irish – namely, to employ the language as a distinguishing characteristic of the newly emergent nation-state. However, this position was eventually to founder both politically and linguistically. In relation to the former, the attempt to promote the language as the unique heritage of *all* Irish people, including long-established English settlers and a much larger segment of 'native Irish' who had abandoned the Irish language in the nineteenth century, inevitably excluded more than it included (Ó Gadhra, 1988). From the start, the changed linguistic demography – coupled with long-standing forms of Irish identity not associated with the Irish language – militated against the successful adoption of the language as a unifying feature of modern Irish nationalism. In relation to the latter, the nationalists' advocacy of Irish did little, if anything, to reverse its linguistic decline. In fact, the language policy subsequently adopted by the nationalists may have further precipitated language loss by limiting itself largely to the promotion of the language's *symbolic* qualities. De Valera illustrates this process well since he himself made little effort to give the language much more than symbolic import (Dwyer, 1980). This limited symbolic emphasis is thus likely to have been a contributing factor in the failure of the language to regain wider communicative currency. The state sector provides a clear example of this process here because while the formal promotion of Irish has long been a key aspect of language policy, actual language use has remained desultory and, despite the long-standing compulsory language components, largely nominal.

More broadly, the Irish example demonstrates just how long it may actually take for the traditionally associated language of a particular ethnie to decline and be replaced – in this case, several centuries. This is not to suggest that language shift always occurs this slowly but it does demonstrate that the process of change is neither insignificant nor peripheral. Such a view is consistent with my previous discussions on the *slow* process of change associated with habitus and encompassing cultures and, relatedly, on the significance of language to ethnic identity. Language shift does clearly occur – it would be foolish to suggest otherwise. However, it is more problematic and traumatic than is often assumed, particularly for those ethnies for whom a certain language represented, at least at one time, an important feature of their collective identity (Taylor, 1994, 1998; Margalit and Raz, 1995). Fishman reiterates this view when he asserts that '[l]anguage shift generally and basic-ally involves cultural change as well indeed, initially, quite devastating and profound cultural change' (1991: 16).[4] This is not to say, using Fishman's terminology, that 'Xmen' cannot be Xmen if they do not speak the language 'Xish'. Indeed, as we have already seen, the detachability of language from ethnic identity is clearly demonstrated by those Xmen who have already come to speak 'Yish' – usually as a result of Yish being a language of greater power and opportunity, as in the Irish context. Nonetheless, we can assert on the basis of the link between language and identity, that it is a *different kind* of 'Xishness' that results. As Fishman concludes:

> The fact that the traditional symbolic relationship between Xish and Xishness can ultimately be replaced by a new symbolic relationship be-tween Yish and Xishness merely indicates that in the fullness of time such transformations are possible and they have, indeed, occurred throughout human history. This does not mean that such symbolic redefinitions and self-redefinitions are either desirable or easily attained, or that Xishness is the same under both sets of linguistic circumstances.
>
> (Fishman, 1991: 34)

Fishman's argument raises another pertinent question, however. Adopting another language may result in a different kind of Xishness but if it is a more powerful and widely used language, if it results in a cultural shift towards greater modernity, surely this is a good thing? Again, this position is one adopted by most sceptics of minority-language rights and it is one that bears remarkable similarities to the broadly pejorative views of ethnicity outlined in Chapter 1. On this view, minority languages are constructed as an impedi-ment to modernisation and social progress. Not only this, proponents of minority languages are dismissed as self-interested and unrepresentative elites who are intent on maintaining such languages solely for nostalgic and/or nationalistic reasons. This, critics suggest, is invariably at the expense of the wider social mobility of those who speak the minority language and, con-comitantly, largely against not only the latter's interests but also their wishes.

Schlesinger's views of bilingualism, discussed in the previous chapter, re-flect well this dual attack on the twin 'perils' of linguistic self-ghettoisation and the self-interested elites who perpetuate it. John Edwards (1985) is likewise dismissive of the apparent disparity between proponents of minority rights and their supposed constituents and uses the Irish case as an exemplar.[5] For the many who actually realise the 'benefits' of shifting to a more 'modern' language, Edwards argues that economic rationality plays a significant part. In effect, this amounts to a linguistic variant of rational choice theory (cf. Chapter 1) – loyalty to a particular language persists only as long as the economic and social circumstances are conducive to it (see also Dorian, 1981, 1982). As Edwards proceeds to observe, this contrasts with what he sees as the clearly regressive interests of minority-language proponents:

> Note here how patronising and naive are attempts to *preserve people as they are*, on the grounds that they are really better off if only they knew it, that progress is not all it is made out to be . . . Little wonder, then, that sensible populations themselves do not accept this line, and that the major proponents of the view are usually securely ensconced within that very segment of society they rail against . . . looking backwards has been a favourite sport for disaffected intellectuals for a long time, but actually moving backwards has not been so popular.

> (1985: 95, 97; my emphasis)

Such views are also echoed in the developing world and are well represented by Kay's (1993) arguments on the 'new African'. Kay's case study of Zambia demonstrates how the country is currently divided into 72 ethnic and 7 regional languages but is united by one official language, English. From this, Kay argues for the displacement of African languages in favour of international languages such as English. African languages, with their reduced communicative power and symbolic purchase, reflect for Kay the old order, while the likes of English now represent the best means of escaping both poverty and the strictures of ethnic identity in Africa. Consequently, language loss is seen as a necessary, perhaps inevitable, aspect of modernisation and development, even if, in the process, it risks the 'destruction' of cultures (see also Mazrui, 1975; Eastman, 1991).

How can one respond to this critique? For a start, it can be argued that the question of minority leadership is largely a red herring – merely a useful stick, in effect, with which to beat proponents of minority-language rights. After all, the charges of self-interest and distinction from the 'rank and file' can be invoked against any leadership, including those advocating a majority language.[6] Likewise, it should be entirely unsurprising that a full range of opinion is expressed within minority groups about such central issues as language maintenance and shift. Internal differences are an inevitable characteristic of *all* groups. It is accordingly a reductio ad absurdum to imply that the presence of such differences negates the legitimacy of minority-language claims. Indeed, critiques along these lines tend simply to obfuscate rather than clarify the competing goals, aims, values and opinions of the various protagonists involved in the minority-language(s) debate (Fishman, 1991). Similarly, the charge of inherent *preservationism* – apparent in John Edwards' earlier comment – does not necessarily follow, as I will argue. Nonetheless, the view presented here of minority languages as a brake on individual social mobility and collective modernisation – as a *problem*, in effect – does seem convincing. It certainly has significant purchase among many actual minority-language speakers themselves, as commentators such as Edwards are more than willing to point out. Relatedly, majority-language advocates generally pose as (and consider themselves to be) both humanitarians and realists, with nothing but the best interests of minority-language speakers at heart (Fishman, 1991). But this position, however benevolent it might seem, also harbours a number of significant problems of its own that are seldom acknowledged or addressed, and it is to these that I now want to turn.

Reevaluating language shift

Language shift appears to be an increasing feature of the modern world. Certainly, there is a noticeably greater tendency for members of ethnolinguistic minorities to bring up their children in a language other than their native one, a process that often leads to the eventual displacement of the former language(s). This process of language displacement usually takes at least three generations. It involves: (1) initial language contact leading to minority status of the historically associated language; (2) bilingualism where the original language is retained but the new language is also acquired; (3) recessive use of the old language, limited largely to intraethnic communication; (4) increasingly unstable bilingualism, eventually leading to monolingualism in the new language (Brenzinger, 1997).

As I discussed in the Introduction, such trends have led to some dire predictions concerning the 'endangered' status of these former languages. J. Hill (1978: 69) estimates, for example, that in the last 500 years at least half of the languages in the world have disappeared, and Krauss (1992: 7), in a much-cited article, argues that as few as 600, perhaps only 300, of the currently estimated 6000 languages in the world will remain secure through the next century. Inevitably perhaps, there are disputes about the accuracy of such projections but the general trend is not in doubt (Grenoble and Whaley, 1996, 1998). To take just one example, when Australia was annexed to Britain in 1770, more than 250 languages were used by different Australian Aboriginal communities. Some 200 years on, only 90 of these languages remain in use, with 70 of these threatened with extinction in the near future. Indeed, in the mid 1980s, only 50 Aboriginal languages had more than 100 speakers, 28 of them more than 250 speakers, and only 9 had more than

1000 speakers (see Lo Bianco, 1987; Smolicz, 1989). Today, only about ten per cent of Australian Aboriginal peoples still speak indigenous languages, that is, 30,000 out of 300,000 (Brenzinger, 1997).

The reference to language 'extinction' here is a pertinent one since, again as noted in the Introduction, parallels are often drawn between endangered languages and endangered species. James Crawford draws such comparisons directly when he argues that endangered languages 'fall victim to predators, changing environments, or more successful competitors', are encroached on by 'modern cultures abetted by new technologies', and are threatened by 'destruction of lands and livelihoods; the spread of consumerism, individualism, and other Western values; pressures for assimilation into dominant cultures; and conscious policies of repression' (1994: 5; see also Hornberger, 1997, 1998). Lest the predatory allusion be taken too far, however, it should be stressed that most language shifts are not solely the result of coercion or 'language murder' (Calvet, 1974). However, neither are they solely the result of a 'voluntary' shift, or 'language suicide' (Denison, 1977), as critics of minority-language rights are wont to suggest. Both internal pull and external push factors are invariably involved – although, as I will argue, it is usually the latter that direct the former. Likewise, it needs to be borne in mind that no two language-contact situations are alike, nor do two language shifts resemble each other exactly (Brenzinger, 1997). Thus, while I will attempt to extrapolate general trends in what follows, it is regionally specific or even community-specific factors that dictate the ultimate patterns and effects of language shift in any given context (Grenoble and Whaley, 1996, 1998).

One further caveat needs to be made before proceeding further. It is often thought that the *number* of actual speakers is the key variable in predicting the likelihood or otherwise of a particular language's survival. While numbers are clearly important – the fewer speakers, the less likely that a language will be maintained over time – this assumption is to some extent misplaced. It is not so much how many speak the language but *who* speaks it (and why) that is of most significance. For example, in a recent report on the current situation of 48 minority language groups in the European Union, Nelde et al. found that 'the demographic size of a language group is no guarantee of the group's [linguistic] vitality, with the existence of some of Europe's largest language groups being severely threatened' (1996: Executive Summary). Two other variables were identified as far more influential in their analysis: the low status of many minority groups and their often related social, cultural and economic marginalisation, and the degree to which minority languages were recognised by the state *and* supported within civil society – what Nelde et al., along with others (see below), have termed the processes of 'legitimation' and 'institutionalisation'. Both these variables highlight the importance of underlying *power relations* in situations of minority-language shift, a key factor that is seldom acknowledged by its many apologists.

Acknowledging power relations

The significance of the often unequal power relations that exist between minority and majority language communities tends to be ignored, or at least downplayed, by proponents of language shift. In this regard, it is interesting to note that language death seldom occurs in communities of wealth and privilege, but rather to the dispossessed and disempowered (Crawford, 1994). Even where unequal sociopolitical conditions are ostensibly recognised as a central factor, as in Edwards' and Kay's accounts discussed earlier, these are legitimised in the name of 'linguistic modernisation'. However, this type of argument exhibits a curious schizophrenia. Edwards (1985), for example, is quite willing to acknowledge that language loss has little to do with linguistic merit and almost everything to do with the (unequal) exercise of social and political power. Yet, at the same time, he is prepared to endorse the arrogation of a majority language on the basis of its greater 'communicative currency'. In other words, the notions of 'communicative currency' or 'languages of wider communication' come to serve as linguistic proxies for the legitimation of the greater sociopolitical status of the majority-language group.

Moreover, attempts to provide a minority language with a greater communicative currency of its own – via, most often, a sympathetic policy of status language planning – are largely derided on the grounds that if another language already has such currency why bother? The best that can be hoped for, it is argued, is the retention of some of the minority language's symbolic or totemic qualities but its continued communicative currency is ruled out of court (see J. Edwards, 1984: 289–291; 1985: 17–18). This is a specious, not to mention historically ill-founded, argument though, since all the current major languages in the world today have at some time undergone a comparable process of communicative expansion. One wonders, for example, what the current status of English would be in Britain, let alone globally, had it not undergone its own significant social and lexical expansion in the sixteenth and seventeenth centuries. In the process, English was transformed within the British Isles from a language with a status lower than both Latin and French to effectively the 'national' language, or at least the accepted language of wider communication. This was a considerable achievement given that, prior to the fourteenth century, English was not even taught as a language. Latin was regarded as the language of record, or the literary language. Moreover, owing to the Norman invasion of 1066, French was the language associated with the nobility and thus social aspiration. Indeed, the first king of England since 1066 to speak English as a first language was Henry IV, who assumed the throne in 1399 (Graddol et al., 1996; see also McCrum et al., 1986).

Thus, while establishing a symbolic/communicative distinction to language may well help to explain the detachability of language from ethnic identity, the implicit assumption that the latter should atrophy and die is inherently a *political* not a *linguistic* judgement. Relatedly, if the loss of a particular language is the result largely of political processes, then apologists of such language shift demonstrate little credibility in their own decrial and/or dismissal of minority-language promotion as 'politically motivated'. If we accept the assumption that the sociopolitical dominates the linguistic when it comes to questions of language shift, then we must also accept that arguments both for *and* against any language shift are inherently political. On this basis, Edwards' arguments, and their like, simply represent a particular *value judgement* – a judgement that equates minority-language loss, and language shift to a majority language, with progress and modernity.

In effect, this position amounts to little more than linguistic social Darwinism – only the languages with the greatest communicative currency should and/or will survive.[7] Concomitantly, any efforts undertaken to protect minority languages from such 'inexorable' processes are viewed as antediluvian; as forlorn attempts to maintain some kind of cultural and linguistic stasis. Edwards' previous comments on the role of elites demonstrate this view clearly and he reiterates this position when he asserts: 'language in its communicative sense is . . . an element of identity very susceptible to change. We may lament the fact, we may wish it were not so – but it is. To expect otherwise is tantamount to asking for change itself to cease' (1985: 97). Yet, as with the comparable criticism of minority rights more generally (see Chapter 3), this argument is simply misplaced. There is no necessary correlation between the continued maintenance of one's minority language and cultural and linguistic stasis – cultural and linguistic continuity and change are always and inevitably intertwined (Fishman, 1991). Likewise, cultural nationalism, which often incorporates a defence of minority-language rights, is principally concerned with the *reconstruction* of tradition – modifying it, where necessary – in order to meet more adequately the demands of modernity (Hutchinson, 1994; see Chapter 2). The key question in both these contexts is thus not one of stasis but rather one of greater *control* and *self-regulation* of the process of cultural and linguistic change. As Fishman argues:

> A call for RLS [reversing language shift] must . . . be seen and explained [principally] as a call for cultural reconstruction and for greater self-regulation . . . RLS is an indication of the dissatisfaction with ethnocultural (and, often, also with ethnopolitical and ethno-economic) life as it currently is, and of a resolve to undertake planned ethnocultural reconstruction. This change does not need to be backward looking in its thrust, regardless of the historical metaphors that it may utilise (because of their recognised symbolic and emotional significance). Indeed, most RLS-efforts are actually syncretistic and modernistic with respect to their cultural implications and goals.
>
> (1991: 17)

This is not to say that all attempts to reverse language shift are shorn of their nostalgic elements. Nor does it preclude the unfortunate potential that still exists to reify language and culture. Nonetheless, the inevitable association of such movements with narrow provincialism is misjudged. As with the conclusions drawn in Chapter 3, maintaining one's minority language does not in any way preclude ongoing cultural and linguistic change, adaptation and interaction. Indeed, it can be argued that those who wish to maintain their historically associated language, usually alongside that of another more dominant language, actually exhibit a greater ability to manage multiple cultural and linguistic identities. Narrower identities do not necessarily need to be traded in for broader ones – one can clearly remain both Spanish-speaking and American, Catalan-speaking and Spanish, or Welsh-speaking and British – and to insist on doing so exhibits its own particular form of ethnocentrism.

But there is still a problem here. Arguments for the maintenance of minority languages are all very well but if increasing numbers of people are voluntarily choosing to opt instead for a majority language, then the cause already appears to be a lost one. This was certainly the case with Irish, it seems. Likewise, Nathan Glazer argues, in the US context, that most immigrants want 'to become Americanised as fast as possible, and this [means appropriating] English language and culture . . . while they often found, as time went on, that they regretted what they and their children had lost, this was *their* choice rather than an imposed choice' (1983: 149). However, it can equally be argued that the degree to which *voluntary* shift actually occurs is extremely problematic. After all, if minority languages are consistently viewed as low status, socially and culturally restrictive, and an obstacle to social mobility, is it little wonder that such patterns of language shift exist? In effect, these widely held views place minority-language speakers in a seemingly intractable dilemma. This dilemma, as Fishman summarises it, is 'either to remain loyal to their traditions and to remain socially disadvantaged (consigning their own children to such disadvantage as well), on the one hand; or, on the other hand, to abandon their distinctive practices and traditions, at least in large part, and, thereby, to improve their own and their children's lots in life via cultural suicide' (1991: 60). Thus, one can reasonably question here the legitimacy of this juxtaposition and the apparently forced choice it entails. To what extent is language shift *on these terms* actually necessary? Moreover, what are the *costs* involved in this process and to what extent can they be regarded as fair or warranted? And finally, what, if anything, can be done to change 'the rules of the game' that constitute this dilemma in the first place? To explore these questions further, we need to examine the central issue of language status and the crucial role of the state in its apportionment. In particular, the role of the state has a significant part to play here with regard both to the official recognition of a language, and its acknowledged and accepted domains of use within civil society.

A question of status

It is surprising the extent to which the relationship between language and politics has been overlooked in much sociological and political analysis. After all, language is a contributing feature in many political conflicts in the world today, including those in the Baltics, Belgium, Canada, Spain, Sri Lanka and Turkey, to name but a few (see Horowitz, 1985: 219–224; Safran, 1999). Yet, as Weinstein (1983) observes, while commentators have had much to say about 'the language of politics', very few have had anything to say about 'the politics of language' (for similar observations, see also Grillo, 1989; Kymlicka, 1995a, b; Blommaert, 1996; Holborow, 1999).

What constitutes the politics of language then? Principally, it is a contest for linguistic control (and, by extension, social and cultural control) of the nation-state. In this regard, 'national' languages are so called because they have been *legitimated* by the state and *institutionalised* within civil society, usually to the exclusion of other languages. Legitimation involves the formal recognition by the state of a particular language variety and this recognition is realised, usually, by the constitutional and/or legislative benediction of official status.[8] Accordingly, 'la langue officielle a partie liée avec l'État' (Bourdieu, 1982: 27) – the legitimate (or standard) language becomes an arm of the state – and other language varieties are consequently relegated to the lower status of 'dialects' (cf. Silverstein, 1996; Collins, 1999). This process of 'language standardisation', as it is known in sociolinguistics, usually comprises four main aspects (see Leith and Graddol, 1996: 139):

1 *Selection*: of an existing language variety, usually that of the most powerful social or ethnic group
2 *Codification*: reduction of internal variability in the selected variety, and the establishment of norms of grammatical usage and vocabulary
3 *Elaboration*: ensuring the language can be used for a wide range of functions
4 *Implementation*: promoting the language variety via print (cf. Anderson's account in Chapter 2), discouraging the use of other language varieties within official domains, and encouraging users to develop a loyalty to and pride in it

Given this, it is important to stress that the often invoked distinction between languages and dialects is not principally a linguistic one. Indeed, to attempt a linguistic distinction of the two is fraught with difficulty. One cannot distinguish, for example, a language and dialect on the basis of mutual intelligibility. There are some languages – such as Norwegian, Swedish and Danish – which are mutually intelligible and there are some languages which encompass dialects that are mutually incomprehensible. Rather, the distinction between language and dialect is primarily a political consequence of the language legitimation processes undertaken by nation-states (cf. Blommaert, 1999a, b). As Haugen (1966) observes, a 'dialect' is usually a language that did not succeed politically. Or, returning to an observation made at the beginning of this chapter, a language can be seen as a dialect with an army and a navy! The boundaries between languages, and the classification of dialects, have invariably followed the politics of state-making rather than the other way around (Billig, 1995; see also Gramsci, 1971; Bakhtin, 1981; Harris, 1981). An inevitable corollary is that the status of languages and dialects may also change as the result of changes in nation-state formation. In the former Czechoslovakia, for example, a common language was deemed to be spoken. However, with the break-up of the former nation-state into the Czech Republic and Slovakia, language differences are now being promoted (Tabouret-Keller, 1997). An even more recent example of this process can be seen in the former Yugoslavia with the nascent re-establishment of distinct Serbian and Croatian language varieties in place of Serbo-Croat (Jakšić, 1995: Grant, 1997). As Grant observes, this has been facilitated, in turn, by the fact that Serbo-Croat was itself the rather artificial product of the Yugoslav federation. In order to balance the two major language constituencies it represented, it was spoken in its Serbian form, but used the Roman alphabet in written form (as Croatian does). Despite attempts to make it the 'national' language of Yugoslavia, its use never reached much beyond the armed forces and diplomatic services.

The legitimation of a language variety is thus an important first step in the political creation of a 'national' language. Moreover, it is a process bestowed upon only a privileged few since, as we saw in the Introduction, of the 6000 or so living languages contained within approximately 200 nation-states, fewer than a hundred actually currently enjoy official status. Even so, legitimation of a language is not, in itself, enough to ensure a central role for that language variety within the nation-state, since it is possible to legitimise a language without this having much influence on its actual use. We saw this clearly demonstrated in the case of Irish, for example. Crucially, what is needed, in addition, is the institutionalisation of the language variety within civil society. Indeed, this may be the more important aspect. By this, the language variety comes to be accepted, or 'taken for granted' in a wide range of social, cultural and linguistic domains or contexts, both formal and informal. The degree to which a language variety comes to be institutionalised in this way will also have a significant bearing on the subsequent status attached to the language in question and, by extension, its speakers. In effect, as Bourhis (1984) has convincingly argued, an ethnic group's cultural vitality, especially its linguistic vitality, is closely related to the degree of institutional support it enjoys. Likewise, Giles et al. (1977) have argued – in a broadly consonant, albeit more elaborate position – that ethnolinguistic vitality is based on a combination of the following components: economic status, self-perceived social status, sociohistorical factors and demographic factors (including institutional support). I will explore some of these other dimensions of ethnolinguistic vitality in my ensuing discussion of Bourdieu's notions of linguistic markets and symbolic violence.

The result of this joint process of legitimation and institutionalisation is to *privilege* a particular language variety over others; imbuing it, in the process, with high status. Not only this, but the privileging of the language becomes *normalised* – it is simply accepted or taken for granted. Consequently, speakers of the dominant language variety are immediately placed at an advantage in both accessing and benefiting from the civic culture of the nation-state. A dominant language group usually controls the crucial authority in the areas of administration, politics, education and the economy, and gives preference to those with a command of that language. Meanwhile, other language groups are limited in their language use to specific domains, usually solely private, and are thus left with the choice of renouncing their social ambitions, assimilating, or resisting in order to gain greater access to the public realm (Nelde, 1997). If language conflict results, this is attributable, at least to some degree, to the differential social status and preferential treatment of the dominant language by the state and within civil society, and the related stigmatisation of other varieties. Indeed, the dynamics of ethnic tension involving language, leading in some cases to political conflict, occur most often *not* when language compromises are made or language rights recognised, but where they have been historically avoided, suppressed or ignored (de Varennes, 1996a). The ongoing linguistic and political tensions in Canada and Belgium provide a case in point here. These two examples are often cited as clear evidence of the inherent instability of multilingual states. However, in contrast, much of the present political instability in these nation-states is attributable to the long-standing *denial* of specific language rights to French and Flemish speakers respectively, and the related socioeconomic and sociopolitical disadvantages that these groups have experienced as a result (for further discussion of Belgium, see Chapter 5; for Québec, see Chapter 6).

Such linguistic and political tensions are exacerbated by the continued assumption that the civic culture of the nation-state is somehow neutral and, relatedly, that the adoption of a national language depoliticises that particular language variety. Yet, as I have argued, the establishment of a state-endowed or 'national' language must be regarded as an inherently deliberate (and deliberative) political act; an act, moreover, that advantages some individuals and groups at the expense of others. Fernand de Varennes summarises the processes and its implications thus:

> By imposing a language requirement, the state shows a definite preference towards some individuals on the basis of language . . . In other words, the imposition of a single language for use in state activities and services is by no means a neutral act, since:

1   The state's chosen language becomes a condition for the full access to a number of services, resources and privileges, such as education or public employment . . .

2   Those for whom the chosen state speech is not the primary language are thus treated differently from those for whom it is: the latter have the advantage or benefit of receiving the state's largesse in their primary tongue, whereas the former do not and find themselves in a more or less disadvantaged position . . . Whether it is for employment in state institutions . . . or the need to translate or obtain assistance . . . a person faced with not being able to use his primary language *assumes a heavier burden.*

(1996a: 86–87; my emphasis)

The public legitimation of a language, and its associated institutionalisation in particular domains, thus become crucial to the ongoing maintenance of the dominant ethnie's cultural and linguistic hegemony within the nation-state. Relatedly, without these same processes being applied to minority languages, it is difficult to envisage a long-term future for minority-language groups in the modern world of nation-states (Nelde et al., 1996). Given the spread of standardised education, the associated literacy demands of the labour force, and the inevitable and widespread interaction required in dealing with state agencies, any language which is not widely used in the public realm becomes so marginalised as to be inconsequential. Using a particular language solely in the home domain, for example, limits its ultimate usefulness since speakers will be unable to deal adequately with the interpenetration of other domains such as talking about work or school at home (Clyne, 1997). The increasing marginalisation of a language in turn limits the linguistic functions of the language itself while the latter, recursively, contributes further to the language's marginalisation. As Florian Coulmas argues: 'Today the future of many languages is uncertain not only because their functional range is scaled down, but because they are never used for, and adapted to, newly emerging functions which are associated with another language . . . Lack of functional expansion is thus a correlate and counterpart of scaled-down use' (1992: 170). Such languages may persist among a small elite, as we have seen demonstrated in the case of Irish, or in a ritualised form, but not as a living and developing language of a flourishing culture (Kymlicka, 1995a).

Linguistic markets and symbolic violence

To explore further the implications of language legitimation and institutionalisation for ethnolinguistic minorities, I want to turn again to the work of

Pierre Bourdieu. Bourdieu has written widely, though disparately, on language, and his work in this regard includes the two seminal essays 'Le fétichisme de la langue' (Bourdieu and Boltanski, 1975) and 'The economy of linguistic exchanges' (1977). Where his thoughts on language (and linguistics) are perhaps most clearly articulated, however, is in *Ce Que Parler Veut Dire* (1982) and its English-language adaptation *Language and Symbolic Power* (1991). His principal concern in these various accounts is to situate language in its proper sociohistorical context. In this regard, he is particularly scathing of the preoccupation in modern linguistics with analysing language in isolation from the social conditions in which it is used. As he comments ironically of this process: 'bracketing out the social . . . allows language or any other symbolic object to be treated like an end in itself, [this] contributed considerably to the success of structural linguistics, for it endowed the "pure" exercises that characterise a purely internal and formal analysis with the charm of a game devoid of consequences' (1991: 34).

For Bourdieu, the inherent formalism of so much modern linguistics rests on a central distinction between the internal form of the language – a 'language system', in effect – and its outworking in speech. This distinction, in turn, arises from the conception of language as a 'universal treasure', freely available to all – a view that was first articulated by Auguste Comte and subsequently adopted by the founding fathers of modern linguistics, Ferdinand de Saussure and Noam Chomsky. De Saussure (1974) invokes the distinction via his celebrated comparison between 'langue' and 'parole', while Chomsky's (1972) notions of 'competence' and 'performance' reflect a similar conception. This is not to suggest that de Saussure's and Chomsky's conceptions are indistinguishable – Chomsky's model, for example, is more dynamic in its attempt to incorporate the generative capacities of competent speakers. However, both approaches rest on the notion that language can be constituted as an autonomous and homogeneous object, amenable to linguistic study (Thompson, 1991). An allied critique of this preoccupation with linguistic formalism at the expense of a wider analysis of the social and political conditions in which language comes to be used can also be found in Vološinov (1973: 77–82) and Mey (1985). Vološinov argued cogently against the 'abstract objectivism' of structural linguistics, as represented by de Saussure, suggesting it created a radical disjuncture between the idea of a language system and actual language history. Mey observes 'that linguistic models, no matter how innocent and theoretical they may seem to be, not only have distinct economical, social and political presuppositions, but also consequences . . . Linguistic (and other) inequalities don't cease to exist simply because their socioeconomic causes are swept under the linguistic rug' (1985: 26).

Bourdieu describes the resulting orthodoxy, which posits a particular set of linguistic practices as a normative model of 'correct' usage, as the 'illusion of linguistic communism that haunts all linguistic theory' (1991: 43). By this,

Bourdieu argues, the linguist is able to produce the illusion of a common or standard language while ignoring the sociohistorical conditions which have established this particular set of linguistic practices as dominant and legitimate – usually, as we have seen, as the result of nation-state formation. However, this dominant and legitimate language – this *victorious* language, in effect – is simply taken for granted by linguists (Thompson, 1991; see also Mühlhäusler, 1996):

> To speak of *the* language, without further specification, as linguists do, is tacitly to accept the *official* definition of the *official* language of a political unit. This language is the one which, within the territorial limits of that unit, imposes itself on the whole population as the only legitimate language . . . The official language is bound up with the state, both in its genesis and its social uses . . . this state language becomes the theoretical norm against which all linguistic practices are objectively measured.
>
> (Bourdieu, 1991: 45; emphases in original)

In addition to habitus (see Chapter 1), Bourdieu employs a number of key concepts that illuminate the processes that underpin language domination and legitimation. These include 'linguistic capital', 'linguistic markets', 'misrecognition' and 'symbolic violence'. Linguistic capital, in Bourdieu's terms, describes the 'value' given to one's linguistic habitus in particular linguistic markets. In a given linguistic market (such as the civic culture of the nation-state), some habitus are valued more highly than others. Accordingly, different speakers will have different amounts of linguistic capital depending on their ability to meet the requirements of the particular linguistic market concerned. Moreover, the distribution of linguistic capital is closely related to the distribution of other forms of capital (economic, cultural, etc.) which define the location of an individual within the social space (Thompson, 1991; cf. Ó Riagáin, 1997; Collins, 1999; Norton, 2000). Those whose habitus are consonant with the demands of the linguistic market are thereby able to secure an advantage, or 'profit of distinction', since the linguistic capital required is far from equally distributed. Concomitantly, those whose habitus are assigned a lesser value by the market come to *accept* this diminution as legitimate, a process which Bourdieu has described as 'symbolic violence'. Bourdieu argues here that symbolic violence occurs when a particular (linguistic) habitus, along with the hierarchical relations of power in which it is embedded, is 'misrecognised' (méconnaissance) as legitimate and tacitly accepted – *even by those who do not have access to it* – as a 'natural' rather than a socially and politically constructed phenomenon. To understand the nature of symbolic violence, Bourdieu argues, it is crucial to see that it presupposes a kind of active complicity, or implicit consent, on the part of those subjected to it; a process, in effect, which induces 'the holders of dominated linguistic competencies to collaborate in the destruction of their [own] instruments of expression' (1991: 49). While by no means limited to such a comparison, Bourdieu's conceptual analysis is clearly helpful here in explicating the unequal relationship that exists between 'majority' and 'minority' languages and the subsequent devaluation of the latter by both majority *and* minority speakers. As he observes:

> In order for one mode of expression among others (a particular language in the case of bilingualism, a particular use of language in the case of a society divided into classes) to *impose* itself as the only legitimate one, the linguistic market has to be *unified* and the different dialects (of class, region or ethnic group) have to be measured practically against the legitimate language or usage. Integration into a single 'linguistic community', which is the product of the political domination that is endlessly reproduced by institutions capable of imposing universal recognition of the dominant language, is the condition for the establishment of relations of linguistic domination.
>
> (1991: 46–47; my emphases)

The single linguistic community, or the unified linguistic market, to which Bourdieu refers is most clearly represented in and by the homogeneous civic culture of the modern nation-state. Indeed, the triumph of official languages and the suppression of their potential rivals are prominent characteristics of the construction of statehood and the achievement of national hegemony, as we have seen. Bourdieu illustrates the particular processes of language domination involved here by tracing the emergence of his own language of French as the 'national' language of post-revolutionary France. It therefore seems appropriate to examine briefly the French example before drawing this chapter to a close.

Vive la France: the construction of la langue légitime

> I express my homage to the lay, Republican school system which often imposed the use of French against all the forces of social and even religious obscurantism . . . It is time for us all to be French through that language. If it is necessary to teach another language to our children, let us not make them waste time with dialects they will only ever use in their villages.
>
> (*Journal Officiel*, 15.4.1994; cited in Ager, 1999: 20)

The above comment was made in the French National Assembly during discussion of the Toubon Act, which, on being passed in 1994, made the use of French obligatory in five domains: education, employment, the media, commerce and public meetings (see also below). The sentiments of the speaker, and of the Act to which it refers, reflect, writ large, the modern French nation-state's historical and ongoing preoccupation with legitimating and institutionalising French as the 'common' national language, and its related vitiation of minority languages. This dual process was most starkly demonstrated at the time of the French Revolution, and has subsequently been systematically reinforced, as the speaker suggests, via the French state education system. However, it was also present, at least in incipient form, well before the advent of the Revolution.

Prior to the French Revolution of 1789, three broad language groups were present in the territory we now know as France. The Langue d'Oïl, comprising a wider range of dialects, was spoken in the North. Of these, the Francien dialect, spoken in and around Paris, was the actual antecedent of modern French. The Langue d'Oc (Occitan), also comprising a wide range of dialects, was spoken in the South. And in central and eastern France, Franco-Provençal was spoken. But not only that, Basque was spoken in the southwest, as was Breton in Brittany, Flemish around Lille, German in Alsace-Lorraine, Catalan in Perpignan, and Corsican (a dialect of Italian and Napoleon's first language) in Corsica (Ager, 1999). In addition, Latin was the administrative language, at least until the sixteenth century (see below), although it was as such largely confined to the church, the university and the royal administration (Johnson, 1993). Premodern 'France', like so many other administrations prior to the rise of political nationalism, was thus resolutely multilingual. As Peyre notes, citing the observations of the sixteenth-century chancellor Michel de l'Hôpital, linguistic divisions were not regarded as a danger to the kingdom. Rather, the key factors of unity were 'one faith, one law, one king': 'What the king demanded above all was loyalty . . . It mattered little then, *up to a certain point*, that custom and usage differed from one province to another' (1933: 10, 16; my emphasis).

The caveat 'up to a certain point' is an important one here because the sixteenth century was also to see the beginnings of a countermovement against multilingualism which would reach its apogee soon after the French Revolution. The first sign of this can be found in the (1538) Ordonnance de Villers-Cotterêts, issued by King Louis XII. Article III of the Act made the 'maternal French tongue' (actually the Francien dialect of the Langue d'Oïl, spoken by the French court) the language of the law. The initial intent of the decree was not to make French the 'national' language – this, as we have seen, is peculiar to the political nationalism of subsequent centuries. It was simply to ensure that the language of the King's court would be used in the quarters significant to his power (E. Weber, 1976). In this sense, the Act's principal target was the replacement of Latin as the language of administration. Nonetheless, the decree's admonition to transact and record all public acts in 'French' presaged the inexorable rise of modern French. In Benedict

Anderson's terms, French came to be seen as the new 'language of power' (cf. Chapter 2). As a result, French began to replace Latin *and* other languages – both in court usage and in much state administration (Lodge, 1993; Schiffman, 1996) – although the various regional languages were still the normal means of communication for the wider population. From the sixteenth century to the time of the French Revolution, most of France thus operated in diglossia, with French colonising the higher-status public-language domains, while other languages were increasingly confined to the lower-status private domains (Ager, 1999).

The establishment in 1635 of the Académie Française was to further reinforce the rise of French in the sixteenth century. Established by Cardinal Richelieu, the principal aim of the Académie was one of corpus planning – to systematically codify, standardise and 'purify' French. The Académie pursued these aims with zeal – as, indeed, it still does to this day. Its early work led to the publication of the *Grammaire Générale et Raisonnée* in 1660 and the first French language dictionary in 1694. More significantly perhaps, the work of the Académie also reinforced a nascent, albeit growing, belief at that time 'in the universality of standard French, in its innate clarity, precision, logic and elegance, and in its superiority over any other language and certainly over any . . . regional language' (Ager, 1999: 23).

Both these developments in the sixteenth century were to foreshadow the eventual proscription of other languages and dialects within France, most notably in the aftermath of the French Revolution. It is thus somewhat ironic that it was only during the early stages of the Revolution that the linguistic diversity of France was fully apprehended. A linguistic survey carried out by the abbé Henri Grégoire in 1790 revealed that over 30 'patois' were spoken in France (for political reasons, he was reluctant to accord them the status of languages; see below). More pertinently perhaps, he concluded that as few as three million people – not more than a tenth of the actual population – could actually speak French with any degree of fluency (Johnson, 1993).

The initial response to this linguistic diversity was cautious magnanimity. For example, the new Assembly agreed on 14 January 1790 a policy of translating decrees into various 'idioms' and 'dialects' in order better to disseminate Republican ideas among the majority non-French-speaking population (Grillo, 1989). But this was soon to change. If we recall the French historian Michelet, and his comment in Chapter 1 advocating the 'sacrifice of the diverse interior nationalities to the great nationality', we can begin to understand why. In short, it soon became apparent to the Jacobins that the ideal of the Revolution lay in uniformity and the extinction of particularisms. For the Revolutionaries, regional languages were increasingly regarded as parochial vestiges of the ancien régime, the sooner forgotten the better. This was reflected in their pejorative labelling as 'patois' rather than as languages. As Bourdieu observes of this process, 'measured de facto against the single standard of the "common" language, they are found wanting and cast into the outer darkness of *regionalisms*'. As a result, 'a system of *sociologically pertinent* linguistic oppositions tends to be constituted which has nothing in common with the system of *linguistically pertinent* linguistic oppositions' (1991: 54; emphases in original).

In contrast, French was seen as the embodiment of civilisation and progress. Consequently, the adoption of French as the single national language, representing and reflecting the interests of the new revolutionary order, was increasingly regarded as an essential foundation for the new Republic and its advocacy of égalité. As the Jacobins came to insist: 'The unity of the Republic demands the unity of speech . . . Speech must be one, like the Republic' (cited in E. Weber, 1976: 72). Bourdieu comments that this perceived imperative 'was not only a question of communication but of gaining recognition for a new *language of authority*, with its new political vocabulary, its terms of address and reference, its metaphors, its euphemisms and the representation of the social world which it conveys' (1991: 48; my emphasis).

The obvious corollary to this also came to be accepted and actively promoted – that the ongoing maintenance of other languages was specifically opposed to the aims of the Revolution. Indeed, Barère, in his Report of 1794, went so far as to assert:

> La fédéralisme et la superstition parlent bas-breton; l'émigration et la haine de la République parlent allemand; la contre-révolution parle l'italien, et le fanatisme parle le basque. Cassons ces instruments de dommage et d'erreur. [Federalism and superstition speak Basque; emigration and hatred of the Republic speak German; counter-revolution speaks Italian, and fanaticism speaks Basque. Let us destroy these instruments of damage and error.]
>
> (quoted in de Certeau et al., 1975; 299)

These sentiments were also reflected, albeit somewhat less iconoclastically, in the final report of the abbé Grégoire on the linguistic state of the new republic. This report was eventually published in 1794, four years after the survey had been commissioned, and concerned itself principally with corpus issues – on 'perfecting' the French language (in a similar way to the Académie). However, its overall position on other languages in France is clearly indicated by its subtitle – 'Sur la nécessité et les moyens d'anéantir les patois et d'universaliser l'usage de la langue française' ['On the need and ways to annihilate dialects and universalise the use of French']. It should come as no surprise then that Grégoire went on to conclude that:

> Unity of language is an integral part of the Revolution. If we are ever to banish superstition and bring men closer to the truth, to develop talent

and encourage virtue, to mould all citizens into a national whole, to simplify the mechanism of the political machine and make it function more
smoothly, we must have a common language.

(cited in Grillo, 1989: 24)

The Grégoire Report proved a watershed. Earlier attempts at translation
were quickly dispensed with in order to expedite this vision of a brave new
world, represented in and through French. More importantly, the legitimation and institutionalisation of French came to be inextricably intertwined in
the minds of the Jacobins with the active destruction of all other languages.
But there was still a problem. Such was the linguistic diversity highlighted
by Grégoire that it could not be easily or quickly displaced. Even as late as
1863, official figures indicated that a quarter of the country's population,
including half the children who would reach adulthood in the last quarter of
the nineteenth century, still spoke no French (E. Weber, 1976). What to do?
The answer lay in a combination of legal enforcement of the language, via a
series of court decisions requiring the use of French in all legal documents
(see Grau, 1992) and, more significantly, a central role for education.

The use of education as a key, perhaps *the* key agency of linguistic standardisation (some might call it linguistic genocide), began as early as 1793. At
that time, French schools were established in the German-speaking Alsace
region, while the ongoing use of German was banned (Grillo, 1989). This
was to provide the template for the use of French education throughout the
nineteenth (and twentieth) century. A central goal of the hussards noirs, the
Republic's teachers, was to eradicate all regional languages, which were by
then regarded as worthless, barbarous, corrupt and devoid of interest
(Bourdieu, 1982). Given the ongoing linguistic diversity, this process took
some time. It was not until the establishment of a fully secularised, compulsory and free primary system in the 1880s that education really began
to have its full effect, principally through the formal proscription of all other
languages from the school. But even prior to that time it had not been for
want of trying. A poignant illustration of this is provided by a prefect in
the Department of Finistère in Brittany who, in 1845, formally exhorted
teachers: 'Above all remember, gentlemen, that your sole function is to kill
the Breton language' (cited in Quiniou-Tempereau, 1988: 31–32).

This state-led 'ideology of contempt' (Grillo, 1989) towards minority
languages has resulted in their inexorable decline in France over the last two
centuries to the point where less than two per cent of the French population
now speak these as a first language (see Héran, 1993; Nelde et al., 1996). It
has also at the same time entrenched deep into the French national psyche a
view that the promotion, and even simply the maintenance, of minority
languages (and cultures) are fundamentally at odds with the principles and
objectives of the French state. As a result, there have been remarkably few
exceptions to this assimilationist imperative in French language and education

policy. One such exception is the (1951) Deixonne Act, which gave formal status in education to four regional languages: Basque, Breton, Catalan and Occitan (see Schiffman, 1996). The Act was limited though in that it did not involve the *active* promotion of these languages, merely *permitting* the languages to be taught in a limited way within schools. (I discuss the distinction between active and permissive language and education rights more fully in Chapter 5.) Moreover, the Act itself was not actually implemented until 1969!

The advent of the Socialist government elected in 1997, however, has seen an apparent change in direction, or at least a discernible shift in emphasis. Almost immediately on taking office, the government commissioned a report on France's regional languages – the first time that any French government had commissioned a report in this area. The Poignant Report, named after its author, was subsequently published in July 1998. While the report continued to uphold the primacy of French, it also advocated that 'the French Republic must acknowledge the existence on its territory of regional languages and cultures which are granted rights in accordance with the laws and regulations. The latter do not pose any threat to national identity' (cited in Louarn, 1998: 5). The report argued that the protection and promotion of France's regional languages was important because such languages constitute an important part of France's cultural and linguistic heritage. However, it also argued that some formal accommodation of regional languages might forestall the rise of potentially troublesome regionalisms at a later point, particularly in light of a growing emphasis on regionalism and devolution within the European Union (Ager, 1999: 38–39; see also Chapter 7). As Poignant concludes: 'The [21st] century will have to deal with strong claims to regional identity. If this republic does not act in response, others will' (see Henley, 1999).

These developments suggest the nascent emergence of a more tolerant approach to minority languages within France. But even this may be overstated. Such is the legacy of French language and education policy that effecting even limited changes in this area remains a process fraught with difficulty. An obvious example of the significant obstacles that still remain in the way of adopting a more tolerant language policy in France is the (1994) Toubon Act. The Act is principally a response to a growing fear of the impact of English as the current world language (see Chapter 6) on French speakers, both within France and beyond it. In particular, the growing fashion for English words, or what has come to be known as 'franglais', was deemed to be such a threat as to necessitate this specific legislative measure in addition to the general policing role performed by the Académie Française. Accordingly, the Toubon Act built upon a previous legislative measure, the (1975) Bas-Lauriol Bill, which was never fully implemented. Among a wide range of measures, it decreed that consumer goods must not be sold without a set of instructions in French, all-English advertisements must not be published either in the French press or in French cinemas, and bilingual signs must not give less prominence to the French part of their message.

It is not hard to see that the Act's aim 'to guarantee to French people the right to use their language and to ensure that it is used in certain circumstances of their everyday and professional life' (cited in Ager, 1999: 8) only serves to reinforce the ongoing legitimation and institutionalisation of French. As such, it would seem to offer little, if anything, for France's minority-language speakers. This is reinforced by the clear belief expressed in the Act that 'the mastery of French . . . is part of the fundamental aims of education' (cited in Ager, 1999: 65). Of course, this conclusion was even more baldly stated by the French Parliamentarian whose comments on the Act began this section. Plus ça change, or so it would seem.

Similar obstacles to any significant change can also be clearly seen in France's varied responses (as yet unresolved) to the formal ratification of the European Charter for Regional and Minority Languages (see Wright, 1999, 2000). The Charter, adopted in 1992 by the Council of Europe, aims to promote the greater formal recognition of regional and minority languages within the European Community and, in so doing, to extend the provision of bilingual education (see also Chapter 5). By December 1998, 18 of the 40 member states of the European Council had signed the charter, but not France. This was because in 1996 the Charter had been declared unconstitutional by the French Council of State (the Constitutional Court). The Council of State concluded that adoption of the Charter would result in the recognition of minorities as *groups* – an anathema to the Republican constitutional tradition – and that it would contravene Article 2 of the Constitution that stipulates French as the 'language of the Republic'. However, as a result of a recommendation in the Poignant Report, a further legal opinion was obtained in 1998. This opinion adopted a more favourable stance, indicating that the minimum requirement necessary to sign up to the Charter – acceptance of 35 of its nearly 100 clauses – could be reached. The opinion also included the attendant observation that a minor change to Article 2 of the French Constitution would be all that would be required to ratify it.

The subsequent expectation was that France would duly sign and ratify the Charter. This would give formal recognition for the first time not only to its historical regional languages but also to the languages spoken in its dependent territories, notably Creoles. Even so, this recognition would be strictly limited. While bilingual provisions within education and the media would be facilitated and extended, French would remain the language of administration and the law. To date, it has achieved the first, signing the Charter in May 1999, but not the second. Within a month of signing the Charter, the French Constitutional Court again ruled that ratification would be unconstitutional, and when the Prime Minister, Lionel Jospin, moved as recommended to amend the Constitution in light of this, Jacques Chirac, the President, refused. Chirac's position has played well among Republican purists who retain an almost visceral fear of minority languages, arguing in a similar way to Schlesinger (see Chapter 3) that it will result in the inevitable 'balkanisation' of France. Suffice it to say that the ongoing debates in France continue to highlight the tenuous and sublimated position of minority languages there.

Legitimating and institutionalising minority languages

But the French example also offers us a useful means of critique. The rise of French provides us with one of the clearest examples of the centrality of power relations and associated language status in the construction of national languages. By implication, it also defuses the charge often levelled against many minority languages, and their related advocacy, concerning the arbitrary and/or artificial link between language and identity. After all, one cannot have it both ways. If there is a certain arbitrariness to the construction of national languages, one might expect a similar pattern to be evident among minority languages also. Moreover, in neither instance do questions surrounding a language's provenance necessarily diminish the affective ties associated with that language. For all their constructedness, evolution and change, both national *and* minority languages remain, for many of their speakers, important indicators of individual and collective identity. To accept this principle for one and not the other is clearly unjust.

Instead, we need to change the terms of the debate. If, as I have argued, the legitimation and institutionalisation of a language are the key to its long-term survival in the modern world, there is a strong moral (and political) argument for providing national-minority languages with these very same attributes. In so doing, national-minority ethnies would be accorded the necessary cultural and linguistic capital to embark on their own process of linguistic modernisation; a modernisation initiated and shaped *from within* rather than from without as has largely been the case until now. Such a process does not preclude individuals from continuing to exercise their own language choices, although, given the continuing balance in favour of dominant languages, and the questions this raises about so-called 'voluntary' language shift, the potential for conflict inevitably remains. Perhaps only when the new-found status of minority languages becomes firmly established might the tendency for individuals to shift to a majority language begin to change. Meanwhile, the association of modernity with one 'common' language and culture needs to be recognised as the nationalist myth-making that it is. Only if language change is separated from the current hegemonic imperatives of the nation-state can the prospect of more representational multinational and multilingual states be secured. The politics of language need not always remain subsumed by the language of politics. As Tollefson concludes:

the struggle to adopt minority languages within dominant institutions such as education, the law, and government, as well as the struggle over language rights, constitute efforts to legitimise the minority group itself and to alter its relationship to the state. Thus while language planning reflects relationships of power, it can also be used to transform them.

(1991: 202)

Changing the language preferences of the state and civil society, or at least broadening them, would better reflect the cultural and linguistic demographics of most of today's multinational (and polyethnic) states. Not only this, it could significantly improve the life chances of those national-minority individuals and groups who are presently disadvantaged in their access to, and participation in, public services, employment and education. As I have consistently argued, linguistic consequences cannot be separated from socioeconomic and sociopolitical consequences, and vice versa. This holds true too, of course, for other ethnic-minority groups. Indeed, in concentrating once again here on national-minority ethnies, I am not wishing to ignore or diminish the language rights attributable to these other groups. After all, the strong arguments in favour of the link between cultural and linguistic identities, which I have outlined in this chapter, clearly point to the right of *all* ethnic minorities to retain and maintain their traditionally associated language should they so wish (see also Chapter 5). Likewise, changing 'the rules of the game' that automatically presume an exclusive relationship between dominant languages and modernity should make the process of maintaining minority languages a little easier. However, as I have also consistently argued throughout this account, one can distinguish the rights of national-minority ethnies from ethnic-minority groups in relation to their *formal* inclusion in, and representation within, the civic culture of the nation-state. As such, the specific emphasis here on the legitimation and institutionalisation of minority languages is necessarily limited to national minorities.

Even so, achieving a greater recognition and acceptance of the languages of national-minority ethnies, let alone those of other ethnic minorities, remains a formidable task. As France illustrates all too starkly, the idea of national (and linguistic) congruence within the current nation-state system remains as deeply entrenched as ever. Crucially, it also continues to be rigorously defended by those who benefit most from it – i.e., majority-language speakers. Indeed, in the long term, one must always concede the possibility of defeat – given the weight of the various forces that continue to arraign themselves against minority ethnies and the languages they speak. Nonetheless, I wish to argue in the next chapter that rethinking the nation-state along more plurilingual lines, and a reconceived role for education within this, also remain real – albeit, in many instances, still distant – possibilities.

Notes

1 Discussions on the Sapir-Whorf theory in linguistics, like discussions of linguistic nationalism in sociology, tend towards caricature on the basis that much of the analysis is predicated solely on the more extreme versions of the position. Concomitantly, the result in linguistic commentary has often been the instant and fatuous dismissal of the central interconnections between language, culture and thought. In the process, much gets distorted. For example, the linguistic merits of Whorf's work have been consistently misrepresented. Likewise, the political motivation of his struggle to support a view of difference and diversity – developed principally in response to the genocide of Native American cultures and languages – has been frequently overlooked (Fishman, 1989d; see also Pennycook, 1994).

2 The term 'Gaeltacht' applies to those Irish-speaking communities that are situated mainly in rural coastal areas in the northwest, west and south of Ireland. It should be noted though that the term is now somewhat problematic since, traditionally, the Gaeltacht was viewed as a composite geographical area whereas currently many parts of Ireland which were once part of the Gaeltacht are no longer so (see Ó Riagáin, 1997; Ch. 3). Accordingly, the plural term 'Gaeltachtaí' is increasingly used to describe present Irish-speaking communities (Ó Gadhra, 1988).

3 Diglossia can be defined as the pattern of language behaviour within a bilingual community where one language is associated with certain (usually high-status) domains of social activity (commerce, for example) while the other language is usually associated with low-status domains (such as family life). Ó Murchú (1988) observes that this appears to be the only instance of bilingual diglossia in Irish history.

4 The sometimes profound cultural dislocation that accompanies language shift for the individual in this context is illustrated well by the personal accounts of Hoffman (1989) and Rodriguez (1983, 1993). Grosjean (1982) also provides examples of the psychological costs of language loss to the individual.

5 This disparity is highlighted in the Irish context by the contrasting efforts of a small bilingual elite in Dublin, who were at the heart of nationalist efforts to promote the Irish language, and the rest of the population, who were far more interested in acquiring English.

6 For a critique of the 'self-interested elite' position with respect to nationalist movements generally, see Brubaker (1998: 289–292).

7 Admittedly, the sophistication of those who argue this position varies widely. John Edwards, for example, provides us with a considered and nuanced defence of this particular view of language shift, although obviously I continue to remain unconvinced by it. However, far cruder versions of this general thesis are evident elsewhere. There is, of course, Schlesinger's account of bilingualism, discussed in Chapter 3. But for one of the crudest (and crassest) of all, see the various contributions in Frost (1997).

8 It should be pointed out, however, that many so-called 'national' languages hold de facto rather than de jure status (see Ruiz, 1990). In the UK, for

example, English is the only accepted language of the state (except in Wales, where Welsh has recently been recognised as having equivalent status; see Chapter 7) but the role of English is not constitutionally or legislatively enshrined. A similar situation pertains in the USA, although there have been recent attempts by pressure groups to have English made the only official language (see the discussion of the 'English Only' movement in Chapter 6).

5

Language, education and minority rights

In the preceding chapter, we encountered an apparent conundrum in relation to the role that education plays in language maintenance and shift. On the one hand, the example of Ireland demonstrates that, however much one might want it to, education is not sufficient in itself to stem societal change. Indeed, a consistent weakness of many minority-language movements has been an overoptimistic view of what education can accomplish in halting, let alone reversing, language shift (see Fishman, 1991; J. Edwards, 1985, 1994; Drapeau and Corbeil, 1996). In short, the fate of a language cannot be borne on the back of education alone.

And yet to dismiss education as simply peripheral to the process of minority-language maintenance is also clearly wrong (cf. J. Edwards, 1985: Ch. 5). After all, education is recognised as a key institution – perhaps *the* key institution – in the apparatus of the modern nation-state, a point that is acknowledged by a wide variety of sociological and educational commentators (see May, 1994a: Ch. 2). To take just one prominent example, Durkheim saw education as a pivotal agency in the inculcation of societal (i.e., nation-state) values, not least because of his own stated commitment to the French Republican tradition. As he argues:

> Society can survive only if there exists among its members a sufficient degree of *homogeneity*; education perpetuates and reinforces this homogeneity by fixing in the child, from the beginning, *the essential similarities* that collective life demands.
>
> (1956: 70; my emphasis)

Durkheim's observation accords closely with the discussion in Chapter 2 of the key role education has played historically in establishing the homogeneous civic culture of the nation-state, a process which has led to the advent of much minority-language shift in the first place. As Gellner (1983) has outlined, the nationalist principle of 'one state, one culture' saw the state, *via its education system*, increasingly identified with a specific language and culture – invariably, that of the majority ethnic group, or dominant ethnie. Indeed, a well-defined, educationally sanctioned and unified linguistic culture was seen as a prerequisite for modernity, a basis of political legitimacy, and a means of shared cultural identity. The example of France, discussed in the previous chapter, clearly illustrates how education was employed to promote a state-sanctioned language, at the expense of other varieties, as a central part of a modernising nationalist project.

If education is used so effectively to these assimilationist ends, its significance as an alternative vehicle for minority-language aspirations should not therefore be underestimated. Those who dismiss the significance of education in this latter regard usually do so on the basis that education cannot be reasonably expected to cater for the language and identity needs of all pupils (see J. Edwards, 1985: 130–131). The Swann Report on multicultural education in Britain clearly outlines this position when it concludes: 'the role of education cannot be, and cannot be expected to be, to reinforce the values, beliefs, and cultural identity which each child brings to school' (1985: 321). However, this begs a key question: given that education accomplishes this for majority group members – whose cultural and linguistic habitus are viewed as consonant with the school's – why can it not do so for minority group members as well? As I have argued consistently elsewhere (May, 1994a, 1995, 1999a), there is a strong argument for schools extending and reconstituting what counts as 'accepted' and 'acceptable' cultural and linguistic knowledge. Moreover, the charge that such recognition would inevitably lead to a rampant cultural and linguistic relativism does not necessarily follow. As we shall see, the differing rights attributable to various minority groups, discussed in Chapters 2 and 3, can be applied with respect to language and education. In short, greater ethnolinguistic *democracy* does not necessarily imply ethnolinguistic *equality* (Fishman, 1995b) – reasonable limits can still be drawn. Likewise, a recognition of minority habitus as cultural and linguistic capital in schools can coexist, albeit not always easily, with an ongoing valuing of a common or 'core' curriculum (see May, 1994a, 1995).

These arguments have been most clearly articulated in recent years by a wide range of ethnic, cultural, linguistic and religious minority groups within education. The advocacy of such groups has focused on two key areas of concern. The first is that, despite their stated intentions to the contrary, previous educational policies have demonstrably failed to address and mitigate the comparative social and educational disadvantages faced by such groups (see May, 1999b). While there are inevitably many intra- as well as intergroup differences here, a general pattern of differential status and achievement is clearly apparent among many minority groups. In short, minorities tend to be overrepresented in unfavourable social and educational indices in comparison with majority group members. As Stacy Churchill observes of this:

Policy-making about the education of minorities must cope with an overriding fact: *almost every jurisdiction in the industrialized world is failing adequately to meet the educational needs of a significant number of members of linguistic and cultural minorities . . . Measured against the criterion of ensuring linguistic and/or cultural survival in the long term, the shortfall is much more serious . . .*

(1986: 8; emphasis in original)

Churchill's concluding comment introduces the second key area of concern – whether an education which requires minority students to dispense with their ethnic, linguistic and/or cultural identities is necessarily an educational opportunity *worth wanting* (K. Howe, 1992).[1] Thus, even if social and educational advancement were to be forthcoming – and, as the first concern suggests, it most often is not – the individual and collective costs of such cultural and linguistic evisceration are increasingly regarded by minority groups as too high a price to pay (see also Chapter 4). Secada and Lightfoot (1993) observe, for example, that the purported 'trade-off' between minority cultures and languages and access to opportunity is increasingly being seen (and rejected) as uneven by minority groups: give up your language and culture and you *might* have opportunity. When the latter is not forthcoming, communal anger has developed in response to prior generations being duped by this promise.

This increasing disenchantment among minority groups, and a related unwillingness to continue to accept the status quo, have contributed to a growing, albeit still tentative, exploration of alternative educational approaches more accommodating of cultural and linguistic diversity. In what still stands as one of the most comprehensive and informed accounts of its kind, Stacy Churchill (1986) highlights these nascent developments by outlining the six principal policy responses to the educational and language needs of minority groups within the OECD. While he suggests that the differences between the various stages are not always clear cut, he attempts the following ranking (in ascending order) by the degree to which such policies recognise and incorporate minority cultures and languages.

- *Stage 1 (Learning Deficit)*: where the educational disadvantages faced by minority groups are associated with the use of the minority language. Accordingly, rapid transition to the majority language is advocated.
- *Stage 2 (Socially Linked Learning Deficit)*: sometimes but not always arrived at concurrently with Stage 1, this stage associates a minority group's educational disadvantage with family status. Additional/supplementary programmes are thus promoted which emphasise *adjustment* to the majority society.
- *Stage 3 (Learning Deficit from Social/Cultural Differences)*: most commonly associated with multicultural education, this stage assumes minority

educational disadvantage arises from the inability of the majority society – particularly the education system – to recognise, accept and view positively the minority culture. However, a multicultural approach does not usually include a commensurate recognition of the minority language.

- *Stage 4 (Learning Deficit from Mother Tongue Deprivation)*: while still linked to the notion of deficit, the need for support of the minority language is accepted, at least as a transitional measure. Accordingly, transitional bilingual education programmes are emphasised.

- *Stage 5 (Private Use Language Maintenance)*: recognises the right of national and ethnic minorities to maintain and develop their languages and cultures in private life to ensure these are not supplanted by the dominant culture and language. A group maintenance approach to bilingual education is the most usual policy response here.

- *Stage 6 (Language Equality)*: the granting of full official status to a national-minority language. This would include separate language provision in a range of public institutions, including schools, and widespread recognition and use in a range of social, institutional and language domains.

Educating for the majority

Stage 1 represents assimilation in its starkest form. For reasons already well rehearsed, it has historically been the predominant approach adopted by modern nation-states, and the mass education systems to which they gave rise. Such 'unitary language policies' (Grant, 1997) ignore or actively suppress minority languages, and view the latter as both a threat to the social mobility of the minority individual, and to the majoritarian controlled institutions of the nation-state.

These policies, again for obvious reasons, had their heyday in the nineteenth century. The Irish and French state education systems are two examples already discussed in Chapter 4. Other examples abound. The Welsh language was formally proscribed from schools in Wales via the (1870) Education Act enacted by the British government in London. This legislation was in turn the culmination of a long-standing vitiation of the Welsh language within Britain which dated back to the time of Henry VIII and the (1536) Act for the English Order, Habite and Language (see Chapter 7). In Aotearoa / New Zealand, a similar legislative pattern emerged in the nineteenth century with the (1847) Education Ordinance requiring that mission schools teach Māori children in English where previously they had taught in Māori. This was followed by the (1867) Native Schools Act, which established state educational provision for Māori and formalised an English-language-only policy (Walker, 1990; A. Durie, 1999; May, 1999c; see Chapter 8). Comparable educational legislation in Australia was enacted after the 1850s, leading to the 'linguistic genocide' of most Australian Aboriginal languages, the end results of which were briefly summarised in the previous chapter (see also Chapter 8).

These educational developments are not confined to the nineteenth century, however. Spain, under Franco's rule, prohibited the Catalan and Basque languages from all formal domains, including education, in favour of Castilian Spanish. These edicts, which were implemented just prior to the Second World War, were draconian to say the least and included the threat to exclude from the profession any teacher – even in private schools – who used a language other than Castilian. As stated in an order issued 18 May 1938: 'the Spain of Franco cannot tolerate aggressions against the unity of its language' (cited in de Varennes, 1996a: 22). With the death of Franco, and the return of democracy to Spain, these laws were revoked and a regional language structure implemented (see Chapter 7). However, other comparable processes of language restriction and/or proscription remain in force to this day.

One such example is Tibet, where, as recently as 1997, Chinese authorities proscribed the Tibetan language in Tibetan schools in favour of Mandarin Chinese. Ostensibly, this measure was aimed at 'improving' the educational attainment of Tibetan children. In reality, it was principally an attempt at curbing Tibet's nationalist aspirations for independence from China, not least because language, along with religion, remains a central feature of a separate Tibetan identity (*Independent*, 5 June 1997).

Another example is the ongoing repression of the Kurdish language within Turkey. Kurdish is an Indo-European language, specifically part of the north-western Iranian language family. As such, it is linguistically far more closely related to Farsi/Persian than to Turkish, an Altaic language. It continues to be spoken predominantly in the territory of Kurdistan, an area with long historical associations for the Kurds that encompasses parts of present-day Turkey, Iran, Iraq and Syria. There are approximately 35 million Kurdish speakers in total and it is currently estimated that, of the 15 million Kurds within Turkey, 3.9 million speak Kurdish as a first language. However, the actual numbers of those who can speak Kurdish in Turkey is much greater than this, due to widespread bilingualism among Kurds and Turks. The ongoing repression of the Kurdish language – in Turkey and elsewhere – does make it difficult though to provide accurate estimates here (see Baker and Prys Jones, 1998: 416–417; Skutnabb-Kangas, 2000: 61).

The active repression and proscription of Kurdish by the Turkish state forms part of a wider denial/rejection of Kurdish nationalist claims to be a distinct people, with attendant rights to secession, or at least greater autonomy. This proscriptive language policy was first enshrined in Atatürk's Constitution of 1923, and reiterated in the Turkish Constitution of 1982 (see Skutnabb-Kangas and Bucak, 1995; Kirisci and Winrow, 1997). In the early 1990s there appeared to be a relaxation of these long-standing proscriptive laws but by the late 1990s they had once again been reinforced. This move was presaged in March 1997 when secret Turkish interior ministry documents were made public which stated that 'administrative and legal measures should be taken against those attempting to propagate the Kurdish language' (*Guardian*, 29 March 1997). Criminal proceedings were subsequently implemented in 1998 against the Foundation for Kurdish Culture and Research – the first nongovernmental organisation (NGO) in Turkey with an overtly Kurdish identity – for its promotion of Kurdish language courses. The key motivation behind this action is summed up in the view of the Turkish National Security Council (NSC). In its view, the ongoing use of the Kurdish language constitutes a danger to 'the existence and independence of the state, the unity and indivisibility of the nation, and the well-being and security of the community' (Skutnabb-Kangas, personal communication). Suffice it to say that the examples of both Tibet and Turkey serve to reinforce Kedourie's well-worn observation concerning the central link between education and state nationalism: 'On nationalist theory . . . the purpose of education is not to transmit knowledge, traditional wisdom, and the ways devised by a society for attending to the common concerns; its purpose rather is wholly political, to bend the will of the young to the will of the nation' (1960: 83–84).

Of course, not all assimilationist policies are so overtly oppressive, and in recent years examples such as these have been limited for the most part to nondemocratic, non-western and/or newly formed states. But the same aims can be achieved as effectively – if not more so – by stealth, a process that Skutnabb-Kangas (2000) has described as 'covert linguicide'. These policies are much more apparent in contemporary western democratic nation-states where 'submersion' or 'sink or swim' forms of language education – that is, requiring minority-language speakers to be educated in the dominant language, come what may – continue to be widely promoted and practised. Assimilation in this sense also retains considerable public support, as we shall see for example in the next chapter when discussing the US 'English Only' movement.

One reason for this ongoing support of assimilationist education, aside from the apparent imperative of maintaining a common language and culture, is the popular conception that the 'family background' of ethnic-minority students may be an obstacle to their educational and wider social mobility. This approach equates with Stage 2 of Churchill's typology and need not detain us long here since it is, in effect, no more than a modified form of assimilation. Language education policies that fall within this category may best be described as *compensatory*; that is, they aim to compensate for the supposed inadequacies of the minority student's 'family background' in order to address, and mitigate, the ongoing relative 'underachievement' of many ethnic-minority students within schools. The variables regarded as most salient with respect to family background vary but may include the immediate family environment, child-rearing practices, and/or the cultural and linguistic repertoires employed within the family (see Valencia, 1997, for a useful review). Whatever variables are focused upon, however, the starting premise is invariably one of cultural and linguistic 'deficit' in relation to majority-group cultural and linguistic 'norms'. It follows from this view that the principal function of educational programmes is to facilitate and/or expedite the minority student's *adjustment* to mainstream schooling and the cultural and linguistic mores of the dominant group which such schooling invariably reflects. One of the most prominent examples of such programmes, still in use today, is the Headstart preschool programme in the USA, aimed primarily at poor, black and Hispanic inner-city children, while the more recent Sure Start is its British equivalent.

Stage 3 includes within it those policies and programmes that come under the rubric of 'multicultural education', broadly defined. I have written at length elsewhere about multicultural education (see especially 1999b) but for the purposes of this present discussion, the following brief analysis will suffice. Multicultural education has its origins in the late 1960s / early 1970s when it arose as a specific policy response to the claims of minority groups for greater recognition within education of their ethnic, cultural, religious and linguistic diversity. It has focused predominantly – indeed, almost exclusively – on the needs of ethnic migrants rather than national minorities, the latter including indigenous peoples. The (1978) Galbally Report, which introduced multiculturalism as public policy into Australia, clearly reflects this emphasis when it states: 'We are convinced that migrants have the right to maintain their cultural and racial [sic] identity and that it is clearly in the best interests of our nation that they should be encouraged and assisted to do so if they wish' (cited in Kane, 1997: 550). As we shall see in Chapter 8, Australia's policy towards its indigenous peoples – Australian Aboriginal peoples and Torres Strait Islanders – was (and still is) far less accommodating of their cultural, ethnic and linguistic identities than this multicultural rhetoric might suggest.

The example of Australia highlights that multicultural education is most common and most prominent in those western nation-states that have regarded themselves historically as 'immigration societies' (Moodley, 1999) or 'polyethnic societies' (Kymlicka, 1995a; cf. Chapter 3). In addition to Australia, these are most notably, the US, Canada and, to a lesser extent, Britain and Aotearoa / New Zealand. Multicultural education continues to be widely practised in these nation-states at local and state level, while multiculturalism has actually come to be adopted as official public policy in both Australia and Canada.[2]

Unlike the two preceding stages in Churchill's typology, multicultural education recognises that the disadvantages faced by minorities are as much a systemic problem as they are a personal and/or familial one. In other words, we see in multicultural education the first glimmer of recognition concerning the historical role that education has played in the *institutionalised* devaluation and marginalisation of minorities within the nation-state. In response, multicultural education offers the concept of 'cultural pluralism', by which the cultural values and practices of minorities come to be specific-ally recognised and included in the school curriculum. The central aim of this approach is to provide minority students with a positive conception of their social and cultural background in order, in turn, to foster their greater educational success. The early rhetoric surrounding multicultural education in Britain provides us with a representative example of this approach. In the early 1980s, the British School Council argued:

> In a society which believes in cultural pluralism, the challenge for teachers is to meet the particular needs of pupils from different religions, linguistic and ethnic sub-cultures . . . All pupils need to acquire knowledge and sen-sitivity to other cultural groups through a curriculum which offers opportun-ities to study other religions, languages and cultures . . . At all stages this may enhance pupils' attitudes and performance at school through develop-ment of a sense of identity and self-esteem.
>
> (1982; cited in Crozier, 1989: 67–68)

The subsequent publication in Britain of the Swann Report (DES, 1985) was to solidify this belief in the ability of cultural pluralism to effect educa-tional change for minority students. However, the Swann Report was also to exemplify another central claim of multicultural education, namely the sug-gestion that cultural pluralism could in and of itself effect a more multicultural and, by implication, less discriminatory society. In this view, multicultural education would be instrumental in achieving 'positive attitudes towards the multicultural nature of society, free from . . . inaccurate myths and stereo-types about other ethnic groups' (1985: 321).

These rather grandiose claims on behalf of multicultural education have also been made widely elsewhere, most notably in the US, Canada and Australia. For example, when Canada adopted multiculturalism as official policy in 1971, the then Prime Minister, Pierre Trudeau, asserted that 'such a policy should help break down discriminatory attitudes and cultural jeal-ousies' (cited in Berry, 1998: 84). But with the passage of time, these claims have come to be regarded by critics as largely illusory. Without wishing to rehearse the already voluminous literature on the merits and demerits of multicultural education, it is worth pointing out briefly two key criticisms that are directly relevant to our concerns here. The first has to do with multicultural education's overemphasis on *lifestyles* at the expense of life *chances*; in other words, that multicultural education overstates the significance of cultural recognition and understates, and at times disavows, the impact of structural discrimination (be it racial, cultural, religious or linguistic) on minority students' lives. Such an approach may in fact serve simply to *reinforce*

it has left to the advocates of bilingual education (see below). Thus, a second key criticism of multicultural education, including critical multiculturalism, is its ongoing unwillingness to engage directly with questions of *linguistic* discrimination, and the continued maintenance of particular linguistic hegemonies within both education and the wider nation-state. This is particularly evident whenever national minorities, including indigenous peoples, agitate for minority-language maintenance within education. Multicultural education's tendency to level all groups to the status of 'immigrants' or 'new minorities' most often results in these claims being ruled out of court since a polyethnic conception of groups does not entail a 'right' to institutional support of a minority language. Indeed, national minorities and indigenous peoples tend to reject multicultural education precisely because they view it as an educational approach that is employed by the state to dilute or contest their demands for separate educational (and language) provision.[3]

Even where language ostensibly forms a part of multicultural educational policy, as in Australia for example, minority-language support does not usually extend much further in practice than the recognition of private minority-language maintenance, usually outside the state education system (Clyne, 1998; May, 1998). This assertion might seem strange to some, given that Australia is well known for its significant attempts at language status planning in favour of minority languages, most notably via the National Policy on Languages (NPL: Lo Bianco, 1987). However, the NPL's broad concern with ethnic identity, language rights, and language diversity as a social, cultural and economic resource – an admirable exception to much of what has been discussed previously – has quickly been eclipsed by a more economically rationalist approach to language within Australia, as seen in the Australian Language and Literacy Policy (ALLP: Dawkins, 1991). The latter has once again peripheralised the issue of minority languages by solely emphasising their (limited) instrumental value as potential 'trading' languages – excluding, in the process, all minority languages (including indigenous languages) that do not meet this criterion (Ozolins, 1993; Herriman, 1996; May, 1998). Meanwhile, all significant activities conducted in the public domain within Australia remain resolutely monolingual, linguistic shift proceeds largely unabated, and minority-language use remains limited to a few restricted (low-status) domains. Suffice it to say, this situation, as with much multiculturalist policy, does little to foster the status and use of minority languages in the longer term. In the end, the essence of the multicultural model is the recognition of the right to be different and to be respected for it, not necessarily to maintain a distinct language and culture.

In contrast, Stage 4 of Churchill's typology does recognise the importance of the link between language, identity and learning, albeit, as we shall see, in an almost solely instrumental way. The promotion of transitional bilingual programmes is characteristic of this stage. Such programmes use the first language in the early stages of schooling so as to facilitate the transition of the minority-language speaker to the majority language. In so doing, these programmes acknowledge the growing linguistic research consensus that instruction in one's first language is both linguistically and educationally beneficial (see Cummins and Swain, 1986; Appel and Muysken, 1987; Romaine, 1995; Baker, 1996; Cummins, 1996; Corson, 1993, 1998). In this sense, it is a significant advance on the preceding approaches to minority-language education. But in other more fundamental respects, transitional bilingualism is little different from its predecessors. Like the latter, transitional bilingual programmes continue to hold to a 'subtractive' view of individual and societal bilingualism. In assuming that the first (minority) language will eventually be replaced by a second (majority) language, bilingualism is not in itself regarded as necessarily beneficial, either to the individual or to society as a whole. This in turn suggests that the eventual atrophy of minority languages remains a central objective of transitional bilingualism. The (1968) Bilingual Education Act in the USA exemplifies the key characteristics of this broad policy approach. I will discuss the Act more fully in the following chapter in relation to the US 'English Only' movement.

Churchill argues that Stages 1–4 all posit that minority groups should seek the same social, cultural and linguistic outcomes as those of the majority group, or dominant ethnie. In other words, the instrumental objectives of education, as defined by the dominant ethnie, should be the same for *all* ethnic groups within the nation-state. The premise is thus the incorporation of minority groups into the hegemonic civic culture of the nation-state with minimal accommodation to minority languages and cultures. This in turn is a result of what I described in Chapter 3 as the underlying 'philosophical matrix of the nation-state'. Churchill proceeds to argue that it is only at Stages 5 and 6 that objectives and outcomes also come to incorporate the cultural and linguistic values of minority groups and, by so doing, begin to question the value of a monocultural and monolingual society. Both these stages assume that minority groups can (and should) maintain their language and culture over time, whereas Stages 1 through 4 clearly take the opposite approach. However, significant differences still remain between these latter two policy approaches.

Educating for the minority

Stage 5 recognises the importance of maintaining minority languages and cultures, at least in the private domain. In order for this to be achieved, however, it also recognises that some measure of *active* protection is required for the minority language if it is not to be supplanted by the dominant (usually, national) language. A group-maintenance approach to bilingual education is thus the most usual policy response here. In contrast to the 'subtractive' view of bilingualism held in transitional bilingual programmes, a group-maintenance approach regards bilingualism as an 'additive' or 'enriching' phenomenon for the individual.[4] However, as its name suggests, the wider cultural and linguistic benefits of maintaining a minority language are also regarded as central, both for minority groups themselves and for their subsequent contribution to the nation-state. Accordingly, maintenance bilingual education is characterised by 'minority language immersion' programmes where school instruction is largely or solely in the minority language. This ensures that the minority language is maintained and fostered, given that the majority language is usually dominant in most other social and institutional domains. Examples of maintenance bilingual programmes are numerous. They can be found in North America (French and heritage language immersion programmes in Canada, and some Spanish language education programmes in the US); in Europe (including Welsh, Basque and Catalan language programmes) and among a wide variety of indigenous groups (including Sámi in Norway and Sweden, Māori in Aotearoa / New Zealand, Inuit in Canada, and Native Americans in North, Central and South America).[5]

Stage 5 recognises that minority languages and cultures may constitute what Margalit and Raz (1995) described in Chapter 3 as an *enduring need* for minority group members; hence, the promotion of ongoing language use in the private domain. However, changes to the formal linguistic uniformity of the nation-state are not usually countenanced at this level. The latter in fact is only addressed at Stage 6, the 'language equality' stage. At this stage, formal multilingual policies are adopted which require the dominant ethnie to accommodate minority groups and their language(s) in all shared domains (at least in theory); a process which has been described elsewhere as *mutual accommodation* (May, 1994a; Nieto, 2000). By this, Stage 6 assumes that the retention of a minority language and culture is an enduring need *for the majority as well*. A prerequisite for this more plurilingual view of the nation-state is the formal legitimation and institutionalisation of minority languages within both the state and civil society, as discussed in the preceding chapter. As one might expect, examples of this approach remain relatively rare, not least because it challenges so directly the 'philosophical matrix' of a common language and culture that underlies nation-state formation and the 'ideology of contempt' towards minority languages attendant upon it.

The granting of some form of language equality at the level of the nation-state is usually based on one of two organising principles. The first is the 'territorial language principle' which grants language rights that are limited to a particular territory in order to ensure the maintenance of a particular language in that area. The most prominent examples of this principle can be found in Québec, which I will discuss in the next chapter, and in Belgium and Switzerland. In Belgium, for example, there had been linguistic conflict between its two principal language groups – the French and Flemish

– since the inception of the Belgian state in 1830. However, much of this had to do with the de facto supremacy of French and the concomitant marginalising of Flemish throughout its history, despite the fact that Flemish speakers were a numerical majority. This ongoing conflict led eventually to the adoption of linguistic legislation in 1962–63 which enshrined the territorial language principle in Belgium, thus ensuring equal linguistic status for Flemish speakers. This legislation divided the country into three administrative regions: Flanders and Wallonia, which are subject to strict monolingualism (Flemish to the north and French to the south), and the capital, Brussels, which is officially bilingual. However, even in Brussels the French/Flemish linguistic infrastructure is quite separate, extending to the workplace as well as to the more common domains of administration and education. In short, this means that in the whole country there are only monolingual educational institutions, while administration is also monolingual, even in multilingual regions. That said, it is also clear that the territorial principle adopted in Belgium has contributed significantly to its sociopolitical and economic stability by ensuring the maintenance of group language rights (Baetens Beardsmore, 1980; Blommaert, 1996; Nelde, 1997). A similar pattern pertains in Switzerland. The Swiss nation-state is officially multilingual in German, French, Italian and Romansch, and, like Belgium, this formal multilingualism is achieved via the enforcement of regional monolingualism. The obvious consequence of this is that many Swiss do not actually become multilingual (Watts, 1997; Grin, 1999). There are also significant infrastructural differences between the four official languages, with German being spoken by 63.6 per cent of the Swiss population, while Romansch is spoken by only 0.6 per cent (Grin, 1999). The consequent difficulties of status and use for Romansch have led to a recent overhaul of Swiss language policy to provide more support for that language (Rossinelli, 1989; Switzerland, 1989; Grin, 1995, 1999).

The second approach to establishing formal language equality is predicated on the 'personality language principle', which attaches language rights to individuals, irrespective of their geographical position. This provides greater flexibility than the territorial language principle in the apportionment of group-based language rights, although it also has its strictures. The most notable of these is the criterion 'where numbers warrant' – that is, language rights may be granted only when there are a *sufficient* number of particular language speakers to warrant language protection. Canada adopts the personality language principle, where numbers warrant, in relation to French speakers outside of Québec, via the (1982) Canadian Charter of Rights and Freedoms, while a similar approach is adopted in Finland with respect to first-language Swedish speakers living there. India though provides perhaps the best example of this principle in operation. On the one hand, we have seen in India the long-standing promotion of English (see Chapter 6), and more recently Hindi, as elite languages. On the other hand, the Constitution of India (Article 350A) directs every state, and every local authority within that state, to provide 'adequate' educational facilities for instruction in the first language of linguistic minorities, at least at primary (elementary) school level. This is in addition to the 18 official languages recognised in India and the division of India's states along largely linguistic lines. These political divisions result in local linguistic communities having control over their public schools and other educational institutions. This, in turn, ensures that the primary language of the area is used as a medium of instruction in state schools (see Pattanayak, 1990; de Varennes, 1996a; Schiffman, 1996). South Africa's establishment in 1994 of formal multilingualism in 11 state languages also has the potential to follow the Indian model in the provision of minority languages (see Heugh et al., 1995; Barkhuizen and Gough, 1996; Language Plan Task Group, 1996). Whether it actually does so, however, is yet to be determined (see Alexander, 2000, and Heugh, 1997, 2000, for their reflections upon, and scepticism about, more recent developments in South African language policy).

Minority-group responses to language-education policies

If we return directly to Churchill's analysis for a moment, while also bearing in mind that any typology is likely to understate significant inter- and intragroup differences, we can also now attempt a broad parallel categorisation of minority-group responses to minority-language education policy (see Churchill, 1986: 48–49):

- *Level 1 (Recognition Phase)*: the minority group seeks to obtain initial recognition of its distinct educational needs and, in many cases, of its very existence as a distinct cultural and/or linguistic group within the nation-state (cf. the distinction between ethnic categories and groups discussed in Chapter 1).
- *Level 2 (Start-up and Extension Phase)*: having obtained some recognition from educational authorities, the minority group seeks to obtain the creation of minority language educational services or, where these already exist, their further legitimation, extension and improvement. At this stage, either transitional or group maintenance bilingual education aims can be pursued. As discussed previously, transitional bilingual education aims to expedite successful transference from the minority to the majority language by employing the minority language in the early years of primary schooling. This acts as a bridge for the child to transfer their first language skills to the replacing language and, while educationally sound, remains essentially assimilative in intent. In contrast, maintenance bilingual education aims 'to the maximum extent possible [to]

involve use of the minority language as a means of instruction [in order] to resist assimilation pressures outside the school environment' (Churchill, 1986: 49).

- *Level 3 (Consolidation and Adaptation Phase)*: If Level 2 is principally concerned with increasing the quantity of minority-language programmes, this level is concerned with enhancing their quality. In transitional terms, the emphasis may be placed on greater, more effective social and economic integration of the minority group within the nation-state (including a greater awareness and acceptance of the minority group by the dominant ethnie). In group maintenance terms, emphasis might be placed not only on fostering the minority language as a medium of instruction but also on employing the minority culture as a specific source and context of instruction.
- *Level 4 (Multilingual Coexistence Phase)*: At this level, distinct minority educational rights are legally and practically enshrined. Different language groups are accorded formal language and education rights on the basis of the principle of *ethnolinguistic democracy* (Fishman, 1995b). As discussed earlier, this may not amount to actual ethnolinguistic equality, nor does it necessarily imply *a lack of friction* between the groups involved. Nonetheless, minority language rights are formally recognised and employed in state and civil society. In this regard, a considerable degree of autonomy is usually accorded to minority groups in relation to the actual control, organisation and delivery of minority-language education.

The consequences of Level 4 for minority groups bear further discussion here. The granting of a measure of educational control at this level clearly holds considerable symbolic purchase for the minority group concerned. However, three other benefits have also been recognised as a consequence of this process.

- While no causal link can be demonstrated, there appears to be a high correlation between greater minority participation in the governance of education and higher levels of academic success by minority students within that system. As Jim Cummins has argued, 'widespread school failure does not occur in minority groups that are positively oriented towards both their own and the dominant culture, that do not perceive themselves as inferior to the dominant group, and that are not alienated from their own cultural values' (1986: 22; see also 1989, 1996; Ferdman, 1990; Corson, 1993, 1998).
- The greater the participation in educational decision-making by minority-group members, the more likely there is to be a match between minority aspirations and subsequent educational provision (see May, 1994a, 1995; Corson, 1999; Ryan, 1999a).

- Direct involvement in the governance of minority education strengthens community links among the members of the minority group themselves. Such involvement may also ameliorate the negative historical experiences of education held by many within the minority community. Examples of this with respect to community-based indigenous education efforts can be found in Corson (1999), Fettes (1999), May (1999c), McCarty and Watahomigie (1999) and Ryan (1999b).

Bridging the gap between policy and practice

I have chosen Churchill's typology as a useful heuristic device for analysing policy responses to minority language and education. Of course, it is not the only one of its kind. Another is Ruiz's (1984, 1990) language typology, which is well known within sociolinguistics. In this, he categorises language-policy orientations into three broad areas, each of which can be equated broadly with Churchill's approach. The first is what Ruiz terms *language-as-problem* (comparable with Churchill's Stages 1–4), where the targets of language policy are construed as a social problem to be identified, eradicated, allevi-ated, or in some other way resolved. The second he describes as *language-as-right* (Stage 5), which confronts the assimilationist tendencies of dominant language communities with arguments about the legal, moral and natural right to local identity. The third, and most accommodative, he terms *language-as-resource* (Stage 6), where language, and the communities which speak them, are viewed as a social resource.

But whatever language typology is employed, it is important to acknow-ledge its limitations. Perhaps the most important limitation here is the inevitable gap that occurs between policy and practice (see Schiffman, 1996). These discrepancies, which are conceded by Churchill in his own study, occur both between and within nation-states and between and within particular minority groups. In relation to different policy approaches, for example, only the very old bilingual or multilingual states (Belgium, Finland and Switzerland) appear to have reached Stage 6. Sweden is at Stage 5, at least in relation to its Finnish minority (Skutnabb-Kangas, 1988; Janulf, 1998). In Canada, Article 23 of the (1982) Canadian Charter of Rights and Freedoms enshrines the right of English and French speakers, who represent 90 per cent of the country's population, to an education in their first language 'where numbers warrant', while the (1968) Bilingual Education Act allows for a Stage 4 approach for Hispanic (and other) minorities in the USA. But even here, all is not as it seems. We have already seen that the official multilingualism of Switzerland and Belgium does not necessarily result in individual multilingualism (Watts, 1997). Similarly, the actual implementa-tion of a stated language education policy within schools and school systems may be far less frequent than assumed. Thus in Canada the actual exercise of minority-language rights, including the right to minority-language education, varies widely from province to province, ranging from Stage 6 to Stage 2 for Francophones outside of Québec. This is a product, in turn, of the federal nature of the Canadian system and the considerable administrative autonomy granted to individual provinces, particularly with respect to education (Corson, 1993; Burnaby, 1996; Coulombe, 1999). An even more marked disparity between policy and practice can be seen in the USA. Here it is probably safe to say that, despite the Bilingual Education Act, most Hispanic children continue to be educated in schools which are still at Stages 1 and 2, promoting the merits of an English-language submersion approach. Even those that promote bilingual education vary widely between a transitional and group-maintenance ethos (J. Edwards, 1985, 1994; Dicker, 1996; see Chapter 6). In similar vein, while the Indian Constitution explicitly allows for, and even actively facilitates, the promotion of minority-language immersion education, there remain strong countervailing pressures to learn English and Hindi via submersion educational approaches (see Pattanayak, 1985, 1986; Tickoo, 1993).

The differences between the delivery of minority-language education to different minority groups within the same nation-state can also be quite marked. We will see in Chapter 8 that the indigenous Māori are moving towards Stage 5, and ultimately to Stage 6 with respect to language and education policy in Aotearoa / New Zealand. However, the approach to other (ethnic) minorities in Aotearoa / New Zealand, such as Pacific Island groups, is not so advanced (Benton, 1996; Maxwell, 1998). A similar pattern pertains in Wales, where the Welsh-speaking national minority are now well served by Welsh-language education, but where ethnic migrant groups, and the languages they speak, are not (Charlotte Williams, 1995, 1997; see Chapter 7). Canada's approach of 'multiculturalism within a bilingual framework' also illustrates well the discrepancies evident between the language education available to different minority groups. Bearing in mind the caveat of provincial variation outlined earlier, Article 23 of the (1982) Canadian Charter of Rights and Freedoms nonetheless protects the rights of English and French speakers to an education in their first language 'where numbers warrant'. However, the linguistic and educational rights of Canada's indigenous peoples are far less clearly endorsed. This is demonstrated poignantly by their initial exclusion from consideration in *The Royal Commission on Bilingualism and Biculturalism* (1963–71). The findings of this Commission, known as the Laurendeau-Dunton Commission (see Chapter 6), led to the adoption of English and French as co-official languages in 1969, and significantly influenced the policy of 'multiculturalism within a bilingual framework' two years later (Burnaby, 1996; see also Maurais, 1996; Ryan, 1999b). This discrepancy is even more evident in Australia, where, as suggested earlier, despite also having an official policy of multiculturalism, its ongoing educational and wider social and political treatment of Aboriginal peoples and Torres Strait Islanders leaves much to be desired (Pilger, 1998; see Chapter 8).

Responses to minority-language education approaches from within particular minority groups are also extremely varied, as one might expect. In the 1980s, the UK broadly adopted a Stage 3 multicultural approach to education, as exemplified in the Swann Report (DES, 1985), although again actual school practice seldom reflected this, tending towards more assimilative models. The responses from within minority groups to even this limited form of multiculturalism, however, have ranged from enthusiastic endorsement (Verma, 1989) to outright rejection (Stone, 1981; Chevannes and Reeves, 1987). Key arguments here have concerned the degree to which multiculturalism mitigated or contributed further to the social and educational marginalisation of ethnic minorities in Britain (cf. Goulbourne, 1991a). Likewise, in the USA some of the most prominent critics of multicultural and bilingual education initiatives are themselves from ethnic-minority groups (cf. Rodriguez, 1983; D'Souza, 1991).

That said, the current variations in approach, and in their delivery, need not be seen as insurmountable. With regard to the latter, discrepancies between policy formulations and actual practice are increasingly being addressed by the concerted political efforts of minority groups themselves. For all their current inadequacies, minority-language education policies *are* being shaped by the growing cultural and linguistic aspirations of minority groups. These aspirations are also, recursively, a product of the growing acceptance of minority rights in the wider social and political arena (cf. Chapter 3). With regard to the former, there is no necessary problem with differing policy approaches being directed at different minority groups. Indeed, it is my general position that variations of approach should exist between, for example, national- and ethnic-minority groups. Thus, while the ideal might be that nation-states provide a *Stage 5 (Private Use Language Maintenance)* minority education policy approach for *all* minority groups, only national minorities could be reasonably expected to be entitled to a *Stage 6 (Language Equality)* policy approach. Likewise, all minorities might expect the right to mobilise to at least *Level 3 (Consolidation and Adaptation Phase)* in terms of their own language and education requirements. However, again, only national minorities could legitimately claim a right to the *Level 4 (Multilingual Coexistence Phase)*.

Minority-language and education rights in international law

The broad position that I have outlined here accords with recent developments in international law with respect to minority-language and education rights. Drawing on the seminal work of Kloss (1971, 1977), two broad approaches can be observed here: *tolerance-oriented* rights and *promotion-oriented* rights (see also Macías, 1979).[6] Tolerance-oriented rights ensure the right to preserve one's language in the private, nongovernmental sphere of national life. These rights may be narrowly or broadly defined. They include the right of individuals to use their first language at home and in public, freedom of assembly and organisation, the right to establish private cultural, economic and social institutions wherein the first language may be used, and the right to foster one's first language in private schools. The key principle of such rights is that the state does 'not interfere with efforts on the parts of the minority to make use of [their language] in the private domain' (Kloss, 1977: 2).

Promotion-oriented rights regulate the extent to which minority rights are recognised within the *public* domain, or civic realm, of the nation-state. As such, they involve 'public authorities [in] trying to promote a minority [language] by having it used in public institutions – legislative, administrative and educational, including the public schools' (1977: 2). Again, such rights may be narrowly or widely applied. At their narrowest, promotion-oriented rights might simply involve the publishing of public documents in minority languages. At their broadest, promotion-oriented rights could involve recognition of a minority language in all formal domains within the nation-state, thus allowing the minority-language group 'to care for its internal affairs through its own public organs, which amounts to the [state] allowing self government for the minority group' (1977: 24). The latter position would also necessarily require the provision of state-funded minority-language education *as of right*.

As one might expect, given the debates around minority rights that I outlined in Chapter 3, both sets of rights – particularly the latter – continue to face considerable opposition from some quarters. In this respect, the long-held liberal antipathy towards separate minority rights and entitlements has been particularly evident where language is concerned. As Fishman observes:

> Unlike 'human rights' which strike Western and Westernized intellectuals as fostering wider participation in general societal benefits and interactions, 'language rights' still are widely interpreted as 'regressive' since they would, most probably, prolong the existence of ethnolinguistic differences. The value of such differences and the right to value such differences have not yet generally been recognised by the modern Western sense of justice . . .

> (1991: 72)

Nonetheless, there is a nascent consensus on the validity of minority-language and education rights. This is predicated on the basis that the protection of minority languages falls within generalist principles of human rights. Concomitantly, there is a growing acceptance of differentiated linguistic and educational provision for minority groups, along with the degree of institutional autonomy that such developments necessarily entail. Accordingly, ongoing disputes are increasingly concerned with the degree to which these activities should be state-funded, not whether they should exist at all.

The debates over minority-language and education rights within international law can be traced back to the minority treaties overseen by the League of Nations – specifically, its Permanent Court of International Justice (PCIJ) – prior to the Second World War (see also Chapter 3). These treaties were primarily concerned with the protection of 'displaced' minorities in other nation-states, the result in turn of the reorganisation of European state boundaries after the First World War (Wolfrum, 1993; Packer, 1999). They included two principal types of measures: (1) individuals belonging to linguistic minorities, amongst others, would be placed on an equal footing with other nationals of the state; (2) the means of preserving the national characteristics of minorities, including their language(s), would be ensured. In the most prominent legal ruling on these provisions – the (1935) Advisory Opinion on Minority Rights in Albania – the PCIJ stated that these two requirements were inseparable. It concluded that 'there would be no true equality between a majority and a minority if the latter were deprived of its own institutions and were consequently compelled to renounce that which constitutes the very essence of its being a minority' (see Thornberry, 1991a: 399–403). On the basis of this judgement, linguistic minorities were confirmed in their right to establish private schools and institutions, a *minimum* tolerance-oriented right. However, where numbers warranted, public funding of minority-language-medium schools was also advanced, a more promotion-oriented right. In respect of this, and other similar decisions, linguistic minorities were defined purely on a numerical basis – that is, as constituting less that 50 per cent of the population. That said, freedom of choice as to membership in a minority also seemed to permeate the treaties, a point to which I will return.

As we have seen, subsequent developments in international law were rapidly to supersede these treaties and the principles upon which they were based. Minority-language and education rights were largely subsumed within the broader definition of human rights adopted by the United Nations since the Second World War. Human rights were thought, in themselves, to provide sufficient protection for minorities.[7] Accordingly, no additional rights were deemed necessary for the members of specific ethnic or national minorities. Nonetheless, even within this more generalist framework of rights, there have been echoes, albeit weak ones, of the principles of minority protection with respect to language and education. The most notable of these has perhaps been Article 27 of the (1966) International Covenant on Civil and Political Rights (ICCPR) which imposes a *negative* duty on nation-states with respect to the protection of the languages and cultures of minority groups:

In those states in which ethnic, religious or linguistic minorities exist, persons belonging to such minorities *shall not be denied* the right, in community with the other members of their group, to enjoy their own culture, to profess and practise their own religion, or *to use their own language*.

(my emphases)

Before proceeding to examine Article 27 in relation to its specific implications for language and education, I should first point out the problematic nature of the initial clause, 'In those states in which ethnic, religious or linguistic minorities exist'. Like many other examples of supranational and/or international law (see below), their successful enactment depends in the end on the compliance of nation-states. But even more than this, nation-states have to agree in the first instance that the legislation is applicable to them. Thus, the initial tentative formulation in Article 27 has allowed some nation-states in the past simply to deny that any such minorities exist within their jurisdiction. As we have seen from the previous chapter, France is one such example where this has occurred, but there are many others, including Malaysia, Thailand, Japan, Burma, Bangladesh and many Latin American nation-states (see de Varennes, 1996a; Thornberry, 1991a, b). This pattern of avoidance has been addressed more recently by new guidelines in the General Comment of the Covenant, adopted in April 1994, which stipulate that the state can no longer solely determine whether a minority is said to exist or not within its territory. However, the 'problem of compliance' remains an ongoing one (see below).

Be that as it may, I want to explore here what the actual obligations entailed in Article 27 might involve – in particular, to what extent these reflect a tolerance or promotion orientation to minority-language rights. Likewise, I am interested in exploring further the degree to which these rights attach to groups and/or to individual members of these groups. Dealing with the latter first, the process of agreeing the particular form of wording in Article 27 provides us with some important clues. As Patrick Thornberry explains, from an initial proposal that 'linguistic minorities shall not be denied the right . . . to use their own language' the final wording of Article 27 was arrived at as follows:

The [UN] Sub-Commission preferred that 'persons belonging to minorities' should replace 'minorities' because minorities were not subjects of law and 'persons belonging to minorities' could easily be defined in legal terms. On the other hand, it was decided to include 'in community with other members of their group' after 'shall not be denied' in order to recognise group identity in some form.

(1991a: 149)

The tension evident here between individual and group ascription is reflected in the question of who exactly can claim rights under Article 27. This question has been tackled on two fronts. First, following the precedent set by the earlier minority treaties, 'minorities' in Article 27 have come to be defined strictly in numerical terms. A minority is defined as a group who share in common a culture, a religion and/or a language and who constitute less than 50 per cent of a *state's* population. Thus a minority may be numerically dominant in a particular province (as, for example, are the Québécois in Québec and the Catalans in Catalonia) but may still be classified as a minority within the nation-state. Second, any person may claim to be a member of a linguistic minority group on the basis of self-ascription. However, to benefit from Article 27 they must also demonstrate that some *concrete* tie exists between themselves and the minority group (cf. the limits of ethnicity discussed in Chapter 1). In relation to a minority language, this would require a real and objective tie with that language. It would not be sufficient, for example, to be a member of a minority ethnic group that is known to speak a particular language if the individual does not speak that language. Nor are particular languages, and the rights associated with them, tied to specific ethnic groups since more than one ethnic group may speak the same language (cf. Chapter 1). Determining that an individual belongs to a particular linguistic minority is thus not an issue of establishing some type of legal or political category, it is principally an objective determination based on some concrete link between an individual and a linguistic community (de Varennes, 1996a).

The definition of what constitutes a linguistic minority for the purposes of Article 27 is important for another reason. It determines whether the rights to minority language and education are tolerance- or promotion-oriented rights. Two opposing schools of thought are clearly evident here. Following the influential review of the scope of Article 27 by Capotorti (1979), some commentators, including myself (see Thornberry, 1991a, b; Tollefson, 1991; May, 1997b, 1999c; Skutnabb-Kangas, 1998, 2000), have argued that while the words 'shall not be denied' could be read as imposing no obligation on a state to take positive action to protect those rights, an alternative and equally compelling view 'is that to recognise a right to use a minority language implies an obligation that the right be made effective' (Hastings, 1988: 19). On this basis, it has been argued that Article 27 can be said to encompass a promotion orientation to language rights, with attendant state support, rather than the more limited tolerance-oriented right that a solely negative duty implies.

This promotion-oriented perspective on language rights can also be linked directly to education. For example, Article 2(b) of the (1960) Convention Against Discrimination in Education specifically provides for the establishment or maintenance, for linguistic reasons, of separate schools, provided attendance is optional and the education is up to national standards. Moreover,

Article 5 of this Convention recognises the *essential* right of minorities to carry on their own educational activities and, in so doing, to use *or teach in* their own language. It subsequently qualifies this right, somewhat contradictorily, by making it conditional on a state's existing educational policies, and by ensuring it does not prejudice national sovereignty and the ability of minorities to participate in national life. However, the right to minority-language education can nevertheless be established (Hastings, 1988).

The question remains though – to what extent should minority language and education be funded by the state, if at all? Promotion-oriented rights suggest they should but also necessarily impose limits on who is eligible. Capotorti's (1979) review, for example, was predicated on the understanding that Article 27 applied solely to national minorities – immigrants, migrant workers, refugees and noncitizens were excluded. In contrast, tolerance-oriented rights imply no such obligation on the state. While necessarily more limited, such rights may at least have the advantage of being able to apply to a wider range of minority groups. And this brings us to the opposing school of thought on Article 27. Fernand de Varennes (1996a) argues that Capotorti's interpretation of a more active obligation by the state on behalf of national minorities, and the subsequent commentary which has endorsed this position, does not reflect the actual intentions of Article 27. Indeed, Capotorti admitted as much at the time of his review. In effect, he set aside what the drafters originally meant because of his concern that a negative duty was not sufficient to protect minority-language and education rights. In hindsight, de Varennes suggests that Capotorti's pessimism may have been misplaced. After all, the minorities' treaties had already established the long-standing principle of *private* language and education for minorities, without any hindrance from the state. Indeed, where sufficient numbers warranted, there was also a recognition that some form of state-funded minority education could be established. As de Varennes concludes: 'Article 27 thus appears to be part of a long-established and continuous legal continuum that the rights of linguistic minorities to use their language amongst themselves must necessarily include the right to establish, manage and operate their own educational institutions where their language is used as the medium of instruction to the extent deemed to be appropriate by the minority itself' (1996a: 158).

The debates on the merits of Article 27 as an instrument for promotion-oriented rights remain ongoing. Be that as it may, we can at the very least conclude that Article 27 sanctions a clear baseline for tolerance-oriented language and education rights. In this respect, Article 27 allows for the *possibility* of Stage 5 minority-language education policy and a Level 3 minority response, as discussed previously, for *all* minorities within the nation-state. This level of protection for minority-language and education rights applies to all minority groups on the basis of the strict numerical interpretation of minorities within international law. As such, protection would be extended to include indigenous and immigrant minorities, as well as established national minorities who are more usually the beneficiaries of such measures (cf. Skutnabb-Kangas and Phillipson, 1995). Indeed, where a minority has sufficient numbers, there remains some additional scope for state-funded language education, although, given the emphases of Article 27, this decision remains at the discretion of the nation-states themselves. Which brings us to the central problem of Article 27 and, indeed, most international law in this area, including more recent developments (see below). In short, much of the implementation of such measures is still dependent on what nation-states *deem appropriate*. The result is thus left to the vicissitudes of internal national politics where the provision of minority rights is viewed principally as one of political largesse rather than a fundamental question of human rights. The consequence of this in turn is, more often than not, the adoption of the bare minimum level of rights required (and sometimes not even that).

Notwithstanding this difficulty, the notion of a more promotion-oriented view of minority-language and education rights does appear to be gaining some ground, at least for national minorities. In this respect, there have been a number of recent instruments in international law which, at least in theory, allow for a more promotion-oriented perspective on language and education rights. These instruments are, in turn, a product of a more accommodative approach to minorities in the post Cold War era (Preece, 1998). One of the most significant of these is the United Nations Declaration on the Rights of Persons Belonging to National or Ethnic or Religious Minorities, adopted in December 1992. This UN Declaration recognises that the promotion and protection of the rights of persons belonging to minorities actually contributes to the political and social stability of the states in which they live (Preamble). Consequently, the Declaration reformulates Article 27 of the ICCPR in the following way:

> Persons belonging to national or ethnic, religious and linguistic minorities . . . *have the right* to enjoy their own culture, to profess and practise their own religion, and to use their own language, in private *and in public*, freely and without interference or any form of discrimination
>
> (Article 2.1; my emphases)

We can thus see here that the phrase 'shall not be denied' in Article 27 has been replaced by the more active 'have the right'. In addition, and significantly, the formulation recognises that minority languages may be spoken in the public as well as the private domain, without fear of discrimination. That said, the 1992 UN Declaration, unlike the ICCPR, remains a recommendation and not a binding covenant – in the end, it is up to nation-states to decide if they wish to comply with its precepts. In a similar vein, the actual article which deals with minority-language education (Article 4.3) qualifies the more general positive intent of Article 2.1 considerably: 'States *should* take *appropriate* measures so that, *wherever possible*, persons belonging to minorities have *adequate* opportunities to learn their mother tongue *or* to have instruction in their mother tongue' (see Skutnabb-Kangas, 2000: 533–535 for an extended discussion).

A second recent and important piece of UN legislation is the (1996) Draft Universal Declaration of Linguistic Rights, accepted in Barcelona in June 1996 (after many years of preparation and numerous previous drafts) and since handed over to UNESCO for further deliberation. In the draft Declaration it is argued that *explicit* legal guarantees be provided for the linguistic rights of individuals, language communities (in effect, national minorities and indigenous peoples) and language groups (other minority ethnic groups). This includes the right of the individual 'to the use of one's language both in private and in public' (Article 3.1). It also includes the right of linguistic communities to have the necessary resources at their disposal 'to ensure that their language is present to the extent they desire at all levels of education within their territory: properly trained teachers, appropriate teaching methods, text books, finance, building and equipment, traditional and innovative technology' (Article 25). What is not clear, or at least not yet, is the extent to which nation-states will be *obliged* to act on these statements of general intent once the Declaration is finally adopted and ratified. Given the pattern of qualified 'discretion' for nation-states, evident in most other international legislation, the answer must be that the Draft is likely to be revised along these more ambiguous lines before being finally accepted (see also Skutnabb-Kangas, 2000: 543–549).

Another example where exactly the same question applies can be found in the (1993) United Nations Draft Declaration on the Rights of Indigenous Peoples. The Draft Declaration was formulated over a ten-year period by the Working Group on Indigenous Populations (WGIP), in turn a part of the United Nations Sub-Commission on the Prevention of Discrimination and Protection of Minorities. I will have much more to say about the Draft Declaration in Chapter 8, but suffice it to say here that it amounts to a strong assertion of indigenous rights, including promotion-oriented language and education rights. Article 15 states, for example, that 'all indigenous peoples have . . . the right to establish and control their educational systems and institutions providing education in their own languages, in a manner appropriate to their cultural methods of teaching and learning'. But the Draft has since been subject to a formal review by the UN Commission on Human Rights Working Group (CHR), prior to its adoption and ratification – a process that began in November 1995 and is still ongoing at time of writing. Given the many substantive objections raised by states in the process of this review (see Chapter 8), the Draft Declaration is also likely to be considerably amended by the time it reaches its final form, almost certainly towards the dilution of its tenets rather than their enforcement.

Recent pan-European law also reflects these competing tensions between, on the one hand, a greater accommodation of promotion-oriented minority-language and education rights, and on the other, the ongoing reticence of nation-states to accept such a view. The (1992) European Charter for Regional and Minority Languages, which has already been discussed to some extent in Chapter 4, is one such example. It provides a sliding scale of educational provision for national and regional minority languages which ranges from a minimal entitlement for smaller groups – preschool provision only, for example – through to more generous rights for larger minority groups such as primary and secondary language education. Again, however, nation-states have discretion in what they provide, on the basis of both local considerations and the size of the group concerned. As discussed previously, these European nation-states also retain considerable scope and flexibility over which articles of the Charter they actually choose to accept in the first place. In this respect, they are only required to accede to 35 out of nearly 100 articles, although three of the 35 articles must refer to education. A similar pattern can be detected in the (1994) Framework Convention for the Protection of National Minorities, which was adopted by the Council of Europe in November 1994 and finally came into force in February 1998. The Framework Convention allows for a wide range of tolerance-based rights towards national minorities, including language and education rights. It also asserts at a more general level that contributing states should 'promote the conditions necessary for persons belonging to national minorities to maintain and develop their culture, and to preserve the essential elements of their identity, namely their religion, language, traditions and cultural heritage' (Article 2.1). That said, the specific provisions for language and education remain sufficiently qualified for most states to avoid them if they so choose (Thornberry, 1997; Troebst, 1998).

Developments in international law then are at once both encouraging and disappointing. The principle of separate minority recognition in language and education is legally enshrined at least as a minimal tolerance-oriented right – that is, when restricted to the private domain. However, more liberal interpretations of tolerance-oriented rights (involving some state support where numbers warrant), and certainly more promotion-oriented rights, remain largely dependent on the largesse of individual nation-states in their interpretation of international (and national) law with respect to minorities. Having said that, there is undoubtedly increasing pressure from minority groups themselves for greater recognition of separate language and education entitlements and, where numbers warrant, for some form of state recognition and funding with respect to these. In this regard, while there may be no watertight legal guarantees to state-funded minority-language education, there *is* an increasing recognition within international and national law that significant minorities within the nation-state have a *reasonable* expectation to some form of state support (de Varennes, 1996a; see also Chapter 4).

In other words, while it would be unreasonable for nation-states to be required to fund language and education services for all minorities, it is increasingly accepted that where a language is spoken by a significant number within the nation-state, it would also be unreasonable not to provide some level of state services and activity in that language. In addition, there are strong arguments for extending the strict numerical definition of minorities within international law, on which this notion of reasonableness is based, to include also the particular claims of *national* minorities (irrespective of number). As de Varennes observes of indigenous peoples, for example, although his argument can be extended here to all national minorities:

> Indigenous peoples, in particular, may have a strong argument that they should receive state services such as education in their primary language, beyond what a strictly 'numerical' criterion would perhaps normally warrant. In the case of indigenous peoples [and national minorities more generally], the state may have a *greater* duty to respect their wishes in view of the nature of the relationship between the two, and of the duties and obligations involved.
>
> (1996a: 97–98; my emphasis)

The claims of national minorities here are based, as we have seen in Chapters 1 and 2, on their historical rights as ethnies. They also gain credence from the wider political developments in relation to national and indigenous minorities discussed in Chapter 3. Given this, such arguments *are* increasingly having to be addressed by nation-states in some form or another. This is both a moral and a political choice for nation-states since the long-held practice of making no accommodations to minority demands is not so readily defensible in today's social and political climate. Ignoring such demands is also unlikely to quell or abate the question of minority rights, as it might once have done. Indeed, it is much more likely to escalate them. Under these circumstances, 'any policy favouring a single language to the exclusion of all others can be extremely risky . . . because it is then a factor promoting division rather than unification. Instead of integration, an ill-advised and inappropriate state language policy may have the opposite effect and cause a levée de bouclier [general outcry]' (de Varennes, 1996a: 91). The potential for unrest as a result of such a policy will be demonstrated in and through the arguments of the 'English Only' movement in the USA, discussed in the next chapter.

The crux of majority opinion

Before turning to this, one further issue needs to be addressed. The ongoing potential for controversy surrounding the question of minority rights returns us to a key feature of these debates, their essentially contested nature. Minority rights will always be controversial, it seems, no matter how valid are the arguments in their favour. For example, ongoing ambivalence about – and, at times, outright opposition to – 'separate' minority-language education initiatives remains prominent, principally (but by no means exclusively) from majority-group members. As Churchill has observed, this is because responding to 'the needs of linguistic and cultural groups outside the majority group . . . often poses a serious threat to the status quo both of school practice and public attitudes to education' (1986: 33). More sceptically, John Edwards asserts:

> The brutal fact is that most 'big' language speakers in most societies remain unconvinced of either the immediate need or the philosophical desirability of officially-supported cultural and linguistic programmes for their small-language neighbours. Some among the minority also share this doubt and it is, in many instances, a minority within a minority who actively endorse the use of schools as instruments of social engineering.
>
> (1994: 195–196)

Setting aside the rather obvious point which seems to escape Edwards – namely, that the *exclusion* of minority languages within education is just as much a process of social engineering as its promotion – the issue of majority opinion remains a crucial one for minority-language education initiatives. In effect, the long-term success of such initiatives may only be achieved (or be achievable) if at least some degree of favourable majority opinion is secured. Churchill, in his OECD study, certainly admits as much when he observes that 'public support seems more important than the objectives of educators or of the minority group members themselves' (1986: 63). On this basis, what is needed is a greater degree of 'tolerability' (Grin, 1995) on the part of wider public opinion towards specific minority initiatives or, more positively, a climate of 'socially enlightened self-interest' (Secada and Lightfoot, 1993). This may be achieved in one of two ways. One potential avenue would be to point out that in this age of increasing globalisation, and with the burgeoning spread of English as the current world language, the question of retaining cultural and linguistic distinctiveness is increasingly becoming an issue for national majority groups as well as for minorities. This is evidenced in the European Union, for example, where its Parliament adopted in December 1990 the 'principle of complete multilingualism . . . consistent with the respect which is owed to the dignity of all languages which reflect and express the cultures of the different peoples who make up the [EU]' (cited in Fishman, 1995b: 49). The central principle involved here is the recognition of state languages as a symbolic reflection of the people who speak them (see Chapter 4). It does not necessarily entail ethnolinguistic equality – English and French still dominate the operations of the European Union – but it is consistent with the notion of greater ethnolinguistic democracy discussed earlier. What is pertinent for our purposes is that this principle can be applied equally to *intra*state languages as to *inter*state languages. If the Netherlands can argue that Dutch has a right to be represented as a working language of the EU, then, by implication, Frisian has a right to be represented as a working language of the Netherlands. After all, it is clearly a national-minority language which is predominantly spoken in the area of Friesland in the Netherlands (Fishman, 1995b). In this way, the language rights of national majorities and minorities can be usefully allied while, at the same time, highlighting the inconsistencies between current interstate and intrastate language policies (see also Dorian, 1998).

Another key avenue to pursue in relation to minority language and education rights is the issue of social justice. While important, it is not enough to argue simply for the merits of cultural and linguistic diversity, if only because this seldom addresses the terms on which such diversity is recognised. As multiculturalist approaches have found out to their cost, recognising diversity is all very well but this in itself does little, if anything, to change hegemonic power relations (see May, 1999b). Moreover, as Edwards has already pointed out, it is highly unlikely that majority-group members will accept minority rights on the basis of self-interest alone. What is needed in addition then is some belief that the dominant ethnie, or Staatsvolk (see Chapter 2), has an *obligation of justice* to accept such rights (Kymlicka, 1995a). It is my view here that the historical disadvantages faced by minority groups, and/or the rights of national minorities as ethnies, constitute a strong basis for such an obligation.

Nonetheless, one should be under no illusion that establishing the validity of minority rights remains a formidable task. As I have also consistently argued, the process of recognising minority rights contests the hegemonic construction of the nation-state and, by implication, the place of the majority ethnic group, or dominant ethnie, within it. By definition, this will engender opposition. Minority-language education is particularly contentious in this regard because it may necessitate changes within a given nation-state to the balance of wider power relations between ethnic groups and the languages they speak. Thus, if significant progress is to be made, the common understanding of the nation-state, deriving from political nationalism, needs to be radically rethought or reimagined. A very few nation-states have already undergone this process, or are presently embarking on such a course, although not without at times considerable difficulty. The remainder though continue to be wedded to the 'philosophical matrix of the nation-state' discussed in Chapters 2 and 3.

For this to change, much still needs to be accomplished. Education *can* play a key role here in promoting more pluralistic and plurilingual aims but it needs to be stressed again that it cannot in itself achieve such change. As Stacy Churchill concludes:

In some cases, the educational response to minorities is in advance of public opinion to a certain extent, but the politicised nature of relations between ethnolinguistic groups and their surrounding societies sets strict limits on how far educational systems can go in responding to minority needs. The root issue is how far societies outside the education system are willing to modify their views of the roles of linguistic and cultural minorities within their countries. Educational systems cannot respond to minority needs unless societies are [also] prepared to respond to those needs.

(1986: 163)

This caveat, and the related importance of overcoming adverse majority (and, at times, minority) opinion, are both borne out starkly in the ensuing chapters, which take particular case studies as their point of focus.

Notes

1 As Kenneth Howe argues: 'The principle of equal educational opportunity can only be realised for cultural minorities by rendering educational opportunities worth wanting, and rendering educational opportunities worth wanting requires that minorities not be required to give up their identities in order to enjoy them' (1992: 469).

2 For analyses of Australia's official policy of multiculturalism, see Ozolins (1993), Kane (1997), Clyne (1998) and Kalantzis and Cope (1999). For analyses of Canada's official multiculturalism, see Fleras and Elliot (1991), Fleras (1994), Moodley (1995), Berry (1998), Kamboureli (1998) and Kymlicka (1998).

3 For examples of indigenous arguments along these lines, see Ignace and Ignace (1998), Perera and Pugliese (1998) and May (1999c, d); see also Chapter 8. For a more general critique of multiculturalism as a form of institutional control, see the iconoclastic account of Australian multicultural policy by Hage (1998).

4 It is now widely recognised that bilinguals mature earlier than monolinguals in acquiring skills for linguistic abstraction, are superior to monolinguals on divergent thinking tasks and in their analytical orientation to language, and demonstrate greater social sensitivity than monolinguals in situations requiring verbal communication (see Romaine, 1995; Cummins, 1995, 1996; Baker, 1996; Corson, 1993, 1998).

5 For recent useful overviews of maintenance bilingual programmes in these and other areas, see Baker and Prys Jones (1998), Cenoz and Genesee (1998), Corson (1998), Freeman (1998), May (1999d) and Skutnabb-Kangas (2000).

6 Macías distinguishes between two broadly comparable sets of rights: the right to freedom from discrimination on the basis of language, and the right to use your language(s) in the activities of communal life (1979: 88–89).

7   As we saw in Chapter 3, this has not actually proved to be the case. Indeed, the United Nations itself has admitted as much in recent times: The *Human Rights Fact Sheet on Minorities* (No. 18, March 1992: 1) states, for example: 'the setting of standards which create additional rights and make special arrangements for persons belonging to minorities and for the minorities as *groups* – although a stated goal of the United Nations for more than 40 years – has made slow progress'.

6

English hegemony and its critics: North American debates

In this chapter I want to explore the various debates surrounding the pre-eminent role of English within North America. In particular, I will examine two quite different responses to the current hegemony of English – the 'English Only' movement in the USA, which seeks to delimit other languages in the public realm, particularly Spanish, and French language laws in Québec, which seek to contain the influence of English itself. The central question I am concerned with here is the extent to which either of these developments can be regarded as *illiberal*. My argument will be that while both examples may appear on the face of it to be employing restrictive language policies, only the former is actually illiberal. Before turning to these questions in detail, however, it is necessary to rehearse briefly the issue of the wider role and influence of English as the current world language, since this frames much of the ensuing debates about English in the North American context, as elsewhere.

Rule Britannia: English in the ascendant

It is indisputable (except perhaps to the French!) that English is the international language of the modern world (Crystal, 1997a). From an estimated four million speakers in 1500 (Jespersen, 1968), limited almost exclusively to the British Isles, English is currently spoken by at least 700 million speakers worldwide. Of these, approximately 300 million use English as a first language, 300 million use English as a second language and a further 100 million use it fluently as a foreign language. This is an increase of 40 per cent since the 1950s and an almost tenfold increase since 1900. Bolder estimates project the number of English speakers at nearer 1–1.5 billion, although this includes those who have lower levels of fluency in English as a foreign language (Crystal, 1997b). While such numbers are undoubtedly significant, they are not the only, or even the principal, reason for the current ascendancy of English (Mandarin Chinese still has far more first- and second-language speakers, for example). Rather, as David Crystal highlights in the *Cambridge Encyclopedia of Language*, the current ascendancy of English is demonstrated by its dominance in a wide range of key areas:

> English is used as an official or semi-official language in over 60 countries, and has a prominent place in a further 20. It is either dominant or well-established in all six continents. It is the main language of books, newspapers, airports and air-traffic control, international business and academic conferences, science, technology, medicine, diplomacy, sports, international competitions, pop music, and advertising. Over two-thirds of the world's scientists write in English. Three quarters of the world's mail is written in English. Of all the information in the world's electronic retrieval systems, 80% is stored in English. People communicate on the Internet largely in English. English [language] radio programmes are received by over 150 million in 120 countries. Over 50 million children study English as an additional language at primary [elementary] level; over 80 million study it at secondary level . . .
>
> (1997b: 360)

Not surprisingly perhaps, a consequence of this increasing global ascendancy of English is that the language has come to be linked inextricably with modernity and modernisation, and the associated benefits which accrue to those who speak it. In particular, the spread of English is linked to modernisation in two key ways. First, it is seen as a central tool by which the process of modernisation can be achieved, particularly in developing societies. Second, and relatedly, monolingualism (preferably in English) is seen as a practical advantage for modern social organisation while multilingualism, in contrast, is viewed as a characteristic of 'premodern' or 'traditional' societies (Coulmas, 1992). We have already seen these arguments developed by Kay (1993) in relation to Africa in Chapter 4, for example. On this view, English is seen as a language which is neutral and pragmatic, beneficial, and freely chosen. Indeed, as Pennycook (1994) has observed, these underlying assumptions continue to inform linguistics, applied linguistics and English-language teaching circles to such an extent that their legitimacy is hardly ever questioned (see also Phillipson, 1992; Canagarajah, 2000). Instead, much of the academic discussion in these areas has, at least until the 1990s, centred largely on the perceived threat to 'standard English' of the proliferation of English (or English*es*) around the world (see Quirk, 1981, 1985; Kachru, 1982, 1986, 1990; Kachru and Nelson, 1996). A similar pattern of ignoring issues of differential power and opportunity can also be found in the more general literature on second-language acquisition (for recent critiques of

SLA along these lines, see van Lier, 1994; Rampton, 1995; Cummins, 1996; Lantolf, 1996; Norton, 2000).

However, this kind of hermetic analysis considerably underplays, if not simply ignores, the more problematic nature of the spread of English. As Pennycook (1994) argues, the view of English as freely chosen fails to address the wider economic, political and ideological forces that shape and constrain such a choice at both the individual and the collective levels. Likewise, treating English as natural and neutral rests on a structuralist and positivist view of language which ignores the wider historical, cultural and political forces that have led to the current dominance of English; a position we have already seen critiqued by Bourdieu in Chapter 4. And finally, the view of English as beneficial assumes, rather naively, that people and nation-states deal with each other on an equal footing when clearly they do not. Consequently, those who advocate the 'benefits' of English largely fail to address the relationship between English and wider inequitable distributions and flows of wealth, resources, culture and knowledge. One obvious example of this can be found in the strong evidence that suggests that the adoption of English as an official language by nation-states has little influence on sub-sequent economic development. The poorest countries in Africa are for the most part those which have chosen English (or French) as an official language, whilst the majority of the Asian 'tiger economies' have opted instead for a local language. In short, there is simply no correlation between the adoption of English and greater economic well-being (Pennycook, 1994; Phillipson and Skutnabb-Kangas, 1994). As Pennycook (1994; see also 1995, 1998b) concludes, other factors, particularly the relative powerlessness and disadvantage experienced by such states within the wider nation-state system, exert far greater long-term influence. Similar critiques along these lines can be found in Bailey (1991), Holborow (1999), Watson (1999), Rassool (1998, 1999, 2000), Tollefson (1995, 2000) and Canagarajah (2000).

Globalisation has clearly played an important part in the rise of English as the current world language, particularly with respect to the rapid expansion of English in the post Second World War period (Crystal, 1997a; see also below). But it is not the whole story, since the current ascendency of English also clearly has longer historical antecedents (see McCrum et al., 1986; Graddol et al., 1996). Indeed, the rise of English to be the preeminent international language has had much to do with the role of Great Britain as the dominant colonial power over the last three centuries. This saw English established as a key language of trade across the globe under the auspices of the expansionist British Empire (Holborow, 1999). With the inexorable decline of Britain as a world power since the mid twentieth century, this mantle has now passed to the United States. The increasing sociopolitical and socioeconomic dominance of the USA, and its preeminent position in cutting-edge media and telecommunications, has ensured that English remains at the forefront of the world's languages. This has been further entrenched by the collapse of the former Soviet Union, and much of communist Central and Eastern Europe along with it, resulting in the exponential growth of English in these areas over the last decade as well. Via US influence, English thus constitutes a key part of the vanguard of globalisation, or at least its most common variant, global Americanisation (cf. Ritzer, 1996, 1997).

Having said that, the British Council continues to play a pivotal role in the widespread promotion of English for economic and political purposes. In any one year, the British Council helps a quarter of a million foreign students to learn English (Crystal, 1997b). The reasons behind this are clear enough and are outlined in the *British Council Annual Report* of 1983–84. The Report states that because the British 'do not have the power we once had to impose our will . . . cultural diplomacy must see to it that people see the benefits of English . . . *and the drawbacks with their own languages* . . . then, consequently [they will] want [to learn] English . . . for their own benefit' (my emphasis). As a result, 'Britain's influence endures, out of all proportion to her economic and military resources' (cited in Phillipson, 1992: 286–287).[1] A more recent statement of intent by the British Council at the launching of *English 2000* (British Council, 1995; see also Seaton, 1997) reflects this just as starkly. The accompanying press publicity for the Report clearly states that the ongoing aim of the Council in promoting the 'role of English as the world language into the next century' was 'to exploit the position of English to further British interest . . . Speaking English makes people open to Britain's cultural achievements, social values and business aims' (cited in Phillipson, 1998: 102). Ndebele's observation, made well over a decade ago now, still holds true it seems: 'the British Council continues to be untiring in its efforts to keep the world speaking English. In this regard, teaching English as a second or foreign language is not only good business . . . it is [also] good politics' (1987: 63).

In short, the English language, and the ideology of modernisation it conveys, are far from neutral. Indeed, it is simply disingenuous to present English as some kind of tabula rasa, available at no cost and for the benefit of all. Rather, this type of reasoning should be recognised for what it is:

> [a] part of the rationalisation process whereby the unequal power relations between English and other languages are explained and legitimated. It fits into the familiar . . . pattern of the dominant language creating an exalted image of itself, other languages being devalued, and the relationship between the two rationalised in favour of the dominant language.
>
> (Phillipson, 1992: 287–288)

Phillipson, in his searing critique of the international English-language-teaching industry (see also Canagarajah, 2000), summarises the 'glorification' of English linguistic hegemony, and the related devaluing of other languages, as outlined in the following table.

Table 6.1   The labelling of English and other languages

Glorifying English	Devaluing other languages
World language	Localised language
International language	(Intra)national language
Language of wider communication	Language of narrower communication
Auxiliary language	Unhelpful language
Additional language	Incomplete language
Link language	Confining language
Window on the world	Closed language
Neutral language	Biased language

(Source: Phillipson, 1992: 282; see also 1997, 1998)

Without wishing to accept the absolute polarisation between English and other languages seemingly implied by Phillipson's analysis (see Holborow, 1999 for a useful critique here), the resonances between these juxtapositions, and those commonly made between national and minority languages, are striking. In effect, the role of English as lingua franca merely extends the latter comparisons to the next level. In Alastair Pennycook's (1994) account of the cultural politics of English as an international language, further aspects of the preeminent position of English are highlighted which also resonate closely with our previous discussions. Employing Pennycook's excellent analysis as a useful point of departure, these include the following:

1 *The promotion of a continuing English language hegemony.* As we have already seen, this acts to reinforce the dominant economic and political position of nation-states such as Britain and the USA in the modern world. It is also facilitated by the role that English has come to assume as the language of international capitalism (Naysmith, 1987; Holborow, 1999). The combined result is the perpetuation of social, economic and political inequality between English and non-English speakers, both within and between nation-states. This process has been termed 'English linguistic imperialism' or, more broadly, 'linguicism' by Phillipson (1992). As he argues, English linguistic imperialism operates when 'the dominance of English is asserted and maintained by the establishment and continuous reconstitution of structural and cultural inequalities between English and other languages'. Linguicism (of which English linguistic imperialism forms a part) is the process by which 'ideologies and practices . . . are used to legitimate, effectuate and reproduce an unequal division of power and resources (both material and immaterial) between groups that are defined on the basis of language' (Phillipson, 1992: 47). As such, linguicism is also equated directly with other forms of inequality such as racism and

ethnicism (see also Skutnabb-Kangas and Phillipson, 1995; Skutnabb-Kangas, 2000).

2   *The dominance of English in prestigious domains* – most notably, in academia, electronic information transfer and popular culture. English is increasingly the language of science and academia, displacing French and German (see, for example, Ammon, 1998, 2000). Information on the Internet or World Wide Web is almost exclusively in English. As one commentator observes, 'the Internet and World Wide Web really only work as great unifiers if you speak English' (quoted in Crystal, 1997a: 107). Likewise, popular culture – in the form of popular music, film and video – is predominantly in English. Crystal estimates that in 1996, 80 per cent of all feature films were in English, while as much as 99 per cent of popular music was written and performed predominantly or entirely in English. Such is the reach of English within popular culture, in fact, that, as we saw in Chapter 4, even nation-states like France are concerned by its impact on French language and culture (Flaitz, 1988; Truchot, 1990; M.-N. Lamy, 1996). The result is a complex set of relationships between English and other local types of culture and knowledge, usually leading to the diminution in value of the latter. As Pennycook argues, 'access to prestigious . . . forms of knowledge is often only through English, and thus, given the status of English both within and between countries, there is often a reciprocal reinforcement of the position of English and the [associated] position of imported forms of culture and knowledge' (1994: 21).

3   *The related threat that English poses to the continuing viability of other languages* – what Day (1985) and Skutnabb-Kangas (2000) have termed the potential for 'linguistic genocide'. In this regard, the pattern of English as a 'replacing language' (Brenzinger, 1997) is increasingly evident, particularly among indigenous and other small and less powerful groups. The fate of Australian Aboriginal languages is one example I have already discussed briefly in the Introduction, others include the Welsh language in Britain (see Chapter 7) and the Māori language in Aotearoa / New Zealand (see Chapter 8). Even when not directly threatening linguistic genocide, however, English may nonetheless contribute significantly to what Pennycook describes as 'linguistic curtailment'; in effect, the restricting of competing languages to particular (usually low-status) domains.

4   *The extent to which English functions as a gatekeeper to positions of prestige within societies.* Due to the central role that English often assumes within many education systems, it has become one of the most powerful means of inclusion into or exclusion from further education, employment or influential social positions. This pattern is particularly evident in many postcolonial countries where small English-speaking elites have continued the same policies as their former colonisers in order to ensure that (limited) access to English-language education acts as a crucial distributor

of social prestige and wealth (Holborow, 1999). Pattanayak (1969, 1985, 1986) and Dasgupta (1993) describe exactly this pattern in relation to India, where English has remained the preserve of a small high-caste elite. This was also the case in Hong Kong, at least until its recent (re)incorporation into China and related moves by the Chinese authorities to further legitimate and institutionalise Mandarin Chinese at the expense of English (see Joseph, 1996; Pennycook, 1998b; S. Evans, 2000). Ngũgĩ (1985, 1993) and Schmied (1991) describe a similar scenario in Africa where, despite English being an official language in eight post-colonial African states, and a semi- or co-official language in a further six, the actual percentage of English speakers in these states does not exceed 20 per cent. Indeed, Alexandre (1972) has gone as far as to suggest that in postcolonial Africa social class can be distinguished more clearly on linguistic than economic lines. However, as we will see, such patterns are by no means limited to postcolonial settings. They are also clearly evident in many developed countries in the western world as well, including arguably the 'most' developed of all, North America.

'Doesn't anyone speak English around here?': the US 'English Only' movement

Which brings us nicely to the so-called 'Official English' movement – or, as I prefer to term it, the 'English Only' movement.[2] I want to begin, by way of background, with two revealing vignettes. The first concerns the New York State constitutional convention in 1916 where, during a debate on an English-literacy requirement for voting, a proponent of the measure traced the connection between the English language and democratic values *directly* back to the Magna Carta: 'You have got to learn our language [English] because that is the vehicle of the thought that has been handed down from the men in whose breasts first burned the fire of freedom' (cited in Baron, 1990: 59). Irrespective of the merits of these sentiments (and there are not many), the key point to be made here is that the Magna Carta was actually written in Latin, not English! As I discussed in Chapter 4, English did not assume any formal prominence in Britain until the fifteenth century.[3]

The second example is far more recent. It concerns a 1995 court case in Amarillo, Texas, where a judge ordered a mother not to speak Spanish to her child at home on the grounds that this was equivalent to a form of 'child abuse':

> If she starts [school] with the other children and cannot even speak the language that the teachers and others speak, and she's a full-blooded American citizen, you're abusing that child . . . Now get this straight: you

start speaking English to that child, because if she doesn't do good in school, then I can remove her because it's not in her best interests to be ignorant.

(cited in de Varennes, 1996a: 165–166)

The only ignorance demonstrated here appears to be the judge's. As de Varennes observes, the reasoning behind the judgement is bizarre, to say the least. However, what is most concerning is that it obviously never occurred to the judge that it may have been the state's school system which was 'abusive' for not meeting adequately the linguistic and educational needs of its large Spanish-speaking population. Instead, he simply places the blame on the parent – and, by extension, the child – for their 'wilful' failure to assimilate.

These examples usefully highlight four significant aspects of the English Only movement. The first is the historical inaccuracy that characterises many of their arguments about the role of English – and, by implication, other languages – within the United States. The second is the explicit link that is made between a lack of English-language facility and subsequent educational failure, along with a related misrepresentation of bilingual education. The third is the inherent nativism of much English Only rhetoric; language is used, in effect, as a convenient proxy for maintaining racialised distinctions in the USA. And the fourth is the assumption that speaking English is a unifying force while multilingualism is by definition destructive of national unity, an assumption we have already seen expressed by Schlesinger in Chapter 3. Each of these characteristics is highly problematic and, as such, bears closer examination. Before that, however, let me briefly sketch the origins of the English Only movement in its current form.

The genesis of a movement

In April 1981, Senator Samuel Hayakawa of California proposed an English Language Amendment (ELA) to the Constitution of the United States which would make English, for the first time, an official rather than a de facto national language. In his initiating speech, the senator gave the following reasons for his ELA (see Marshall, 1986: 23):

- 'a common language can unify; separate languages can fracture and fragment a society'
- learning English is the major task of each immigrant
- only by learning English can an immigrant fully 'participate in our democracy'

Hayakawa's proposal was to set the tone and the broad parameters of much of the subsequent 'English Only' debates in the USA in its assertion of the unifying power of a common language, its (convenient) elision of ethnic and national minorities – treating all such groups as if they were immigrants or new minorities (see Chapter 2) – and its faith in the role of English as the principal agent of social mobility. On this basis, Hayakawa proceeded to argue that his principal concern in making English the official language of the USA was to help clarify the 'confusing signals' being sent to 'immigrant' groups over the preceding decade. Such signals included the provision of bilingual (voting) ballots which he considered 'contradictory' and 'logically conflicting' with the requirements of naturalised citizens to 'read, write and speak' English. Group-maintenance approaches to bilingual education were also regarded as 'being dishonest with linguistic minority groups'. Accordingly, he was determined that only transitional forms of bilingual education should be allowed, if that, in order to 'end the false promise being made to new immigrants that English is unnecessary to them'.

The themes expressed by Hayakawa at the beginning of the 1980s were to spawn a movement. While his ELA failed, the publicity that it garnered led Hayakawa to join forces with Dr John Tanton to establish the organisation 'US English' in 1983. US English is not the only organisation of its type ('English First' is another) but it is certainly the most prominent, having grown rapidly in both number and profile from the time of its inception.[4] During the 1980s, a further five ELAs were tabled under the auspices of the English Only movement, a pattern that has continued into the 1990s. The latest variant of the ELA – the English Language Empowerment Act – was tabled to Congress in 1996. To date, none of these proposals has been successful, largely due to the care and caution with which constitutional amendments are treated (see Marshall, 1986). However, the English Only movement has continued to lobby vigorously for restrictionist language policies at the federal level while also increasingly focusing on changing state-level language policies (Nunberg, 1989; Ruiz, 1990). As Daniels observes of the latter, 'the overall strategy [here] seems to be to get some official-English law on the books of a majority of states and to continually fan public resentment over schooling policies that "degrade English" and "cater" to immigrants' (1990: 8). In this regard, they have been far more successful. Using their considerable organisational, lobbying and media skills, the English Only movement has effectively used the vehicle of popular state referenda (originally implemented as a progressive measure to avoid the special-interest lobbying endemic to US politics) to endorse and implement restrictionist language policies. The first of these, California's Proposition 63, was passed in 1986 by a majority of 73 per cent to 27 per cent – albeit on a very low voter turnout – and included a significant degree of Hispanic voter support (MacKaye, 1990). Since then, 23 states (as well as 40 cities) have adopted English as their official language (*Observer*, 4 August 1996). These statutes and amendments vary considerably from state to state. However, all are concerned to declare English as the official language of the state and most are concerned with ensuring that English is the only language of government activity (see Adams and Brink, 1990). While such laws have

subsequently been repealed in one state (Arizona) and are the subject of ongoing legal challenge in two others (Alabama, Alaska), their overall popularity,
and the growing momentum behind them, are not in doubt. In summary,
the key objectives of the English Only movement, which have remained
constant since its inception, are to:

1   adopt a constitutional law establishing English as the official language of
     the United States
2   repeal laws mandating multilingual ballots and voting materials
3   restrict federal funding of bilingual education and, if possible, eliminate
     all forms of group-maintenance bilingual education
4   strengthen the enforcement of English-language civic and immigration
     requirements for naturalisation (see Tarver, 1994)

It should be stressed that these concerns are not particularly new in
themselves. The primacy of English, and the links with nativist concerns
about immigration, were clearly evident in the 'Americanisation Movement'
at the time of the First World War (Higham, 1963; see also Baron, 1990;
Piatt, 1990; Crawford, 1989, 1992a, 1992b). Indeed, the above example of
the New York State constitutional convention in 1916 suggests as much.
However, what is distinct about the present English Only movement is its
national profile and organisation (previous debates about language were
usually confined to local or state arenas) and, relatedly, the increasingly wide
support that it seems to have found among the American public (A. Padilla,
1991; Donahue, 1995). Much of the success of the English Only movement
here has been in its ability to articulate forcefully a particular view of the
USA as a resolutely monolingual, English-speaking country, currently
threatened by the (recent) rise of multilingualism. This multilingualism is
also linked implicitly, and sometimes explicitly, with the growing number of
Spanish-speaking Hispanic communities within the USA who, despite comprising a wide range of disparate groups, including national minorities (Puerto
Ricans and Chicanos), are conveniently viewed as an homogeneous mass of
(often illegal) 'immigrants'. The often alarmist rhetoric promulgated by the
movement is thus endemically racist, as I will argue in due course. Here I
want to explore further the historical amnesia that attends so much of this
rhetoric. As we saw Ernest Renan observe in Chapter 2, 'forgetting, I would
even go so far as to say historical error, is a crucial factor in the creation of
a nation' (1990: 11). The nationalist myth-making of the English Only movement certainly bears this out.

Historical amnesia: the 'forgotten' languages of the USA

The English Only movement makes three principal claims in relation to the
language history of the USA. The first is that the USA is a monolingual,

English-speaking country *and always has been*. The second is that the English language is a central and indispensable symbol of American national identity; a view, moreover, that has been consistently supported by historical language policy and practice. The third is that English is under serious threat for the first time as a result of the recent rise of bilingual voting and bilingual educational developments. Each of these propositions is fundamentally misplaced.

First, it is clear that English is, and has been historically, the dominant language in the USA. This point is not in doubt. However, to extrapolate from this the myth of English *monolingualism* is another story entirely (cf. Silverstein, 1996). And story it is, for the USA is not and never has been a monolingual country. Indeed, multilingualism has been a feature of US society since the colonial times of the eighteenth century (Kloss, 1977), a feature which should not surprise us given the USA's status as the largest immigrant country of them all. In American colonies between 1750 and 1850, non-English-speaking European settlers made up one quarter of the white population and Dutch (New York), Swedish (Delaware) and German (Pennsylvania) were widely spoken. Indeed, in 1790 German speakers comprised 8.7 per cent of the total US population (Zentella, 1997). Native Americans, and their languages, were also still numerous and widespread at this time (see below). And Black Americans – mostly slaves, and with their many African languages – numbered more than one fifth of the total population (Shell, 1993). Moreover, outside of the early colonies, Spanish- and French-language speakers predominated. Many of these language speakers were eventually incorporated into the United States as it expanded. For example, the (1803) Louisiana Purchase saw this territory, which included a majority of French speakers, acquired from France. Likewise, the (1848) Treaty of Guadalupe Hidalgo saw Mexico cede nearly half of its predominantly Spanish-speaking territory to the US, including areas of present-day New Mexico, Texas, Arizona, Colorado and California.

To take just one example of the historical language diversity apparent in the United States, the case of Native American languages bears closer examination. When the Spanish first arrived on the North American continent in the early sixteenth century (see Conklin and Lourie, 1983), it is estimated that at least 500 Native American languages were spoken (Leap, 1981). The subsequent impact of European colonisation on Native Americans – along with its usual corollaries of introduced diseases, land dispossession and genocide – were to change all that. By 1920, the Native American population reached a nadir of 400,000, having fallen from an estimated 30–40 million at time of contact (see McKay and Wong, 1988). An educational policy over this period of actively repressing Native American languages, and replacing them with English, also contributed significantly to the related decline and extinction of many Native American languages. As a federal commissioner of Indian Affairs, J. D. C. Atkins, observed in his annual report for 1887:

'schools should be established, which [Native American] children should be required to attend, [and where] their barbarous *dialects* should be blotted out and the English *language* substituted' (reprinted in Crawford, 1992b: 48; my emphases). Note here, the deliberate relegation of Native American language varieties to mere 'dialects' in contradistinction to the English 'language', along with all this implies about language hierarchy (see the discussion on language and dialects in Chapter 4). Although the Bureau of Indian Affairs formally rescinded this assimilationist education policy in 1934, punishment for native language use in schools continued through to the 1950s (Crawford, 1989).[5] Notwithstanding this sorry history, Native American languages are still spoken today in the USA, although they are seldom commented upon. In the 1990 census, 1,878,275 people identified as Native Americans, of whom 331,600 over the age of five years reported speaking a Native American language. Altogether, 26 such languages were identified in the 1990 census as having at least 1000 speakers (Ricento, 1996).

So much for the myth of a monolingual USA. But what of the pivotal role of English in US society, and the language policies and practices which have supposedly *consistently* supported this? Again, all is not as it seems. There are actually two clear countervailing tensions apparent historically in the USA's approach to status language policy and planning. On the one hand, there has certainly been a clear drive towards English linguistic uniformity at various times in the USA's history. This drive has been characterised most often by a prominent advocacy of the role of English as a central organising symbol of American identity. In this context, much has been made of John Jay's assertion at the time of America's independence 'that Providence has been pleased to give this one connected country, to one united people; a people descended from the same ancestors, *speaking the same language*, professing the same religion' (cited in Shell, 1993: 103; my emphasis). Likewise, Theodore Roosevelt's famous appeal 'The Children of the Crucible' in 1917 is often invoked: 'we have room for but one language here, and this is the English language, for we intend to see that the crucible turns our people out as Americans, of American nationality, and not as dwellers in a polyglot boarding house' (cited in J. Edwards, 1994: 166).

Like Hayakawa's more recent English Only arguments, Roosevelt's notion of the American crucible assumes that *all* Americans are *willing* immigrants. At the risk of repetition, this completely ignores the subjected status of African Americans, and the various national minorities – including Native Americans and Puerto Ricans – who have been incorporated by conquest into the United States. Be that as it may, such sentiments accord with a strong emphasis historically in American federal policy on fostering English as the language of administration, education and the legislature, a feature the English Only movement is only too willing to point out. In effect, from the time of the Louisiana Purchase, English has been promoted as the language of government, voting and the courts, often in the face of strong local opposition. English has also been the recognised language of instruction in schools since the Constitution of 1868 (Hernández-Chávez, 1995). The example of the trenchant assimilationist language and education policies directed towards Native Americans, described earlier, would also seem to bear out the general significance attributed to English in the educational domain.

On the other hand, there have also been significant examples where minority-language rights – albeit limited ones – have been specifically accommodated. These examples have simply been ignored by the English Only movement (as they were by Roosevelt before them) but they cannot just be wished away, much as some might want them to be. The historical language context of the USA is thus far more complex than English Only advocates would care to admit. For a start, one of the principal reasons that the English Only movement places such store in a constitutional amendment is because of the *deliberate* ambiguity of the Declaration of Independence and the Constitution in relation to the role of English in US society. Although the documents were written in English, neither the Declaration of Independence nor the Constitution specified an official language for the United States. This was not an oversight, as the English Only movement argues, but a planned political strategy (Heath, 1977, 1981). Underpinning this decision of the 'Founding Fathers' was the centrality of the principle of individual choice. This was exemplified in the notion of free speech, and the related adoption of a laissez-faire language policy, deriving from the British model, which eschewed the legislative formality of granting 'official status' to English (see Marshall, 1986; Nunberg, 1992). Coupled with the widespread multilingualism described earlier, 'the intellectual climate of the times, which depended upon communication across language groups . . . supported maximum flexibility in language use' (Heath, 1977: 270).

This 'flexibility of language use' was also reflected in the well-established practice of granting limited minority-language rights to (some) minority-language speakers in the USA. The territory of Louisiana is a case in point. When Louisiana was annexed from France to the US in 1803, the then President, Thomas Jefferson, initially made few accommodations to the territory's Francophone majority. His first act, in fact, was to appoint a territorial governor who spoke no French and who proposed that English be the official language of the local government (Leibowitz, 1969). In the face of strong opposition, this policy was subsequently modified. After Louisiana joined the Union in 1812, Louisiana's laws and other public documents were printed in French, and the courts and legislature operated bilingually. These concessions, along with the right to bilingual schooling, survived in Louisiana law until 1921 (Crawford, 1992a). However, despite the relatively liberal language policy adopted over this time, the eventual demise of French as a public language was seldom in any doubt (Ricento, 1996).

The German-speaking minority in the USA was also accorded a measure of minority-language protection, both prior and subsequent to the country's declared independence in 1776. Indeed, the strength of the German language in Pennsylvania led the essayist and publisher Benjamin Franklin to complain bitterly in 1750: 'Why should *Pennsylvania*, founded by the *English*, become a colony of *Aliens*, who will shortly be so numerous as to Germanise us instead of our Anglifying them, and will never adopt our Language or Customs' (cited in Crawford, 1992a: 37; emphases in original).[6] Official proclamations were published in German until 1794 and at least 32 German-language newspapers were published between 1732 and 1800 (Crawford, 1992b; for a wider account of the multilingual nature of American literature, see Sollors, 1998). While the process of anglicisation and assimilation had reduced the influence of German in public life by 1815, the language remained a strong, unofficial presence throughout the nineteenth century, both in Pennsylvania and elsewhere. The ongoing strength of the German language was attributable here largely to a new influx of German migrants, beginning in the 1820s, who settled in cities such as St Louis, Milwaukee and Cincinnati as well as in the rural heartlands (R. Daniels, 1991). The German language dominated cultural and educational institutions in these areas and resulted in the widespread establishment of German-language schools, both private *and* public. Beginning in 1839, a number of states passed laws allowing German as the language of instruction in public schools, where numbers warranted, a clear tolerance-oriented language right (Dicker, 1996).

The growing acceptance of German-language education might have continued well into the twentieth century had it not been for two events. From the 1880s, state legislation was passed in several states mandating English as the only language of public (and even private) education. These clearly restrictionist policies were directed principally against German-language schools and formed part of a wider anti-immigration 'Americanisation movement' that emerged at this time (Crawford, 1989; Baron, 1990; Piatt, 1990). Although many of these laws were subsequently rescinded by the courts, the deleterious effects on German bilingual schooling were reinforced by the subsequent anti-German hysteria surrounding the First World War. The most (in)famous case of language restrictionism at this time occurred in Nebraska. A 1913 state law required public schools to provide instruction in any European language if 50 or more parents requested it; German was the only language ever requested. In 1918 the law was repealed on the basis that it was pro-German and thus un-American. The legislation that replaced it went so far as to prohibit any public- or private-school teacher from teaching a subject in a foreign language or, indeed, from teaching a foreign language *as a subject* (Dicker, 1996). The severity of the approach is not dissimilar to those adopted in totalitarian regimes such as Franco's Spain. The new law was overturned in the Supreme Court in 1923 in the *Meyer v. Nebraska* case (see below). However, by then, the damage was done. By the 1930s, bilingual instruction of any type in German had all but disappeared in the United States, while the study of German as a foreign language had fallen from 24 per cent of secondary-school students nationally in 1915 to less than one per cent in 1922 (Crawford, 1989).

One further example of the formal recognition of minority-language rights can be explored with regard to the use of Spanish in the state of New Mexico. While Hawai'i is the only US state which has actually declared itself to be officially bilingual (an example conveniently 'overlooked' by the English Only movement), New Mexico comes closest to this position in its recognition and use of both Spanish and English as languages of the state government. Like Hawai'i's official recognition of the indigenous Hawaiian language, the de facto endorsement of bilingualism in New Mexico acknowledges that Spanish is the language of a historical ethnie not (simply) an immigrant language. When the area was ceded to the United States by Mexico at the end of the Mexican-American war, via the (1848) Treaty of Guadalupe Hidalgo, over half its population were Spanish-speaking. As with the incorporation of French speakers in Louisiana before it, local language use was at first ignored. However, Spanish soon came to play a more prominent role within the territory when the US Congress in 1853 authorised the New Mexico Assembly to hire translators and interpreters to conduct its affairs. Subsequent funding was provided in 1884 for the translation and publication of the Assembly's proceedings into Spanish (Marshall, 1986) and a school law passed in that year permitted either Spanish or English as the language of instruction (Hernández-Chávez, 1995).

With the eventual granting of statehood in 1912,[7] these provisions were further formalised in New Mexico's Constitution. All laws could be published in both English and Spanish on a 20-year 'trial basis' and thereafter 'as the legislature may provide'. Given the relatively hostile climate towards minority languages at that time in the USA (see above), the ensuing decades saw the gradual ascendancy of English. Nonetheless, provisions for training teachers in both languages were established for the purposes of better serving Spanish-speaking pupils. Likewise, guarantees were provided to ensure that Spanish-speaking children were not discriminated against or segregated in schools. State statutes also called for the use of Spanish in a wide range of governmental activities, including elections, the posting of legal notices and bilingual/multicultural education (Dicker, 1996). In this last respect, the state's (1978) Bilingual-Multicultural Act specifically endorsed group-maintenance approaches to bilingual education and has facilitated the ongoing formal presence of Spanish within New Mexico's schools. This applies predominantly to Spanish, as one might expect. However, the recognition of other minority-language groups, including Native Americans, is also included (see Marshall, 1986: 43). Needless to say, as a result Spanish is still widely spoken in New Mexico, *alongside* English, in a wide range of language domains.

Before examining the English Only movement's third claim in relation to the language history of the United States – that bilingual practices such as these threaten for the first time the ascendancy of English in the US – I want to refer briefly to two key Supreme Court cases in the twentieth century which also support some accommodation of minority rights. The first has already been mentioned, *Meyer v. Nebraska* (1923), which challenged the restrictionist language policies adopted by Nebraska at the end of the First World War – one of many states to do so at the time. The Supreme Court ruled in this case that the state *was* able to restrict the language of instruction to English in state-funded schools but could not do so for private schools. The Court based its argument on the due process clause of the 14th Amendment which protects certain substantive individual liberties from restrictive state policies. The relevant part of the 14th Amendment reads: 'No states shall make or enforce any law which shall abridge the privileges or immunities of citizens; nor shall any state deprive any person of life, liberty, or property, without due process of law; nor deny any person within its jurisdiction to equal protection of laws'.

Since language is not specifically mentioned in this clause, an important precedent was thus established with regard to the protection of private minority-language education.[8] That said, the judgement was also clearly sympathetic to the general tenor of the state language policy in question, with its strong emphasis on the centrality of English: 'Perhaps it would be highly advantageous if all had ready understanding of our ordinary speech, but this cannot be coerced by methods which conflict with the Constitution – a desirable end cannot be promoted by prohibited means' (cited in Marshall, 1986: 15). Thus, the decision upholds only the most minimal interpretation of tolerance-oriented language rights, although this in itself remains an important guarantee in the US context.

Another landmark decision was *Lau v. Nichols* (1974) where the Supreme Court ruled in a case brought by Chinese-American parents that the English-only education policy in the San Francisco Unified School district effectively excluded Chinese-speaking children from meaningful participation in the education system. The Court concluded that this constituted a violation of equality of treatment under the (1965) Civil Rights Act: 'Under these state-imposed standards there is no equality of treatment merely by providing students with the same facilities, textbooks, teachers, and curriculum; for students who do not understand English are effectively foreclosed from any meaningful education' (cited in de Varennes, 1996a: 197). The decision was interpreted by proponents and opponents alike as at least tacit endorsement of bilingual education. However, the Court specifically refrained from ordering any particular educational remedy. As the judgement clearly states: 'No specific remedy is urged upon us. Teaching English to the students of Chinese ancestry who do not speak the language is one choice. Giving instructions to this group in Chinese is another. There may be others. Petitioners ask only that the Board of Education be directed to apply its expertise to the problem and rectify the situation' (cited in Crawford, 1989: 36).

Thus Macías has observed that while 'it is tempting to say that somehow the *Lau* decision created some [minority] language rights . . . it did not. The plaintiffs sought no specific remedy [from] the School District and the Court demanded none' (1979: 92; see also Schiffman, 1996: 269–270). In effect, the court did not make it a legal requirement for schools to provide bilingual education but simply ruled on the illegality of excluding minority-language students from such programmes.

While still limited, this position does nevertheless extend *Meyer v. Nebraska* considerably. *Lau* at least allows for the *possibility* of some state-funded provision of bilingual education even if the nonspecificity of the decision has meant that the standards of compliance associated with it remain somewhat varied (see Feinberg, 1990). However, more recent developments, notably the acceptance in 1998 of Proposition 227 in California which specifically delimits publicly funded bilingual education, may foreclose the possibility of such programmes being made available in the future (see below).

Nonetheless, there is clearly some precedent in both law and state policy and practice for a limited recognition of minority language and education rights in the USA. But this might appear to confirm the fear expressed by the English Only movement that such concessions, along with the provision of bilingual voting ballots, threaten the ascendancy of English in the USA (see, for example, Bikales, 1986: 84–85). Not so. If it is not already apparent by now, such an assertion is simply nonsense. Linguistic shift *from* minority languages *to* English – what Gorlach (1986) has described as 'reduced multilingualism' – is the dominant pattern in the USA. In this regard, less than four per cent of the population are actually non-English speakers (Amastae, 1990). According to the 1990 census, 80 per cent of those over the age of five for whom English is not a first language speak English 'well' or 'very well' (Ricento, 1996). Immigrants are actually currently shifting to English at a faster rate than was true of European immigrants at the turn of the century (Baron, 1990). Indeed, 75 per cent of all Hispanic immigrants – who cause the most 'concern' for English Only advocates – speak English frequently each day (Veltman, 1983, 1988; Portes and Hao, 1998). The only distinction of Hispanic communities to this general pattern of language shift is that it takes perhaps one further generation to occur fully – that is, four as opposed to two or three – given the continued influx of monolingual Spanish speakers (Fishman, 1992). As Veltman sensibly concludes, the only languages that are threatened in the USA are languages *other than* English.

Misrepresenting bilingual education

The historical fictions perpetuated by the English Only movement in relation to minority-language policy and practice are thus plain to see. However, it does not end there. A similar approach is adopted in arguing about the link between English-language facility and subsequent educational achievement.

Not only this, English Only advocates also proceed to *actively* misrepresent the educational (and psychological) merits of bilingual education; an approach which has been aptly described by Cummins (1995) as a deliberate 'discourse of disinformation'. This dual strategy can now be examined.

A key tenet of much English Only rhetoric is that English is essential for social mobility in US society, or rather, that a lack of English *consigns* one inevitably to the social and economic margins. As Linda Chávez, a former President of US English, has argued: 'Hispanics who learn English will be able to avail themselves of opportunities. Those who do not will be relegated to second class citizenship' (cited in Crawford, 1992c: 172). Guy Wright, a prominent media supporter of English Only policies, takes a similar line in a 1983 editorial in the *San Francisco Examiner*, asserting that 'the individual who fails to learn English is condemned to semi-citizenship, condemned to low pay, condemned to remain in the ghetto' (cited in Secada and Lightfoot, 1993: 47). A more recent example can be found in US English advertising in 1998: 'Deprive a child of an education. Handicap a young life outside the classroom. Restrict social mobility. If it came at the hand of a parent it would be called child abuse. At the hand of our schools . . . it's called "bilingual education"' (cited in Dicker, 2000: 53). We have also seen this argument (if one can call it that) expressed by our judge in Amarillo, Texas, and, in only slightly less iconoclastic terms, by Schlesinger in Chapter 3 in relation to the 'ghettoisation' of minorities. Broadly similar positions have also been articulated with respect to bidialectalism – notably, in response to the controversy surrounding the attempts by California's Oakland School Board in 1996–97 to formalise the recognition and use of Ebonics (African American Vernacular English) within its education district (Collins, 1999).

There is certainly a measure of truth in the claim that learning standard English in the USA is an important prerequisite for participating in the social and economic 'mainstream'. Moreover, this conception is not the sole preserve of conservative commentators (see Macedo, 1994; McLaren, 1995; May, 1994a, 1999a). Donaldo Macedo, a trenchant critic of English Only, has argued, following Gramsci, that bilingual 'educators should understand the value of mastering the standard English language of the wider society. It is through the full appropriation of the standard English language that linguistic-minority students find themselves linguistically empowered to engage in dialogue with various sectors of the wider society' (1994: 128). However, where the intellectual dishonesty of the English Only movement becomes apparent, and where critics such as Macedo and I would beg to differ, is in the two allied claims that are then made:

1   that a mastery of English is *the* key determinant in effecting the social and economic 'betterment' of marginalised minority-language speakers
2   that the best means of achieving such mastery is via English-only 'submersion' educational policies

Arguments asserting that English is the key to social mobility, and conversely that its lack is the principal cause of social and economic marginalisation – like the debates on English as an international language, discussed previously – conveniently overlook the central question of the wider *structural* disadvantages facing minority-language speakers. Indeed, on this question, English Only advocates are almost wholly silent. Mastery of English, while important, is only *one* variable in the equation. After all, African Americans have been speaking English for two hundred years and yet many still find themselves relegated to urban ghettos (Macedo, 1994). Likewise, English is almost as inoperative with respect to Hispanic social mobility as it is with respect to black social mobility. Twenty-five per cent of Hispanics currently live at or below the poverty line, a rate that is at least twice as high as the proportion of Hispanics who are not English-speaking (Fishman, 1992; Garcia, 1995; San Miguel and Valencia, 1998). Macedo concludes of this:

> It would be more socially constructive and beneficial if the zeal that propels the US English movement to spread the 'English only' gospel were diverted toward the struggle to end violent racism, to alleviate the causes of poverty, homelessness, and family breakdown, among other social ills that characterise the lived experience of minorities in the United States. If these social issues are not dealt with appropriately, it is naive to think that the acquisition of the English language alone will, somehow, magically eclipse the raw and cruel injustices and oppression perpetrated against the dispossessed class of minorities in the United States.
>
> (1994: 128; see also Kozol, 1991)

As for sustaining the merits of an English-only 'submersion' approach to education, this is only achieved by a deliberate misrepresentation of, and polemical attack on, bilingual education. The strategy adopted here by the English Only movement is effected on two key fronts. First, English Only advocates imply that, given sufficient motivation, anyone can master English in an English-only environment, a position which is usually tied to the related lament that bilingual education has replaced the beloved 'sink or swim' approach (see Imhoff, 1990; R. Porter, 1990). In effect, the argument is that 'children of normal intelligence' are sure to learn English if they are exposed to it. As Donahue (1985) argues, this position conveniently blames the victim and, in so doing, masks a deeply racist attitude to non-English speakers (see also Zentella, 1997). Second, the English Only movement continues to argue on this basis that bilingual education disadvantages minority children both educationally and socially. The position adopted here stands in sharp contrast to the bulk of academic research on the topic which points strongly to the attested social and educational merits of learning in one's first language and to the particular benefits of maintenance bilingual programmes. Such research began with UNESCO's (1953) unequivocal endorsement of 'mother-tongue teaching' and has been consistently reinforced since (for useful summaries, see Genesee, 1987; Baker, 1996; Cummins, 1996; Corson, 1993, 1998; Baker and Prys Jones, 1998; see also my discussion in Chapter 5). Given this, the only way that the English Only movement can sustain its position is by deliberately ignoring these widely attested conclusions. As Cummins (1995) observes, drawing on Chomsky (1987), the 'threat of the good example' must be neutralised. This is achieved by the use of a limited number of deeply flawed US government-sponsored research studies which cast (some) doubt on bilingual education (see also Cummins, 1996, 1999a, b; Krashen, 1996, 1999). To explore these studies further, and their inherent limitations, it is necessary to sketch briefly the political background that led to their commissioning.

Much of the concern expressed by English Only advocates about the emergence of bilingual education relates to its apparent endorsement in the (1968) Bilingual Education Act. The Act was actually an extension (Title VII) of an earlier one – the (1965) Elementary and Secondary Education Act (ESEA) – established by Lyndon Johnson in his 'war against poverty' programme. In this respect, both its remit and underlying philosophy were directed at rectifying the poor educational performance of 'limited English-speaking ability' students, rather than with issues of bilingualism per se (Shannon, 1999). Indeed, the phrase 'limited English-speaking ability', which has continued to be used in the USA until quite recently, clearly denotes a deficit, subtractive view of bilingualism – describing students in relation to their *lack* of English, rather than their knowledge and command of other languages.

Nonetheless, critics such as Hayakawa argued that the Bilingual Education Act facilitated the development of not only transitional bilingual programmes but also group-maintenance bilingual approaches, depending on how one interpreted its rather vague remit. In fact, there is a convincing argument that this was not the case. Initially, these broad provisions did allow for the establishment of federally funded group-maintenance bilingual programmes, developments that were reflected in the 1974 reauthorisation of the Act. However, with the increasing political hostility towards group-maintenance bilingual education over the course of the 1980s, allied with the Reagan presidency of the time, the emphases increasingly shifted to transitional and English-only programmes. By the time of the 1988 reauthorisation of the Act, these views had become so firmly entrenched that advocates of bilingual education were having to fight to defend even transitional programmes. In this respect, the vagueness of the Act's remit has actually militated against, rather than fostered, the extension of bilingual-education initiatives (Moran, 1990; Secada and Lightfoot, 1993). The implicit deficit approach underlying what remit there is within the Act also lends itself far more easily to a subtractive view of bilingualism and bilingual education than to an enrichment perspective. Add to this a pattern of consistent underfunding for what was to begin with only a modest grant-in-aid programme anyway, and it is not hard to see that the Act's influence on group-maintenance bilingualism is far less than is often claimed by its opponents.

Part of the success in neutering what little impact the Bilingual Education Act might have had is related to the English Only movement's mobilisation of two high-profile federally funded reports critical of bilingual education. The first of these, the American Institute for Research's (AIR) evaluation of bilingual education programmes, was commissioned by the United States Office of Education and published in 1978. It provided an overview of federally funded bilingual programmes operating at the time and found that such programmes had no significant impact on educational achievement in English, although they did enhance native-like proficiency. It furthermore suggested that pupils were being kept in transitional bilingual programmes longer than necessary, thus contributing to the segregation of such students from 'mainstream' classes (Moran, 1990). Despite significant criticism of its methodology (see below), these findings dealt a considerable blow to bilingual education advocates and led Congress in 1978 to begin the process of shifting the remit of the Bilingual Education Act towards a more English-only approach.

The conclusions of the AIR study were seemingly replicated by a second piece of federally commissioned research by Baker and de Kanter (1981, 1983; see also Rossell and Baker, 1996). They reviewed the literature and likewise concluded that bilingual education was not advancing the English-language skills and academic achievements of minority-language students. In short, Baker and de Kanter argued that students had no clear advantage over those in English-only programmes. Given the increasingly sceptical political climate of the time, this research generated enormous publicity and exerted even more influence on subsequent federal policy. However, as Crawford (1989) observes, while the Baker and de Kanter (1983) report is easily the most quoted federal pronouncement on bilingual education, it is probably the most criticised as well. As with its predecessor, much of this criticism had to do with the methodology that was employed. For example, as with the AIR study, Baker and de Kanter specifically rejected the use of data gathered through students' first languages. They also failed to account for the fact that two thirds of the comparison group in English-only education programmes *had previously been in bilingual programmes* where, presumably, they had benefited from first-language instruction (Crawford, 1992a). Moreover, in failing to differentiate between transitional and maintenance bilingual programmes in their analysis, the somewhat lesser educational effectiveness of the former, which constituted the majority of the programmes under review, inevitably subsumed the better educational results of the latter (Cummins, 1995, 1996). Overall, the inadequacy of Baker and de Kanter's findings has been confirmed by Willig's (1985, 1987) subsequent meta-analyses of their data. Willig controlled for 183 variables that they had failed to take into account. She found, as a result, small to moderate differences in favour of bilingual education, even when these were predominantly transitional programmes.

Willig's conclusions, which confirm what is elsewhere widely acknowledged, are also replicated in the most recent federally funded bilingual research. In the largest study yet, Ramírez et al. (1991) compared English-only programmes with transitional and group-maintenance bilingual programmes, following 2,300 Spanish-speaking students over four years. The findings clearly supported bilingual education and found that the greatest growth in mathematics, English-language skills and English reading was particularly evident among students in late-exit [group-maintenance] bilingual programmes where students had been taught predominantly in Spanish. By implication, the Ramírez study also confirmed another feature which is widely corroborated by other research on bilingual education, that minority-language students who receive most of their education in English rather than their first language are *more* likely to fall behind and drop out of school. In fact, it is important to note here that the English-only programmes used for comparison in the Ramírez study were not typical to the extent that while the teachers taught in English, they nonetheless understood Spanish. This suggests that in the far more common situation where the teacher does not understand the students' first language, the trends described here are likely to be further accentuated. What is so interesting here is that this research has generated far less interest and had far less impact on subsequent federal policy than its two predecessors (see McQuillan and Tse, 1996; Krashen, 1996, 1999). As Ricento observes of this, in spite of an impressive amount of both qualitative and quantitative research now available on the merits of bilingual education, 'the public debate (to the extent that there is one) [in the USA] tends to focus on perceptions and not on facts' (1996: 142).

The English Only movement thus continues to insist in the face of consistent published research to the contrary that English-only programmes are the best educational approach to adopt for minority-language students. In so doing, it uses to great effect the few high-profile but methodologically suspect studies which appear to support its case. This would seem to amount to little more than cynical (although highly successful) political manipulation, an assertion that is confirmed when one looks at the movement's failure to fund the English-only programmes for minority students that it so vociferously advocates. In this respect, English Only is clearly found wanting. Many of the members of the public who supported the establishment of official state-level English policies logically assumed that a principal concern of the legislation was to expand the opportunities for immigrants to learn English. However, logical or not, this has proved not to be the case. While US English spent lavishly to get these measures on the ballot, in 1988 it declined to support legislation creating a modestly funded federal programme

for adult learners of English (Crawford, 1992c). As a result of public criticism, US English did make some subsequent effort to fund similar ventures,
but these efforts have remained largely desultory and continue to constitute
only the barest minimum of their total funding efforts (Dicker, 2000). The
attitude adopted here appears to be that English-language programmes should
be the sole responsibility of Spanish-speaking volunteers! Guy Wright, whom
we have already encountered, wrote somewhat wistfully along these lines in
his media column in 1986, suggesting that a grassroots volunteer movement
was by far the best solution since 'the legislature will balk when it realises how
much it would cost to hire enough credentialed teachers and professional
administrators to cope with the waiting lists for English classes'. Taking the
latter route was also not necessary in his view since 'the immigrant doesn't
need to learn perfect English . . . [only] survival English'. Accordingly, 'volunteers will need some guidance from the state. But not too much. A simple
briefing and a handbook that set out the lessons should do' (cited in Tollefson,
1991: 124).

Wright's ruminations contradict (albeit unwittingly) a central tenet of the
English Only movement – that non-native English speaking immigrants
(particularly Hispanics) are *unwilling* to learn English. This is flatly contradicted by the facts, as Wright's comments on 'waiting lists' implicitly
suggest (see Dicker, 2000: 55 for specific details of the high demand among
migrants for English-language courses). His sentiments concerning 'survival
English' also clearly illustrate the underlying racism and indifference towards
minority language speakers that are evident in so much of English Only
rhetoric (see below). As Crawford concludes:

> One thing is clear. Rather than promote English proficiency, 99 per cent
> of the organisation's efforts go toward restricting the use of other lan-
> guages. Certainly there is nothing in Official English legislation to help
> anyone learn English. On the other hand, there is much to penalise those
> who have yet to do so . . . English Only is a label that has stuck, despite the
> protests of US English, because it accurately sums up the group's logic:
> That people will speak English only if they are forced to. That the crutch
> of bilingual education must be yanked away or newcomers will be perman-
> ently handicapped. That immigrants are too lazy or dim-witted to accept
> 'the primacy of English' on their own.
>
> (1992c: 176)

The result of this misinformed, disingenuous but nonetheless highly
politically effective rhetoric on bilingual education can be seen starkly in the
adoption of Proposition 227 in California in June 1998. Proposition 227 –
entitled, 'The English Language Education for Children in Public Schools
Initiative' – characterised California's previous record on educating immigrant

children (aka bilingual education) as a failure. In its place, it required that all children for whom English is not a first language be educated in 'sheltered' English-only programmes, for one year only, after which they would be transferred into mainstream classes. Limited exceptions to this model are allowed but only by parental request, and on being granted written waivers (see Orellana et al., 1999; Dicker, 2000). All reputable research in bilingual education, as should be clear by now, suggests that this submersion English-only approach, with only short-term specialist support, represents the worst of all possible worlds for such (predominantly Hispanic) students.

The return of the nativist

If US English is not actually concerned with extending opportunities to minority-language speakers to learn English, or when it does, it only does so via what is widely attested by bilingual research as the *least* effective educational approach, there must be another, more sinister agenda at work. In this respect, it is interesting to note that all previous movements that advocated English-only policies did so as part of a wider nativist and anti-immigrationist agenda. The current English Only movement, despite its disavowals, is no exception to this trend – in effect, it provides us with a modern variant of the Americanisation movement which swept the country around the turn of the last century. The links that the organisation US English has with anti-immigrationist groups would appear to confirm this, not least because the co-founder of US English, John Tanton, was also previously the founder of a smaller anti-immigration organisation, 'Federation for American Immigration Reform' (see Jaimes and Churchill, 1988).

The principal concern of Tanton, and other anti-immigrationists involved in the English Only movement, if it is not already all too clearly apparent, is the rapidly rising Hispanic population in the United States. Spanish speakers currently number 17 million in the USA, and US census forecasts suggest that by the year 2005 Hispanic Americans will surpass Black Americans as the largest minority. It is further suggested that by the year 2050 Hispanic communities will have increased from 10.7 per cent of the total population to 25 per cent, outnumbering the combined total of African Americans, Asian Americans and Native Americans. This will coincide with a concomitant decline in the number of white Americans (*Guardian*, 31 March 1997). It is this population growth – what Tanton has termed 'the Latin onslaught' on the USA – which is the real concern of many English Only advocates. Zentella (1997) has coined the term 'Hispanophobia' to describe it.

Tanton's own Hispanophobia was exposed when an internal memorandum he wrote in 1986 was made public two years later, causing his resignation from US English. In it, he discusses a range of cultural threats posed by 'Spanish-speaking immigrants', including a lack of involvement in public affairs, Roman Catholicism, low 'educability', high school-dropout rates and 'high fertility'. Among a range of questions raised in relation to these concerns were: 'Perhaps this is the first instance in which those with their pants up are going to get caught with their pants down'. 'Will the present [white] majority peaceably hand over its political power to a group that is simply more fertile?' 'As whites see their power and control over their lives declining, will they simply go quietly into the night? Or will there be an explosion?' (cited in Crawford, 1992c: 173). A number of notable public supporters of the organisation also resigned at the time because of the anti-Hispanic and anti-Catholic sentiments expressed, including Linda Chávez, the then President of US English.

Despite this setback, US English has continued to garner increasingly wide support. And this is where the present English Only movement differs from its predecessors. In short, it cannot *simply* be a nativist movement – or, rather, it cannot just be a simple (transparent) nativist movement – since, one would expect, it would not have generated the broad following that it has. This would appear to be confirmed by the extent of the movement's appeal to many minority-language speakers themselves, as we saw previously with the success of California's Proposition 63. Indeed, its prominent minority supporters have been regularly paraded by the movement as the epitome of the 'good alien' (Tarver, 1994); the success stories of immigration and the embodiment of the American dream. These have included Hayakawa himself – although, as Donahue (1985) points out, he actually came from British Columbia – Gerda Bikales, and Linda Chávez.

How is the movement able to generate this wide appeal, among both majority- and minority-language speakers? One way it does so is by *inverting* the usual immigration and language axis. Where previous movements concentrated primarily on concerns over immigration, from which arose (subsequent) language policies, the English Only movement attempts the reverse, thus making it far more politically palatable. In short, it concentrates almost solely on the status of the English language in the USA as a convenient proxy for a more overtly racial politics. The approach adopted here is similar to the 'new racism' which substitutes (at least ostensibly) culturalist arguments about 'race' for biological ones (see Barker, 1981; Donald and Rattansi, 1992; Small, 1994; Gillborn, 1995; Rattansi, 1999; see also Chapter 1). Deutsch has observed that 'language is an automatic signalling system, second only to race, in identifying targets for privilege or discrimination' (1975: 7; see also Chapter 4). James Crawford argues along more specific lines:

> The English Only movement, an outgrowth of the immigration-restrictionist lobby, has skilfully manipulated language as a symbol of national unity and ethnic divisiveness. Early in [the twentieth] century, those who sought to exclude other races [sic] and cultures invoked claims of Anglo-Saxon superiority. But in the 1980s, explicit racial loyalties are no longer acceptable in political discourse. Language loyalties, on the other

hand, remain largely devoid of associations with social injustice. While race is [supposedly] immutable, immigrants can and often do exchange their mother tongue for another. And so, for those who resent the presence of Hispanics and Asians, language politics has become a convenient surrogate for racial politics.

(1989: 14)

Certainly, this could explain why states such as California, where Hispanics will constitute a two-thirds majority by 2040 (*Independent*, 4 June 1998), appear so enamoured with the English Only movement's agenda.[9]

The 'curse' of multilingualism

Which brings us to the fourth and final dimension of the English Only movement that I want to examine here, its argument that multilingualism and minority-language rights are inherently destabilising to the nation-state. As we saw in Chapter 3, this is a view that is widely shared by both liberal and conservative commentators. Given its commonsense assumptions, it also finds considerable support among the wider public, providing another reason for the English Only movement's wide appeal. Thus, Kathryn Bricker, former executive director of US English, can assert:

> Language is so much a part of our lives that it can be a great tool either for unity or disunity. And we are getting close to the point where we have a challenge to the common language that we share . . . We are basically at a crossroads. We can reaffirm our need for a common language, or we can slowly go down the road of division along language lines.

(cited in Secada and Lightfoot, 1993: 46)

Other assertions are even more apocalyptic – emphasising the potential nightmares of separatism and civil strife apparent in prominent 'ethnic conflicts' elsewhere in the world. Gary Imhoff, for example, baldly states that 'language diversity has been a major cause of [international] conflict . . . Any honest student of the sociology of language should admit that multilingual societies have been less united and internally peaceful than single-language societies' (1987: 40). Likewise, Hayakawa has argued:

> For the first time in our history, our nation [sic] is faced with the possibility of the kind of linguistic division that has torn apart Canada in recent years; that has been a major feature of the unhappy history of Belgium, split into speakers of French and Flemish; that is at this very moment a bloody division between the Sinhalese and Tamil populations of Sri Lanka.

(cited in Nunberg, 1992: 492)

However, as I have already indicated in the preceding chapter, the position painted here is simply wrong – both in its historical and comparative dimensions. Historically, the principal cause of most language-based conflicts has been the *denial* of legitimate minority-language rights rather than their recognition. This is true of Canada, Belgium and Sri Lanka. We have already seen this to be the case with respect to Belgium, and I will outline shortly why the Canadian context, with particular reference to Québec, can also be regarded in the same light. The conflict in Sri Lanka between the Sinhalese majority (comprising 75 per cent of the population) and the Lankan Tamils (who comprise 12.5 per cent of the remaining Tamil-speaking population) was also largely precipitated by, but not limited to, the language question. In 1956, eight years after independence, Sinhala was made the sole official language, replacing English. This language law created much discontent among Tamil speakers who, with limited access to land, had previously looked to the civil service for employment. With the implementation of the official language law, this option was increasingly denied to them also. Moreover, the language measure was the first of many that restricted the rights and opportunities of Tamil speakers. The subsequent Tamil independence movement, which emerged formally in 1973, thus draws its grievances from this wider background of the apparent denial of minority Tamil aspirations by the majority Sinhalese (Fishman and Solano, 1989; see also Little, 1994).

If this degree of historical inaccuracy were not enough, the comparisons drawn between the USA and these examples are also misplaced and misleading. In Canada and Belgium, minority-language claims centre on the rights of historical ethnies who are formally recognised, at least ostensibly, in the bicultural and bilingual frameworks of the countries concerned. The question is thus not about the eventual linguistic assimilation of these minority-language speakers, and the best way(s) this might be achieved, as in the USA. Rather, it concerns how separate language recognition as befits their status as ethnies can be achieved, and how past injustices that have militated against such recognition can be rectified.[10] Although there are also historical ethnies within the USA, notably Native Americans and some Spanish speakers, the principal concerns of the language debates there remain focused on immigrants or new minorities. Likewise, the erosion and infringement of existing *constitutional* minority-language rights, leading to the threat of conflict and secession, has no precedent in the USA, not even with the Louisiana Purchase or the Treaty of Guadalupe Hidalgo (Magnet, 1990).

Contrasting Québec

These distinctions can be highlighted further by a brief examination of the language debates in Québec, along with their broader impact on Canada.

Francophones in Québec at the time of the 1990 census constituted a clear majority (83 per cent) in the province, and a considerable minority (23 per cent) throughout the whole of Canada (Forbes, 1993; Barbaud, 1998). This makes French a 'regional majority language' in the area of Québec (Maurais, 1997), although it still clearly remains a minority language throughout Canada as a whole. Along with the historical status of Francophones as one of the two colonial charter groups of Canada, the apparent strength of French, particularly in Québec, might suggest a measure of cultural and linguistic security for the language. Not so. The history of Francophones in Canada conforms broadly to the experiences of minority-language speakers elsewhere. Since the defeat of the French in 1759 in what was then called New France, and with its subsequent incorporation into the Canadian Confederation in 1867, Francophones have clearly been the minority partner in Canadian institutional life. In short, they have been subject to the political, cultural and economic dominance of English speakers (Anglophones) throughout Canada and, until recently, in Québec itself. Consequently, it has been only within the last 50 years that significant linguistic accommodations have been made towards Francophones. For example, it was only in 1958 that simultaneous translation became available in the Canadian House of Commons. It was not until 1969 that bilingualism in the Canadian federal civil service was formalised with the passing of the first Official Language Act (revised in 1988). And it was not until 1982 that the right to minority-language education in French outside of Québec was entrenched via the Canadian Charter of Rights and Freedoms (Réaume, 1999; see also Chapter 5).

However, it is true to say that, over time, Francophones, at least in Québec, have also consistently achieved, and been able to maintain, a considerable degree of institutional autonomy (Colin Williams, 1994). This measure of institutional autonomy was initially based upon their status as French Canadians or 'Canadiens', which, in turn, was perceived in primarily ethnic and religious terms, rather than in language terms (Juteau, 1996). Identification via the French language was only to come much later (see below). Nonetheless, in carving out an institutional niche for themselves in Québec, French Canadians were also able to safeguard an ongoing role for French within the civic realm, albeit indirectly at first. That said, developments immediately after the conquest of New France by the British suggested a far less promising picture. This was because the first significant piece of legislation – the (1763) Royal Proclamation – was specifically punitive towards the French Canadian majority in the region (cf. US legislation in Louisiana, discussed earlier). The Proclamation imposed English law and effectively barred French Canadians from public office by requiring them first to abjure, or formally renounce, their Catholicism. This punitive approach, however, was quickly replaced by a more accommodating one in the actual practice of provincial administration. The latter tendency was further confirmed by the (1774) Québec Act, which, in attempting to ensure the loyalty of French Canadians at the time of the American War of Independence, reinstated civil laws and institutions (including the right for Catholics to hold public office) and indirectly recognised the use of French alongside English in their application. This process of accommodation was furthered by the (1791) Constitutional Act, which recognised the regional majority rights of French Canadians by dividing the territory into Upper and Lower Canada (corresponding today to the southern portions of Ontario and Québec respectively). In the latter, French Canadians were able to exercise considerable autonomy in political and civil administration, while French was also able to continue in its de facto role as the language of that administration. After rebellions in the late 1830s in both areas, Britain attempted to reimpose a more overtly assimilationist approach. Following a report by Lord Durham in 1839, which situated the problems of the region in the continued cultural and linguistic existence of the French Canadian community, the (1840) Union Act was implemented. This reunited the two areas of Upper and Lower Canada and specifically proscribed French as a language of public record or of debate in the new legislative assembly. However, actual practice again proved to be more accommodating, leading to a reunified Anglo- and French-Canadian political administration in 1847, and the reinstatement of French as an administrative language in 1848 (Magnet, 1995). This accommodation of bilingualism was subsequently to be reflected in the (1867) British North American Act, which established Canada in its modern form and which in Section 133 recognised a limited administrative and judicial role for French/English bilingualism. While Canadian courts were subsequently to delimit the provisions of Section 133 even further (see Réaume, 1999), it nonetheless provided an important precedent, leading to the eventual further extension of minority-language rights in the (1982) Canadian Charter of Rights and Freedoms.

The institutional autonomy carved out by the French-Canadian community in Québec was aided, until the 1950s, by the relative geographical isolation of Québec, by its predominantly rural outlook and, primarily, by its Catholicism. Indeed, from the time of the conquest of New France until the 1950s, it was the Catholic Church rather than the provincial administration which was the principal protector and defender of French language and culture (Guibernau, 1999, Heller, 1999). However, with the emergence of the 'Quiet Revolution' in the 1950s and 1960s – which saw the transformation of Québec into a modern western economy – the role of the church faded rapidly. In its place, a new territorial conception of 'Québécois' identity as a 'distinct society' was established, thus excluding French Canadians from outside Québec, while 'joual', or Québec French, came to be seen as its principal marker (see Handler, 1988: 163–166; see also Balthazar, 1990; McRoberts, 1988, 1997). This new Québécois identity replaced the previous nostalgic celebration of rurality and French-Canadian Catholicism with a modernist political outlook centred on the economic, political, cultural and linguistic liberation of

Québec (Juteau, 1996; Heller, 1999). As Juteau argues, it transformed 'a past-oriented, static and essentialist orientation into an ideology emphasising control over one's destiny and modernity' (1996: 47), a process that equates closely with cultural nationalism, as discussed in Chapter 2.

These developments, and the central role of language within them, led to the establishment of the Office de la langue française in 1961, whose principal function was to protect and standardise the use of French within Québec (Handler, 1988; Barbaud, 1998). Two important commissions at that time also reaffirmed the significance of language. The Parent Commission of 1966 recommended that the major responsibility of the provincial government was to protect the French language, regulate its use, encourage its improvement, and ensure the fullest possible development of the culture it expressed (Mallea, 1989). The Laurendeau-Dunton Commission, which first reported in 1967, found that the wider principle of French/English language equality enshrined in the Canadian Confederation could only realistically be achieved within Québec, let alone elsewhere in Canada, when the marked economic and educational disparities between Francophones and Anglophones were addressed. In Québec, for example, the Catholic Church had historically discouraged Francophones from involvement in the business sector. This had resulted in a cultural division of labour in which an Anglicised elite dominated the economy, and where English had accordingly become inextricably associated with social mobility. Indeed, the Laurendeau-Dunton Report found that, on the basis of average income, monolingual Anglophone males in Québec constituted the most economically privileged group in all of Canada. In contrast, their Francophone counterparts earned 35 per cent less in comparison (Barbaud, 1998). French was further threatened by a declining birth rate among the Francophone population, by increased emigration to other provinces, and by an increasing pattern of new minorities in Québec choosing to send their children to English-speaking schools, given the higher status of English within Canada. In this last respect, it was found that in 1971–72, fully 85 per cent of new minorities were being educated in English-language schools, while in 1973 even 25,000 French-speaking students were enrolled in such schools (Maurais, 1997). These immediate concerns over the fate of the language were also framed within a wider scepticism towards the Canadian federal government's bilingual policy, which seemed to be doing little to redress the decline of French throughout Canada (Heller, 1999). Indeed, given the predominance of English elsewhere in Canada, and in prestigious institutional domains within Québec, only an active promotion-oriented language policy in favour of French could redress the balance. This was the conclusion of the Laurendeau-Dunton Commission since, in its view, 'the life of the French-Canadian culture necessarily implies the life of the French language' (cited in Coulombe, 1995: 75).

As a result of this increasing focus on language as the core of Québécois identity, a range of significant language legislation actively promoting French

was enacted in the 1970s. These legislative developments were also facilitated by the rise of the nationalist Parti Québécois (PQ) to provincial government for the first time in 1976. The most prominent of the language laws
passed at this time, Bill 101 (Charte de la langue française, 1977), has also
been the most controversial. The Bill aimed to address the historical cultural
division of labour in Québec by formalising French in economic, educational and political domains. As the Bill's architect, Camille Laurin, argued:

> The Québec we wish to build will be essentially French. The fact that the
> majority of its population is French will be clearly visible – at work, in
> communications and in the countryside. It will also be a country in which
> the traditional balance of power will be altered, especially in regard to the
> economy . . . this will accompany, symbolise and support a reconquest by
> the French-speaking majority in Québec of that control of the economy
> that we ought to have.

> (Laurin, 1977; cited in Colin Williams, 1994: 196)

Specifically, the Bill entailed that all children in state education, except
those whose parents had themselves been taught in English *in Québec*, attend
Francophone schools – requiring, in effect, all Francophones, new minorities and other Canadians to be educated in French. Freedom of choice with
respect to language of instruction would now be available only at the Cegep
(pre-university) and university levels (Maurais, 1997). In addition, all commercial signs were required to be solely in French. And all businesses with
over 50 employees had to undertake 'francisation' programmes so as to
ensure the right of any Quebecer to be able to work in French, in both the
public and the private sectors. The process of francisation, in particular,
provided Francophones with significant linguistic capital in business and
commerce and, in so doing, opened up higher-status occupations to them –
both of which had been, until then, traditionally denied them (Keating,
1997; Heller, 1999). The Office de la langue française was given responsibility for the application and enforcement of Bill 101 and was subsequently
backed up by the Commission de surveillance. In 1983, the latter became
the Commission de protection de la language française and was endowed
with formal powers of inquiry to investigate any shortfalls in the francisation
programmes of companies within Québec (Barbaud, 1998).

Needless to say, the Bill's requirements, and its enforcement, generated
considerable opposition, particularly from the Anglophone minority in
Québec and the Anglophone majority elsewhere in Canada. Subsequently,
aspects of Bill 101 were ruled unconstitutional. The educational restrictions
were deemed by the Canadian Supreme Court in 1984 to contravene Article
23 of the (1982) Canadian Charter of Rights and Freedoms protecting the
rights of minority-language speakers (although Québec had not actually been

involved in its endorsement; see below). Thus, the Supreme Court ruled that, in addition to the exemptions outlined in Bill 101, children whose parents had received elementary instruction in English *anywhere in Canada*, and the siblings of a child who had received, or was receiving, elementary or secondary instruction in English in Canada, could also attend English-language schools in Québec. The commercial signage restrictions were also deemed discriminatory by the Supreme Court in the *Ford v. Québec* (1988) case, although a comparable case brought before the United Nations Human Rights Committee (UNHRC) the following year, *Ballantyne, Davidson and McIntyre v. Canada*, was more favourable towards the policy. In this respect, the UNHRC acknowledged that, under Article 27 of the International Covenant on Civil and Political Rights (ICCPR; see Chapter 5), the Québec government could validly seek to protect French within Québec as long as such a policy was not used to delimit the use of other minority languages in the private domain (see also below). Similarly, the UNHRC ruled that the litigants, who were Anglophones living in Québec, were *not* a linguistic minority under Article 27, as they claimed, because 'English-speaking citizens *of Canada* cannot be considered a linguistic minority' (cited in de Varennes, 1996: 142; my emphasis).

In response to the contested legal nature of their language policy, the Québec provincial government initially disregarded the Canadian Supreme Court's rulings by invoking the 'notwithstanding clause' of Canada's Constitution, arguing that Bill 101 was in the best interests of Québec's distinct character (Lemco, 1992; Tully, 1995; Coulombe, 1999). However, over time, and in light of the actual success of the francisation programme in cementing French within the civic and commercial domains (see below), language restrictions were gradually relaxed. For example, most of the machinery for enforcing francisation was abolished in 1993, along with the legislation restricting non-French advertising (Keating, 1997).

The tensions between the francisation programme of the Québec government and the wider Canadian polity have nonetheless remained ongoing. The general scepticism in Canada towards the arguments employed in defence of Bill 101 was, for example, to result in the eventual failure of the (1987) Meech Lake Accord. The Accord had attempted to reconcile Québec's aspirations as a 'distinct society' with the federalism of the Canadian state as represented by the Canadian Charter of Rights and Freedoms. This was regarded as extremely important by both sides, not least because the provincial Québec government had never formally agreed to the latter, viewing it as too weak on the question of French language rights. However, the Meech Lake Accord lapsed when Manitoba and Newfoundland failed to sign it over concerns about the 'distinct society' clause. The Accord's failure, and the subsequent failure of a similar attempt, the (1992) Charlottetown Accord, have had ongoing ramifications for the increasingly fraught question of Québec's relationship with the rest of Canada, fuelling calls among Québec nationalists, particularly members of the Parti Québécois (PQ), for independence. This culminated in the October 1995 referendum on the question of Québec's sovereignty, which was lost by only 54,288 votes, or 1.6 per cent (Guibernau, 1999), although since that time support for sovereignty appears to have receded. Lest the issue of secession be given too much emphasis, however, one further caveat can be added here. Even at its most strident, the PQ's vision of a sovereign Québec was (and continues to be) highly attenuated, emphasising ongoing close economic and political partnership with Canada (Keating, 1996, 1997). Moreover, the principal concerns of the PQ, *in practice*, have focused primarily on questions of cultural nationalism – notably, on the question of language – rather than on secession as such, and this continues to be the case in the present.

To return then directly to the question of comparison, can one argue that the restrictionist Québec language laws are in the same (illiberal) league as those advocated by the English Only movement in the USA? The short answer is no. In fairness to the English Only movement, the language laws of Québec are far from unproblematic, certainly. However, it is surely ironic that the most problematic aspects of these language policies – and certainly, the most criticised – are those which most closely reflect the majoritarian tendencies of the English Only movement itself. The Québec language laws have largely achieved their intention of raising the public profile of French within Québec. In effect, the previously marginalised status of French within the economy and within education has been reversed. French now features as both a functional and legitimate language in commerce and industry (Colin Williams, 1994), while there is a pattern of increasing enrolment in French-language schools, even by those eligible for English-language education (Coulombe, 1995). But these results have been achieved, it seems, only at the expense of certain individual freedoms with regard to language choice. In relation to Will Kymlicka's distinction between external protections and internal restrictions, discussed in Chapter 3, it is clear that the Québec language laws are *primarily* an external protection. In other words, they relate to *inter*group relations where a national minority group seeks to protect its distinct identity by limiting the impact of the decisions of the larger society. However, they necessarily involve internal restrictions on members of that community as well, and the degree to which the latter is actually valid remains open to serious question. Kymlicka himself suggests it might not be when, in his own discussions on these issues, he describes Bill 101 as 'an over-restrictive external protection' (1995a: 205).

These concerns notwithstanding, it can nonetheless be argued that the Québec laws are not as exclusionary as they might at first appear. First, access to English is not being denied in Québec, not least because it clearly remains the *majority* language of Canada and because Francophones are thus invariably bilingual in English as well. Rather, it is ongoing monolingualism *in English* that is being circumscribed. We have already seen that 'unfettered' language choice inevitably results in the loss of minority languages, grounded as it is in wider asymmetrical sociopolitical and socioeconomic power relations. Consequently, advocates of Bill 101 argue that the only way that individual bilingualism can be maintained and fostered is by, counterintuitively, setting strict limits on the extent of institutional bilingualism (Maurais, 1997).

Second, indigenous peoples in Québec are accorded distinct language rights on the basis that they are also, along with Francophones, historical ethnies in the territory. The architect of Bill 101, Laurin, admitted as much when observing: 'the Amerindians and the Inuit are the only ones who . . . can consider themselves as peoples separate from the totality of Québécois and in consequence [can] insist on special treatment under the law' (cited in Coulombe, 1995: 119). To be sure, this has not stopped French acting as a 'replacing language' with respect to indigenous languages in Québec, in much the same way as English has elsewhere in Canada (see Drapeau and Corbeil, 1996; Maurais, 1997; Hamers and Hummel, 1998). Nor are the broadly comparable rights claims of French and indigenous languages without their tensions (see Salée, 1995). Nonetheless, Québec's approach does specifically allow for the ongoing *active* protection and promotion of indigenous languages, particularly via education.

And this points to a third key distinction. The intent of the Québec language legislation is *not* to curb the use of other minority languages, as is the case with English Only (or, for that matter, in France itself; see Chapter 4). Indeed, the (1975) Québec Charter of Rights and Freedoms specifically recognises that persons belonging to new minorities – who are termed 'cultural communities' in Québec – have the right to continue to maintain and develop their own languages and cultures. This was followed by a 1978 White Paper, 'La politique québécoise du développement culturel', which stipulated a clear and active role for the state in support of minority languages and cultures. It was further formalised by the 1981 Québec government publication *Autant de Façons d'être Québécois*, which promoted the notion of 'interculturalism' as a stronger form of multiculturalism, specifically stating that its central aim was 'to ensure the survival and development of [Québec's] cultural communities as well as their individuality' (cited in Handler, 1988: 178).

In other words, cultural and linguistic pluralism are actively fostered while, at the same time, the use of the *majority* French language *within Québec* is legitimated and institutionalised within all public domains. One might add here that this formal promotion of French in the civic realm also constitutes a central part of the wider political question raised by Francophones' *minority* position within Canada – a position confirmed by the UNHRC case, discussed earlier. As such, it is entirely consistent with the granting of promotion-oriented rights in international law to minority-language speakers, *where numbers warrant*. In this respect, the questions raised here are inevitably related to the broader issue of the degree to which Francophone speakers in

Québec (and elsewhere in Canada) can maintain their autonomy, and the language and cultural rights attendant on this, as a legitimate part of the historical power-sharing agreement with Anglophone Canadians. Any ongoing discontents concern the *failure* adequately to ensure these protections; a failure, moreover, that continues to be evidenced in Canada by the ongoing decline of French in the majority of those provinces that do not accord French civic status (see Joy, 1992).

A question of (ethnolinguistic) democracy

It should thus be clear that the example of Québec bears little actual relation to the alarmist claims invoked by English Only advocates, both in substance and effect. While clearly not without its tensions, it should be stressed again that, where these do arise, they relate principally to the denial rather than the recognition of minority-language claims. Such a conclusion also points to a second fundamental weakness of the English Only position on multilingualism. If this contra-indicated position is actually the case, then far from ensuring national unity, restrictionist language policies such as those of the English Only movement are much more likely to precipitate *disunity*. In short, attempting to enforce linguistic homogeneity is far more likely to foster disunity than to ameliorate it. Indeed, of all possible scenarios, this one is likely to be the most divisive, the most contentious and fractious (Donahue, 1985). As Donahue asserts: 'The final irony of [the English Only] approach to the matter of language use is that by . . . aligning itself with a theory which holds that all ethnic intergroup behaviour is inevitably conflict producing, [it] forecloses itself from the possibility of unifying American society' (1985: 107).

In contrast, a 'language competent society' (A. Padilla, 1991) – where all minority-language speakers are able to learn English, while also retaining their first language – is far more likely to result in both social mobility for minority speakers and a more flexible and less contentious national language policy overall. As Marshall and Gonzalez conclude, 'it is not multilingualism itself that is disruptive, but denying a group that speaks a different language from participating in greater social mobility' (1990: 33). Given the distinctions that I have consistently drawn between national- and ethnic-minority groups, one can also add here the historical claims of ethnies which, while they may incorporate issues of social mobility, are not principally dependent upon them.

Which brings me to my final point in this chapter. Why does the English Only movement persist in peddling its position in the face of seemingly insurmountable evidence to the contrary? 'Why', as Fishman despairingly asks, 'are facts so useless in this discussion?' (1992: 167). The answer returns us to the wider social, economic and political context within which all debates on minority language and education are embedded. The principal motivation that underlies the rationale of so much of the English Only movement is to ensure that the dominant group, or Staatsvolk, maintains political, social and economic control of the civic realm of the United States. After all, what else could explain the deliberate amnesia about minority-language rights in the USA, the spurious association of multilingualism with conflict and fragmentation, and the rejection of the educational approach – group-maintenance bilingualism – that has been widely attested as most likely to benefit minority-language students? Jim Cummins candidly observes of this last feature that such empowerment pedagogy will continue to be resisted simply because empowered people are more difficult to exploit: 'if minority groups develop the confidence in their own identity [which includes valuing their language and culture] and the knowledge and critical awareness to articulate their rights, then they become resistant to exploitation at the hands of the dominant group' (1995: 160).

I am not suggesting, by this, some kind of grand conspiracy theory, although conspiratorial (anti-immigrationist) elements do clearly exist within the English Only movement. Rather, I wish to reiterate that the question of minority rights is not about a neutral, disinterested state responding to the claims of vociferous, 'politically motivated' minorities. It is about a *contest* in which *all* players are culturally and politically *situated* and one in which much is at stake on all sides. Specifically, it is a contest for recognition, for resources, and for justice, fairness and equity. As such, it is perhaps not surprising that many within the dominant ethnie are unwilling to renegotiate the terms of agreement which have served them so well in the past. However, do so they must. Otherwise, the greatest fear of many opponents of minority-language and education rights will be realised; the eventual break-up of the nation-state that they are so intent on defending. This is simply because national- and ethnic-minority groups are increasingly unwilling to settle for the degree of marginalisation and cultural and language evisceration which have historically characterised their incorporation into modern nation-states. As I have argued in Chapter 2, many of these groups are not actually seeking independent statehood – the sine qua non of political nationalism – but they *are* seeking greater *ethnocultural* and *ethnolinguistic democracy*.

The litmus test facing the USA and so many other nation-states today is thus their capacity to move from political democracy to this wider recognition and incorporation of cultural and linguistic democratic rights. Such change involves *reimagining* the nation-state and the role of minority languages and cultures within it. It means balancing the, at times, countervailing demands of individual and group rights. And it requires broadening the conception of what constitutes social, cultural and linguistic capital, and how these may be defined and used in the private and public realms. At stake here are questions of individual and collective social mobility. Also at stake, however, are the wider questions of minority inclusion within, and exclusion from, the nation-state, and the historical power relations upon which these are predicated. Accordingly, no one is suggesting that reimagining the nation-state along these lines will be an uncontested and unproblematic task – or, indeed, a panacea once accomplished – Québec, alone, suggests as much. But if the obstacles are complex and daunting, and the implications of a reconstituted nation-state remain uncertain, the possibilities that inhere in such a task – for *both* minorities *and* majorities – are nonetheless significant enough to warrant a serious attempt. The stakes are high but the potential rewards are even more so. Just how high – in both respects – can be seen in the following chapter, where I explore the principle of greater ethnolinguistic democracy in the European context, with specific reference to Catalonia and Wales.

Notes

1   France's 'mission to civilise' strategy is also a variant of this same theme.

2   'Official English' movement is the preferred designation adopted by its proponents in the USA. However, opponents use the phrase 'English Only' movement in order to highlight the exclusionary linguistic (and political and social) motives behind the movement. These motives will be highlighted in what follows.

3   A far more recent, although perhaps apocryphal, example of this kind of historically inadequate thinking is the story told of the US congressman who argued on a talkback show that 'if English was good enough for Jesus, it's good enough for me'!

4   In 1983, US English reported having 300 members, in 1984, 35,000 (Marshall, 1986). By 1994, its numbers had grown to some 400,000 members (J. Edwards, 1994) while, over the course of this time, the organisation has also attracted to its ranks many well-known public figures.

5   As one might expect from our discussions in Chapter 5, this assimilationist approach fostered both Native American language loss and educational 'underachievement'. Interestingly, it also stands in sharp contrast to a Cherokee educational initiative implemented prior to this policy. This self-managed policy, based on first-language principles, achieved a 90 per cent literacy rate in Cherokee *as well as* 'a higher English literacy level than the white populations of either Texas or Arkansas' (Crawford, 1989: 25; see also Fuchs and Havighurst, 1972; Szasz, 1974; and Chapter 8).

6   There is some suggestion that Franklin's increasingly trenchant views on multilingualism were linked to his bitterness over a business failure in publishing. In the 1730s, Franklin did not seem at all averse to multilingualism, teaching himself French, German, Italian, Spanish and Latin. He also launched the first *German*-language newspaper in North

America, the *Philadelphische Zeitung*. It was only after this venture failed, and a 'better qualified German printer' cornered the German book market, that his writings about American 'foreign'-language speakers took its sharply xenophobic turn (Shell, 1993).

7   Because New Mexico comprised predominantly 'mexicanas' (a term of self-identification among the Spanish-speaking population) and was also poor, it had to wait some 64 years for statehood. Statehood was only granted after 50 previously unsuccessful petitions to Congress (Hernández-Chávez, 1995).

8   However, the downside of this is that because language is not specifically mentioned in the 14th Amendment, some subsequent Supreme Court decisions have simply refused to address the issue of language discrimination at all. In *Garcia v. Spun Steak* (1993), for example, a claim of discrimination on the grounds that the employer prohibited Spanish speakers from speaking privately in Spanish to each other while at work was unsuccessful. This was because the Court declined to examine the principal point raised by the Spanish-speaking workers: that is, if some employees have the privilege of conversing with others privately at work in their primary language, they should not be denied the same privilege (de Varennes, 1996a).

9   The argument that English Only may appeal to racist beliefs is supported by a study by Huddy and Sears (1990). The authors examined the attitudes of white Americans towards bilingual education and found that opposition was strongest among those who looked down on minority groups, particularly on immigrants, and who opposed any federal support for them. In addition, these attitudes were most strongly represented in areas with a high Hispanic population (see also MacKaye, 1990).

10   With respect to Canada, see Taylor (1994), Tully (1995), Coulombe (1995, 1999) and Réaume (1999).

7

Extending ethnolinguistic democracy in Europe

If Europe was the locus of the modern nation-state as we know it, then it is also currently a prominent example of the rise of supranationalism. Most notable here of course is the growing influence of the European Union, which currently comprises 15 European nation-states and which is set to expand again in the near future to 21, as it begins to incorporate nation-states from Central and Eastern Europe. The EU has proved to be a focus of controversy in the politics of some European nation-states, Britain being one prominent example, for its avowed agenda of greater European integration. Anti-European parties in Britain, and elsewhere, have made much of the EU's potential to 'supersede' the sovereign functions of the traditional nation-state. The particular concerns of anti-European groups, which are usually but not exclusively on the right of the political spectrum, tend to focus on two key areas. One is the impending loss of economic sovereignty, a prospect that has been made more likely by the recent establishment of the 'Euro' pan-European currency. A second focuses on the potential loss of political sovereignty, via the increasing incorporation of member states into the administrative and political structures and functions of the EU bureaucracy.

These ongoing debates are not of principal concern to me here, except perhaps in as much as they point to the growing influence of supranational organisations such as the EU over the affairs of nation-states. However, unlike political opponents of the EU, as well as some academic commentators (see, for example, Hall et al., 1992; Robertson, 1992; Bauman, 1993; Soysal, 1994; Held, 1995), I do not believe that it signals the end of the modern nation-state as we know it (see also Chapter 1). Of course, nation-states *are* clearly subject to wider trends towards greater economic and political interdependence in this age of late capitalism, not least because of the rapid growth of globalisation (cf. Chapter 6). To suggest otherwise would be foolish. But the idea that this is an entirely new phenomenon would also appear to be misplaced, since nation-states have always been subject to wider economic and political forces of one form or another. As Hinsley observes, the idea of complete economic and political sovereignty is a 'situation to which many states may have often aspired, but have never in fact enjoyed' (1986: 226). Moreover, it can be argued that, far from replacing nation-states, supranational organisations such as the EU may serve, at least in some key respects, to reinforce them. Certainly, the two countervailing political views on European integration that have been promoted over the last decade – the idea of the federal European 'super state' versus the national 'opt out' – both perpetuate the notion of nationhood. The former simply transfers nationhood to a wider entity, adopting in the process many of its key political apparatus and symbols (territorial boundaries, immigration controls, parliament, currency and an electorate). The latter continues to define membership of the EU in terms of existing nation-states and national boundaries (Shore and Black, 1994; Billig, 1995; A. Smith, 1998). Indeed, some have gone so far as to argue that the European Union has been a key bulwark of the nation-state. As Milward argues, 'it has been its buttress, an indispensable part of the nation-state's post-war construction. Without it, the nation-state could not have afforded to its citizens the same measure of security and prosperity which it has provided and which has justified its survival' (1992: 3).

Thus, the impending demise of nation-states via the emergence of supranational organisations may be overstated, although such organisations can also clearly act both as catalysts and as intermediaries in relation to other forms of identity – particularly at the local and regional level. The latter is apparent within the EU in the growing emphasis on regional identities, and the allied promotion of greater political devolution and regional control within European Union member states (see Petschen, 1993; Bullman, 1994; Jones and Keating, 1995). As we shall see, such developments provide a potential political 'space' in which alternative identities, including those of minority-language speakers, may be promoted.

A multilingual European Union?

Be that as it may, the record of the EU with respect to minority languages is not a strong one. One only need remember the report by Nelde et al. (1996), discussed in Chapter 4, which indicated that many of the 48 minority-language groups within the EU are seriously threatened. Of course, part of the reason for this is that many EU member states continue at national levels to ignore and/or oppose the extension of minority-language rights – France being the most obvious example here. The example of France also highlights the limits of any pan-European legislation in support of minority languages – as seen, for example, in relation to the (1992) European Charter for Regional and Minority Languages, discussed in Chapter 5. In addition, there is the tricky question of accommodating language rights and multilingualism within the formal workings of the EU itself. At one level, the accommodation of multilingualism is clearly quite extensive, not least because, again as we saw in Chapter 5, the European Parliament formally adopted in 1990 the 'principle of complete multilingualism'. The treaties of accession guarantee that speakers of the 11 official languages of the EU (in effect, the dominant languages of the 15 current member states) have the right to use these languages in the European Parliament and the European Commission, the administrative centre of the EU. Similarly, official EU documents must be made available in all of these languages, where required. The result is that the EU has the largest translation and interpretation service in the world (Labrie, 1993; Phillipson, 1998). But with its ongoing further expansion, the prospect of maintaining this degree of multilingualism seems less and less likely. Even now, it is hardly sustainable, with 40 per cent of the EU administrative budget committed to translation and interpretation alone (Skutnabb-Kangas, 2000). As Fishman (1995b) observes, the logistical cost of interpretation to and from all official languages in the EU is formid-able, with currently 210 possible combinations for the 15 member states. With the inclusion of the likely 6 new member states, this would grow to 420. Add to this those states still wishing to join the EU, notably in the former Yugoslavia and former Soviet Union, and the potential combinations would quickly exceed 600.

Given these difficulties, we are already seeing in the EU a retrenchment of formal multilingualism, with, for example, the European Commission adopting only English and French, and to a lesser extent German, as its working languages for all internal documents (Phillipson, 1998). While the Parliament and Council of Ministers still use all 11 official languages for formal sessions and key documents, this rule is usually abandoned in less formal situations, where English and French dominate. In effect, English and French are now the principal languages within the EU – English be-cause of its global reach, and French because many of the EU institutions are situated on French-speaking territory (Wright, 1999). Thus, even within the multilingual apparatus of the EU, linguistic rationalisation in favour of dominant languages is at work. Consequently, the working languages of the EU are increasingly facing the same scenario at the supranational level that many minority languages face at a national level – linguistic marginalisation and allied perceptions of lower status, value and use. As I argued in Chapter 5, this development might prove a useful point of comparison in the quest for greater minority-language rights within European nation-states as well.

To this latter end, there are also countervailing tendencies in favour of multilingualism and minority-language rights within the EU. The Commit-tee of Regions and the Bureau for Lesser Used Languages are both active in promoting regional identities, and regional and other minority languages, respectively. More significantly perhaps, the EU has allowed national minority groups within Europe, or what I described in Chapter 2 as 'nations without states', an alternative political forum in which to operate, independent of (or at least in conjunction with) the nation-states in which they are currently subsumed. As Esteve notes, 'the dynamics of the present-day situation suggest that Europe may evolve into a complex association of autonomous communities in which the supranational unifying process is accompanied by a reinforcement of . . . regional autonomies' (1992: 259).

One prominent example here is Catalonia, which is currently one of the 'autonomías' (autonomous regions) of the Spanish state. However, the Catalonian Generalitat, or government, is also a vocal supporter of the Europe of the Regions and, within the narrow constraints of the intergovernmental system of policy-making, participates as fully as it can in the formal workings of the EU (Keating and Hooghe, 1996; Keating, 1996, 1997). Wales and Scotland, both of which have recently been granted devolved political and economic powers within Britain, are currently less active in European affairs but are nonetheless increasingly looking to Europe as an alternative sphere of influence (McCrone, 1992; May, 1999e; Taylor and Thompson, 1999). These developments at the sub-state level may also provide considerable scope and institutional space for the fostering of minority languages. Again, both Catalonia and Wales are exemplars here of just what can be achieved in this respect. The move towards greater devolution in the once highly centralised states of Spain and Britain has facilitated the (re)legitimation and institutionalisation of Catalan and Welsh, respectively. In so doing, a long history of derogation, proscription and neglect of these historically associated languages has begun to be redressed, leading to their current revival after many years of language shift and loss and, just as significantly, their reentry into, and reestablishment within, the civic realm. Having said that, and given all that we have discussed thus far, it should perhaps not come as too much of a surprise that these developments have also generated their fair share of controversy.

Catalonia: the quest for political and linguistic autonomy

Catalan is a regional majority language in the area of Catalonia (Catalunya in Catalan) that currently boasts over 5 million speakers in Catalonia and throughout Europe. It is currently spoken outside of Catalonia in Valencia, the Balearic Islands, Andorra, the city of l'Alguer in Sardinia, and the French Departement of Pyrénées-Orientales (also known as the French Roussillon) (see Fishman, 1991). However, it also clearly remains a minority language in relation to the wider Spanish state in which it is situated (cf. Chapter 6). Strubell (1998) argues in fact that Catalan is unique within Europe because it is the only language of that size that has managed to survive three centuries of nation-state ideology – what I termed in Chapter 3, the 'philosophical matrix of the nation-state' – without actually having a state to back it. It is also the only language in that circumstance that has not entered into an irreversible demographic decline (although, as we shall see, it has clearly suffered periods of decline). A large part of the reason for the resilience of Catalan has to do with its prominent role in the long history of Catalonia, which is the territory of a historical ethnie, and subsequently a nation, that can trace its roots back to before the tenth century (Castells, 1997). This history, in turn, is characterised by a repeated quest for greater political and linguistic autonomy for Catalonia, often in the face of highly centralist policies that actively repressed Catalan political institutions, and the Catalan language along with it.

The rise and fall of Catalunya

In the tenth century, the territory now known as Catalonia gained de facto independence from the Franks (Miller and Miller, 1996), while the actual name of 'Catalunya', as a political entity with its own language, was first recorded in 1176 (Hoffmann, 1999). By the thirteenth and fourteenth centuries, Catalonia, as part of the Kingdom of Aragon, had established itself as a maritime and Mediterranean region of some considerable influence and power. In the process, it had incorporated Mallorca (1229), Valencia (1238), Sicily (1282), Sardinia (1323) and Naples (1442), as well as parts of Greece (including Athens) and Roussillon beyond the Pyrénées in modern-day France. Catalan had also become well established by that time, having emerged from the fragmentation of Latin to become one of the original Romance languages, along with, among others, Galician and Castilian (Spanish). Indeed, by the thirteenth century, Catalan had already replaced Latin as the language of record within the Catalonian region – providing us with the first European feudal code in a vernacular language, the oldest European maritime code, and the first Romance language to be used in science and philosophy (Fishman, 1991).

Catalonia, and Catalan, began to decline in power and influence, however, from the time of the 1412 Compromiso de Caspe between Catalonia and Castile – the latter, of course, being the precursor of modern Spain. This began a process of political convergence which was formalised by the marriage and subsequent accord of Isabel of Castile and Fernando of Aragon, in 1469 and 1475 respectively. This political merger was meant to see the language, customs and institutions of both regions respected. However, this did not prove to be the case as Castile, increasingly guided by the power and wealth of the Spanish Crown, and the fundamentalist Catholic Church of the CounterReformation, quickly adopted a centralist approach. The increasingly centralist approach adopted by Castile led eventually to the rebellion of Catalonia and Portugal in 1640 against the Spanish King Philip IV.

While Portugal, supported by the English, succeeded in gaining its independence, Catalonia was defeated, with the consequence of the loss of most of its political freedoms (although it retained Catalan as its official language). This inevitably led to further discontent, and Catalonia again attempted to regain greater autonomy via the Spanish War of Succession (1705–14), siding with the Austrians against Philip V. But Catalonia was again defeated, following the siege of Barcelona in 1714. As a consequence, it lost all its political institutions of self-government – established, as we have seen, since the early Middle Ages – with Philip V abolishing the Catalan Parliament (the Corts) and government (Diputació Generalitat) of the time (Strubell, 1998). At the same time, a history of 500 years of Catalan as the official language of Catalonia was brought unceremoniously to an end. The ensuing period thus saw Catalonia's first experience of active institutional, cultural and linguistic repression from a centralised Spanish state. It was not to be its last. In this period, the Spanish state attempted to replace Catalan with Castilian, progressively proscribing Catalan as the language of administration, the language of commerce, and the language of education. In the end, the only domains left to Catalan were the family and the Church (Castells, 1997). Consequently, the nobility, higher clergy, military and civil servants quickly became completely 'Castilianised'. The middle classes retained spoken Catalan for informal use and only the illiterate rural population remained monolingual in Catalan (Hoffmann, 1999). Catalan thus experienced the usual processes of stigmatisation and peripheralisation associated with the 'minoritisation' of a language by a hegemonic state (cf. Chapter 4).

These setbacks were ameliorated somewhat in the nineteenth century, when Catalonia successfully industrialised, one of the few areas of Spain to do so. Industrialisation contributed to the rise of a strong middle class and established a pattern that was to characterise Catalonia's position within the wider Spanish state until well into the twentieth century. In effect, while Catalonia remained politically marginalised, it increasingly became the economic powerhouse of Spain. Concomitantly, while Catalan continued to be formally proscribed from the civic realm, it (re)gained credence as the preferred language of a highly educated and economically successful Catalan bourgeoisie. The status of Catalan was also reaffirmed by the nineteenth-century Catalan language movements, 'Renaixença' and 'Modernista'. These cultural nationalist movements emphasised the long (and strong) historical links of the language with a cosmopolitan political administration, and a high-status culture, and promoted the widespread use of Catalan in literary fields, journalism and education. Catalan thus came to be increasingly viewed as the focal point, and principal medium of expression, of Catalan cultural nationalism (Miller and Miller, 1996), and was further bolstered at the beginning of the twentieth century when, as a result largely of this cultural nationalism, the language was standardised and modernised (Yates, 1998; DiGiacomo, 1999).

From Franco to federalism

If the nineteenth century saw Catalan regain some of its lost cultural and linguistic status, the early twentieth century saw Catalonia itself reestablish its political status on two occasions, albeit briefly in both instances. In 1914–25, Catalonia was granted a degree of home rule under the presidency of Enric Prat de la Riba, but the first of Spain's twentieth-century dictators, Primo de Rivera, who led a successful military coup in 1923, quickly returned Catalonia to centralised Spanish control. The Second Republic (1931–36) restored a degree of political autonomy to Catalonia – granting it a Statute of Autonomy in 1932, while at the same time granting Catalan co-official language status. But this was also to be shortlived. With the success of Franco in the Spanish Civil War (1936–39), Catalonia was subjected once again to absolute political, cultural and linguistic repression – this time for a period of nearly 40 years. Catalonia's political autonomy was annulled and the region was divided into four provinces which were administered by the central government in Madrid. As I have already briefly discussed in Chapter 5, Franco's years of repression also included the official proscription of Catalan in all public domains – administration, commerce, education, the media, and even, this time, the Church – and the ruthless enforcement of these linguistic strictures. Even Catalan names and toponyms were banned and replaced by Spanish (Castilian) equivalents. Catalan itself was declared a 'mere dialect' and official propaganda of the period described its speakers as 'barking like dogs' or as 'non-Christian' (Fishman, 1991). Only after some 20 years were these restrictions eased, at least to a degree, with some latitude allowed for the use of Catalan within the Church. By 1970 an education law permitting the teaching of (but not in) Catalan was also proposed, but was not actually implemented until 1975, the year of Franco's death (Fishman, 1991). These late and limited concessions aside, Franco's 'glorioso Movimiento nacional' was clearly a centralist Spanish nationalist movement that had as a key aim the repression of Catalan, and its replacement with Castilian Spanish or 'la lengua del Imperio' (Strubell, 1998).

One consequence of Franco's years of repression, and his centralist Spanish nationalism, was the further strengthening of Catalan cultural nationalism, with the Catalan language its central motif and point of resistance. Anti-state nationalism was also a feature of the Basque Country which was similarly oppressed by Franco. However, Basque nationalism has principally been preoccupied with the question of secession, seen most prominently in the ongoing terrorist activities of the ETA movement (Euzkadi 'ta Askatasuna). Catalan nationalism, in contrast, has always sought greater political autonomy *within* Spain, rather than secession as such, in line with the key tenets of cultural nationalism discussed in Chapter 2 (see also Conversi, 1997; Grugel and Rees, 1997).

Despite the growing strength of Catalan cultural nationalism, and the fact that the language continued to be spoken privately by a wealthy middle class, Catalan did inevitably suffer at the hands of Franco. There was an undeniable negative impact on Catalan use, and even Catalan competence, among native Catalan speakers (Fishman, 1991). Generations of Catalans were taught to be literate only in Castilian, while the scope and functions of Catalan were inevitably delimited, preventing the language from adapting to new situations and communicative requirements (Hoffmann, 1999). The influx of Spanish-speaking migrants from other areas of Spain over this period, who came seeking work in Catalonia's prosperous industries, was also to have a major impact on the health of the Catalan language. Since the rise of industrialisation, in-migration from other areas of Spain had always been on a much smaller scale, with the result that most in-migrants were able to adopt successfully, and without contradiction, dual Catalan and Spanish identities. This was particularly the case during the two previous periods of political autonomy in the twentieth century, where the Catalan language was actively promoted, principally via education, and was seen by in-migrants as the language of social mobility. The combination of Franco's repression, which meant in-migrants had no incentive to learn Catalan, and the sheer scale of in-migration, particularly during the period 1950–75, was to change all this. Thus, the number of Catalan speakers in Catalonia fell from 90 per cent in 1939 to 60 per cent in 1975 (Miller and Miller, 1996). It was also to see the establishment of linguistic differences along broadly class lines, as the in-migrants who spoke Castilian Spanish were predominantly working class, while Catalan remained a language of prestige closely associated with the economically prosperous middle class. This ongoing association of Catalan with economic dominance, even during the years of its political marginalisation, is certainly a key factor in its survival – amounting, in effect, to a form of reverse diglossia within Catalonia (although, of course, not within Spain itself). But the class-based juxtaposition of Catalan and Castilian was also to have its own deleterious consequences in the subsequent reestablishment of Catalan within Catalonia post-Franco, as we shall see.

After the death of Franco, democracy was quickly restored to Spain and a new Constitution agreed by all the main political parties that emerged from the first democratic election, a not inconsiderable achievement in itself. But more radically still, the (1978) Spanish Constitution moved away, to some considerable extent, from the centralist and overtly assimilationist policies that had dominated Spanish politics for so much of the preceding two centuries. In this respect, the Constitution accomplished a delicate balancing act. On the one hand, it continued to emphasise the ongoing unity and social cohesion characteristic of the traditional centralist conception of the (Spanish) nation-state, what I described as 'civism' in Chapter 3, most notably by its proclamation of Spanish as its sole official language, to be spoken by all its citizens. On the other hand, the Constitution also specifically recognised Spain's cultural and linguistic pluralism – granting specific cultural and linguistic rights, as well as a considerable degree of political autonomy, to the different historical ethnies within the Spanish state. The latter moved Spain much closer to the model of a multinational (and multilingual) state. Article 2 of the Constitution encapsulates both these features:

> The Constitution is founded upon the indissoluble unity of the Spanish nation [sic], the common and indivisible patria of all Spaniards, and recognizes and guarantees the right to autonomy of all the nationalities and regions integrated in it and the solidarity among them.

> (cited in Guibernau, 1997: 93)

The new Constitution was to facilitate the subsequent establishment of 17 'autonomías' (autonomous regions), which were granted various degrees of devolution and autonomy. Those granted the greatest degree of political autonomy – termed 'autonomías históricas' – included Catalonia, the Basque Country and Galicia. These three regions were regarded as having the strongest historical claims to a separate identity, based centrally on their language and culture. They had also enjoyed political autonomy (in the case of Catalonia) in the Second Republic (1931–36), or would have (in the case of the Basque Country and Galicia) had the Spanish Civil War not intervened. Consequently, Catalonia was the first of the autonomías to be so recognised when it was granted its Statute of Autonomy in 1979, while the Basque Country and Galicia followed in 1980. Other regions within Spain, with lesser historical claims, had first to fulfil a five-year 'restricted autonomy' period. However, once 'full autonomy' is achieved, the Constitution makes no distinction between the various autonomous regions (Guibernau, 1997).

The Catalan Statute of Autonomy is significant for its stress on the historical origins of Catalonia, particularly its language and culture, *coupled with* their restoration within a specifically modern and modernising democratic political project. These are both key attributes, as I argued in Chapter 2, of cultural nationalism. Thus the Preamble states: 'In the process of regaining their democratic freedom, the people of Catalonia also recover their institutions of self-government' (cited in Guibernau, 1997: 94). The Statute is also significant for its specific recognition of collective identity and freedom – or more accurately, group-differentiated rights (cf. Chapter 3) – a recognition that is implicit in the following:

> The *collective freedom* of Catalonia finds in the institutions of the 'Generalitat' [government] a link with a long history of emphasis on and respect for the fundamental rights and public freedoms of individuals *and peoples*: a history which the people of Catalonia wish to continue, in order to make possible the creation of a forward-looking democratic society.

> (cited in Guibernau, 1997: 95; my emphases)

A concrete example of just such a group-differentiated right is the right to speak Catalan within Catalonia. Here the Statute is unequivocal, asserting that Catalan is 'la llengua pròpia de Catalunya' (Catalonia's own language) and that 'Catalan is the official language of Catalonia as Castilian is the official language of the whole of the Spanish state' (Art. 3.2; see Artigal, 1997: 135; Guibernau, 1997: 96). But as we already know, the legitimation of a language (though important) is one thing, its institutionalisation quite another (cf. Chapter 4). Thus the Statute also stipulates a specific plan of action:

> The Generalitat . . . will guarantee the normal and official use of both languages, adopt whatever measures are deemed necessary to ensure both languages are known, and create suitable conditions so that full equality between the two can be achieved as far as the rights and duties of the citizens of Catalonia are concerned.
>
> (Art 3.3; cited in Strubell, 1998: 163)

As Strubell observes, this amounts to a clear social contract between Catalan and Castilian language speakers – a process of mutual language accommodation that is evident in only Stage 6 of Churchill's typology, as discussed in Chapter 5. The task of bringing this about was given to the nationalist coalition 'Covergencia i Unio' (CiU), led by Jordi Pujol and elected to lead the Generalitat in the first postdemocratic regional elections. The CiU, which still remains in power some 20 years on, insists on the distinct political character of Catalonia, but emphasises that this can be effectively maintained within the multinational Spanish state, rather than by secession (see Guibernau, 1997 for an extended discussion). The CiU also places considerable store on the importance of fostering and maintaining a distinct Catalan identity. Its definition of who is Catalan includes all those who live and work in Catalonia – no ethnic, religious or racialised distinctions are made. But the CiU does add the key caveat 'and wants to be Catalan', and the sign of 'wanting to be' Catalan is to learn to speak the language (Castells, 1997). As Pujol asserts: 'our identity as a country, our will to be, and our perspectives for the future depend on the preservation of our language' (cited in Guibernau, 1997: 101). As such, much of the subsequent political efforts of the CiU have focused both on maximising Catalonia's political autonomy within Spain and reestablishing Catalan fully as the language of the state and civil society within Catalonia, in line with the Statute's recommendations.

The quest for greater political autonomy is demonstrated by the considerable (opponents would say, disproportionate) influence that the CiU has wielded at the level of Spanish national politics over the last 20 years, and particularly in the last 10 years. For example, the CiU formed a coalition with the Socialist government in 1993, and then with the Conservatives when they first came to power in 1996, after both had failed to gain a working majority on their own. In both instances, Pujol was able to extract significant concessions that further bolstered Catalonian autonomy – for example, being granted direct control of 30 per cent of its income taxes, as well as exclusive control of education, health, environment, communications, tourism, culture, social services and most police functions (Castells, 1997). The granting of these further concessions to Catalonian autonomy was all the more remarkable in the latter instance, given that the Conservatives, the Partido Popular, initially campaigned for the retrenchment of devolution, and against the perceived 'nationalisms' of autonomous regions (while, of course, completely ignoring their own; see DiGiacomo, 1999; see also below). The recent reelection of the Partido Popular with a sufficient mandate to govern on its own may change this state of affairs. Only time will tell. However, the Conservatives may well decide against the wholesale retrenchment of Catalan gains, not least because the degree of success achieved by the CiU over the years might also explain why the civic culture of Catalonia leaves little room for extremism. In this respect, separatist groups continue to have only a small following in Catalonia, in sharp contrast to the Basque Country (Giner, 1984; Conversi, 1997). Indeed, as a 1982 survey found, Catalans self-identify most often as 'equally Catalan and Spanish' (Stepan, 1998), seeing no necessary contradiction between the two forms of identity (see my discussion of multiple identities in Chapter 2). This was also confirmed by a subsequent survey in 1990, which indicated that Catalans continued to remain largely sceptical of independence as a feasible or necessary political option for Catalonia (Strubell, 1998).

The reestablishment of Catalan as a civic language, which I will focus upon in what follows, has been achieved by embarking on an extensive language status planning programme within Catalonia itself. The principal instrument of this programme, at least initially, was the (1983) Llei de Normalització Lingüística (Law of Linguistic Normalisation), also known as the 'Charter of the Catalan Language'.

Linguistic normalisation

Linguistic normalisation in the Catalonian context was first described by the Congress of Catalan Culture (1975–77) as 'a process during which a language gradually recovers the formal functions it [has] lost and at the same time works its way into those social sectors, within its own territory, where it was not spoken before' (cited in Torres, 1984: 59). In this light, and following Fishman (1991), the process of linguistic normalisation subsequently embarked on in Catalonia can be described as having three broad initial aims:

1   to achieve the symbolic promotion and functional institutionalisation of Catalan in all key public- and private-language domains

2   to redress illiteracy in Catalan, and any remaining sense of inferiority attached to Catalan, both legacies of the Franco years

3   via a 'policy of persuasion' (Woolard, 1985, 1986, 1989), to gain the commitment of first-language Spanish speakers to Catalan, while at the same time countering any hostility towards Catalan as a perceived 'threat' to Spanish as the language of the Spanish state

Over the course of the last 20 years, Catalonia has been largely successful in achieving the first two objectives although, as we shall see, the third still remains in the balance. Today Catalonian citizens have the right to use Catalan on all (public and private) occasions, while virtually all written and oral work in the Generalitat and local authorities is now undertaken in Catalan. A 1991 census found that 94 per cent understood, 68 per cent spoke, and 40 per cent could write in Catalan (Artigal, 1997), a considerably more favourable position for the language than in 1975 (see above).[1] Of course, these changes did not happen overnight and the most prominent feature of Catalan language planning, particularly in its early stages, was its graduated approach. Education provides us with a representative example here (see Miller and Miller, 1996; Artigal, 1997).

Catalan-language education

Catalan was first legally reinstated as a language that could be taught in schools in 1978, although this was largely limited, at least initially, to teaching Catalan as a subject (in 1978, only 3.3 per cent of schools actually taught in Catalan). Nonetheless, this initial development acknowledged the possibility in the longer term of extending teaching in Catalan – i.e., the more widespread adoption of group-maintenance language-immersion programmes. The latter possibility was further solidified in the (1983) Law of Linguistic Normalisation, which stated categorically: 'Education centres are obliged to make Catalan the normal vehicle of expression' (cited in Webber and Strubell, 1991: 34). Thus, from 1983 to 1993, Catalan was given priority in education. Three models were available at preschool and elementary schools, described by Artigal (1997) as 'predominantly Catalan-medium', 'bilingual instruction' and 'predominantly Spanish-medium'. The first approach was encouraged wherever possible, although schools always had the final choice of which language education approach to adopt (at secondary level, the choice of language medium remained entirely open). Nonetheless, nearly 90 per cent of preschools and elementary schools did in fact opt for predominantly Catalan-medium programmes, not least because of the wide and careful dissemination of their educational advantages to both parents and teachers. Drawing in particular on the experiences of French-Canadian immersion programmes, the Catalonian Department of Education argued that the formal promotion of Catalan within schools, as the still socially weaker language, would allow Spanish speakers to become bilingual, given that Spanish remained dominant in the wider social setting. This obviated the (misplaced) fear of many Spanish-speaking parents that immersion in Catalan might have led to their children losing their Spanish. These developments were supported by an extensive programme of in-service language support for teachers (itself part of a wider programme within the civil service), given the initial lack of Catalan-speaking teachers. Bilingual textbooks and other supporting curriculum materials were also developed over this period, along with training in the theory and methodology of immersion language education.

Since 1993, a single model of Catalan immersion for all schools has been adopted at preschool and elementary levels (although at secondary level free choice continues). This extension of Catalan immersion programmes was predicated, in turn, on the demonstrable success of such programmes over the preceding decade in teaching Spanish-speaking students Catalan, particularly in the industrialised, predominantly Spanish working-class areas where Catalan had very little social presence. There remains some element of choice within the preschool/elementary programme, as Spanish-speaking parents can demand that the first stage of teaching (from 3 to 7 years old) be in Spanish, with only the minimum of Catalan required by law. But the latter 'opt out' can only now be claimed on an individual family basis, and involves individual rather than classroom-based instruction. Thus the unified nature of the new Catalan immersion system remains intact, a position subsequently reinforced by the implementation of a new language law, the (1998) Catalan Linguistic Policy Act.

The Catalan Linguistic Policy Act: controversy and contention

The Catalan Linguistic Policy Act has three main objectives. The first is to support the legal consolidation of Catalan language policies in schools and the wider civil service, the former by fully implementing the unified Catalan immersion education approach discussed earlier, the latter by further strengthening formal Catalan-language requirements for civil servants working in the Generalitat and in local authorities. The second objective is to increase the presence of Catalan in the media and commerce fields (in which Spanish remains dominant), principally via the introduction of minimum Catalan-language quota systems in the media, and the requirement of bilingual service provision in the commercial sector. In this latter respect, the Act specifically calls for private companies to implement programmes and measures in support of the further use of Catalan at work. The third objective of the Act is a more broad-based one, to achieve full equality or comparability between Catalan and Spanish in all formal language domains. This includes not only the devolved areas of administration currently regarded as the responsibility of the Generalitat but also those areas that still remain under the jurisdiction of the Spanish central government, notably the judicial system, law and order, and tax administration (Costa and Wynants, 1999).

While the (1993) Law of Linguistic Normalisation was concerned principally with the extension of the knowledge of Catalan within Catalonia, particularly within education and the wider civil service, the (1998) Catalan Linguistic Policy Act is thus concerned primarily with the further extension of its legal status and institutional reach. These measures constitute, in effect, the 'next stage' of the legitimation and institutionalisation of Catalan within Catalonia – with a movement away from a more gradualist, 'politics of persuasion' approach to one much closer to the Québec model of legislative enforcement, à la Bill 101. Inevitably, such a 'change of pace' has generated controversy and opposition, despite the widespread acceptance of Catalan language measures up to this point. However, a significant feature of this opposition is that it has largely been initiated and fostered from elsewhere in Spain, rather than from within Catalonia itself. It has also tended to be firmly located within a broader conservative political agenda advocating the return of a traditional centralist Spanish nationalism (DiGiacomo, 1999). Thus Catalan language laws, as the most visible manifestation of an alternative Catalan nationalism, and as a demonstrable example of the wider federalism of Spain, have become something of a cause célèbre for these traditional Spanish nationalists. Before proceeding to a brief analysis of their campaign, I should point out that these oppositionalists almost never actually see themselves as nationalists – their avowedly 'anti-nationalist' stance obviously does not extend to a critique of their own. The subsumption of majoritarian forms of nationalism at work here is a process we saw Billig describe in Chapter 2 as 'banal nationalism', where the nationalism of the dominant ethnie 'not only ceases to be nationalism . . . it ceases to be a problem for investigation' (1995: 17). There are none so blind, it seems, as those who cannot see.

The campaign mounted against Catalan language laws has been played out in the Spanish media and in the Spanish courts over the course of the last decade (DiGiacomo, 1999). The general tenor of this campaign is captured well by the following banner headline in a national Spanish paper in 1993: 'como Franco pero al revés: Persecución del castellano en Cataluña' (the same as Franco but the other way round: Persecution of Spanish in Catalonia) (quoted in Costa and Wynants, 1999). The inference here is abundantly clear – minority-language rights constitute 'special treatment' and may well be illiberal – a position that is also broadly congruent with the charges of 'reverse apartheid' that characterise more general dismissals of group-differentiated minority rights (cf. Chapter 3). Consequently, much of the subsequent vocal and often vituperative debates on Catalan language laws have focused on the supposed threat they pose to the right to speak the majority language, (Castilian) Spanish. In this respect, oppositionalists have termed themselves, without any degree of irony it seems, 'bilingüistas' (see

Strubell, 1998). I say without any degree of irony because, as with the comparable campaigns in North America, opponents of Catalan language laws are specifically *not* arguing for bilingualism at all but, rather, for the right of majority (Spanish) language speakers to remain monolingual.

Thus, when the single model of Catalan immersion education was adopted in 1993, opponents took the Catalonian government to the Spanish Constitutional Court, arguing that the measure contravened the individual language right to speak Spanish, enshrined within the Constitution. Unfortunately for the plaintiffs, the Constitutional Court ruled in December 1994 that the Catalan immersion education model *was* constitutional, given that its stated aim was the acquisition of both Catalan and Spanish, and given that this goal is clearly reached because of the broad presence of Spanish in the wider social milieu (see Artigal, 1997: 140). This particular decision was broadly congruent with a previous one reached by the same court in February 1991, concerning the formal requirement of a working knowledge of Catalan within the civil service in Catalonia. Catalan-language opponents had also argued before the Court on that occasion that such a requirement discriminated against Spanish speakers on the grounds of language, while limiting the freedom of movement that the Spanish Constitution guarantees all its citizens. However, the Constitutional Court ruled that the command of an official language within a given autonomous region was neither an unreasonable nor disproportionate requirement (Miller and Miller, 1996). Returning to Kymlicka's distinction, discussed in Chapter 3, internal restrictions imposed by Catalan language laws were deemed not to be so great as to render those laws, and their basis as an external protection, illiberal.

These legal setbacks have not stopped opponents of the language laws continuing their campaign on other fronts, most notably in attempting to complicate the language question in Catalonia by recourse to class. Here, the approach has been to argue that the denial of language rights to 'immigrants' within Catalonia (by which is almost always meant, Spanish-speaking in-migrants from other areas of Spain) is a reflection of class as well as linguistic discrimination, since such immigrants are also invariably working class. In contrast, Catalan speakers, as we have seen, are strongly represented in the middle classes. These arguments are almost certainly disingenuous, not least because the majority of in-migrants actually accept and support 'Catalanisation' policies (Keating, 1997; Strubell, 1998; Costa and Wynants, 1999; DiGiacomo, 1999). But they have nonetheless proved useful as another potential cause of friction with respect to Catalan language laws (Atkinson, 1997, 1998).

If there is a valid point to be made in relation to the language claims of 'immigrants' within Catalonia, it is not one made by opponents of the Catalan laws, nor is it about Spanish. Rather, it is that the promotion of Catalan, while not necessarily problematic in itself, does not as yet extend to the *active* recognition of other minority languages and cultures within Catalonia, 'where numbers warrant' – Stage 5 of Churchill's minority-language typo-logy. In this respect, there have been long-settled communities of Roma in Catalonia (Tarrow, 1992) and more recent migrants from North Africa (Yates, 1998; Hoffmann, 1999), whose languages and cultures have been almost en-tirely ignored. There have been a few 'compensatory' (Stage 2) educational programmes aimed at Roma, but nothing more (Tarrow, 1992). In other words, like many other European minority-language policies, the pressing claims of particular national minorities have meant that wider polyethnic or multicultural claims have been given far less priority.

This important caveat aside, the clear weight of evidence in debates on Catalan language laws suggests that the arguments of oppositionalists are almost entirely invalid. The formal promotion of Catalan does *not* threaten either the position of Spanish or the rights of Spanish speakers. Unlike Québec's formal proscription of English in commerce and advertising, for example, Spanish has never been officially proscribed in Catalonia in any domain (not least because the Spanish Constitution forbids it), nor for that matter has any other language. Indeed, Spanish is specifically enshrined as the *only* official language of the *whole* Spanish state, while Catalan only has co-official rights within the autonomous region of Catalonia. And Spanish still remains the dominant language in the media, as well as in fields such as justice, commerce and taxation within Catalonia. As Yates sensibly con-cludes, 'by any objective standards, Catalan is still a subordinate language in a process of "reverse shift", with a long way to go towards normalisation in key areas' (1998: 207). One might also add here the rather obvious point that if Spanish speakers in Spain can regard the formal recognition of their language, within their own historic territory, as an inalienable right (with no question of illiberality), why cannot Catalans as well?

This campaign highlights once again the intractable nature of the opposi-tion that attends any attempt to legitimate and institutionalise a minority language, no matter how misplaced the former, or how justified the latter, may be. In this sense, the issue of gaining (and then keeping) a sufficient degree of 'tolerability' (Grin, 1995; see Chapter 5), particularly among majority-language speakers, continues to be a crucial factor in, and potential obstacle to, the successful long-term adoption of a minority-language policy. And the issue of tolerability *is* clearly made more difficult when a politics of consensus is replaced by a politics of legislative enforcement – Québec's Bill 101 and the 1998 Catalan Linguistic Policy Act suggest as much (Yates, 1998; Hoffmann, 1999; Myhill, 1999). But critics of the latter also presuppose that consensus, left to its own devices, will achieve the same result, albeit much more slowly. This is simply naïve, not least because it ignores, or at least significantly underplays, the ongoing powerful influence of the 'philo-sophical matrix of the nation-state' to undermine and subvert such attempts. Wales, and the successes and limitations of recent Welsh-language bilingual policy, provide us here with another useful case in point.

Wales: the development of a bilingual state in a 'forgotten' nation

The Welsh, as a people, were born disinherited.

(Gwyn Williams, 1985: 45)

Wales is one of the three constituent nations of the multinational British state, alongside England and Scotland. If one adds Northern Ireland to this triumvirate, we also get the United Kingdom. But of these constituent members, Wales is the one most often overlooked. The difficulties in Northern Ireland have dominated the British political landscape since the mid twentieth century, as did the concerns of Ireland as a whole and 'Irish Home Rule' in the nineteenth century. Scotland, though united by treaty with England in 1707, has since retained intact much of its civil society (including its own legal, church, and education systems). Consequently, it has enjoyed a far greater degree of institutional autonomy, and therefore maintained a considerably higher profile within both British politics and the corpus of British history itself. And England, of course, has been the dominant partner – or, simply, dominant – for much of the modern history of the British state. Which leaves Wales; unremarked and, to many, unremarkable.[2] As Kenneth Morgan, the noted Welsh historian, poignantly observes in an essay written in 1971 on the origins of Welsh nationalism:

'For Wales – see England'. This notorious directive in the early editions of the *Encyclopaedia Britannica* crystallises all the emotion, the humiliation, and the patronising indifference which helped to launch the national movement in Wales.

(1995: 197)

That these attitudes still remain today within Britain is clearly illustrated by the controversial English literary critic and columnist A. N. Wilson. Writing in the London daily paper the *Evening Standard* in 1994, he comments disparagingly on the cultural contribution of the Welsh (or lack thereof) to British life:

The Welsh have never made any significant contribution to any branch of knowledge, culture or entertainment. Choral singing – usually flat – seems to be their only artistic achievement. They have no architecture, no gastronomic tradition and, since the Middle Ages, no literature worthy of the name. Even their religion, Calvinistic Methodism, is boring.

(cited in Moss, 1994: 26)

The misplaced attempt at humour aside, Wilson's comments are simply wrong. The one thing, above all else, that *has* distinguished the Welsh from their other British partners has been their cultural distinctiveness; most significantly, their language. The fault lies then not so much with a lack of Welsh cultural expression, as Wilson speciously suggests, but with the failure historically to recognise and accord value to it. A key reason for this failure resides in the long history of political and institutional incorporation of Wales within the British state.

Incorporating Wales

The degree of Welsh political incorporation into the British state is clearly illustrated by the administrative term 'England and Wales' which is employed to describe a wide range of shared institutions and programmes. It is also exemplified by the fact that Wales was not recognised as a constituent nation of Britain until the late nineteenth century, the last of the constituent nations of Britain to be so. Prior to this time, Britain was regarded for formal purposes as comprising only three nations – England, Scotland and Ireland. There simply was no 'Welsh question' in British politics comparable to the question of Irish Home Rule, for example, and the reiterated litany of Westminster politicians was that 'there was no such place as Wales' (Morgan, 1995). Even the eventual recognition of Wales as a nation, in 1886, had its origins elsewhere, being precipitated by the Irish crisis of 1885–86. In the wake of the Irish crisis, Gladstone – the British Prime Minister at the time – was led to reexamine his assumptions and publicly recognise Welsh nationality for the first time (E. Williams, 1989).

The reasons for this reticence are not hard to find – long regarded as a 'non-historic nation', Wales was simply not seen as having a necessary, sufficient or legitimate claim to independent statehood. To this end, Friedrich Engels – whose views on non-historic nations we have already encountered in Chapter 1 – avers:

> The Highland Gaels and the Welsh are undoubtedly of different nationalities to what the English are, although nobody will give to these remnants of people long gone the title of nations [nation-states] . . . [To do so would mean] the Welsh . . . , if they desired it, would have an equal right to independent political existence, absurd though it be, with the English! The whole thing is absurdity.

> ([1866]; cited in Fishman, 1989e: 14)

Setting aside the clearly pejorative tone of Engels' assertions, there is some basis for this view. Wales was brought increasingly into the ambit of English rule from the time of the Norman King Edward I (1239–1307). The subsequent colonisation of Wales in the fourteenth and fifteenth centuries led to the area's increasing anglicisation, particularly with respect to trade (Kearney, 1989). Relatedly, while much of Wales continued to speak Welsh – a language spoken since the sixth century and for which written records exist from the eighth century[3] – Welsh/English bilingualism became an increasing feature in these areas (P. Jenkins, 1992). These developments were the prelude to the area's formal incorporation within the British state in the sixteenth century. The (1536) Act of Union, and the related Act of 1542, instigated by Henry VIII (1491–1547), firmly situated Wales within the political, legal and administrative jurisdiction of the British Crown and Parliament. As a result of these Acts, the Welsh language was proscribed from the courts, and from all official domains, in favour of English, while virtually all separate Welsh institutions were eliminated (see also below).

The instructions of the Acts of Union directly affected only a small number of Welsh elite – those who held or sought property or position. However, with the dismantling of any separate institutional focus, the establishment of a political norm soon became a powerful social norm as well (Butt Philip, 1975). As we saw Iris Marion Young observe in Chapter 3, if particular groups 'have greater economic, political or social power, their group related experiences, points of view, or cultural assumptions will tend to become the norm, biasing the standards or procedures of achievement and inclusion that govern social, political and economic institutions' (1993: 133). This describes well the English–Welsh relationship. In effect, the Welsh elite became assimilated into the English class and political system – adopting its mores and its language (Colin Williams, 1982). Concomitantly, Welsh language and culture – still strongly evident among the peasantry (Y Werin) – were deemed of little value, both by the Welsh elite themselves and by the English political system to which they were increasingly beholden. As Morgan concludes of this: 'Wales continued to be regarded as a remote tribal backwater, economically backward, adhering obstinately to its antique language in the face of the "march of intellect"' (1995: 198).

It was not until the rise of religious Nonconformity in the early half of the nineteenth century, and the industrialisation of Wales in the latter half, that this state of affairs was to change significantly. These two developments provided the basis for a new Welsh nationalist movement – a movement whose characteristics have been much discussed elsewhere (Morgan, 1995; Gwyn Williams, 1985; see also Chapter 2). For the purposes of this present discussion, it is enough to point out that an important consequence of the rise of nineteenth-century nationalism in Wales was the *reestablishment* of separate Welsh institutions and legislative measures. These were primarily cultural, religious and educational – reflecting the particular emphases of the nationalist movement of the time.[4]

Yet, despite these advances, the basic political and social organisation of Wales remained largely indistinguishable from England's. For example, it was not until 1956 that a Welsh capital (Cardiff) was officially designated. Indeed, it was only after the Second World War that a specifically Welsh institutional framework was to emerge. As Charlotte Davies (1989) argues, this development was tied principally to the expansion of the British welfare system, which saw many government departments reorganised on a regional basis. In most cases, Wales came to be treated as a single administrative unit, resulting in the steady growth of Welsh bureaucracy and, for the first time, a degree of coordinated economic planning in Wales. That said, such developments still fell well short of the idea of regional government in the wider European sense (Jones and Keating, 1995).

Easily the most prominent of the newly emergent regional organisations was the Welsh Office, established in 1964 and headed by a Welsh Secretary of State. The Welsh Office was initially regarded as a symbolic rather than a substantive bearer of Welsh interests by the still highly centralist British government of the day. However, once established, it gradually began to aggrandise power (Charlotte Davies, 1989). This gradual enlargement of the Welsh Office's administrative responsibilities led, in turn, to the introduction of a range of legislative measures specific to Wales and, in particular, the Welsh language. These measures, which began to lay the basis for a bilingual state, and which will be discussed in more detail shortly, include the (1967) Welsh Language Act, offering 'equal validity' for English and Welsh in Wales; the (1988) Education Reform Act, which incorporated a specifically Welsh (and Welsh-language) dimension into the newly established National Curriculum for England and Wales; and the (1993) Welsh Language Act, which extended the 1967 Act considerably in its support for Welsh in the public domain. In short, the institutional infrastructure administered by the Welsh Office came to be increasingly identified with the reemergence of the Welsh language in the public or civic realm.

This process was also supported, and expedited, by the emergence in the 1960s of Cymdeithas yr Iaith Gymraeg (the Welsh Language Society), an organisation that employed nonviolent direct action in support of the extension of Welsh in the civic realm (see Butt Philip, 1995; Gwyn Williams, 1985; Charlotte Davies, 1989; Colin Williams, 1994). The activities of Cymdeithas yr Iaith Gymraeg contributed, at least in some measure, to the normalisation of bilingual public signs, the establishment of a Welsh-language media (notably, the Welsh-language television channel Sianel Pedwar Cymru [S4C]) as well as a Welsh Language Board, and to an increasing demand for public services available in Welsh. The (1993) Welsh Language Act, as well as its 1967 predecessor, also owe much to the political advocacy of the language movement (A. Thomas, 1997).

The most recent development in Wales' long and slow march towards greater institutional differentiation from England occurred in September 1997 when Wales voted in a national referendum in favour of a devolved Welsh Assembly. The Welsh referendum was part of a wider programme of constitutional change, implemented by the British Labour government elected in that year, which also included a devolved Parliament for Scotland. But while Scotland voted overwhelmingly in its referendum for devolution (74.3 per cent to 25.7 per cent), Wales only did so by the narrowest of margins (50.3 to 49.7 per cent; an actual majority of only 6000). The closeness of the Welsh referendum notwithstanding, both institutions were formally established in May 1999.

However, the closeness of the Welsh referendum vote also highlights the ongoing consequences of the long history of political and institutional incorporation of Wales within Britain, with many within Wales remaining ambivalent about the need for greater political autonomy. This history of incorporation is also reflected in the different devolution packages offered to Scotland and Wales in the first place. In contrast to Scotland's 129-seat Parliament – with its ability to enact primary legislation and vary taxes – the Welsh were only offered a 60-seat Assembly, with all that the difference in nomenclature implies. The Welsh Assembly has since assumed responsibility for the administrative powers previously exercised by the Welsh Secretary in the Westminster British Parliament – a not insignificant development since it involves direct control of an annual budget presently estimated at £7 billion. Unlike the Scottish Parliament, however, it has no legislative and tax-varying powers beyond the enactment of secondary legislation.

Thus, the long history of Wales' incorporation within Britain continues to limit both the possibility of, and the commitment to, greater political devolution (May, 1999e; Taylor and Thompson, 1999). But this may also have its advantages, since it can be argued that *political* incorporation has actually facilitated the *cultural* distinctiveness of the Welsh – principally, through the maintenance of their language and cultural traditions. Richard Jenkins (1991) argues, for example, that Welsh incorporation within the British state may have actually *created* the social and economic space within which the Welsh language and culture could survive. The Welsh language may have been formally proscribed from the civic realm from the time of the (1536) Act of Union, and may have been regarded, along with its culture, as antediluvian. However, it was not viewed as a threat to the state. In contrast, the far more problematic (and contested) political incorporation of Scotland and Ireland – and, relatedly, the close association of Gaelic language and culture in these areas with Catholicism – may have contributed to the more rapid and widespread decline of the latter within the (Protestant) British state.

Vitiating Welsh

Be that as it may, the anglicisation of Wales remains perhaps the most prominent feature of the nation's history. In this respect, the Welsh nationalist R. S. Thomas despondently observes of the English language: 'this is the major language, spoken by hundreds of millions of people with enormous resources devoted to it, that our small, bullied and embattled nation is called upon to maintain itself in the face of. And that is the way of it' (1992: 15; see also N. Thomas, 1992). Although perhaps not entirely, since it is not the *spread* of English which has been crucial in anglicising Wales, at least not up until the advent of the twentieth century. Indeed, Wales remained 90 per cent Welsh-speaking in the sixteenth and seventeenth centuries (P. Jenkins, 1992) and as late as 1880, three out of four Welsh people still spoke the Welsh language by choice (Morgan, 1981). This compared dramatically with the mere ten per cent in Scotland who still spoke Gaelic by the late nineteenth century (P. Jenkins, 1992) and, as we saw in Chapter 4, the same low percentage in Ireland who still used Irish regularly by the turn of the twentieth century.

Rather, it has been the diminution of the status of Welsh and its restriction to private, low-status language domains which has proved to be more debilitating historically (cf. Chapter 4). It is this, more than anything else, which led to the rapid loss of the Welsh language over the course of much of the twentieth century. During this period, the once strong Welsh-speaking heartland (Y fro Gymraeg) retreated in the face of English into the western and northern rural margins of Wales. This retreat was also reflected in the overall percentage of Welsh speakers in Wales, which diminished from 43.5 per cent of the population in 1911 to only 18.7 per cent at the time of the 1991 census – approximately 600,000 speakers.[5] Not only that, Welsh monolingual speakers – who, in 1911, still constituted 8.5 per cent of the population – have now all but disappeared. Put simply, virtually all Welsh speakers today are bilingual in English as well (Aitchison and Carter, 1994).

The attrition of the Welsh language, however, is by no means a recent historical phenomenon, beginning as early as the Norman colonisation of Wales in the late eleventh century. During that time, the prestige languages were Latin and French and to speak a local vernacular language such as Welsh was seen as a mark of bondage (Kearney, 1989). Consequently, Latin and French quickly acquired the status of formal languages of administration and documentation in Wales, a mantle which English would assume by the fourteenth century. This marked the first significant restriction of Welsh within formal language domains, since previously Welsh had been used as the language of customary law. Thus, with the emasculation of legal and administrative systems in Welsh, such as they were, only the literary tradition remained as a formal linguistic indicator of Welshness (Aitchison and Carter, 1994).

The complete exclusion of Welsh from the public realm was formalised by the (1536) Act of Union. The language provisions outlined in the Act made English the sole language of government. In so doing, the Act was unequivocal about the status (or lack thereof) of the Welsh language, viewing it as a key obstacle to successful incorporation of the new dominion within Britain:

because the people of the same Dominion [Wales] have and do daily use a speech nothing like or consonant to the natural mother tongue used within this Realm [England] . . . to reduce them to perfect order notice, and knowledge of the laws of this, his Realm . . . and *utterly to extirpate all and singular the sinister usages and customs differing from the same* . . . bringing all the citizens of this Realm to amiable concord and unity . . . From henceforth, no person or persons that use the Welsh speech or language shall have or enjoy any manor, office or fees . . . unless he or they use and exercise the speech or language of English.

(Henry VIII, Acts of Incorporation of Wales with England, 1536; cited in Williams and Raybould, 1991: 2, my emphasis)

The effect of the Act was to exclude Welsh from the public realm for the next four centuries. The only formal arena where the Welsh language continued to be recognised – that is, beyond the private and low-status domain of the family – was the Church. Ironically, this was because Henry VIII's successor, Elizabeth I, had authorised a Welsh translation of the Bible in 1563. While this authorisation of the Welsh translation of the Bible might thus appear contrary in intent to the prior Act of Union, it was not actually so. The principal reason for the concession – as for the Act – had to do with facilitating integration of the Welsh into Britain (Williams and Raybould, 1991). More pertinently, the authorisation was *not* an endorsement of the Welsh language but was, again, specifically assimilationist in intent. The provisions for the authorisation state clearly that its purpose was that 'such as do not understand the said Language [Welsh] may be conferring both Tongues together, the sooner attain to the Knowledge of the English Tongue' (cited in Jones, 1997: 15). In this it was to some extent successful, since bilingualism became an increasing feature of life in Wales from this time. However, it also had the effect of maintaining the Welsh language in the face of English – something not countenanced by its proposers. Indeed, the translation which was to emerge subsequently in 1588 became the 'sheet-anchor' (Gwyn Williams, 1985) of the language. Crucially, it allowed Welsh to remain a standardised literary language, with the *capacity* to be used in any domain (even if it was not so used). Despite the fact that it was still regarded as a low-status language (see below), the literary standard provided by the 1588 translation prevented the language from diverging into mutually incomprehensible dialects and/or atrophying altogether (Morgan, 1981).

That said, the Welsh language continued to face considerable opposition and consistent negative attribution as a perceived low-status language. While Wales remained predominantly Welsh-speaking up until the advent of the twentieth century, the Welsh landed gentry were the first to adopt English as first an additional, and then a substitute, language. This pattern was well established by the eighteenth century (P. Jenkins, 1992). Concomitantly, the use of Welsh was invariably equated with backwardness and inferiority (Morgan, 1995; Miles, 1996). This pejorative view of the Welsh language (not to mention the Welsh themselves) is ably demonstrated by William Richards, in his *Wallography* of 1682:

> The Native Gibberish is usually prattled throughout the whole of Taphydome, except in their Market Towns, whose inhabitants being a little raised, and (as it were) pufft up into Bubbles, above the ordinary scum, do begin to despise it . . . "Tis usually cashier'd out of Gentlemen's Houses . . . the Lingua will be Englishd out of Wales.

> (cited in Aitchison and Carter, 1994: 27)

These sentiments continued to be echoed in succeeding centuries. In 1866, *The Times* newspaper thundered that 'The Welsh language is the curse of Wales' (Mayo, 1979). Likewise, the nineteenth-century English education-alist and literary critic, Matthew Arnold, while paying tribute to the Welsh literary classics in his *Study of Celtic Literature*, could also state:

> The fusion of all the inhabitants of these islands into one homogeneous, English-speaking whole, the breaking down of barriers between us, the swallowing up of provincial nationalities, is a consummation to which the natural course of things irresistibly tends. It is a necessity of what is called modern civilisation . . . *The sooner the Welsh language disappears as an instrument of the practical, political, social life of Wales, the better; the better for England, the better for Wales itself.*

> (cited in Griffith, 1950: 71; my emphasis)

Similar views on the Welsh language were also clearly apparent in an influential nineteenth-century review of the state of education in Wales. Published in 1847 as *Reports of the Commissioners of Enquiry into the State of Education in Wales*, it has since come to be known as 'Brad y Lyfrau Gleision' (The Treachery of the Blue Books). The Reports were compiled by three young English, Oxford-educated lawyers and their terms of reference were to conduct 'an inquiry . . . into the state of education in . . . Wales, especially into the means afforded to the labouring classes of acquiring a knowledge of the English language' (cited in Jones, 1997: 14–15). To this end, they made some well-merited criticisms of the limited and variable educational provi-sion of the church-based schools in Wales at that time (Morgan, 1995; Jones, 1997). However, they also proceeded to include an excoriating wider attack on Welsh language and culture as the principal explanation for these inadequacies. Indeed, all the social, cultural and economic disadvantages the three commissioners saw in Wales were, in one way or another, attributed to the language: 'His language keeps him under the hatches, being one in which he can neither acquire nor communicate the necessary information'. They concluded: 'The Welsh language is a vast drawback to Wales, and a manifold barrier to the moral progress and commercial prosperity of the people . . . It dissevers the people from intercourse which would greatly advance their civilisation, and bars the access of improving knowledge to their minds' (cited in E. Evans, 1978: 14).

The conclusions of these Reports with respect to Welsh were to provide the intellectual background and rationale for the (1870) Education Act. This Act, which established the joint state elementary system in England and Wales, formally excluded Welsh from the pedagogy and practice of Welsh schools. The subsequent valorisation of English within state education – and, concomitantly, the specific proscription of Welsh – continued well into the twentieth century. It has been only in the last 60 years that Welsh has effectively reemerged as a school language (see below). In this respect, the educational policy of Welsh-language proscription was itself merely a reflection of the wider, long-established hierarchising of English over Welsh, along with the accompanying belief that in the English language lay the route to social and economic mobility. However, a monolingual English educational policy was also to entrench the view among many that the very *retention* of Welsh itself was actively *dis*advantageous. Thus, where previously Welsh monolingualism and de facto bilingualism had been the norm, English monolingualism was increasingly to replace them both. Many Welsh-speaking parents, for example, while continuing to speak Welsh among themselves, stopped speaking it to their children. The result at the individual level, as for so many other minority-language speakers (cf. Chapters 4 and 5), was a generational loss of the language. As Gwyn Thomas poignantly observes of this process: 'My father and mother were Welsh-speaking, yet I did not exchange a word in that language with them. The death of Welsh ran through our family like a geographical fault' (quoted in Osmond, 1988: 149).

To many this decline was viewed as a positive trend – English was perceived as the language of progress, equality, opportunity, the media and mass entertainment (Colin Williams, 1990). Even today, the practice of unfavourably comparing the utility and status of Welsh to English remains commonplace. One contemporary example can be found in the assertions of the Welsh sociologist Christie Davies:

> English became a world language . . . as part of a spontaneous order emerging from the free interaction of individuals and corporations. Men and women have voluntarily learned to speak English because there are gains to them as individuals that stem from the world's dominant patterns of spontaneous interactions. The ancestors of today's Welsh people shifted from speaking Welsh to speaking English, not because of external political pressure, but in order to take advantage of economic and educational

opportunities. English and Welsh are, in a quite objective sense, not equal languages. Welsh people who become fluent in English gain enormously, whereas English people learning Welsh gain very little.

(1997: 42)

Davies' comments bring us up to date with this particular perception of the Welsh language. Their facility and fatuousness aside, his views stand well within the long tradition of negative attribution towards Welsh that I have briefly outlined here. I do not want to deconstruct his or the preceding arguments further since I have already dealt at length in previous chapters with the misconceptions and misrepresentations within them as they relate to minority languages in general: notably, the unquestioned primacy of a homogeneous, unilingual nation-state, the equation of majority languages – particularly, English – with modernity, progress and social mobility, and the notion of 'free', 'spontaneous' language choice. What I do want to highlight again briefly here is the process of symbolic violence, as described by Bourdieu (see Chapter 4), which has occurred historically in relation to Cymraeg – the Welsh language. In effect, the English language came to be seen by the Welsh as a form of cultural and linguistic capital, an escape from primitivism, and a demonstration of having embraced the 'modern' way of life (Miles, 1996). Concomitantly, a Welsh linguistic habitus was increasingly regarded as having little cultural, social and economic value. As Bourdieu argues, to understand the nature of symbolic violence, it is crucial to see that it presupposes a kind of active complicity, or implicit consent, on the part of those subjected to it. This is clearly the case historically in Wales, where Welsh speakers themselves came to 'collaborate in the destruction of their [own] instruments of expression' (Bourdieu, 1991: 49).

This is not to apportion blame in any way. After all, as Joshua Fishman has argued, the choice facing minority-language speakers such as the Welsh has often been presented as an intractable one: 'either to remain loyal to their traditions and to remain socially disadvantaged (consigning their own children to such disadvantage as well), on the one hand; or, on the other hand, to abandon their distinctive practices and traditions, at least in large part, and, thereby, to improve their own and their children's lots in life via cultural suicide' (1991: 60; see Chapter 4). R. S. Thomas echoes this analysis, in relation to class, when he observes: 'A Welshman or woman was faced with a partial choice. He could, by remaining loyal to his or her native speech, be dubbed a member of an inferior class, or by assiduously imitating the English upper class could be admitted to it, generally at the expense of Welsh' (1992: 13). Given the long historical vitiation of Welsh, that so many adopted this latter option should not surprise us. It certainly helps to explain the process of rapid language loss that occurred throughout the twentieth century. What *is* surprising is that it took so long for them to do so, and that despite it all, Welsh remains a living language, still spoken today as a language of everyday life by 20 per cent of the Welsh population. Moreover, in the 1991 census, this decline was, if not exactly reversed, at least abated (Aitchison and Carter, 1994). This encouraging countertrend is related to the influence of Welsh-medium education, and the wider institutionalisation of Welsh of which it is a part.

Relegitimating Welsh

Despite the long history of political incorporation of Wales by England, and its attendant historical anglicisation, the Welsh language is currently experiencing a significant revival. The results of the 1991 census, for example, revealed a *reduction* in the decline of Welsh speakers over the previous intercensal period (1981–91) – the first time this had occurred in nearly a century. While Welsh language loss continued to occur between the intercensal period 1981–91, the decrease was only 1.4 per cent compared with 6.3 per cent for the previous intercensal period (1971–81). As Colin Williams comments, 'this is a welcome arrest in the . . . pattern of decline and should be seen as the turning of the tide [as well as the] beginning [of] significant long-term shifts in the distribution and structure of the Welsh-speaking population' (1994: 136).

A second key feature of recent language trends has been the growing urban base of the Welsh language. The traditional Welsh-speaking areas within Y fro Gymraeg continue to decline but still remain proportionately the strongholds of the language – accounting for 55 per cent of all Welsh speakers. However, the majority of Welsh speakers, in absolute terms, are now to be found in urban and suburban areas. Most notable among these is the capital city, Cardiff, which has become the administrative centre of the Welsh language. The growing urbanisation of the Welsh language thus highlights the significance of the institutionalisation of Welsh, particularly in the public sector, where the ability to speak Welsh is beginning once again to be viewed as a form of linguistic and cultural capital. Here, Aitchison and Carter observe that while the long-demonstrated detraction of the language is still extant, 'it is by no means as powerful as it was, and there is [now] a widespread awareness of the advantages of a knowledge of Welsh, especially in public employment' (1994: 115). These developments also present us with a central irony, since the decline of the traditional Welsh-speaking heartland is continuing apace at the same time as the language is being regenerated in urban contexts (Colin Williams, 1995).

Also significant is the fact that the most rapid growth in the Welsh language can be found in the 3–15 year age group. The burgeoning use of the Welsh language in this age group – which now constitutes 22 per cent of the Welsh-speaking population – is largely attributable to the influence of Welsh-medium education, particularly in the anglicised areas of south and north-east Wales. Accordingly, many of these speakers are second-language learners of Welsh, a feature that is increasingly evident in the adult population as well, where language courses for adult learners are growing in popularity.

As a result, the prospects for the Welsh language itself, and the possibilities of successfully developing a bilingual Welsh state, have never looked better. A recent national survey on attitudes to the language, for example, found widespread support across Wales (71 per cent) for the use of Welsh. Similarly strong support (75 per cent) was found for making Welsh co-equal in status with English in Wales, while almost nine out of ten (88 per cent) agreed that the Welsh language is something to be proud of (NOP, 1995). This remarkable turn around in the fortunes of the Welsh language, and for the prospects of state bilingualism, are underpinned by recent legislation in Wales – notably, the (1993) Welsh Language Act and the (1988) Education Reform Act.

The Welsh Language Act

Colin Williams has argued, in relation to Wales, that 'if a fully functional bilingual society [is to be achieved], where choice and opportunity are the twin pillars of individual language rights, then clearly that possibility has to be constructed through both the promotional and regulatory powers of the state' (1994: 162). A significant step in establishing such rights in Wales occurred in October 1993, when a new Welsh Language Act (Mesur yr Iaith Gymraeg) passed into law. The Act replaced its more limited 1967 predecessor and repealed all previous legislation to do with the Welsh language, including the original Acts of Union. The new Act's genesis, under the then Conservative government, was the result of a more sympathetic approach to Wales and the Welsh language by the British government in general, and of the cumulative influence of the Welsh-language lobby in particular (A. Thomas, 1997). While still limited in some respects, as we shall see, it nonetheless clearly reflects the significant advances made on behalf of the Welsh language in recent times.

In the Act, Welsh is treated for the first time as having 'a basis of equality' with English within Wales although it qualifies this equality as being that which is appropriate within the circumstances and 'reasonably practicable'. To this end, the new Act provides for the right to use Welsh in courts, given suitable notice, and also states that public documents in Welsh should carry the same legal weight as those in English. However, perhaps its most significant feature is the *statutory* recognition provided to Bwrdd yr Iaith Gymraeg (the Welsh Language Board). Bwrdd yr Iaith had originally been established in July 1988, although merely as an advisory body on the language, with little status and power. In this respect, it was not too dissimilar initially to its Irish equivalent, Bord na Gaeilge (Irish Language Board; cf. Chapter 4). Under the Act's aegis, however, Bwrdd yr Iaith is now authorised not only to promote and facilitate the use of the Welsh language but also to ensure its adoption within the public sector. The latter is to be achieved via formal language schemes which public organisations have to submit to the Board. These schemes are to specify the measures each organisation aims to take in order to provide effective bilingual public services in Wales. Again, there is the caveat invoked that such bilingual services will be provided 'so far as is both appropriate in the circumstances and reasonably practical'. However, as the subsequent Draft Guidelines for implementation of the Act outline, it is Bwrdd yr Iaith, crucially, not the organisations, which determines the parameters of reasonableness and practicality: 'It will not be acceptable for those preparing schemes to adopt a highly subjective and restricted view of what is appropriate in their circumstances or reasonably practicable' (Welsh Language Board, 1995: 6). Likewise, the Draft Guidelines stipulate that organisations should not rely on the *current* demand for services in Welsh as a basis for their schemes, on the premise that once more effective bilingual services become available, demand will increase:

> It is acknowledged that, in the past, many Welsh speakers turned to English in dealing with public organisations because they were not certain what services were available in Welsh. Some were also concerned that using Welsh could lead to delay or a lower standard of service. Therefore, *whatever their experience to date*, organisations should plan for an increase in demand and respond accordingly.
>
> (1995: 5; my emphasis)

The end result envisaged for each organisation is that public-service provision through Welsh should be a natural, integral part of the planning and delivery of that service. For this to occur, a sufficient number of Welsh-speaking staff is required, particularly in anglicised areas where the number of Welsh speakers from which to draw has been traditionally low. This, in turn, will require the active recruitment of Welsh-speaking staff. As the Guidelines again state: 'Organisations may need to adopt positive action strategies which publicise the fact that job applications from Welsh speakers are welcomed. This will reflect the fact that Welsh will increasingly be a regular part of public life – especially as organisations implement the requirements of the Welsh Language Act through their individual Welsh language schemes' (1995: 24). Moreover, in the context of the language schemes, if an organisation concludes that it cannot reasonably meet its obligations under the Act without having Welsh speakers in certain posts 'then, as a general rule, appointing persons able to speak Welsh to these posts will be justifiable' (1995: 24).

As with comparable debates in Québec and Catalonia, this position has proved to be controversial. Indeed, the question of whether a knowledge of Welsh can be stipulated as a requirement of employment has faced a number of legal challenges in Wales. In one prominent case, *Jones v. Gwynedd County Council* (1985), Gwynedd county council was taken to court by two monolingual English-speaking applicants when they failed to secure a council position working with senior citizens (many of whom were Welsh-speaking). They argued that the Welsh-language requirement for the position was discriminatory under the British (1976) Race Relations Act. The initial Industrial Tribunal upheld the complaint on the basis that Welsh speakers formed a 'sub-ethnic' group – thus suggesting that differentiation on the basis of ethnicity had occurred. This was later overturned on appeal. In this latter ruling (in 1986), it was concluded that language differences within an ethnic group were not applicable under the Race Relations Act.

The Welsh Language Board Draft Guidelines also specifically adopt this position, stating that 'distinguishing between Welsh people on the grounds of their ability or inability to speak Welsh does not . . . amount to racial discrimination' (1995: 24). The Guidelines further assert that 'under the law of the European Union, it will not be discriminatory to insist that a post-holder should be able to speak a specific language if linguistic knowledge is required to fulfil the duties of the post' (1995: 24). In other words, language qualifications in the labour market are no more or less restrictive than other professional qualifications required for specific forms of employment and are entirely applicable, and defensible, when bilingualism and/or multilingualism are a functional necessity.

That said, there remain limitations in the scope of the (1993) Welsh Language Act and in the related remit of Bwrdd yr Iaith. Conspicuously, the Welsh Language Board's remit does not extend to the private business sector – unlike in Québec, for example (cf. Chapter 6). This means that businesses may, if they choose, remain largely untouched by Welsh-language requirements. While many are beginning to respond positively to such requirements, often as the result of local pressure, the opposition to the mandatory use of Welsh by industry and business on grounds of practicality and profitability remains strong and consistent (Aitchison and Carter, 1994). Moreover, even in the state sector, the Board only has the right to investigate organisations that fail demonstrably to meet the requirements outlined under the Act and, subsequently, to *recommend* remedial action. There is also no general clause which guarantees an individual the right to use the Welsh language in their interactions with any public body (unlike in Catalonia), or to insist on a Welsh-medium education for their children.

Nonetheless, the significance of the Welsh Language Act and the functions of Bwrdd yr Iaith Gymraeg should not be underestimated. As Colin Williams argues, 'the reconstituted Welsh Language Board looks set to become the most critical government agency yet in the social history of Wales' (1995: 65). In effect, Bwrdd yr Iaith is in the vanguard of a new approach to language planning in Wales which now centres increasingly on the *relegitimation* of Welsh in a specifically *bilingual* context.

Welsh-medium education

Much of the educational interest in Wales has centred until recently on Welsh-medium education (see, for example, Baker, 1985; Colin Williams, 1994; Jones, 1997). This has been largely the result of the movement's success in fostering the Welsh language within schools over the last 60 years, beginning in 1939 when the first (initially) private Welsh-language elementary school was established. This first Welsh-medium school was established in Aberystwyth by local Welsh-speaking parents. Despite initial scepticism, it quickly achieved academic success – attracting, in the process, children from English-speaking homes. However, it was not incorporated into the state education system (and thus financially supported) until 1951. By then, the success of the Aberystwyth venture had also led to the development of state-funded Ysgolion Cymraeg (Welsh-medium schools) elsewhere in Wales. As Charlotte Davies argues, the Aberystwyth school's 'primary contribution to the postwar development of the Welsh schools movement was to demonstrate the feasibility of Welsh-medium education and, through the support given it by middle-class parents, to help dispel fears that children in such a school might be retarded in general academic growth' (1989: 52).

Subsequently, the greatest growth of Welsh-medium education – and, by extension, of Welsh speakers – has occurred in the historically anglicised areas of Wales. Thus, Welsh-medium education has been crucial in providing an expanding base of Welsh-speakers in these anglicised areas and, more broadly, in contributing to the abatement of the long history of Welsh-language decline. The increasingly widespread support for Welsh-medium education – among both Welsh- and non-Welsh-speaking parents, many of whom are middle class – also has much to do with the educational success of the movement (Lyon and Ellis, 1991; Packer and Campbell, 1993; cf. my discussion of Catalonia).

As for the actual growth of Welsh-medium education, particularly in recent years, this can be regarded as nothing short of spectacular. Cylchoedd meithrin (nursery groups), for example, have seen a growth throughout Wales from a base of 67 in 1971 to 617 in 1992. In 1992, these groups reached over 10,000 children, 60 per cent of whom came from non-Welsh-speaking backgrounds (PDAG, 1993a). Similarly, in 1993 there were 538 Welsh-medium primary schools, constituting 33.3 per cent of the total number of primary schools in Wales and 19.8 per cent of the total primary-school population (PDAG, 1993b). Moreover, the majority of pupils being educated in these Welsh-medium schools (59 per cent) actually spoke English at home (PDAG, 1994). A similar story is evident in secondary education, where 58 secondary schools (25.5 per cent of the total number of secondary schools) are designated as Welsh-medium schools (PDAG, 1993b). Welsh-medium education is also increasingly available at tertiary level, albeit still in a limited capacity, while there is special provision for training teachers through the medium of Welsh at designated teachers' colleges.

However, there remain limits to both the influence and efficacy of Welsh-medium education. One key limitation relates to the extent to which education can influence wider language use. As we know from Chapter 4, education cannot compensate for society, or remediate, at least on its own, long-standing language loss (Fishman, 1991). Welsh-medium education is no exception here, not least because even now it still only reaches, at most, approximately 20 per cent of the school population of Wales. Similarly, the strength of Welsh-medium schools in anglicised areas of Wales is both a benefit and a curse. Such schools may well have contributed to the creation of a new generation of Welsh speakers in the post Second World War period. However, they also epitomise the fragmentation of the wider bilingual community within Wales since these schools often provide the only significant domain where a predominantly Welsh-medium milieu can be experienced (Colin Williams, 1995; cf. Harley, 1993). But perhaps most significantly, Welsh-medium education, prior to 1988, remained part of a state system of education controlled and directed by England. Consequently, any distinct educational provision in Wales remained primarily dependent on internal advocacy from parents and educationalists and, more crucially, external largesse from the British government (Jones, 1997). The (1988) Education Reform Act was to change all this, albeit accidentally.

The Education Reform Act

The Act, a notable feature of the Conservative Thatcher administration, established a National (sic) Curriculum for England and Wales. The deliberate qualification in the title of the 'National' Curriculum is important here. Like all previous major educational reform affecting 'England and Wales', the whole thrust of the Act was actually concerned with the needs of the English (national) curriculum (Jones, 1997). Ironically, as it turns out, this is perhaps where it has been least successful. The New Right ideology underpinning the Act – an unwieldy combination of laissez-faire economics and social conservatism – led on the one hand to an emphasis on the increased marketisation and commodification of education and, on the other hand, to the promotion of a centralised, highly prescriptive, 'traditional' curriculum. This dual emphasis, and its sometimes conflicting demands, resulted in both considerable controversy about, and active opposition to, the subsequent implementation of the National Curriculum within England (see Ball, 1990, 1994; Flude and Hammer, 1990; Lingard et al., 1993; Short and Carrington, 1999).

In marked contrast, the Act has been received in Wales with considerably more enthusiasm. Many of its more controversial New Right elements have simply been disregarded in Wales, thus avoiding the controversies apparent in England, while debates about curriculum content have also proved less problematic (Daugherty, 1993; Reynolds, 1994). More crucially, the Act has achieved what no other previous major legislation had come near to doing – the establishment of a Welsh education system in its own right. That this development was not envisaged by its original proponents makes the end result even more remarkable. In short, the 1988 Act has accomplished a fundamental transformation of Welsh education within the last decade. This is most evident in the curriculum where the Welsh language is now not only formally recognised as a principal language of instruction within Welsh-medium schools, but also as a *national* language that should be taught *as of right* to *all* pupils within Wales.

The formal recognition of Welsh throughout all schools in Wales occurred because at the time of the drafting of the National Curriculum in the mid 1980s there was a sufficient number of Welsh-medium schools to ensure that the government of the day could not define the core language component of the National Curriculum (at least in Wales) as solely English. Conceding that Welsh was now the language of instruction and initial study for a significant minority of schools in Wales meant that Welsh had to be recognised as a 'core subject' in these schools under the Act (Williams and Raybould, 1991). Following from this, Welsh has also been given the status of a 'foundation subject' within all other schools in Wales, to be compulsorily studied as a subject by all non-Welsh-speaking children (National Language Forum, 1991). As an official report on the place of Welsh within the National Curriculum summarised it at the time: 'Our objective is to ensure that non-Welsh-speaking pupils in Wales, by the end of their compulsory schooling at 16, will have had the opportunity to learn sufficient Welsh to enable them to use it in their everyday life and to feel part of a bilingual society' (cited in D. Edwards, 1993: 264). The result is that for the first time Welsh has been established as a compulsory element of the curriculum within all schools in Wales. In contrast, the earlier advances of Welsh-medium education, important though they were, remained dependent on sufficient local parental demand and/or the beneficence of individual local head-teachers for their successful enactment (Rawkins, 1979, 1987; Baker, 1995). Similarly, the group-maintenance bilingual education pioneered by the Welsh-medium education movement is now officially recognised, and normalised, as a key part of Welsh state education.

Ongoing challenges and possibilities

The Welsh Language Act and the Education Reform Act reflect, writ large, the enormous institutional changes that have occurred in the last decade in Wales with respect to the legitimation and institutionalisation of Welsh in the public domain. These developments augur well for the reconstruction of a Welsh national identity that once again includes the Welsh language as an important (but not necessarily preeminent) component. As David Miller, writing on national identity, observes:

> a national identity helps to locate us in the world; it must tell us who we are, where we have come from, what we have done. It must then involve an essentially historical understanding in which the present generation are seen as heirs to a tradition which they then pass on to their successors. Of course the story is continually being rewritten; each generation revises the past as it comes to terms with the problems of the present. Nonetheless, there is a sense in which the past always constrains the present: present identities are built out of materials that are handed down, not started from scratch.
>
> (1995: 165)

Bhikhu Parekh argues, along similar lines: 'A community's identity is subject to constant change . . . Every community must wrestle with it as best it can, and find ways of reconstituting its identity in a manner that is both deeply sensitive to its history and traditions and fully alive to its present and future needs' (1995b: 267). These positions have a close resonance with my discussion of habitus in Chapter 1. Moreover, they appear to encapsulate what is currently occurring in Wales with respect to the development of a formal bilingual state. The construction of a bilingual Wales, based on a new set of urban Welsh identities (Colin Williams, 1995), rejects both a narrow language-based conception of Welshness *and* its opposite, the disavowal of any public role for Welsh within contemporary Wales. The result, as Fiona Bowie outlines, is that

> Wales is increasingly looking out, towards Europe, as well as within, at its own mixed population, its bilingualism, and its cultural roots. I perceive a new confidence and determination by Welsh-speakers, incomers and English-speaking people alike, to forge a Welsh identity which builds on all these disparate groups and experiences. It will be different from the Wales of the imagination and from the Wales of the past, but it will also be distinctively and assertively Welsh.
>
> (1993: 191)

But that is not to suggest that there is nothing more to be done. Like Catalonia, the new conception of Welshness apparent in Wales has yet to be extended to the formal recognition of the cultural and linguistic histories of its various ethnic minorities (see Bourne, 1989; Tarrow, 1992; Charlotte Williams, 1995, 1997). Predominantly of South Asian ancestry, these ethnic minorities currently comprise 1.3 per cent of the Welsh population (OPCS, 1991). The majority live in Cardiff (where they constitute 6 per cent of the local population) and include, as well as South Asians, a long-established African Caribbean community. Relatedly, while the formal development of Welsh/English bilingual education is no bar necessarily to the recognition and use of other minority languages within Welsh education, such languages have to date received little formal recognition. Indeed, even at the ostensibly more superficial level of multiculturalism, there has been little actual progress made in establishing a consciously multicultural curriculum in Wales. Norma Tarrow argues, for example, that the major barrier to implementing effective multicultural policies 'is the widely held belief that there is little representation in Wales of groups other than English, Welsh and long-standing assimilated ethnic minorities' (1992: 502).

Moreover, the attitudes of majority-language speakers in Wales towards these changes remain febrile, *despite* the apparent widespread support for them at a general level (cf. the NOP (1995) survey discussed earlier). Thus, in my own recent language-attitude survey in Wales (May, 2000), I found, alongside this widespread support of Welsh at a general level, a more complex and contested picture. In particular, more specific questions of language compulsion in education, or the requirement to be bilingual for certain employment positions, continued to elicit considerable scepticism, and at times outright opposition from majority-language speakers. Indeed, in this respect, the survey demonstrated a remarkable congruence with anti-Catalan language discourses, with many non-Welsh speakers articulating a discourse of individual language rights as a means of *opting out* of bilingual requirements. Pejorative attitudes about minority languages more generally, particularly in relation to their 'adequacy' in and 'relevance' to the modern world, were also clearly apparent, as was the notion that bilingual requirements were somehow in themselves 'racist' and illiberal. Thus, as one respondent observed:

> A bilingual requirement for public service employment is by no means a fair system, it promotes cultural insularity, is divisive and fails to recognize individual merit. It is, in effect, an expression of the Welsh 'ghetto' mentality that predominates in many levels of society.
>
> (quoted in May, 2000: 120)

While another could similarly assert:

> I would have thought it does turn out to be a racial issue if you can prove that a job where you're forced to speak both Welsh and English, say, doesn't really require that skill.

Interviewer: What about jobs that do require it?

I would have thought that it's a very subjective issue, being able to prove that . . . *You're always going to have people that want to speak English*. I would have thought that it's going to be very difficult to prove that satisfactorily in law.

(quoted in May, 2000: 122; my emphasis)

The advocacy of individual language rights for majority-language speakers implicit in these responses was not based on any perceived threat to English as the majority language in Wales, but rather upon the implicit, sometimes explicit, wish of these English speakers to remain monolingual. Levelling charges of 'racism' with regard to language requirements for employment, for example, can be seen in this light, rather than as a legitimate or a sustainable argument (Glyn Williams, 1994). Certainly, the requirement to be bilingual in English and Welsh does not at any point threaten the individual's ability and scope to use English within Wales; quite the reverse, in fact, since English remains dominant in all language domains.[6] The unwillingness to learn Welsh must thus be predicated on the long-standing derogation and vitiation of minority languages and, conversely, the association of so-called 'national' languages with modernity and progress. However one views the constructedness of national languages, drawing a distinction between majority and minority languages on this basis can only be construed as part of the wider historical prejudice exhibited towards the latter. This of course helps to explain why majority-language speakers can accept without question the requirement that everyone speak their own language within a given territory, but suddenly decide that it is 'illiberal' when the same principle is applied to a minority language (even though the latter will inevitably lead to bilingualism, not monolingualism). It also helps to explain why much of the oppositional discourse to Welsh bilingual policy (as elsewhere) continues to assume that any process of linguistic accommodation should remain the sole responsibility of minority-language speakers.

These ongoing frictions again point (if we need reminding) to the contest and conflict that necessarily attach to any attempt to legitimate and institutionalise a minority language. Thus, with respect to Wales, achieving a Welsh bilingual state requires far more than the public, formal acknowledgement of language rights, public services and educational opportunities, important though these are. Rather, as Colin Williams observes, its legitimacy 'will always be subject to fierce debate about a contested social reality, namely the sort of Wales we are constructing together' (1995: 67). In this sense, while much *has* clearly been accomplished by the recent institutional changes in Wales, much more still needs to be accomplished if the significant progress made thus far in legitimating and institutionalising Welsh is not to be undone within the crucible of majority-language speakers' attitudes.

Notes

1   This dramatic change in the fortunes of Catalan was greatly facilitated by the linguistic closeness of Catalan and Spanish as adjacent Romance languages, thus making the learning of Catalan relatively straightforward for Spanish speakers.

2   Apart from the efforts of Welsh historians themselves – most notably, in recent times, Gwyn Williams (1985) and Kenneth Morgan (1995) – Wales has been disproportionately underrepresented in accounts of British history. Most, as Kearney (1989) and Crick (1991, 1995) point out, have been preoccupied historically with England. Hugh Kearney's (1989) excellent revisionist account of British history was the first to provide some semblance of balance here, by specifically including the different, and at times competing, historical trajectories of Scotland, Wales and Ireland. This welcome trend has been reinforced by subsequent British histories, notably Linda Colley (1992) and Keith Robbins (1997).

3   Welsh emerged in the sixth century when the Brythonic branch of Celtic began to separate into distinct languages. While the first written records date back to the eighth century, it was not until the Middle Welsh period (1150–1400) that a standardised language began to develop; the result, principally, of bardic writings (V. Edwards, 1991).

4   Legislation specific to Wales included the (1881) Welsh Sunday Closing Act, the (1888) Local Government Act and the (1889) Welsh Intermediate Education Act. A range of national institutions was also created over this period, including the University of Wales (1883), the Board of Education, a national library and a national museum (all 1907), and a Department of Agriculture (1912).

5   A more recent, non-census-based social survey of 19,000 households conducted by the Welsh Office (1993) actually estimated a higher percentage of Welsh speakers in the total population at 21.5 per cent. The difference between this and the census figures (at 18.7 per cent) is attributable perhaps to the tendency of many Welsh speakers to under-report to the census their ability in the language (Williams and Raybould, 1991).

6   Of course, in this case, English benefits not only from being the historically associated 'national' language in the British context, but also from its current (and equally constructed) ascendancy as the world language (see Chapter 6).

8

Indigenous rights: self-determination, language and education

This chapter begins with a brief review of the debates surrounding the rights and standing of indigenous peoples within national and international law, with particular emphasis on the issues of self-determination, language and education. I will then proceed to discuss the example of Māori in Aotearoa / New Zealand in specific relation to these issues.

Indigenous peoples are at the forefront of developments regarding the recognition of group-differentiated minority rights, not least because their own status within modern nation-states has been, and continues to be, so problematic. After all, indigenous groups have in nearly all cases a long history of colonisation which has seen such groups faced with systematic disadvantage, marginalisation and/or alienation in their own historic territories (cf. Chapter 2). As a result, they have been undermined economically, culturally and politically, with ongoing, often disturbing, consequences for their individual and collective life chances. At the same time, indigenous peoples have been viewed extremely pejoratively in relation to modernisation – i.e., as 'primitive' or premodern. Consequently, they have been subjected in many cases to forced assimilation, on the misplaced assumption that this was the only viable option for their social and cultural survival and/or advancement. The shocking case of the 'stolen generations', recently brought to light in Australia, illustrates the extremes of such a position all too starkly. For 60 years, from 1910 to 1970, the Australian authorities enforced a systematic policy of 'resettlement' which saw up to a third of Aboriginal and Torres Strait Island children forcibly removed from their families and adopted out to white families or, more often, simply fostered or institutionalised. In the process, original family records were deliberately destroyed because, it was thought, any life was better than a traditional Aboriginal one (see Edwards and Read, 1992; Perera and Pugliese, 1998; Pilger, 1998).[1]

Thus, indigenous peoples have not had access, in many instances, to even the most basic rights ostensibly attributable to all citizens in the modern nation-state. Aboriginal peoples and Torres Strait Islanders, for example, were only granted full citizenship rights in Australia in 1967 – some two hundred years after the advent of European colonisation. Where indigenous peoples have had such access, they have, more often than not, been treated solely as a disadvantaged ethnic-minority group rather than as a national-minority ethnie within the nation-state. That said, indigenous peoples have been granted, in certain circumstances, some 'special privileges' and protection not afforded 'regular' citizens. Traditional systems of social order, for example, including the right to very limited forms of governmental autonomy (e.g., tribal or band government on Native American reservations) have been preserved in some cases in order to *allow* indigenous peoples to exercise a modicum of control over their traditional territories and ways of life (Churchill, 1986; Kymlicka, 1989). However, it is perhaps not surprising that protectionism in this form has also simply been used as a variant of assimilation. As Hartwig argues, concerning Māori in Aotearoa / New Zealand and Aboriginal and Torres Strait Islanders in Australia: 'whatever the differences between "amalgamationist" and "protectionist" strategies, the ultimate aim of the state for long periods in both countries was the disappearance of Aboriginal and Māori societies as distinguishable entities' (1978: 170; cited in Harker and McConnochie, 1985). Joshua Fishman is also particularly critical of this kind of 'protectionism'. As he argues, 'even in such settings indigenous populations are robbed of control of the natural resources that could constitute the economic bases of a more self-regulatory collective life and, therefore, robbed also of a possible avenue of cultural viability as well' (1991: 62).

The extremely limited nature of these concessions has also tended to place indigenous peoples in a double bind. On the one hand, such concessions have done little, if anything, to redress the extreme marginalisation facing indigenous peoples in modern nation-states. On the other hand, the granting of even very limited local autonomy to indigenous peoples is usually viewed with a good deal of suspicion, and often with outright opposition, because it may infringe on the individual rights of majority group members. Again drawing on Australia as an example, the recent rise (and, thankfully, even more recent decline) of the populist and overtly racist politician Pauline Hanson, with her 'One Nation' Party and her specifically anti-Aboriginal policies, illustrates the extreme antagonisms which such a position can promote (see May, 1998).

Given this historical background of colonisation, and the ongoing reticence of many nation-states to recognise its legacy, indigenous groups have become increasingly disaffected with their treatment by national majorities and have sought the right to greater *self-determination* within nation-states, via both national and international law. In this respect, the definition of what constitutes an indigenous people becomes important. However, as we saw in Chapter 2, such definitions are not entirely unproblematic and indigenous groups themselves, like all broad groupings, exhibit a range of significant inter- and intragroup differences. These caveats notwithstanding, the International Labour Organisation's (ILO) Convention 169 (Article 1.1), formulated in 1989, may serve as a useful starting point:

a) tribal peoples in independent countries whose social, cultural and economic conditions distinguish them from other sections of the national community, and whose status is regulated wholly or partially by their own customs or traditions or by special laws or regulations;

b) peoples in independent countries who are regarded as indigenous on account of their descent from the populations which inhabited the country, or a geographical region to which the country belongs, at the time of conquest or colonisation or the establishment of present state boundaries and who, *irrespective of their legal status*, retain some of their own social, economic, cultural and political institutions.

(my emphasis)

Lest objectivist definitions be accorded too much weight, however, Article 1.2 adds the rider that 'self-identification as indigenous or tribal shall be regarded as a fundamental criterion for determining the groups to which the provisions of this Convention apply' (cf. Chapter 1). Suffice it to say at this point that self-identification, along with the qualification 'irrespective of their legal status' highlighted previously, are both central to any discussion of indigenousness since not all nation-states are willing to recognise indigenous groups in their territories. Indeed, governments in Malaysia, India, Burma and Bangladesh have at times claimed that everyone is indigenous and that no one is thus entitled to any special or differential treatment (de Varennes, 1996a). This unwillingness on the part of national governments to recognise indigenous peoples is also extended to minorities more generally, as we saw in the discussion of Article 27 of the (1966) International Covenant on Civil and Political Rights in Chapter 5.

The ILO Convention 169 is also significant for another reason. It replaces an earlier convention (107), drawn up in 1957, which exhibited a much more paternalistic approach to indigenous peoples. These differences are reflected in both the wording and the general intent of the two conventions. With regard to wording, for example, Convention 107 (a) uses the phrase 'tribal populations' whereas 169 (a) employs 'tribal peoples'. This is significant, given the connotations of the term 'peoples' in international law (see below). Convention 169 (a) also states that the social, cultural and economic conditions of tribal groups are *distinguished* from other sections of the national community whereas 107 (a) employs the more pejorative phrase 'at a less advanced stage'. Likewise, where Convention 169 (b) states that indigenous peoples 'retain some of their own social, economic, cultural and political institutions', 107 (b) specifically equates these institutions with premodern practices and contrasts them with 'the [modern] institutions of the nation to which they belong'. These differences are not simply semantic ones. More broadly, Convention 107 clearly views indigenous culture as a temporary obstacle to modernisation. As such, it is as much concerned with the assimilation of indigenous peoples as with their protection. In contrast, Convention 169 reflects a far more positive view of indigenous cultures and is specifically anti-assimilationist in intent (see Thornberry, 1991b: 18; de Varennes, 1996a: 252–253).

Indigenous peoples, self-determination and international law

The distinctions between the two ILO Conventions illustrate the different status that has gradually come to be accorded to indigenous peoples in international law over the intervening 40-year period, and subsequently to the present day (see Anaya, 1996, for a full review; see also Stamatopoulou, 1994; Tennant, 1994). Central to this change has been the argument of indigenous groups themselves that they are not simply one of a number of ethnic-minority groups, competing for the limited resources of the nation-state, and therefore entirely subject to its largesse, but are *peoples*, with the associated rights of self-determination attributable to the latter under international law. This argument has been articulated by such organisations as the World Council of Indigenous Peoples (WCIP) and the Working Group on Indigenous Populations (WGIP), the latter being established in 1982 as part of the United Nations Sub-Commission on the Prevention of Discrimination and Protection of Minorities. The work of the WGIP has been particularly influential here and has contributed to a growing tendency to regard indigenous peoples 'as a separate issue [from other minority groups] in international and constitutional law' (Thornberry, 1991b: 6). The culmination of these developments thus far has been the (1993) United Nations Draft Declaration on the Rights of Indigenous Peoples, a document that clearly outlines the key legal and political demands of indigenous peoples. Article 8 of the Declaration states, for example: 'Indigenous peoples have the collective and individual right to maintain and develop their distinct identities and characteristics, including the right to identify themselves as indigenous and to be recognised as such'. Article 3 is even more unequivocal: 'Indigenous peoples have the right to self-determination. By virtue of that right they freely determine their political status and freely pursue their economic, social and cultural development'.

Such demands, if accepted, would involve a fundamental reconceptualisation of national and international law and practice. It is perhaps not surprising, then, that, despite the more favourable view adopted towards indigenous peoples in recent times, there remains considerable reticence about the right of self-determination being accorded to them. Thus, in the ILO Convention 169 – which is clearly positive towards indigenous peoples – there is also a clear caveat which states: 'The use of the term "peoples" in this Convention shall not be construed as having any implications as regards the rights which may attach to the term under international law' (Article 1.3). Much of this reticence has to do with the specific meaning of self-determination in international law. As we saw in Chapter 3, the right of minority national groups (including indigenous peoples) to self-determination is not actually inconsistent with international law since the (1945) United Nations Charter clearly states that 'all peoples have the right to self-determination'. However, the term 'peoples' is not defined by the UN and the injunction has tended to be interpreted only in relation to the recognition of postcolonial states (the 'salt water thesis') rather than to national minorities within existing nation-states, even though the latter may have been subjected to broadly the same processes of colonisation. Self-determination has thus been limited *in practice* to existing states in the post Second World War era (Thornberry, 1991a; Clark and Williamson, 1996). This widely accepted practice has been further reinforced by the implicit assumption that the right of self-determination includes, crucially, the right to secession (Scott, 1996; see also below).

The contested nature of these debates around self-determination and its applicability, or otherwise, to indigenous peoples is ably demonstrated by the workings of the subsequent United Nations Commission on Human Rights (UNCHR) Working Group, whose brief it is to agree a final (and, by definition, politically acceptable) version of the (1993) Draft Declaration on the Rights of Indigenous Peoples. The first session of the UNCHR Working Group was convened in November 1995 to review the Draft Declaration. Unlike that document, which had been the result of a decade-long dialogue between indigenous peoples and the UN legal representatives on the WGIP subcommittee, the UNCHR Working Group was to be dominated once again by the interests of states. This was because the UNCHR Working Group, as part of the formal apparatus of the UN, was restricted in its membership to attested nongovernment organisations. As a result, many indigenous groups involved in the formulation of the Draft Declaration were excluded, while, at least theoretically, any state could veto an objectionable element of the draft under review. In this latter respect, state representatives on the UNCHR did endorse the WGIP text as a 'sound basis' for future drafting. However, subsequent proceedings saw many substantive objections raised by states about specific principles outlined in the Draft Declaration. Indeed, some states, notably Japan and the US, contended that the text as a whole was 'not a reasonable evolution of human rights law' (Barsh, 1996: 788). The full range of contentions raised by the various states need not concern us (for an extended discussion, see Barsh, 1996) – here I want to concentrate solely on the issue of self-determination.

As I have already indicated, the key problem for many states in this respect was that any claim to self-determination by indigenous peoples (the term 'peoples' rather than 'people' being, in itself, an indication of this) carried with it an implication of secession. On this basis, the potential threat of secession that self-determination implied could simply not be accepted by many states (although, interestingly, international law nowhere says that 'peoples' have the right to secede from existing states by virtue only of the right to self-determination; see Scott, 1996: 818). However, in the course of discussion, some states argued for a more restricted view of self-determination, termed by some as 'internal self-determination', and by others as 'autonomy'. Thus, Chile argued that the idea of internal self-determination allowed:

> [a] space within which indigenous peoples can freely determine their forms of development, [including] the preservation of their cultures, languages, customs and traditions, in a manner that reinforces their identity and characteristics, in the context and framework of the States in which indigenous peoples live.
>
> (cited in Barsh, 1996: 797)

Similarly Australia argued that the right of indigenous peoples to self-determination could be accepted, 'subject to the understanding that the exercise of this right should [remain] within existing State boundaries, that is not [including] a right to secession'. Nicaragua agreed that 'autonomy' captured the 'sense and meaning of the concept of self-determination, without affecting the unity of the State' (both cited in Barsh, 1996: 799). While some states, notably France, Japan, and to a lesser extent the USA, continued to oppose any notion of self-government for indigenous peoples, *in principle*, the general position which emerged from this first session of the UNCHR Working Group was one of qualified support for greater 'internal self-determination' or 'autonomy' for indigenous peoples. An earlier observation by the Aotearoa / New Zealand government on the conclusions of the WGIP provides us with a useful summary of this position:

> There is no indication at present that governments will recognise a right of *external* self-determination for indigenous peoples, that is, including the right to secede from a state. Any 'right of self-determination' for indigenous people would therefore have to be understood differently from its traditional meaning in international law if it were to be acceptable to governments. [In this regard] international law may be moving towards recognition of an 'aboriginal right to self-determination' or autonomy which does not include the right of secession.
>
> (Te Puni Kōkiri, 1994: 9; my emphasis)

In effect then, we are seeing the emergence, however tentatively, of an intermediate position in international law with respect to self-determination which acknowledges the right to greater *autonomy* within the nation-state for indigenous peoples but which does not necessarily include the right to secession (see Clark and Williamson, 1996). This form of 'internal self-determination' emphasises *negotiated* power-sharing, both through constitutional reform and within existing institutions, and extends well beyond the desultory measures of local autonomy already established for some indigenous groups. As Madame Daes, the UN rapporteur for the WGIP, has observed of this: 'the existing state has the duty to accommodate the aspirations of indigenous peoples through constitutional reforms designed to share power democratically. It also means that indigenous peoples have the duty to try and reach an agreement, in good faith, on sharing power within the existing state and to exercise their right to self-determination by this means to the [fullest] extent possible' (cited in Te Puni Kōkiri, 1994: 11). More broadly, Craig Scott has observed that rethinking the notion of self-determination has required us 'to begin to think of self-determination in terms of people existing *in relationship with each other*' (1996: 819; my emphasis; see also Anaya, 1996). This view echoes the relational aspects of ethnicity, discussed in Chapter 1, and Iris Marion Young's arguments with respect to the relational basis of group-differentiated rights, discussed in Chapter 3 (see also Young, forthcoming).

This is not to say that the debate is over – any consensus over this issue, let alone others raised by the Draft Declaration, remains a long way off (see Barsh, 1996: 804–813). Indeed, the process of ratification may well take us past the officially designated International Decade of the World's Indigenous People (1995–2004; note the use of the term 'people' here). There also remains some reticence about the applicability or usefulness of self-determination to the claims of indigenous peoples, even in reconceived form. Corntassel and Primeau (1995) argue from a legal perspective, for example, that the use of self-determination, in whatever form, is unhelpful in debates about indigenous rights because of its intrinsic association with secession. Moreover, since the central questions that actually concern indigenous peoples have to do with cultural preservation and integrity (see also Sanders, 1989), these can be better ensured by existing human-rights legislation. I disagree with this argument for reasons that should already be clear – not least, the long-standing inability of existing human-rights law to ensure adequately exactly these kinds of cultural and linguistic protections.

Will Kymlicka (1999c) raises some concerns about indigenous self-determination from a different angle. He argues that the emergent distinction between national minorities (or nations without states) and indigenous peoples within international law, with only the latter being accorded a right to self-determination (albeit in delimited form), is inconsistent and unnecessary. Consequently, he argues that all national minorities (including indigenous peoples) should be accorded the same rights to greater political, cultural and linguistic autonomy, with the implication, at least in my reading of him, that invoking self-determination may not be the best way forward here. I am much more sympathetic to this more inclusive line of argument, not least because it accords so closely with my own position on cultural nationalism, which, as I argued in Chapter 2, may apply as much to 'nations without states' as to indigenous peoples (see also below). Where I would differ from Kymlicka is in still thinking that the notion of 'internal self-determination', rather than the more limited minority rights enshrined in, say, Article 27 of the (1966) International Covenant on Civil and Political Rights (see Chapter 5), provides us with a stronger basis for protecting those rights for *all* national minorities within international law. In other words, rather than retrenching on the rights of 'internal self-determination' for indigenous peoples, national minorities should also be included within these claims.

Indigenous peoples and national law

Despite these ongoing debates, developments in international law since the Second World War clearly signal a more accommodative approach to indigenous peoples, and their claims to greater self-determination. This approach has also been paralleled, at least to some extent, within the laws of (some) nation-states. Thus, in Brasil, the adoption in 1988 of a new constitution recognised for the first time the indigenous Indians' social organisation, customs, languages, beliefs and traditions, along with the right of native title to their lands (*Constituição* Chapter VIII, Art. 231; Brasil, 1996; see also Hornberger, 1997). After a century of enforcing a stringent 'Norwegianisation' (read assimilationist) policy towards the indigenous Sámi, their languages and their culture, Norway also moved in 1988 to revise its Constitution in order to grant greater autonomy for Sámi. As the amendment to the Constitution stated: 'It is incumbent on the governmental authorities to take the necessary steps to enable the Sámi population to safeguard and develop their language, their culture and their social life' (cited in Magga, 1996: 76). The effects of this new amendment are most apparent in the regional area of Finnmark, in the northernmost part of Norway, where the largest percentage of the Sámi live. The formal recognition accorded to Sámi has led to the subsequent establishment of a Sámi Parliament in Finnmark (in 1989), while the Sámi Language Act, passed in 1992, recognised Northern Sámi as its official regional language. The Act saw the formal promotion of the language within the Sámi Parliament, the courts of law, and all levels of education (see Corson, 1995; Magga, 1995, 1996; Huss, 1999; Todal, 1999). However, as Todal (1999) points out, it is only in Finnmark that this degree of autonomy has been achieved since in the other areas in Norway where

Sámi can be found, they live in relatively isolated settlements. Accordingly, the language varieties spoken by these groups of Sámi, notably Lule Sámi and Southern Sámi, and their cultural practices, have far less institutional support.

The precedent of regional autonomy for indigenous peoples set by Finnmark has been built upon considerably in more recent times in Canada. In December 1997, the Canadian Supreme Court ruled in a landmark decision (subsequently referred to as the Delgamuukw Decision) in favour of the recognition of indigenous land rights. This ruling coincided with an initiative entitled 'Gathering Strength', developed over the course of the 1990s by the Canadian Liberal government of Jean Chrétien, that aimed to redress and, crucially, make actual restitution for the colonial appropriation of the lands and resources of Canada's indigenous peoples (Purvis, 1999a). The culmination of both these developments, at least thus far, has been twofold. First, an autonomous Inuit-led government was created in April 1999 as part of the formal establishment of the new Arctic province of Nunavut. And second, the Nisga'a Agreement, requiring the return of a proportion of the traditional lands of this Native Canadian tribe in Northern British Columbia, was formally ratified by the Canadian Parliament in December 1999 (having first been signed the previous year).

The establishment of Nunavut, the first formal subdivision of territory in Canada for 50 years, is the end result of a 20-year negotiation process with the 22,000 Inuit of the region (out of a total regional population of 25,000). In return for ceding wider claims to their traditional territories across the north of Canada, the Inuit have been granted 22,000 square kilometres of territory to the immediate northwest of Hudson Bay, a comparable degree of autonomy to Canada's other provinces, and a current annual budget of C\$620 million. The new provincial administration is dominated by Inuit and it is proposed that the local Inuit language, Inuktitut, be made co-official with English and French in the region, as well as being the first working language of the provincial government (Purvis, 1999b). Given the scale of these developments, it is perhaps surprising that so little controversy has actually attended them (at least thus far) – although, no doubt, the remoteness of the territory, and the relatively sparse nonindigenous population within it, have played their part here.

In contrast, the Nisga'a Agreement has proved to be far more controversial. Originally agreed in 1998, again after a 20-year period of negotiation, it called for the transfer of nearly 2000 square kilometres of land to the 5500-member Nisga'a band (who now describe themselves as a 'nation') in Northern British Columbia. Restitution amounting to \$C330 million, and the granting of substantial powers of self-government – including an autonomous legislature responsible for citizenship and land management – were also central features of the Agreement (Purvis, 1999a). This, in turn, was based on a long-standing claim – first raised in the nineteenth century – against the colonial appropriation of Nisga'a lands. However, the subsequent ratification of the agreement in the Canadian Parliament was characterised by strong and vituperative opposition from the Reform Party, a conservative, anglocentric 'one nation' party that has also been prominent in opposing any separate recognition of Québec. The Reform Party claimed that the Agreement would give the Nisga'a too much power over local businesses and nonindigenous peoples and that it would set a precedent for the establishment of similar treaties with Canada's 50 other Native Canadian bands. Consequently, the Reform Party tried to derail the legislation by tabling 471 amendments and required the Liberal-led Canadian Parliament to sit in session for over 42 hours before managing to pass the Agreement in its original form (*Guardian*, 11 December, 1999: 23). Setting aside the clear inconsistency that seems to have escaped the Reform Party – that non-indigenous control of indigenous peoples is regarded as legitimate without question, whereas the reverse is not – this opposition highlights, once again, the strong antipathy to any notion of group-differentiated rights within modern nation-states. The effects of the latter are also graphically illustrated by the successes, and subsequent reverses, in Australian policy towards Aboriginal land rights over the course of the 1990s.

In 1992 the High Court of Australia ruled in favour of Koiki Mabo and four other plaintiffs over their claims that a common-law property right of 'native title' had existed prior to European colonisation and the subsequent annexation of their lands by the Queensland government (see R. Hill, 1995; Patton, 1995). The Mabo Decision (*Mabo v. Queensland* (no. 2), 1992) set a major new precedent since, as we saw in Chapter 2, up until that time European colonisation of Australia had been predicated on the convenient legal fiction of terra nullius (empty land). Consequently, indigenous land rights were never acknowledged and did not evolve as part of Australian land and property law – in contrast to Aotearoa / New Zealand, for example (see below). The consequence of the Mabo Decision was the belated recognition that Australia's indigenous peoples could lay claim to native title on the 25 per cent of Australia that remained Crown or public land. The (1993) Native Land Act, implemented by the Australian Labor Party, formalised and clarified this position. The Mabo Decision also required that indigenous peoples had to demonstrate a continued (and continuous) association with their traditional lands. However, this caveat was modified somewhat by the Wik Decision of the High Court in 1996, which ruled that where land had been given to white farmers under a colonial pastoral lease scheme, native title was not *automatically* extinguished.[2]

The response to these decisions, particularly the latter, can be seen in a high-profile campaign of 'white hysteria' (Perera and Pugliese, 1998) that has been waged subsequently. This is most apparent in the rise of Pauline Hanson's 'One Nation' Party with its overtly anti-Aboriginal policies, and in the orchestrated opposition of the National Farmers Federation (NFF) to the Wik Decision. With respect to the latter, the NFF have disingenuously argued that it would give carte blanche to Australia's indigenous peoples to make claims on private land – although what is actually at stake is the land granted under the colonial pastoral lease scheme. At the same time, the NFF campaign has continued to promote the 'myth' of the centrality of the white pioneers to Australia's 'national' (read colonial) heritage and identity. In response to this often vitriolic campaign, and with the subsequent election of a conservative government, a significantly delimited Native Title Act was implemented in 1998, retrenching much of the gains achieved for Aboriginal peoples in the Mabo and Wik decisions.

To reiterate, it is clear from the above examples that recent developments towards greater 'internal self-determination' for indigenous peoples, both at national and international levels, have been significant. As de Varennes comments of these developments: 'Whilst there is certainly no unanimity, both international and national law appear to be heading towards increased recognition of the special position which indigenous peoples occupy within a [nation-state's] legal and political order' (1996a: 274). But just as clearly, these gains remain fragile and subject to ongoing, often debilitating, opposition. This is despite the fact that indigenous claims are not principally concerned with the politically contentious question of secession. Indeed, internal self-determination bears a remarkable resemblance to the concept of cultural nationalism, discussed in Chapter 2, with its emphasis on the transformation of national communities from *within* the nation-state, rather than with secession per se. Indigenous peoples are not consumed with questions of secession since, generally, their limited socioeconomic, demographic and political strength precludes such an option. Rather, indigenous peoples are advocating a right to separate representation, *alongside* national majorities, on the basis that they constitute a distinct ethnie in the nation-state. Indeed, as we have seen, many nation-states already acknowledge as part of their internal law, however begrudgingly, that indigenous peoples have either retained some degree of inherent sovereignty that has not been extinguished by conquest and/or colonisation, or have a continuing legal status that sets them apart (de Varennes, 1996a, b).

These national-minority claims thus contrast with the usual polyethnic concerns of (immigrant) ethnic-minority groups for the abolition of barriers that lead to disadvantage and preclude greater integration into the nation-state (see Chapter 2). This is not to say, of course, that these concerns are not shared by indigenous peoples – they clearly are. However, polyethnic claims are not their *principal* preoccupation. Thus, state policies that address only these concerns, on the basis that indigenous peoples are simply one of many disadvantaged ethnic-minority groups, do little to allay their specific demands.

Indigenous language and education rights

The cultural nationalist emphases of indigenous claims are also significant for our purposes because, in addition to questions of land restoration and the granting of greater political autonomy, they often have, as a central concern, issues of language and education. In this respect, Articles 14 and 15 of the (1993) Draft Declaration of Indigenous Peoples are most pertinent:

> 14. Indigenous peoples have the right to revitalize, use, develop and transmit to future generations their histories, languages, oral traditions, philosophies, writing systems and literatures, and to designate and retain their own names for communities, places and persons.
>
> States shall take *effective* measures, whenever any right of indigenous peoples may be threatened, to ensure this right is protected . . .
>
> 15. . . . All indigenous peoples . . . have . . . the right *to establish and control* their educational systems and institutions providing education in their own languages, in a manner appropriate to their cultural methods of teaching and learning.
>
> Indigenous children living outside their communities have the right to be provided access to education in their own language and culture.
>
> States shall take effective measures to provide appropriate resources for these purposes.

> (my emphases)

The clear desire of indigenous peoples for greater linguistic and educational *control* apparent in these articles is, in turn, a product of colonial histories of cultural and linguistic proscription, particularly within education, that must be regarded as being at the most extreme end of such practices. The comments of J. D. C. Atkins with respect to Native American education in the USA (see Chapter 6), are testimony enough to this, as are the wider historical attempts at the 'resocialisation' of indigenous children (of which education formed a key part), discussed at the beginning of this chapter. The result, not surprisingly, has been not only the loss of indigenous languages but a long history of educational 'failure' for indigenous students within education (see May, 1994a; Corson, 1998).

Given this history, it is thus also not surprising that education has now come to be seen as a key arena in which indigenous peoples can reclaim and revalue their languages and cultures and, in so doing, improve the educational success of indigenous students. As a result, we have seen over the last 20–30 years the emergence of numerous indigenous community-based education initiatives where indigenous-community control and a central role for indigenous languages and cultures are prominent features (see McCarty and Zepeda, 1995; Henze and Davis, 1999; May, 1999d). While still in many cases small-scale, and while still facing considerable odds, these initiatives *are* beginning to have a positive effect on the specific educational futures of indigenous students and, more broadly, the retention of indigenous language and cultures. In the process, the normalisation and valorisation of European languages and cultures, and their representation within education, are being critiqued and contested. In particular, indigenous language education proponents argue that the long historical dominance of European norms and values in schooling has nothing to do with their greater intrinsic value or use, but rather with the exercise and legitimation of unequal power relations which privilege such languages and cultural practices over all others, indigenous ones in particular. There is clearly potential in these arguments for the reinforcement of a static and reified view of (indigenous) languages and cultures, and their unhelpful juxtaposition with dominant 'European' cultural and linguistic practices (see Fettes, 1999; Hornberger and King, 1999). But emergent practice has tended to demonstrate a more contextual, relational approach – one that incorporates a dynamic and ongoing process of 'cultural negotiation', rather than a simple return to, or retrenchment of, past practices. An exemplar of the latter can be found in the recent emergence of Māori-language education in Aotearoa / New Zealand – a development that is itself both a product and illustration of a wider repositioning of identity and minority-rights issues within this once 'British settler society' (see Larner and Spoonley, 1995; Fleras and Spoonley, 1999; Pearson, 1990; 2000).

Aotearoa / New Zealand: a tale of two ethnicities

When one significant section of the community burns with a sense of injustice, the rest of the community cannot safely pretend that there is no reason for their discontent.

(Waitangi Tribunal, 1986: 46)

Until the 1960s, Aotearoa / New Zealand had regarded itself, and been regarded by others, as a model of harmonious 'race' relations; a rare success story of colonisation. Pākehā (European)[3] New Zealanders, in particular, looked back with pride at a colonial history of mutual respect, cooperation and integration with the indigenous Māori iwi (tribes). This colonial history began with Pākehā settlement of Aotearoa / New Zealand in the late eighteenth century, although prior to the arrival of the first Pākehā, Māori had been resident in Aotearoa / New Zealand for approximately 1000 years (Walker, 1990). Colonial relations between Māori and Pākehā were subsequently formalised by the British Crown in the nineteenth century and were interrupted by only brief periods of antagonism, notably the Land Wars in the 1860s. The foundational colonial document, Te Tiriti o Waitangi (the Treaty of Waitangi) – signed on 6 February 1840 between the British Crown and Māori chiefs – was a surprisingly progressive document for its time. The Treaty specifically attempted to establish the rights and responsibilities of both parties as a mutual framework by which colonisation could proceed. Captain Hobson, the Crown's representative, was instructed to obtain the surrender of Aotearoa / New Zealand as a sovereign state to the British Crown, but only by 'free and intelligent consent' of the 'natives'. In return, Māori iwi were to be guaranteed possession of 'their lands, their homes and all their treasured possessions (taonga)'. Consequently, the Treaty had come to be commemorated as the central symbol of this apparently benign history. The words 'he iwi tahi tātou' (we are all one people) – spoken by William Hobson at the Treaty's signing – provided its leitmotif. In short, while undeniably a white settler colony in origin, the emergence of Aotearoa / New Zealand as a nation-state was seen to have avoided the worst excesses of colonialism. Māori were highly regarded, intermixing and miscegenation were common, and Māori language and culture were incorporated, at least to some degree, into Aotearoa / New Zealand life. Or so the story went.

From the 1970s, a quite different story emerged into the public domain. A generation of young, urban and educated Māori articulated a history of continued conflict and oppression of Māori by the Pākehā (Sharp, 1990); a theme that was to be taken up in subsequent revisionist histories of the country (see Orange, 1987; Kawharu, 1989; Walker, 1990: Sinclair, 1993; Belich, 1986, 1996). It was a history that had been consistently told by many Māori over previous generations but one that had seldom actually been *heard* before. In this view, the Treaty of Waitangi was a fraud; an inconvenient document that had been quickly and ruthlessly trivialised by Pākehā settlers in their quest for land.

The issue of legitimacy centres on the question of whether the informed consent of Māori was ever obtained at the signing of the Treaty. Much of this has to do with the discrepancies between the English-language version of the Treaty and the Māori-language version that the Chiefs actually signed. The Treaty comprises three articles. In the 1st Article, for example, there is a distinction between the ceding of 'all the rights and powers of *Sovereignty*' in the English version – equating to the term 'tino rangatiratanga', or absolute Chieftainship, in Māori – and the actual use in the Māori text of the lesser term 'kāwanatanga', or governorship. In the 2nd Article this discrepancy is reinforced. In the official English translation Māori are granted 'exclusive and undisturbed possession of their Lands and Estates, Forestries, Fisheries and other properties which they may individually and collectively possess'. In the Māori translation, this becomes 'the absolute Chieftainship [tino rangatiratanga] of their lands, of their homes and all their treasured possessions'. The Chiefs are thus likely to have understood Article 2 as confirming their own sovereign rights in return for a limited concession (granted in Article 1) of Pākehā 'governorship'. The 3rd Article – the least contentious – extends to Māori the rights of British citizens, although the Māori version talks again of governance, rather than sovereignty – reinforcing the previous emphases (see Orange, 1987; Kawharu, 1989; Walker, 1990; Belich, 1996).

The ruthless quest for land is supported by any considered reading of New Zealand history. While a period of prosperity and relative stability between Māori and Pākehā followed the signing of the Treaty, this ended with the land wars of the 1860s in which the Settler Government (established in 1852) invaded the Taranaki and Waikato districts of the North Island. The ostensible aim of these campaigns was to move against iwi supporters of Kīngitanga (the King movement) – a confederation of tribes under the Māori king Te Wherowhero – who supposedly posed a threat to law and order. The actual aim was to remove the opposition of Kīngitanga to the expropriation of Māori land for the rapidly growing numbers of Pākehā settlers (Walker, 1990). When military means proved inconclusive, the government resorted to legislation which transformed communally owned Māori land into individual titles – as in English law – in order to expedite the further sale of the land. This proved so successful that by the turn of the century almost all New Zealand territory was in European hands. Meanwhile, the Pākehā population had risen from 1000 in 1838 to 770,000 by 1900 while the Māori population had fallen from an estimated 100,000–200,000 at the time of European settlement to the nadir of 45,549 in 1900; in effect, a 75 per cent population collapse of Māori over the course of the nineteenth century (Stannard, 1989; Walker, 1990). As Claudia Orange concludes: 'In many respects New Zealand, in spite of the treaty, has been merely a variation in the colonial domination of indigenous races [sic]' (1987: 5).

Indeed, the degree to which Treaty obligations came to be overtaken by 'events' is reflected by the New Zealand Chief Justice Sir James Prendergast, who in 1877, in *Wi Parata v. Bishop of Wellington*, could declare the treaty 'a simple nullity'. This legal view was to hold sway until the 1980s. As Orange's previous comment suggests, what resulted for Māori were the usual deleterious effects of colonisation upon an indigenous people – political disenfranchisement, misappropriation of land, population and health decline, educational disadvantage and socioeconomic marginalisation. The cumulative weight of this historical process, allied with the rapid urbanisation of Māori since the Second World War,[4] had seen their economic and social incorporation into a metropolitan-based cultural division of labour, usually at the lowest point of entry, that of surplus unskilled labour (Miles and Spoonley, 1985; Pearson, 1990; Spoonley, 1996). The economic downturn precipitated by the oil crisis in the 1970s, and the New Right economic agenda of successive New Zealand governments since the 1980s, exacerbated further the disparities between Māori and Pākehā on most social and economic indices. Thus, while Māori comprised 14 per cent of the total population of

3.5 million in Aotearoa / New Zealand at the time of the 1991 census, they were significantly over-represented in social and economic 'at risk' categories.[5] Māori workers, for example, were heavily under-represented in high-income, high-skilled and growing sectors of the economy. Conversely, they were over-represented in low-paid, low-skilled, declining occupations, and among beneficiaries and those not in paid employment (Manatū Māori, 1991). The emasculation of low-skilled, semi-skilled occupations over the last two decades, under the New Right economic agenda, has also resulted in a disproportionately high level of unemployment for Māori; 24 per cent of all Māori over 15 years compared with 11 per cent for the total population. Young Māori, in particular, have borne the brunt of the depressed labour market. In 1991, 43 per cent of all Māori teenagers (15–19 years) were unemployed. Moreover, given that 52 per cent of this group did not hold a school qualification, future employment prospects appear limited (Davies and Nicholl, 1993).

Some are suggesting, from this, the emergence of an increasing Māori underclass (Jarden, 1992; McLoughlin, 1993). When these economic statistics are linked to social and educational statistics for Māori, this pattern seems to be confirmed. In 1991, 56 per cent of Māori aged between 15 and 59 years were receiving some form of income-support benefit and Māori were also proportionately over-represented on all other welfare benefits, except for the pension. With respect to the latter, 4.3 per cent of the Māori population received a pension compared with 17.1 per cent of non-Māori. David McLoughlin (1993) argues that while some of this has to do with the young age structure of the Māori population, it is also because too few Māori live long enough. Health indicators here present a disturbing picture. Māori do not live, on average, as long as non-Māori. The immunisation rates of Māori children – less than 60 per cent compared with 90 per cent for most other 'developed' countries – see Māori children suffer disproportionately from preventable diseases. Half of all Māori over 15 years smoke (compared with about a quarter of the non-Māori population). This includes 45 per cent of men and 57 per cent of women, with Māori women having one of the highest lung-cancer rates in the world.

Educational status completes the picture of comparative disadvantage for Māori. Though increasing numbers of Māori have been completing school and pursuing tertiary education, particularly in the last decade (Chapple et al., 1997; see also below), 60 per cent of Māori aged more than 15 years still held no formal educational qualifications in 1991. This compared with 40 per cent for non-Māori. At the same, Māori were nearly half as likely as the total population to hold a tertiary qualification. This low level of educational attainment is also a central explanatory variable for the current poor position of Māori in the labour market (Davies and Nicholl, 1993).

In light of these clearly unfavourable social and economic indicators, Māori activists have increasingly rejected the liberal individualist tenets of assimilation upon which colonisation, and much public policy towards Māori, had historically been based (cf. Chapter 3). Drawing initially on contemporary notions of ethnic nationalism (Mulgan, 1989) and subsequently on the right as indigenous peoples to self-determination (Wilson and Yeatman, 1995; M. Durie, 1998; Fleras and Spoonley, 1999), they have argued, instead, for the separate recognition by the state of Māori political culture and social organisation, and for the recognition of the cultural and linguistic *distinctiveness* of Māori.

As one might expect, these claims have not gone uncontested by the Pākehā majority, with the usual proclamations of 'reverse apartheid' that accompany oppositional majoritarian discourses towards the recognition of group-differentiated rights. But such was their momentum that by the early 1980s they had set the platform for a significant realignment of Māori–Pākehā relations. This realignment took the form of a constitutional revolution that saw the Treaty of Waitangi returned to centre stage in Aotearoa / New Zealand public life after more than a century of neglect. As a result of increasing Māori advocacy and political protest, greater emphasis was placed on pursuing legal and constitutional redress for Māori iwi in relation to the Treaty. In this regard, the principal constitutional vehicle for arbitrating Māori claims has been the quasi-legal body, the Waitangi Tribunal. Originally set up in 1975, with limited powers to hear Māori grievances, it was invested in 1984 with the retrospective power to settle Māori claims against the Crown, dating back to 1840. While land issues have been the principal focus of the Tribunal's subsequent deliberations, the Tribunal has also ruled on the status of the Māori language (see below). The Waitangi Tribunal has thus been central to reinvesting moral and legal authority in the Treaty of Waitangi. The Tribunal has defined the Treaty, through its deliberations, as 'the foundation of a developing social contract, not merely a historical document' (Sorrenson, 1989: 162). More tangibly, it has led, both directly and indirectly in recent years, to considerable restitution by the Crown to iwi claimants.

As a result of the Treaty's return to prominence, the concept of biculturalism has come increasingly to the fore in Aotearoa / New Zealand (Wilson and Yeatman, 1995; M. Durie, 1998; Bishop and Glynn, 1999; Fleras and Spoonley, 1999). While retaining an emphasis on some degree of separate development and/or autonomy for Māori, the concept has been employed increasingly to describe a *partnership* between Māori and Pākehā, under the Treaty's auspices, rather than separation of one group from the other (see, for example, New Zealand Ministerial Advisory Committee, 1986). This clearly accords with Iris Young's emphasis on the relational nature of group-differentiated rights, discussed in Chapter 3, as well as reflecting accurately the close and symbiotic relationship between Māori and Pākehā since the time of colonisation. The partnership model also emphasises the Crown's *active* commitment to redressing past injustices towards Māori, and its commitment to the inclusion of Treaty 'principles' within the constitutional and administrative framework of the nation-state. Where the government has balked at its own rhetoric, it has been kept to its task by the judiciary. In June 1987, for example, the New Zealand Court of Appeal, in a landmark judgement, ruled against a key piece of government legislation – the State Owned Enterprises Act – which would have seen the transfer of Crown land to semi-privatised 'state owned enterprises' (SOEs). The central legal point of the case concerned the Treaty. Section 9 of the SOE Act stated that nothing in the Act shall permit the Crown to act in a manner inconsistent with the principles of the Treaty. Accordingly, the five appeal judges were unanimous that the Treaty of Waitangi prevented the Crown from transferring land without entering into proper arrangements to protect Māori rights. It was a historic judgement. As Ranginui Walker observes, in the space of just a few years, the Treaty had been transformed 'from "a simple nullity" to the level of a constitutional instrument in the renegotiation of the relationship between Māori and Pākehā in modern times' (1990: 266). In short, the doctrine of biculturalism had become established in political and public discourse by the late 1980s, and institutionalised to some considerable extent in law.

These developments notwithstanding, there remain a number of attendant difficulties with the debates surrounding biculturalism. First, the politics of biculturalism has clear implications for other ethnic-minority groups within Aotearoa / New Zealand, who tend inevitably to be overlooked in such a bifurcated construction (see also below). Indeed, with its recognition of the central place of indigenous Māori language and culture, biculturalism is seen by many opponents to overlook the interests of other minority ethnic groups. Instead, multiculturalism, where Māori would be seen merely as one claimant among many, has at times been advocated as a 'fairer' and more inclusive policy. While the view that all minority cultures should be recognised equally within Aotearoa / New Zealand might appear attractive, proponents of biculturalism reject this position. In their view, multiculturalism, in practice, would simply work in favour of the numerically dominant Pākehā group. Minority groups would be encouraged to fragment and to compete with one another for limited resources, thus maintaining current Pākehā dominance (Spoonley, 1993; cf. Chapter 5). Specifically, relegating Māori to the status of a single group among many (albeit a large and influential one) disadvantages Māori in two ways:

> it denies Māori people their equality as members of one among two (sets of) peoples, and it also tends to deny the divisions of Maoridom their separate status while exaggerating the status of other immigrant groups. In the end, Māori interests become peripheral, combined with other special problem areas.
>
> (R. Benton, 1988: 77)

The Waitangi Tribunal is equally clear on this point:

We do not accept that the Māori is just another one of a number of ethnic groups in our community. It must be remembered that of all minority groups the Māori alone is party to a solemn treaty made with the Crown. None of the other migrant groups who have come to live in this country in recent years can claim the rights that were given to the Māori people by the Treaty of Waitangi. Because of the Treaty Māori New Zealanders stand on a special footing reinforcing, if reinforcement be needed, their historical position as the original inhabitants, the tangata whenua [people of the land] of New Zealand . . .

(1986: 37)

Here again, biculturalism emphasises the right of Māori to exist and persist as a distinct and unique people – an ethnie (cf. Chapter 1) – on equal terms with Pākehā (Sharp, 1990). This position is reinforced by an awareness that support for multiculturalism amongst some Pākehā arises less out of a valuing of diversity, and/or a concern for the interests of minority groups, than from a fear of the possible fulfilment of Māori bicultural aspirations (Simon, 1989). However, as these definitional disputes between biculturalism and multiculturalism already suggest, another difficulty with the concept of biculturalism is its potential for reifying culture. Class and gender divisions in Aotearoa / New Zealand, and their complex interrelation with ethnicity (at both intra- and intergroup levels), are consequently consistently understated (Larner, 1996; Maxwell, 1998). And yet, notwithstanding these reservations, there is a very real sense in which Māori ethnicity and culture *can* be regarded as distinct from Pākehā. For example, in the *April Report* of the Royal Commission on Social Policy (Royal Commission on Social Policy, 1988), the following values were held to be representative of Māori culture: Te Ao Tūroa (guardianship of the natural environment), Whanaungatanga (the bonds of kinship), Manaakitanga (caring and sharing), Mana (authority and control among themselves), Kotahitanga (an emphasis on group commitment rather than individualism), Taonga-tuku-iho (cultural heritage) and Tūrangawaewae (a place to stand; a piece of land inalienably one's own). Even sceptics and critics broadly accept this description. As Andrew Sharp argues, in relation to the Commission's summary, 'irritating, unsubtle, simplifying, romantic, and naive as such a summary gloss of any culture must be . . . [this] nevertheless does capture much of the way things were' (1990: 53).

Current Māori identity has inevitably been constructed out of colonialism and a symbiotic interaction with Pākehā. Following Anthony Smith's formulation of an ethnie (see Chapter 1), Māori may be said to have drawn on shared historical memories, myths of common ancestry, and a growing sense of solidarity, in order to develop a common ethnic and cultural parlance in the face of a colonising power. Indeed, the construction of a pan-Māori identity (where previously none had existed) was the principal means by which Māori came to distinguish themselves from Pākehā. A pan-Māori ethnic identity has not, however, replaced previous forms of identity formation among Māori, notably whānau (family), hapū (subtribe) and iwi (tribal) affiliations. Rather, it has emerged as an additional form of identity that both accommodates and is in tension with more particularistic and traditional affiliations (Pearson, 1990). The continued interaction – and, at times, discontinuities – between these different levels of identity for Māori highlight the multifaceted nature of identity formation, as discussed in Chapter 1.

Despite these various tensions, Māori also clearly have a sufficient basis and claim to be recognised as a separate ethnie within Aotearoa / New Zealand. Their political assertiveness is based on some form of unity, implied or actual, and the claims to resources and rights have been made on the basis of their rights as indigenous peoples. The politicisation of Māori ethnicity then can perhaps be best described by the aphorism 'old symbols, new meanings' – the phenomenon of going into the future by way of reclaiming the past (Greenland, 1991). One clear example of this process of cultural reclamation *and* adaptation – of cultural nationalism, in effect – can be seen in the development of Māori-language education.

Language, culture and education in Aotearoa / New Zealand

While many of the claims before the Waitangi Tribunal have had to do with expropriation of land under colonial rule, they have also, crucially, encompassed other 'non-material' possessions such as the Māori language. In the Māori-language case of 1985/86, for example, the Waitangi Tribunal ruled that the Māori language could be regarded as a taonga (treasured possession) and therefore had a *guaranteed* right to protection under the terms of the Treaty (Waitangi Tribunal, 1986). In its ruling, the tribunal defined the term 'guarantee' as 'more than merely leaving Māori people unhindered in their enjoyment of the language and culture'; it also required 'active steps' to be taken by the guarantor to ensure that Māori have and retain 'the full exclusive and undisturbed possession of their language and culture' (Waitangi Tribunal, 1986: 29). This is consistent with interpretations in international law, as discussed in both this chapter and Chapter 5, on the *active* right to minority-language protection. However, the Tribunal also found with respect to Māori-language education, an equality right in the Treaty independent of minority-language rights (Hastings, 1988):

> the education system in New Zealand is operating unsuccessfully because too many Māori children are not reaching an acceptable level of education . . . Their language is not protected and their scholastic achievements fall

short of what they should be. The promises in the Treaty of Waitangi of equality of education as in all other human rights are undeniable. Judged by the system's own standards Māori children are not being successfully taught, and for this reason alone, quite apart from the duty to protect the Māori language, the education system is being operated in breach of the Treaty.

(Waitangi Tribunal, 1986: 51)

The Tribunal's conclusions, allied with the wider political climate in Aotearoa / New Zealand of which it forms a part, has led to significant changes in the areas of language and education. In 1987, the Māori Language Act was passed – recognising, for the first time, Māori as an official language of Aotearoa / New Zealand. This legal recognition of the language is still somewhat limited. In particular, the right to use or to demand the use of Māori in the public domain does not extend beyond the oral use of the language in courts of law and some quasi-legal tribunals (R. Benton, 1988). Nonetheless, it still stands as the *only* example where the first language of an indigenous people has been made an official state language (Sámi still only has regional official status; see my earlier discussion). The Act also provided for the establishment of a Maori Language Commission, Te Taura Whiri i te Reo Māori. Closely modelled on the Irish Bord na Gaeilge (see Chapter 4), the Commission's role is to monitor and promote the use of the language, although its staff and resources are limited. A recent Draft National Languages Policy has continued these positive developments by highlighting, as its top priority, the reversal of the decline in the Māori language (Waite, 1992), although as yet further action in implementing the Draft Report has not been forthcoming (R. Benton, 1996).

More significantly still, the 1980s saw the rapid (and highly successful) emergence of Māori-medium language education. After well over a century of prejudice and proscription from Pākehā administrators (see below), Māori language and culture are now being reasserted visibly within education. Moreover, this reassertion has come from Māori initially prepared to work outside the state education system until their language and educational needs, and *rights*, were recognised and acted upon.

The educational assimilation of Māori

From the beginnings of the state education system in Aotearoa / New Zealand in the 1860s–1870s, an assimilationist agenda was adopted towards Māori. Accordingly, the teaching of English was considered to be a central task of the school, and te reo Māori (the Māori language) was often regarded as the prime obstacle to the progress of Māori children (R. Benton, 1981). The inevitable result was the marginalisation of Māori, and the Māori language, within the educational process. In particular, Māori have historically had very little meaningful influence in educational policy decision-making

(G. Smith, 1990a). As Linda Tuhiwai Smith observes, schooling came to be seen as 'a primary instrument for taming and civilising the natives and forging a nation which was connected at a concrete level with the historical and moral processes of Britain' (L. Smith, 1992a: 6). Ironically, in this process, Pākehā were not only to repudiate and replace Māori language and knowledge structures within education but were also to deny Māori full access to European knowledge and learning.

This was not always so. Prior to the arrival of Pākehā, Māori had practised a sophisticated and functional system of education based on an extensive network of oral tradition, and with its own rational and complex knowledge structure (G. Smith, 1989; Nepe, 1991). Moreover, upon European colonisation, Māori actively sought to complement their own educational knowledge, and their long-established oral tradition, with 'Pākehā wisdom'. Largely for these reasons they turned to the early mission schools, which, while they taught only the standard subjects of the English school curriculum, did so through the medium of Māori. As a result, the period in which these schools were most influential – 1816 to the mid 1840s – saw a rapid spread of literacy among Māori *in both Māori and English*. The initial aim for Māori in incorporating Pākehā learning was one of enhancing their traditional way of life. However, from the 1840s this outlook was increasingly modified as Māori came to perceive European knowledge as a necessary defence against the increasing encroachment of Pākehā society upon Māori sovereignty and resources (J. Williams, 1969; Simon, 1992). As Ward observes,

> the Maori response to Western contact was highly intellectual, flexible and progressive, and also highly selective, aiming largely to draw upon the strengths of the West to preserve the Maori people and their resources from the threat of the West itself, and to enjoy its material and cultural riches co-equally with the Westerners.
>
> (1974: viii)

The growing fear among Māori of Pākehā encroachment was, as we have already seen, well founded. It was also to coincide in the 1840s with a change to a much more overtly assimilationist policy towards Māori in education. As Barrington and Beaglehole argue:

> Education was to be deliberately out of touch with the Maori environment in the belief that formal schooling could transform the Maori and fit him for a different environment. The Maori was to be lifted from one society to another.
>
> (1974: 4)

The (1844) Native Trust Ordinance stated, for example, that the 'great disasters [that] have fallen on other uncivilised nations on being brought into contact with Colonists from the nations of Europe' would only be avoided by 'assimilating as speedily as possible the habits and usages of the Native to those of the European population'. The (1847) Education Ordinance Act reinforced this sentiment by making state funding of mission schools dependent on English being the medium of instruction, effectively ending Māori-medium teaching. As the Auckland Inspector of Native Schools, Henry Taylor was to argue in 1862:

> The Native language itself is also another obstacle in the way of civilisation, so long as it exists there is a barrier to the free and unrestrained intercourse which ought to exist between the two races [sic], it shuts out the less civilised portion of the population from the benefits which intercourse with the more enlightened would confer. The school-room alone has power to break down this wall of partition . . .
>
> (*AJHR*, E-4, 1862, 35–38)

This position was further formalised in 1867 when the state established a system of village day schools in Māori rural communities, ten years prior to the establishment of a parallel public system. While some privately funded Māori schools remained independent, Māori schooling was now effectively controlled by the state. The Native School system, as it came to be known, operated a modified public-school curriculum, with a particular emphasis on health and hygiene. Initially, teachers were expected to have some knowledge of the Māori language, which was to be used as an aid in teaching English. However, by the turn of the twentieth century, the Māori language had all but been banned from the precincts of the schools; a prohibition, often enforced by corporal punishment, that was to continue until the 1950s.

But this was not all. Another theme which came to dominate state educational policy for Māori over this time was their unsuitability for 'mental labour'. The aim of assimilation was ostensibly 'to lift Māori from one society to another', but only as long as they were not lifted *too* high. A key objective of native schooling thus came to be the preparation of Māori for labouring-class status; an objective which was rationalised largely through racial ideologies (Simon, 1992). As the Director of Education, T.B. Strong, observed in 1929, Māori education should 'lead the Maori to be a good farmer and the Maori girl to be a good farmer's wife'. Barrington has argued that such views 'included the assumption that Maori rural communities should be preserved and that Maori should stay within them, a biological and racist assumption that the "natural genius" of Maori lay in manual labour, and a strategy to reduce competition for expanding bureaucratic, commercial and professional positions in urban areas by putting impediments in the way of Maori students' (1992: 68–69). That Māori were to become largely proletarianised after the Second World War, as the needs of industry drew them to the urban areas in rapidly increasing numbers, must be seen as the logical outcome of these education policies, along with those directed at land alienation (Simon, 1989, 1992). It certainly goes some considerable way to explaining the current unfavourable socioeconomic and educational indices of Māori.

Education and language loss

Assimilationist policies in education also contributed significantly to the rapid decline of the Māori language over the course of the twentieth century. This, despite the fact that the English-only policy of Native schools was not initially seen as in any way threatening the Māori language and culture, and was strongly supported by some Māori (A. Durie, 1999). Since the 1940s, however, there has been a growing concern among Māori about the state and status of the Māori language. In 1930, for example, a survey of children attending Native schools estimated that 96.6 per cent spoke only Māori at home. By 1960, only 26 per cent spoke Māori. The rapid urbanisation of Māori since the Second World War has been a key factor in this language decline. While the Māori language had been excluded from the realms of the school for over a century, it had still been nurtured in the largely rural Māori communities. The effects of urbanisation were to undermine both these communities and the language they spoke. By 1979 the Māori language had retreated to the point where language death was predicted (R. Benton, 1979, 1983; see also N. Benton, 1989).

With this growing realisation came an increased advocacy of the need for change in educational policy towards Māori. New approaches to language and education were sought. Assimilation was replaced in the 1960s by a brief period of 'integration'. Heralded by the 1961 Hunn Report, integration aimed 'to combine (not fuse) the Maori and Pakeha elements to form one nation wherein Maori culture remains distinct' (see Hunn, 1961: 14–16). While an apparently laudable aim, integration proved little different in either theory or practice from its predecessor. It was less crude than assimilation in its conceptions of culture but a clear cultural hierarchy continued to underpin the model. Hunn, for example, clearly regarded those aspects of the Māori culture that were to 'remain distinct' as 'relics' of a tribal culture of which 'only the fittest elements (worthiest of preservation) have survived the onset of civilisation'. Compared with this 'backward life in primitive conditions', he argued that 'pressure [should] be brought to bear on [Māori] to conform to . . . the pakeha mode of life', which he equated with modernity and progress. This 'deficit' view simply reinforced the previous assimilationist agenda and resulted in the continued perception of Māori as an educational 'problem' (cf. Stages 1 and 2 of Churchill's typology, discussed in Chapter 5).

In the face of mounting criticism from Māori, integration was replaced in the 1970s and 1980s by multicultural education. This latter approach

– representing Stage 3 of Churchill's typology – came to be known as taha Māori (literally, the Māori side). In what was, by now, an integrated state education system, it attempted to incorporate a specifically Māori dimension into the curriculum that was available to *all* pupils, Māori and non-Māori alike. As its official definition outlines: 'Taha Māori is the inclusion of *aspects of* Māori language and culture in the philosophy, organisation and the content of the school . . . It should be a normal part of the school climate with which all pupils should feel comfortable and at ease' (New Zealand Department of Education, 1984a; my emphasis). While the emphasis here was clearly on biculturalism, this was also seen as a first step to the incorporation of other cultures within the curriculum along similar lines. As a related publication states: 'an effective approach to multicultural education *is through* bicultural education' (New Zealand Department of Education, 1984b: 31; my emphasis). But for reasons already discussed, Māori remained sceptical of multiculturalism in the form of taha Māori. One key criticism here was that the process of limiting biculturalism to support for 'aspects of Māori language and culture' within schools fell far short of the biculturalism that many Māori seek; a biculturalism concerned primarily with institutional transformation and social change. In this sense, multiculturalism was also seen as a useful ideology for *containing* the conflicts of ethnic groups within existing social relations rather than as the basis for any real power-sharing between Māori and Pākehā and, from that basis, other ethnic groups. Second, the peripheral and selective treatment of Māori language and culture does little, if anything, to change the cultural transmission of the dominant group within schooling; a criticism that has been directed at multicultural education more widely (May, 1994a, 1999a; cf. Chapter 5). And third, the control of the policy, as with all previous educational approaches, remained firmly with Pākehā educationalists and administrators (Bishop and Glynn, 1999). The very process of cultural 'selection' highlights this lack of control for Māori in educational decision-making. However well intentioned, cultural 'selection' is a paternalistic exercise which must, inevitably, reflect more the interests and concerns of Pākehā than those of Māori. This irony is illustrated by the conclusion of many Māori educationalists that the main beneficiaries of taha Māori have actually been Pākehā children (Irwin, 1989; G. Smith, 1990b).

Education and language reversal

The result of these educational policies with respect to language loss for Māori is self-evident. Currently more than nine out of ten of Aotearoa / New Zealand's 3.5 million inhabitants are first-language speakers of English – a figure that makes it one of the most linguistically homogeneous in the world today. Even among those of Māori ancestry, only one in ten, 50,000 people in all, are now adult native speakers of Māori, and the majority of these are middle-aged or older (Te Taura Whiri i te Reo Māori, 1995).

However, two recent educational developments have begun to halt the process of language loss for Māori. First, the establishment of bilingual schools in the late 1970s saw the beginnings of a more positive approach to the Māori language within education, after a century of neglect and proscription. Secondly, and more significantly, the emergence of alternative Māori-medium (immersion) schools – initiated and administered by Māori – during the course of the 1980s has led to the rapid reemergence of Māori as a medium of instruction in Aotearoa / New Zealand schools. The latter movement, in particular, has combined with the wider political developments discussed earlier to spearhead the beginnings of what Christina Paulston has described as 'language reversal'; a process by which 'one of the languages of a state begins to move back into more prominent use' (1993: 281).

The beginnings of this language reversal within education can be found in the early 1960s, when a formal review of the education system, the Currie Commission, included in its recommendations the teaching of Māori as an optional subject at secondary-school level. This first tentative step to reintroduce te reo Māori into the school curriculum initiated a period of renewed debate on the merits of bilingual schooling in Aotearoa / New Zealand. It was to culminate, in 1977, with the first officially sanctioned English/Māori bilingual primary school at Ruatoki – one of the last predominantly Māori-speaking communities in the country. Other schools were to follow – providing, primarily, a 'transition' approach to bilingualism (Stage 4 in Churchill's typology; see Chapter 5). By 1988, 20 such bilingual schools had been established, predominantly in Māori rural communities. In addition, 67 primary schools and 18 secondary schools by this time operated with at least some bilingual classes, catering for approximately 3000 students (R. Benton, 1988; Hirsh, 1990). By 1991, this had risen rapidly to 251 primary schools and 54 secondary schools offering some form of bilingual education to 13,000 primary students and 2500 secondary students respectively (Davies and Nicholl, 1993). By 1996, the overall number of students in bilingual programmes had more than doubled to 33,438, the vast majority of whom were Māori (New Zealand Ministry of Education, 1998). While these developments have been very encouraging, the rationales for bilingual programmes, and the degree to which they incorporate Māori as a medium of instruction, continue to vary widely (Ohia, 1990; Jacques, 1991; New Zealand Ministry of Education, 1998). This degree of variability, and a continuing lack of both teaching and material resources for bilingual education, remain a cause for concern (Spolsky, 1987; New Zealand Ministry of Education, 1998).

Given the developments in bilingual education that the Currie Commission precipitated, it is no doubt ironic that the Commission itself remained deeply ambivalent about any greater role for the Māori language in the educational process (R. Benton, 1981). It certainly did not envisage the development of Māori/English bilingualism in schools in the ways just described (Hirsh, 1990). In a close echo of the Swann Report, in fact, the

Commission states that the school 'is not, nor can it ever be, the prime agency in conserving the Māori cultural heritage'. This is, of course, true to a point. However, it begs a question – if the school clearly performs this function, at least to some degree, for Pākehā children, why can it not do so also for Māori (Harker, 1980; R. Benton, 1987)?

If the Currie Commission was surprised by the subsequent development of these bilingual schools and bilingual programmes in light of its own, far more tentative, recommendations, it would surely have been agog at concurrent developments, initially outside the state education system, which have since come to overshadow them significantly. Indeed, much of the growing enthusiasm for bilingual education within state schooling can be attributed to an independent movement for the establishment of Māori-medium preschools – Te Kōhanga Reo – instigated in 1982 by a small group of Māori parents. So successful has this movement been, in fact, that in the space of just twenty years it has changed the face of education in Aotearoa / New Zealand – affecting, in the process, all other levels of schooling.

Relative autonomy and community control: Te Kōhanga Reo and Kura Kaupapa Māori

Te Kōhanga Reo

Te Kōhanga Reo – meaning literally 'language nest' – was launched as a movement with the opening of its first centre in April 1982. At the time of its inception, the continued survival of Māori language and culture was looking bleak. As Irwin states:

> The proposed Te Kōhanga Reo movement, an initiative aimed at reviving traditional Māori knowledge and cultural practices, seemed like an impossible dream to some. Crucial elements which contributed to this doubt were a cultural base which was said to be too fragmented to support such an initiative, and a people whose alienation from this traditional base was considered to be such that they could no longer, nor would they wish to, take part in its reaffirmation.
>
> (1990: 115–116)

And yet, Te Kōhanga Reo has proved to be, by any comparative measure, a phenomenal success. In 1982, less than 30 per cent of Māori children aged 2–4 years participated in early childhood (preschool) education, compared with 41 per cent for non-Māori. By 1991, the Māori participation rate had risen to 53 per cent, largely as a result of Te Kōhanga Reo (Davies and Nicholl, 1993). Indeed, between 1983 and 1993 there was a demonstrated growth rate in kōhanga student numbers of 250 per cent (O'Rourke, 1994). This has been matched by the proliferation of kōhanga around the country so that by 1996 there were 767 kōhanga catering for over 14,000 Māori children (New Zealand Ministry of Education, 1998).

The kaupapa (philosophy; set of objectives) of Te Kōhanga Reo can be summarised as follows:

- total immersion in te reo Māori at the Kōhanga Reo
- the imparting of Māori cultural and spiritual values and concepts to the children
- the teaching and involvement of the children in Tikanga Māori (Māori customs)
- the complete administration of each centre by the whānau (extended family; see below)
- the utilisation of many traditional techniques of child care and knowledge acquisition (Sharples, 1988)

From this, three aspects can be highlighted as key organising principles (see Kā'ai, 1990).

1 Te Reo
   'He kōrero Māori' (speaking in Māori) is a central organising principle of Te Kōhanga Reo. An environment where only Māori is spoken is seen as the best means by which 'language reversal' can be achieved. Only by this can the current dominance of English in almost every other domain in Aotearoa / New Zealand life be effectively contested. This accords with a 'maintenance' view of bilingualism (cf. Baker, 1996; Cummins, 1996), or Stage 5 of Churchill's language-policy typology, discussed in Chapter 5. Culturally preferred styles of pedagogy – such as teina/tuakana roles (peer tutoring) and collaborative teaching and learning – also feature prominently in the ethos and practice of Kōhanga (see Metge, 1990, and May, 1994a, for a fuller discussion here).

2 Whānau
   Te Kōhanga Reo has been, from its inception, a parent-driven and resourced initiative based on whānau (extended-family) principles. Kōhanga are staffed by fluent Māori-speaking parents, grandparents and caregivers, often working in a voluntary capacity, and are supported by the wider whānau associated with the preschool. Whānau are usually constituted on traditional kinship grounds but have also come to include, in urban centres, a more generic concept in which criteria for affiliation have moved from kinship ties to that of commonality of interests and/or residence (Nepe, 1991). The latter amounts to a contemporary form of cultural adaptation. The significance of kaumātua (elders) is also highlighted in the whānau structure. Kaumātua are regarded as active participants in

the educational process. They are used not just as repositories of knowledge but also as teachers who can model the language, and other forms of cultural practice and behaviour, to Kōhanga children (L. Smith, 1989).

3   Mana motuhake (self-determination)
The central involvement of whānau in Te Kōhanga Reo has meant that Māori parents have been able to exert a significant degree of *local* control over the education of their children. The whānau approach is characterised by collective decision-making and each whānau has autonomy within the kaupapa (philosophy) of the movement (Irwin, 1990). Meaningful choices can thus be made over what children should learn, how they should learn, and who should be involved in the learning (L. Smith, 1989). Individual whānau are also supported at a national level by the Kōhanga Reo Trust, which was established in the early 1980s to develop a nationally recognised syllabus for the purposes of gaining state funding. This latter objective was achieved in 1990. Prior to this, kōhanga had been almost entirely funded by whānau themselves. While state funding presents some contradictions here (see below), the principle of 'relative autonomy' (G. Smith, 1990a, b, 1992) remains a key feature of Te Kōhanga Reo.

Te Kōhanga Reo represents a major turning point for Māori perceptions and attitudes about language and education. Its success has also had a 'domino effect' on the provision of Māori-medium education at other levels of schooling as kōhanga graduates have worked their way through the school system over the course of the last 15 years. This is particularly evident at the primary (elementary) level with the development of bilingual schooling, already discussed, and the emergence of Kura Kaupapa Māori, which I will examine shortly. These developments are also now beginning to extend to higher educational levels with the establishment in 1993/94 of the first Wharekura (Māori-medium secondary schools) and Whare Wānanga (tertiary institutions) (O'Rourke, 1994). By 1997 there were four such Wharekura and three Wānanga (New Zealand Ministry of Education, 1998; A. Durie, 1999). However, the primary-level Kura Kaupapa Māori (literally, 'Māori philosophy schools') provides us with a representative example here of the ongoing gains being made by Māori-medium education.

Kura Kaupapa Māori

The first Kura Kaupapa Māori, entirely privately funded, opened in February 1985. Five years of political advocacy by Māori followed before a pilot scheme of six Kura Kaupapa Māori was approved for state funding in 1990. With the success of this scheme (see Reedy, 1992), rapid development has occurred. By 1999, 59 Kura Kaupapa Māori had been established, serving approximately 4000 students, with five new kura being approved each year (New Zealand Ministry of Education, 1998).

The development of Kura Kaupapa Māori is largely attributable to the success of Te Kōhanga Reo and the increasing demand that it created for Māori-medium education at the primary level. The inability of the state education system effectively to meet these demands, beyond the limited options provided in bilingual programmes (see above), had led by the mid 1980s to the advocacy of Kura Kaupapa Māori as an alternative schooling option. A principal concern of kōhanga parents was to maintain the language gains made by their children. Kura Kaupapa Māori, in adopting the same language and organisational principles as Te Kōhanga Reo, could continue to reinforce these language gains within a Māori cultural and language-medium environment. More broadly, the importance of 'relative autonomy' and 'community control' featured prominently in the advocacy of Kura Kaupapa Māori during the 1980s and 1990s (see G. Smith, 1992, 1997). Te Kōhanga Reo had served to politicise Māori parents with regard to the education of their children (L. Smith, 1989, 1992b; G. Smith, 1990b) and the advocacy of Kura Kaupapa was the natural extension of this. In 1984, for example, the Māori Education Conference brought together Māori teachers, community leaders and educationalists from across the political spectrum to discuss Māori educational concerns. The consensus from the conference was that only significant structural reform of the state education system could change the educational circumstances of Māori children. If this did not occur, the Conference urged 'Māori withdrawal and the establishment of alternative schooling modelled on the principle of Kōhanga Reo'. In 1988, another hui (conference) produced the Mātawaia Declaration, which states:

> our children's needs cannot be met through a continuation of the present system of Pākehā control and veto of Māori aspirations for our children. It is time to change. Time for us to take control of our own destinies. We believe this development is both necessary and timely.

These calls from Māori for greater autonomy, and structural change, within education were to coincide with the reorganisation of the state education system in 1988/89. The reforms emphasised parental choice, devolution and local school management. While many of the changes which have resulted can be seen as problematic (see Dale and Ozga, 1993), the reforms did provide Māori with a platform to argue for separate recognition of Kura Kaupapa Māori. Initially, the government responsible for the reforms was reticent to apply its own rhetoric of local control to the Kura Kaupapa Māori case. However, after a considerable degree of prevarication, and as a result of consistent and effective lobbying by Māori, Kura Kaupapa Māori was eventually incorporated into the (1990) Education Amendment Act as a recognised (and state-funded) schooling alternative within the Aotearoa / New Zealand state education system. The principles which have since come to characterise it can be summarised as follows (see G. Smith, 1992: 20–23; see also Bishop and Glynn, 1999).

1   Rangatiratanga (relative-autonomy principle)
    A greater autonomy over key decision-making in schooling has been
    attained in areas such as administration, curriculum, pedagogy and Māori
    aspirations.
2   Taonga Tuku Iho (cultural-aspiration principle)
    In Kura Kaupapa Māori to be Māori is taken for granted. The legitimacy
    of Māori language, culture and values is normalised.
3   Ako Māori (culturally preferred pedagogy)
    Culturally preferred forms of pedagogy such as peer tutoring and
    collaborative teaching and learning are employed. These are used in
    conjunction with general schooling methods where appropriate.
4   Kia piki ake i ngā Raruraru o te Kainga (mediation of socioeconomic
    difficulties)
    While Kura Kaupapa Māori (or education more generally) cannot, on
    its own, redress the socioeconomic circumstances facing Māori, the col-
    lective support and involvement provided by the whānau structure can
    mitigate some of its most debilitating effects.
5   Whānau (extended-family principle)
    The whānau structure provides a support network for individual mem-
    bers and requires a reciprocal obligation on these individuals to support
    and contribute to the collective aspirations of the group. It has been
    most successful in involving Māori parents in the administration of their
    children's schooling.
6   Kaupapa (philosophy principle)
    Kura Kaupapa Māori 'is concerned to teach a modern, up to date,
    relevant curriculum (within the national guidelines set by the state)'
    (G. Smith, 1990b: 194). The aim is not the forced choice of one culture
    and/or language over another but the provision of a distinctively Māori
    educational environment that is able to promote effectively bilingualism
    and biculturalism.

Some caveats

A number of caveats need to be outlined briefly in conclusion. First, it needs
to be reiterated that education cannot compensate for society (cf. Chapter
4); a reality also recognised by those directly involved in Māori-medium
education. The developments in Māori-medium education must thus be
situated clearly within the much wider social, economic and political framework of change that has occurred in Aotearoa / New Zealand over the last
20 years. This has had, at its heart, the restoration of the Treaty of Waitangi
to its central role in mediating Māori–Pākehā relations.
    Second, it is important also to reiterate that these educational developments
are neither separatist nor a simple retrenchment in the past. Nothing in the
assertion of indigenous rights – or, as I have argued throughout this book,

minority rights more generally – precludes the possibilities of cultural change and adaptation. The specific aim of Māori-medium education is, in fact, to accomplish this very process, *but on its own terms*. The crucial question then becomes one of control rather than retrenchment or rejection. Te Kōhanga Reo and Kura Kaupapa Māori provide the opportunity for Māori parents, working within national curriculum guidelines, to 'change the rules' that have previously excluded Māori language and culture from recognition as cultural and linguistic capital in schools, and beyond (cf. Chapter 4). Māori knowledge and language competencies thus come to frame, but do not exclude, those of the dominant Pākehā group, and they are themselves the subject of negotiation and change. The stated outcomes of Kura Kaupapa Māori clearly highlight this process of mutual accommodation with their emphasis on bilingualism and biculturalism. As Graham Hingangaroa Smith argues, 'Kura Kaupapa Māori parents . . . want for their children the ability to access the full range of societal opportunities' (1990b: 194). Moreover, Kura Kaupapa Māori remains only one option among many and, at this stage at least, still very much a minority one. In 1996, for example, only 2.3 per cent of Māori school students were enrolled in a kura. Proponents of Kura Kaupapa argue that the crucial point is that Māori-medium education *is made available* as a legitimate schooling choice, not that it is the answer to everything.

Third, the incorporation of Te Kōhanga Reo and Kura Kaupapa Māori into the state system does present some contradictions, particularly with regard to the notion of relative autonomy. While state funding has underwritten these initiatives and, crucially, facilitated their expansion, there is an increasing possibility of state encroachment and appropriation on what were originally local whānau-based initiatives. However, it would seem that the benefits of state involvement outweigh their disadvantages. In particular, the state education system is now beginning to address the critical shortage of material and teaching resources for Māori-medium schools, and for bilingual initiatives more broadly. This has already led to the rapid expansion of Māori/English bilingual training programmes within teacher education and a slow but growing expansion of Māori-language teaching material, both of which augur well for the long-term future of Māori-medium education. Incorporation within the national curriculum and assessment framework has also lent legitimacy to Māori-medium initiatives. This legitimacy has been reinforced by initial assessments which suggest that the academic progress of children in Kura Kaupapa is comparable with their mainstream peers, while providing the added advantage of bilingualism (Reedy, 1992; Hollings et al., 1992; Keegan, 1996).

Fourth, there remains the ongoing issue of the institutional/educational support (or, rather, relative lack thereof) of the languages and cultures of other ethnic-minority groups within Aotearoa / New Zealand. These groups comprise small, albeit long-standing, Asian (e.g., Chinese, Indian) and European language communities (e.g., Dutch, German, Greek, Polish). Pacific

Islanders (e.g., Samoan, Tongan, Cook Islands Māori) have also increasingly migrated to Aotearoa / New Zealand since the 1960s. South East Asian refugees (particularly from Cambodia and Vietnam) came in the 1970s, while more recent Asian migration – reaching its height in the mid 1990s – has come from the likes of Japan, Singapore, Hong Kong, Korea, Malaysia and Taiwan. At present, the language and education provision for such groups remains very limited, the result largely of the predominance of English in Aotearoa / New Zealand and, the reemergence of Māori aside, the ongoing valorisation of English as both the preeminent national and international language. Consequently, an assimilationist imperative and a subtractive view of bilingualism are clearly apparent in the majority of language policies, and language education policies, aimed at ethnic-minority groups (New Zealand Ministry of Education, 1994; R. Benton, 1996).

That said, a more accommodative viewpoint has been advanced in recent years recognising a responsibility (and need) for more active state support of the first languages of other ethnic-minority groups, particularly within education. Thus, the New Zealand Ministry of Education recently made the following assurance: 'students whose mother tongue is a Pacific Islands language or a community language will have the opportunity to develop and use their own language as an integral part of their schooling' (1996: 10). In this respect, Māori-medium education appears to have provided a template that other minority groups are moving increasingly to adopt (see Bishop and Glynn, 1999: 86–96). These developments are reflected in the nascent emergence of comparable Pacific Islands preschool language nests (modelled on Te Kōhanga Reo). In 1993, 177 such language nests, catering for 3877 children, were receiving government funding (R. Benton, 1996). At the very least, such developments indicate that the promotion of Māori-medium education need not be at the expense of other ethnic-minority groups in Aotearoa / New Zealand and, indeed, may well be instrumental in facilitating the latter's expansion along comparable lines.

To conclude, there is still much to be accomplished in the arenas of language and education in Aotearoa / New Zealand – of that there is no doubt – while the wider political struggle for group-differentiated rights for Māori continues. However, in the areas of language and education, Te Kōhanga Reo and Kura Kaupapa Māori represent, for the first time since 1840, a genuine educational alternative that meets the terms outlined in the Treaty of Waitangi of 'guaranteed [and active] protection' of Māori language and culture. The aims of Kōhanga Reo and Kura Kaupapa are also consistent with developments in international law and other national arenas, discussed in this chapter, concerning the language and education rights of indigenous peoples. Moreover, they are contributing to Aotearoa / New Zealand's slow move towards a genuinely bilingual and bicultural society – Stage 6 of Churchill's typology, as discussed in Chapter 5. As Graham Hingangaroa Smith concludes of these developments:

The advent of Te Kōhanga Reo and its politicising effects on Māori parents has created a new interest and optimism in regard to Māori language
and culture revival and survival. Kura Kaupapa Māori is a manifestation of
[this] renewed Māori interest in schooling and education. The opportunity
to capitalise on the potential of Kura Kaupapa Māori should not be lost in
terms of . . . meeting Māori needs and aspirations related to language and
cultural survival, and in terms of building a fair and just New Zealand
society in the future.

(1990b: 195)

After two centuries of European colonisation, which has seen the attendant proscription, derogation and vitiation of Māori language and culture, a
whākatauki (Māori proverb) sums up this nascent sense of renewed optimism:

'Tera te haeata e takiri ana mai i runga o Mata-te-ra'
The rays of the morning sun strike a new dawn on the mountain

Notes

1   For discussion of a comparable example in the USA, see McCarty and
    Watahomigie (1999).
2   Pastoral leases were first granted to European farmers in 1848, allowing
    them access to Aboriginal lands for the purposes of (limited) grazing and
    cultivation. While they were not intended to deprive Aboriginal peoples of
    their rights to roam and hunt on the land, this is what happened very
    quickly. Many farmers began to treat the land as private property and began
    commandeering Aboriginal peoples as free labour. The ongoing genocide of
    Aboriginal peoples, apparent throughout the nineteenth century and well
    into the twentieth century, was also 'vindicated' on the basis of the 'protec-
    tion' of these pastoral leases (see Perera and Pugliese, 1998: 68).
3   'Pākehā' is the Māori term for New Zealanders of European origin. Its
    literal meaning is 'stranger', although it holds no pejorative connotation in
    modern usage.
4   Prior to the Second World War, less than 10 per cent of Māori had lived in
    cities or smaller urban centres. Currently, 82 per cent of Māori live in urban
    areas (Te Taura Whiri i te Reo Māori, 1995). Māori have thus undergone
    what is perhaps the most comprehensive and certainly the most rapid urban-
    isation process in modern times.
5   I am aware that any discussion of unfavourable social, economic and educa-
    tional indices can, by its very nature, lend itself to a pathological conception.
    This has certainly been the case in many past analyses of Māori, for ex-
    ample. However, it is not my intention here. Rather, I am simply wanting to
    demonstrate in what follows how Māori have come to be *unequally placed*
    within Aotearoa / New Zealand, and its key institutions, as the result of
    these historical processes.

9

Minority languages and the nation-state

It is clear that nation-states remain the bedrock of the international inter-state system and look likely, despite many predictions to the contrary, to be around still for some time to come. Like Mark Twain's famous retort to the premature media report of his death, the imminent demise of nation-states is obviously greatly exaggerated. But if this is the case, it certainly does not necessarily follow that the traditional organisation of nation-states should remain unchanged. Indeed, the forces of economic and political globalisation, and the associated rise of multinational companies and supranational organisations, have already had a considerable effect in renegotiating the parameters of the economic and political sovereignty of nation-states. This is all well and good. But my argument is that, if we accept this process of change for the nation-state from above so to speak, there is no reason why we should not accept pressure for change from below as well. In this latter respect, the principle of nation-state congruence, and the allied notion of cultural and linguistic homogeneity – both of which are the specific products of the political nationalism of the last three centuries – have been brought increasingly into question by national and ethnic minorities within nation-states. What such minorities are asking is simple and direct – why should the notion of a homogeneous national identity, represented by the language and culture of the dominant ethnie, invariably *replace* cultural and linguistic identities that differ from it? This 'intolerance of difference' (Billig, 1995: 130) embedded within the structural organisation of nation-states has resulted in the historical subjugation and, at times, evisceration of the traditional languages and cultures of minority groups. For centuries this process has been 'validated' on the basis that it is necessary for establishing social and political cohesion, or 'civism' (Bullivant, 1981) within the nation-state (see Chapter 3). But it is a cost that many minority groups are simply no longer prepared to pay.

When this is recognised, it becomes clearer why alternative ethnic, linguistic and/or national identities and affiliations – what Castells (1997) has called 'resistance identities' – continue to be a source of identity and mobilisation for many minority groups, confounding the 'liberal expectancy' (Fenton, 1999) that they would atrophy in the face of modernity. In this respect, my central contention throughout this book has been the reverse of much academic and popular commentary (cf. Chapter 1). It is not the cultural, linguistic and political expression or mobilisation of (minority) ethnicities and nationalisms which are the cause of so much contemporary mayhem in the modern world, but their *disavowal*. We ignore their ongoing influence and purchase at our peril.

Addressing constructivism

In adopting this position, I want to reiterate that we do not need to abandon the social constructionist consensus on ethnic and national identities. Clearly, all collective forms of identity (indeed, *all* forms of identity) are permeable, fluid and subject to change. They vary in salience depending on the individual, the immediate context, their complex articulation with other identities, and the wider vicissitudes of history. There is certainly nothing inherent about them – the constructivist case has clearly won the day here. But there are two important caveats to this position. The first is that while identities may well be constructed, they are no less meaningful for all that. Thus it is clear that particular ethnic and/or linguistic identities continue to exert considerable influence, both individually and corporately, in the world today. I have argued that this apparent conundrum can be explained by the fact that such identities, constructed though they may be, are also at the same time an embodied set of dispositions, or habitus (Bourdieu, 1990a). In this sense, they are not simply representations of some inner psychological state, nor even particular ideologies about the world (Billig, 1995). Rather, they are social, cultural and political forms of life – material ways of being in the modern world (see Chapter 1).

The second caveat is that if all identities are constructed, then this recognition applies as much to majoritarian forms of (national) identity as it does to minority identities. We cannot have one without the other. Thus, there is no reason why we cannot rethink nation-states, and the national identities therein, in more plural and inclusive ways (cf. Parekh, 2000). Indeed, doing so is congruent with the allied recognition that individuals have access to, and value, a wide range of different identities (cf. Chapter 1). Given this, advocacy of group-differentiated minority rights need not lead inevitably to cultural reification and essentialism, as its many critics suggest, but can actually lead to its opposite, the central recognition of the significance of plural or multiple identities. But advocates of minority rights are quick to point out that a recognition of multiple identities does not necessarily entail

the postmodernist view that such identities are equal and interchangeable –
one may still retain a primary or 'encompassing group' identity (see Chapter 3). They also make the important point that these identities need not
always be in conflict, although inevitably there will be times when they are.
Narrower identities do not necessarily need to be traded in for broader ones
since one can clearly remain, for example, Welsh-speaking and British,
Catalan-speaking and Spanish, or Spanish-speaking and American. Where
the holding of such multiple identities has been problematised or polarised,
it is invariably at the instigation of the nation-state, rather than minority
group members themselves.

Recognising and acknowledging the constructedness of all ethnic and
national identities is also important for a related reason. It requires us to
consider critically why it is that the constructedness and contingency of
majoritarian forms of ethnic and/or national identity (and the languages that
are associated with them) tend so often to escape such recognition. In this
sense, ethnicity and nationalism do not simply lurk *out there* – the sole
preserve of 'extremist' nationalists or malcontented national or ethnic minorities, although they are often painted as such. Rather, they inhabit the very
structures of the civic societies in which we live. In effect, both the political
and administrative structure of the state and its civil society are *ethnicised*.
This is achieved principally, as I have argued throughout this book, via
the artificial establishment of a 'common' civic language and culture. This
supposedly common language and culture in fact represents and is reflective
of the *particular* cultural and linguistic habitus of the dominant ethnie, or
Staatsvolk. It is a majoritarian particularism masquerading as universalism
(see Taylor, 1994; cf. Chapter 3).

This recognition leads in turn to another. We need to examine and critique the specific historical processes by which particular ethnic and/or
national identities, and their historically associated languages, have come to
be legitimated and normalised in this way while others specifically have
not. As I have argued, the rise of political nationalism, and the 'philosophical
matrix of the nation-state' which is its product, are the principal catalyst
and agent in this process of selective identity construction. Following
from this, the valorisation of national languages, and the stigmatisation of
minority languages, can be seen for what they are – a move in the wider
politics of nationalism and ethnicity (of which the politics of language forms
a part), nothing more. Consequently, the unfavourable juxtaposition of
majority national languages and minority languages is neither inevitable
nor inviolate.

And this brings us to one further key issue that we need to consider. We
must never lose sight of the central importance of (unequal) power relations,
and the means by which these have come to be articulated within modern
nation-states – particularly, for our purposes, with respect to language. A
critical perspective of power relations helps to explain why, for example,

in Bourdieu's terminology, the cultural and linguistic habitus of majority group members are accorded cultural and linguistic capital while other (minority) habitus specifically are not. It also helps to explain why the principal consequence for many minorities – at both the individual and collective levels – has been the enforced loss of their own ethnic, cultural and linguistic habitus as the necessary price of entry to the civic realm of the nation-state. As we saw Peter McLaren observe in Chapter 3, a prerequisite of 'joining the [national] club' is to become denuded, de-ethnicised (or, rather, *re*-ethnicised) and culturally stripped. There are numerous examples where this act of defenestration has been achieved by state coercion – Wales and Catalonia provide us with two clear historical examples here (see Chapter 7). But we also still see contemporary examples of these coercive processes, with the overt proscription of Albanian within Serbia, Tibetan in Chinese-controlled Tibet and Kurdish in Turkey being prominent examples. If the US English Only movement has its way, as discussed in Chapter 6, such will also be the case for Spanish-speaking Hispanic communities in the USA.

However, it is via civil society that the marginalisation and stigmatisation of minority languages have been most widely and effectively achieved (although, it must be said, often in conjunction with more coercive measures). Language and education play central roles here. Indeed, the construction of national languages, and their reinforcement via mass education, have become a sine qua non of modern nation-states. These linguistic and educational processes have also linked dominant language varieties inexorably to modernity and progress, while consigning their minority counterparts to the realms of primitivism and stasis. The cultural and linguistic capital ascribed to dominant language varieties also inevitably leads to the view that they are of more value and use in the modern world. Such associations operate on the international stage as well – with the dual status of lingua franca and world language currently ascribed to the English language being a reflection largely of the sociopolitical dominance of those western nation-states (notably the USA) with which it is most closely associated (see Chapter 6).

It is perhaps not surprising then that, in light of all of the above, many minority group members have come to accept and internalise the view that their own cultural and linguistic habitus have little or no value. This, in turn, leads many to become active participants in the jettisoning of their traditionally associated languages and cultures. Bourdieu (1991) describes this process as one of méconnaissance (misrecognition) – assuming the greater value accorded the dominant language and culture to be a 'natural' rather than a socially and politically constructed phenomenon. As Bourdieu argues, the resulting 'symbolic violence' that is visited upon particular minority languages and cultures is often sustained by an active complicity, or implicit consent, on the part of those subjected to it.

Moving forward: from principles to practice

> We need a little less pietistic articulation of political principle ... a little
> more of the principle of political negotiation.
>
> (Bhabha, 1994: 28)

So how can we change this state of affairs? Not easily is the simple answer. But the examples discussed in this book demonstrate that real progress *can* be made on behalf of minority languages and their speakers. The nation-state can be reconfigured – reimagined, in effect – to accommodate greater cultural and linguistic diversity. Or rather, as Homi Bhabha argues, it can be reimagined in order to accommodate greater cultural and linguistic *difference*. The distinction Bhabha makes is crucial here. The former, most evident in the rhetoric of multiculturalism, treats culture as an *object* of empirical knowledge – as static, totalised and historically bounded, as something to be valued but not necessarily *lived* (see also May, 1994a, 1999a). The latter is the process of the *enunciation* of culture as 'knowledg*able*', as adequate to the construction of systems of cultural identification. This involves a *dynamic* conception of culture – one that recognises and incorporates the ongoing fluidity and constant change that attends its articulation in the modern world.

A formal recognition of cultural and linguistic difference along these lines is what is presently occurring in the likes of Québec, Catalonia, Wales and Aotearoa / New Zealand. In each of these examples, minority languages are in the process of being legitimated and institutionalised in the public domain – after centuries of proscription, derogation and neglect – alongside the majority national language. These developments are often allied with, and framed within, a wider cultural nationalism that aims to build on, and where necessary transform, the minority language and culture in question in order more adequately to meet the demands of modernity. However, as we have also seen, this process remains a highly contested one, and the contest is perhaps most virulent at the intersection of group-differentiated and individual rights. Majority-language speakers in particular are often loath to accommodate minority-language rights, arguing that such rights infringe on their individual right to continue speaking the majority language in all contexts and language domains.

I have argued that this assertion of continued monolingualism has no real or legitimate basis – certainly, at least, not under the auspices of individual rights, since the opportunity and right to continue to speak the dominant language is in no way threatened by minority-language recognition (see also below). Nonetheless, it presents an ongoing problem of 'tolerability' for minority-language rights. In light of this, how might we proceed? For a start, by recognising that these issues are never likely to be entirely resolved. More significantly, it is not necessary that they should be. As Bhabha (1994) again observes, an alternative minority discourse amounts to a strategy of intervention which is similar to what British parliamentary procedure recognises as a supplementary question. A supplementary strategy suggests that *adding 'to' need not be the same as adding 'up'*. In other words, what we may have here in the end are *incommensurable* discourses – 'abseits designating a form of social contradiction or antagonism that has to be negotiated rather than sublated' (1994: 162). We cannot, and perhaps should not, evacuate tension and conflict from these negotiations about minority-language rights (and minority rights more generally), since real and substantive differences continue to underlie the various positions involved (see Taylor, 1994; Coulombe, 1995; Modood, 1998b).

Indeed, the continuing debates around individual and group-differentiated rights may help to guard against the possibility of, and potential for, social and political closure – of simply substituting one kind of totalising and exclusionary (national, ethnic and/or linguistic) discourse for another. After all, the world is replete with examples of minority groups who, on attaining greater sociopolitical and sociocultural status for themselves, promptly deny it to others. The tenets of international law concerning minority groups are pivotal here. With regard to language, for example, three key tenets can be highlighted. The first principle, which is widely accepted, is that it is not unreasonable to expect from national members some knowledge of the common public language(s) of the state. On this basis, it is possible to argue for the legitimation and institutionalisation of the languages of national minorities within nation-states, according to them at least some of the benefits that national languages currently enjoy.

A second principle is that in order to avoid language discrimination, it is important that where there is a sufficient number of other language speakers, these speakers should be allowed to use that language as part of the exercise of their *individual* rights as citizens. That is, they should have the *opportunity* to use their first language if they so choose. As de Varennes argues, 'the respect of the language principles of individuals, *where appropriate and reasonable*, flows from a fundamental right and is not some special concession or privileged treatment. Simply put, it is the right to be treated equally without discrimination, to which everyone is entitled' (1996a: 117; my emphasis). Again, this principle can clearly be applied to minority-language speakers within particular nation-states. Ostensibly, this can also be applied to majority-language speakers on the same grounds. However, a crucial caveat needs to be added here. The formal promotion of a minority language does not *preclude* the ongoing use of the majority language, given that it is most often dominant anyway in all key language domains. Thus, what is being promoted is not a new monolingualism in the minority language – indeed, this is usually neither politically nor practically sustainable – but the *possibility* of bilingualism or multilingualism. As such, the claims of language discrimination by majority-language speakers are both misplaced and inapplicable. The majority language is not generally being precluded from the public realm, nor proscribed at the individual level, nor are majority-language speakers actually penalised for speaking their language.[1] Rather, monolingual majority-language speakers are being asked to accommodate to the ongoing presence of a minority language and to recognise its status as an additional language of the state – a process that I described in Chapter 5 as 'mutual accommodation'.

The third principle arises directly from the previous one – how to determine exactly what is 'appropriate and reasonable' with regard to individual language preferences. The distinction between national-minority and poly-ethnic rights (see Chapter 3) is useful in this respect. I have consistently argued that only national minorities – as historical ethnies – can demand *as of right* formal inclusion of their languages and cultures in the civic realm. However, this need not and should not preclude other ethnic minorities from being allowed *at the very least* to cultivate and pursue unhindered their own historic cultural and linguistic practices in the private domain. In relation to language, this has been articulated by Kloss (1977) as the distinction between promotion-oriented and tolerance-oriented rights (see Chapter 5). In relation to Churchill's (1986) typology of minority-language-policy approaches, also discussed in Chapter 5, it is illustrated by the distinction between the maintenance of languages for private use (Stage 5) versus the widespread institutional recognition of languages (Stage 6).

Thus, while continuing to recognise the rights attributable to other minorities, this distinction allows us to avoid the problem of cultural relativism. In short, greater ethnolinguistic democracy is not necessarily the same as ethnolinguistic equality. It also addresses the question, to which I have alluded on a number of occasions, of the role of multiculturalism. In this respect, a common argument has been that bicultural/bilingual policies privilege one particular minority group over others and are therefore both disadvantageous and discriminatory towards the latter. In this view, differential treatment of minorities is illiberal – either all minority groups should be so recognised, or none should be.

However, this argument can be challenged on a number of grounds. First, as with much discussion of minority rights, no distinction is made here between the differing rights attributable to national and ethnic minorities. National-minority rights are thus treated as merely equivalent to the rights of all other competing groups. What is being advocated, in effect, is the applicability of *polyethnic* rights (and only these) to *all* minorities. In the process, and this is my second point, the demands of multiculturalism come to be articulated as an *alternative* to national-minority rights – i.e., as a means of *avoiding* biculturalism/bilingualism. This suggests, in turn, the distinct possibility that the articulation of multiculturalism along these lines is not seriously countenanced by at least some of its proponents. Remembering Bhabha's earlier distinction, the rhetoric of cultural and linguistic *diversity* is used as a spoiling device against the articulation of cultural and linguistic *difference*. Support for multiculturalism may thus arise less out of a valuing of diversity, and/or a concern for the interests of minority groups, than from a fear of the possible fulfilment of bicultural and bilingual aspirations. Pierre Coulombe makes this point, albeit somewhat more forcefully, in relation to Canada's official French/English bilingualism:

> Those who object to bilingualism often do so because they fear differences and are unable to reconcile themselves with the loss of their hegemony over society. Needless to say, it is an attitude that is not receptive to multi-culturalism and the maintaining of differences. There is no way that the cultural imperialists who wrap themselves in the language of moral outrage in denouncing bilingualism will open their arms to multiculturalism... They will, in other words, profess their tolerance towards a diversity of languages and cultures, so long as that diversity is consigned to the private sphere. Ethnic minorities ought to be cautious when they too oppose official bilingualism, for they may be unwillingly supporting an attitude that will turn against them.
>
> (1995: 104)

As such, we should treat the competing claims of multiculturalism with considerable scepticism. But having said that, it is unwise to dismiss multi-cultural claims out of hand, as Coulombe comes close to doing. Multicul-turalism may still have an important, perhaps essential, part to play as an *addition* or *complement* to bicultural/bilingual policy. Certainly, in the ex-amples of bicultural/bilingual policy that have been discussed at length in this book – Québec, Catalonia, Wales and Aotearoa / New Zealand – much still needs to be done in order to address adequately the cultural and linguistic needs and rights of other ethnic-minority groups within these territories. In short, the development of formal bilingualism *must* remain sensitive to, and accommodating of, other ethnic-minority groups and the languages they speak.

Likewise, there is a continuing necessity to guard against essentialism and reification in the articulation of minority cultural and language rights. Multiculturalism may thus usefully ensure against the objectification of ethnicity and the hardening of ethnic and national boundaries, while contrib-uting at the same time to ongoing debates about a more open, evolving conception of ethnic and national identities. Bourdieu argues, to this end, that one needs 'to keep together what go together in reality: on the one hand the objective classifications . . . and, on the other hand, the practical relation to those classifications, whether acted out or represented, and in particular the individual and collective strategies . . . by which agents seek to put these classifications at the service of their material or symbolic interests, or to conserve or transform them' (1991: 227).

And this brings me to my final point. It has been my argument throughout this book that in order to rethink or reimagine the nation-state along more plural and inclusive lines we must first (and somewhat counterintuitively) acknowledge the cultural-historical dimensions of the ethnic and national identities which comprise it. As Stuart Hall argues, a positive conception of ethnicity must begin with 'a recognition that all speak from a particular place, out of a particular history, out of a particular experience, a particular culture, *without being contained by that position*' (1992b: 258; my emphasis). Moreover, if a particular language has played an important part in that historical positioning (and it may well not have), there is no reason why it cannot continue to do so.

However, Hall's qualification points to the second key aspect of my argument here – that the recognition of our cultural and historical situatedness should not set the limits of ethnicity and nationality, nor act to undermine the legitimacy of other, equally valid forms of identity. This requires a reflective, critical approach to ethnic and national identity, and the role of languages within them. Such an approach would have to engage with the present and the future as well as the past, and would have to remain open to competing conceptualisations, diverse identities, and a rich public discourse about controversial issues (Calhoun, 1993b).[2] As Peter McLaren observes, echoing Renan's conception of the 'will to nationhood' (see Chapter 2): 'rather than searching for the origins of our identities as historical agents of struggle, we need to focus more on what we can achieve together. What we might become takes precedence over who we are' (1995: 109). Likewise, Terry Eagleton asserts: 'Any emancipatory politics must begin with the specific . . . but must in the same gesture leave it behind. For the freedom to question is not the freedom to be [this or that particular identity], whatever this might mean, but simply the freedom now enjoyed by certain other groups *to determine their identity as they wish*' (1990: 30; my emphasis).

Such a position recognises the ongoing interspersion of groups, the complex interconnections between ethnic and national identities and other forms of identity, and the ambiguities, tensions, and competing demands that inevitably arise as a result. But even more importantly, it recognises that these can be outworked from within (or centrifugally), rather than always being determined from without (or centripetally). Or, to put it another way, they can be negotiated on one's own terms, rather than the terms set by others, as has so often been the case historically for minority groups. Thus, the arguments of minority groups for the retention of their ethnic, cultural and linguistic identities are most often *not* characterised by a retreat into traditionalism or cultural essentialism but, rather, by a more *autonomous* construction of group identity and political deliberation (Kymlicka, 1995a).

It is about time that we started paying much closer attention to these arguments, and their emancipatory possibilities, not least because they present perhaps the only significant hope for the ongoing survival of many of the world's minority languages over the course of this new century. This is an important political imperative that we should not side-step in the name of academic 'disinterestedness' since, as I argued at the beginning of this book, the latter tends simply to reinforce the ongoing exponential loss of the world's minority languages. But if this remains an unpalatable prospect for some, there is also a more straightforward intellectual reason for taking far greater cognisance of these arguments. We simply cannot continue to promote uncritically the current intellectual orthodoxy that rejects language as a key factor in identity politics without at the same time being able to explain more adequately *why* questions of language, and language rights, continue so patently to play a significant (even central) part in many of the political disputes in the world today.

Notes

1   The examples where this has occurred as the result of a minority-language policy remain extremely rare. The post-Soviet language policies of Latvia and Estonia, however, may be said to fall into this category. This is because the significant majority Russian-speaking population in these areas have been denied citizenship rights since independence unless they can demonstrate a conversational ability in Latvian or Estonian (see de Varennes, 1996a; Laitin, 1998).

2   In a parallel argument drawn from feminist discourse, Nira Yuval-Davis describes this process as one of 'transversal politics' in which 'perceived unity and homogeneity are replaced by dialogues that give recognition to the specific positionings of those who participate in them, as well as to the "unfinished knowledge" . . . that each such situated positioning can offer' (1997b: 204). Central to this idea of transversal politics is the interrelationship between 'rooting' and 'shifting'. Each participant in the dialogue brings with them the rooting in their own grouping and identity, but tries at the same time to shift in order to put themselves in a situation of exchange with those who have different groupings and identities.

Bibliography

Acton, J. (1907). Nationality. In J. Figgis and R. Lawrence (eds.), *The History of Freedom* (pp. 270–300). London: Macmillan (original, 1862).

Adams, K., and Brink, D. (eds.) (1990). *Perspectives on Official English: The Campaign for English as the Official Language of the USA*. Berlin: Mouton de Gruyter.

Ager, D. (1999). *Identity, Insecurity and Image: France and Language*. Clevedon, England: Multilingual Matters.

Ahmad, A. (1995). The politics of literary postcoloniality. *Race and Class* 36, 3, 1–20.

Aitchison, J., and Carter, H. (1994). *A Geography of the Welsh Language 1961–1991*. Cardiff: University of Wales Press.

AJHR. *Appendices to the Journals of the House of Representatives 1858–1939*. Wellington, New Zealand.

Alba, R. (1990). *Ethnic Identity: The Transformation of White America*. New Haven, CT: Yale University Press.

Alexander, N. (2000). Language policy and planning in South Africa: some insights. In R. Phillipson (ed.), *Rights to Language. Equity, Power and Education* (pp. 170–173). Mahwah, NJ: Lawrence Erlbaum.

Alexandre, P. (1972). *Languages and Language in Black Africa*. Evanston: Northwestern University Press.

Alter, P. (1989). *Nationalism*. London: Edward Arnold.

Amastae, J. (1990). Official English and the learning of English. In K. Adams and D. Brink (eds.), *Perspectives on Official English: The Campaign for English as the Official Language of the USA* (pp. 199–208). Berlin: Mouton de Gruyter.

Ammon, U. (1998). *Ist Deutsch noch internationale Wissenschaftssprache? Englisch auch für die Lehre an den deutschsprachigen Hochschulen*. Berlin: Mouton de Gruyter.

Ammon, U. (ed.) (2000). *The Dominance of English as the Language of Science: Effects on other Languages and Language Communities*. Berlin: Mouton de Gruyter.

Anaya, J. (1996). *Indigenous Peoples in International Law*. New York: Oxford University Press.

Anderson, B. (1991). *Imagined Communities: Reflections on the Origin and Spread of Nationalism* (rev. edn). London: Verso.

Anthias, F. (1992). Connecting 'race' and ethnic phenomena. *Sociology* 26, 421–438.

Anthias, F., and Yuval-Davis, N. (1992). *Racialized Boundaries: Race, Nation, Gender, Colour and Class and the Anti-Racist Struggle*. London: Routledge.

Anzaldúa, G. (1987). *Borderlands / La Frontera: The New Mestiza.* San Francisco, CA: Aunt Lute Books.

Appel, R., and Muysken, P. (1987). *Language Contact and Bilingualism.* London: Edward Arnold.

Armstrong, J. (1982). *Nations Before Nationalism.* Chapel Hill, NC: University of North California Press.

Artigal, J. (1997). The Catalan immersion program. In R. Johnson and M. Swain (eds.), *Immersion Education: International Perspectives* (pp. 133–150). Cambridge: Cambridge University Press.

Atkinson, D. (1997). Attitudes towards language use in Catalonia: politics or sociolinguistics? *International Journal of Iberian Studies* 10, 5–14.

Atkinson, D. (1998). Normalisation: integration or assimilation? A response to Miquel Strubell. *Current Issues in Language and Society* 5, 3, 210–214.

Baetens Beardsmore, H. (1980). Bilingualism in Belgium. *Journal of Multilingual and Multicultural Development* 1, 145–154.

Bailey, R. (1991). *Images of English: A Cultural History of the Language.* Ann Arbor, MI: University of Michigan Press.

Baker, C. (1985). *Aspects of Bilingualism in Wales.* Clevedon, England: Multilingual Matters.

Baker, C. (1995). Bilingual education and assessment. In B. Morris Jones and P. Singh Ghuman (eds.), *Bilingualism, Education and Identity* (pp. 130–158). Cardiff: University of Wales Press.

Baker, C. (1996). *Foundations of Bilingual Education and Bilingualism* (2nd edn). Clevedon, England: Multilingual Matters.

Baker, C., and Prys Jones, S. (eds.) (1998). *Encyclopedia of Bilingualism and Bilingual Education.* Clevedon, England: Multilingual Matters.

Baker, K., and de Kanter, A. (1981). *Effectiveness of Bilingual Education: A Review of the Literature.* Washington, DC: US Department of Education.

Baker, K., and de Kanter, A. (eds.) (1983). *Bilingual Education: A Reappraisal of Federal Policy.* Lexington, MA: Lexington Books.

Bakhtin, M. (1981). *The Dialogic Imagination: Four Essays.* C. Emerson and M. Holquist (trans.). M. Holquist (ed.). Austin, TX: University of Texas Press.

Balibar, E. (1991). The nation form: history and ideology. In E. Balibar and I. Wallerstein (eds.), *Race, Nation, Class: Ambiguous Identities* (pp. 86–106). London: Verso.

Ball, S. (1990). *Politics and Policy Making in Education.* London: Routledge.

Ball, S. (1994). *Education Reform: A Critical and Post-Structuralist Approach.* Buckingham, England: Open University Press.

Balthazar, L. (1990). *Bilan du Nationalisme au Québec.* Montreal: L'Hexagone.

Banton, M. (1980). Ethnic groups and the theory of rational choice. In *Sociological Theories: Race and Colonialism* (pp. 475–483). Paris: UNESCO.

Banton, M. (1983). *Racial and Ethnic Competition.* Cambridge: Cambridge University Press.

Banton, M. (1987). *Racial Theories.* Cambridge: Cambridge University Press.

Barbaud, P. (1998). French in Québec. In J. Edwards (ed.), *Language in Canada* (pp. 177–201). Cambridge: Cambridge University Press.

Barker, M. (1981). *The New Racism: Conservatives and the Ideology of the Tribe.* London: Junction.

Barkhuizen, G., and Gough, D. (1996). Language curriculum development in South Africa: what place for English? *TESOL Quarterly* 30, 453–472.

Barnard, F. (1965). *Herder's Social and Political Thought: From Enlightenment to Nationalism*. Oxford: Clarendon Press.

Baron, D. (1990). *The English-Only Question: An Official Language for America?* New Haven, CT: Yale University Press.

Barrington, J. (1992). The school curriculum, occupations and race. In G. McCulloch (ed.), *The School Curriculum in New Zealand* (pp. 57–73). Palmerston North, New Zealand: Dunmore Press.

Barrington, J., and Beaglehole, T. (1974). *Maori Schools in a Changing Society*. Wellington, New Zealand: New Zealand Council for Education Research.

Barsh, R. (1996). Indigenous peoples and the UN Commission on Human Rights: a case of the immovable object and the irresistible force. *Human Rights Quarterly* 18, 782–813.

Barth, F. (1969a). Introduction. *Ethnic Groups and Boundaries: The Social Organization of Culture Difference* (pp. 9–38). Boston, MA: Little, Brown and Co.

Barth, F. (1969b). *Ethnic Groups and Boundaries: The Social Organization of Culture Difference*. Boston, MA: Little, Brown and Co.

Barth, F. (1989). The analysis of culture in complex societies. *Ethnos* 54, 120–142.

Bauman, Z. (1973). *Culture as Praxis*. London: Routledge and Kegan Paul.

Bauman, Z. (1993). *Postmodern Ethics*. London: Routledge.

Belich, J. (1986). *The New Zealand Wars*. Auckland, New Zealand: Auckland University Press.

Belich, J. (1996). *Making Peoples*. Auckland, New Zealand: Allen Lane.

Bentahila, A., and Davies, E. (1993). Language revival: restoration or transformation? *Journal of Multilingual and Multicultural Development* 14, 355–374.

Bentley, G. (1987). Ethnicity and practice. *Comparative Studies in Society and History* 29, 24–55.

Benton, N. (1989). Education, language decline and language revitalisation: the case of Māori in New Zealand. *Language and Education* 3, 65–82.

Benton, R. (1979). *Who Speaks Māori in New Zealand*. Wellington, New Zealand: New Zealand Council for Educational Research.

Benton, R. (1981). *The Flight of the Amokura: Oceanic Languages and Formal Education in the South Pacific*. Wellington, New Zealand: New Zealand Council for Educational Research.

Benton, R. (1983). *The NZCER Māori Language Survey*. Wellington, New Zealand: New Zealand Council for Educational Research.

Benton, R. (1987). Fairness in Māori education: a review of research and information. In *Report of the Royal Commission on Social Policy* Vol. 3 (pp. 287–404). Wellington, New Zealand: Government Printer.

Benton, R. (1988). The Māori language in New Zealand education. *Language, Culture and Curriculum* 1, 75–83.

Benton, R. (1996). Language policy in New Zealand: defining the ineffable. In M. Herriman and B. Burnaby (eds.), *Language Policies in English-Dominant Countries* (pp. 62–98). Clevedon, England: Multilingual Matters.

Berry, J. (1998). Official multiculturalism. In J. Edwards (ed.), *Language in Canada* (pp. 84–101). Cambridge: Cambridge University Press.

Best, G. (1982). *Honour among Men and Nations: Transformations of an Idea*. Toronto: Toronto University Press.

Best, G. (ed.) (1988). *The Permanent Revolution: The French Revolution and its Legacy*. Chicago, IL: Chicago University Press.

Bhabha, H. (1994). *The Location of Culture*. London: Routledge.

Bikales, G. (1986). Comment: the other side. *International Journal of the Sociology of Language* 60, 77–85.

Billig, M. (1995). *Banal Nationalism*. London: Sage.

Birch, A. (1989). *Nationalism and National Integration*. London: Unwin Hyman.

Bishop, R., and Glynn, T. (1999). *Culture Counts: Changing Power Relations in Education*. Palmerston North, New Zealand: Dunmore Press.

Blommaert, J. (1996). Language and nationalism: comparing Flanders and Tanzania. *Nations and Nationalism* 2, 235–256.

Blommaert, J. (1999a). The debate is open. In J. Blommaert (ed.), *Language Ideological Debates* (pp. 1–38). Berlin: Mouton de Gruyter.

Blommaert, J. (1999b). The debate is closed. In J. Blommaert (ed.), *Language Ideological Debates* (pp. 425–438). Berlin: Mouton de Gruyter.

Blommaert, J. (ed.) (1999c). *Language Ideological Debates*. Berlin: Mouton de Gruyter.

Blommaert, J., and Verschueren, J. (1992). The role of language in European nationalist ideologies. *Pragmatics* 2, 355–375.

Blommaert, J., and Verschueren, J. (1998). *Debating Diversity: Analysing the Discourse of Tolerance*. London: Routledge.

Bloom, A. (1987). *The Closing of the American Mind: How Higher Education Has Failed Democracy and Impoverished the Souls of Today's Students*. New York: Simon and Schuster.

Bonnett, A. (2000). *Anti-Racism*. London: Routledge.

Bourdieu, P. (1977). The economy of linguistic exchanges. *Social Science Information* 16, 645–668.

Bourdieu, P. (1982). *Ce Que Parler Veut Dire: L'Économie des Échanges Linguistiques*. Paris: Arthème Fayard.

Bourdieu, P. (1984). *Distinction: A Social Critique of the Judgement of Taste*. Cambridge, MA: Harvard University Press.

Bourdieu, P. (1990a). *In Other Words: Essays Towards a Reflexive Sociology*. Cambridge: Polity Press.

Bourdieu, P. (1990b). *The Logic of Practice*. Cambridge: Polity Press.

Bourdieu, P. (1991). *Language and Symbolic Power*. Cambridge: Polity Press.

Bourdieu, P., and Boltanski, L. (1975). Le fétichisme de la langue. *Actes de la Recherche en Sciences Sociales* 4, 2–23.

Bourdieu, P., and Passeron, J.-C. (1990). *Reproduction in Education, Society and Culture* (2nd edn). London: Sage.

Bourdieu, P., and Wacquant, L. (1992). *An Invitation to Reflexive Sociology*. Chicago, IL: Chicago University Press.

Bourhis, R. (ed.) (1984). *Conflict and Language Planning in Quebec*. Clevedon, England: Multilingual Matters.

Bourne, J. (1989). *Moving into the Mainstream*. Windsor, England: NFER Nelson.

Bowie, F. (1993). Wales from within: conflicting interpretations of Welsh identity. In S. Macdonald (ed.), *Inside European Identities: Ethnography in Western Europe* (pp. 167–193). Oxford: Berg Publishers.

Bowman, G. (1994). Xenophobia, fantasy and the nation: the logic of ethnic violence in the former Yugoslavia. In V. Goddard, J. Llobera and C. Shore (eds.), *The Anthropology of Europe* (pp. 143–171). Oxford: Berg.

Brah, A. (1992). Difference, diversity and differentiation. In J. Donald and A. Rattansi (eds.), *'Race', Culture and Difference* (pp. 126–145). London: Sage.

Brasil (1996). *Constituição da República Federativa do Brasil (CF/88)*. São Paulo: Editora Revista dos Tribunais.

Brass, P. (ed.) (1985). *Ethnic Groups and the State*. London: Croom Helm.

Brenzinger, M. (1997). Language contact and language displacement. In F. Coulmas (ed.), *The Handbook of Sociolinguistics* (pp. 273–284). Oxford: Blackwell.

Breuilly, J. (1993). *Nationalism and the State* (2nd edn). Manchester: Manchester University Press.

British Council (1995). *English in the World: The English 2000 Global Consultation*. Manchester: The British Council.

Brown, G. (1984). *Colin McCahon: Artist*. Wellington, New Zealand: Reed.

Brubaker, R. (1996). *Nationalism Reframed: Nationhood and the National Question in the New Europe*. Cambridge: Cambridge University Press.

Brubaker, R. (1998). Myths and misconceptions in the study of nationalism. In J. Hall (ed.), *The State of the Nation: Ernest Gellner and the Theory of Nationalism* (pp. 272–306). Cambridge: Cambridge University Press.

Bullivant, B. (1981). *The Pluralist Dilemma in Education: Six Case Studies*. Sydney: Allen and Unwin.

Bullman, U. (ed.) (1994). *Die Politik der dritten Ebene. Regionen im Europa der Union*. Baden-Baden, Germany: Nomos.

Burnaby, B. (1996). Language policies in Canada. In M. Herriman and B. Burnaby (eds.), *Language Policies in English-Dominant Countries* (pp. 159–219). Clevedon, England: Multilingual Matters.

Burtonwood, N. (1996). Culture, identity and the curriculum. *Educational Review* 48, 227–235.

Butt Philip, A. (1975). *The Welsh Question: Nationalism in Welsh Politics, 1945–1970*. Cardiff: University of Wales Press.

Byram, M. (1986). Schools and ethnolinguistic minorities. *Journal of Multilingual and Multicultural Development* 7, 97–106.

Caglar, A. (1997). Hyphenated identities and the limits of 'culture'. In T. Modood and P. Werbner (eds.), *The Politics of Multiculturalism in the New Europe: Racism, Identity and Community* (pp. 169–185). London: Zed Books.

Calhoun, C. (1993a). Nationalism and ethnicity. *Annual Review of Sociology* 19, 211–239.

Calhoun, C. (1993b). Nationalism and civil society: democracy, diversity and self-determination. *International Sociology* 8, 387–411.

Calhoun, C. (1997). *Nationalism*. Buckingham, England: Open University Press.

Calhoun, C., LiPuma, E., and Postone, M. (eds.) (1993). *Bourdieu: Critical Perspectives*. Cambridge: Polity Press.

Calvet, L.-J. (1974). *Linguistique et Colonialisme: Petite Traité de Glottophagie*. Paris: Payot.

Canagarajah, A. (2000). *Resisting Linguistic Imperialism in English Teaching*. Oxford: Oxford University Press.

Cannadine, D. (1983). The context, performance and meaning of ritual: the British monarchy and the 'invention of tradition' c. 1820–1977. In E. Hobsbawm and

T. Ranger (eds.), *The Invention of Tradition* (pp. 101–164). Cambridge: Cambridge University Press.

Capotorti, F. (1979). *Study on the Rights of Persons Belonging to Ethnic, Religious and Linguistic Minorities.* New York: United Nations.

Carter, A., and Stokes, G. (1998). *Liberal Democracy and its Critics.* Cambridge: Polity Press.

Castells, M. (1997). *The Power of Identity.* Oxford: Blackwell.

Cenoz, J., and Genesee, F. (eds.) (1998). *Beyond Bilingualism: Multilingualism and Multilingual Education.* Clevedon, England: Multilingual Matters.

Chapman, M., McDonald, M., and Tonkin, E. (1989). Introduction: history and social anthropology. In E. Tonkin, M. McDonald and M. Chapman (eds.), *History and Ethnicity* (pp. 1–21). London: Routledge.

Chapple, S., Jeffries, R., and Walker, R. (1997). *Māori Participation and Performance in Education. A Literature Review and Research Programme.* Wellington, New Zealand: Ministry of Education.

Chevannes, F., and Reeves, M. (1987). The black voluntary school movement: definition, context and prospects. In B. Troyna (ed.), *Racial Inequality in Education* (pp. 147–169). London: Tavistock.

Chomsky, N. (1972). *Language and Mind.* New York: Harcourt Brace Jovanovich.

Chomsky, N. (1979). *Language and Responsibility.* London: Harvester.

Chomsky, N. (1987). *On Power and Ideology: The Managua Lectures.* Boston, MA: South End Press.

Churchill, S. (1986). *The Education of Linguistic and Cultural Minorities in the OECD Countries.* Clevedon, England: Multilingual Matters.

Churchill, S. (1996). The decline of the nation-state and the education of national minorities. *International Review of Education* 42, 265–290.

CILAR (Committee on Irish Language Attitudes Research). (1975). *Report.* Dublin: Stationery Office.

Clark, D., and Williamson, R. (eds.) (1996). *Self-Determination: International Perspectives.* London: Macmillan.

Claude, I. (1955). *National Minorities: An International Problem.* Cambridge, MA: Harvard University Press.

Clyne, M. (1990). *Community Languages: The Australian Experience.* Cambridge: Cambridge University Press.

Clyne, M. (1997). Multilingualism. In F. Coulmas (ed.), *The Handbook of Sociolinguistics* (pp. 301–314). London: Blackwell.

Clyne, M. (1998). Managing language diversity and second language programmes in Australia. In S. Wright and H. Kelly-Holmes (eds.), *Managing Language Diversity* (pp. 4–29). Clevedon, England: Multilingual Matters.

Cohen, A. (1974). *Two-Dimensional Man.* London: Tavistock.

Colley, L. (1992). *Britons: Forging the Nation 1707–1837.* London: Pimlico.

Collins, J. (1999). The Ebonics controversy in context: literacies, subjectivities, and language ideologies in the United States. In J. Blommaert (ed.), *Language Ideological Debates* (pp. 201–234). Berlin: Mouton de Gruyter.

Conklin, N., and Lourie, M. (1983). *Host of Tongues: Language Communities in the United States.* New York: Free Press.

Connor, W. (1978). A nation is a nation, is a state, is an ethnic group, is a . . . *Ethnic and Racial Studies* 1, 377–400.

Connor, W. (1991). From tribe to nation? *History of European Ideas* 13, 5–18.

Connor, W. (1993). Beyond reason: the nature of the ethnonational bond. *Ethnic and Racial Studies* 16, 374–389.

Conversi, D. (1997). *The Basques, the Catalans and Spain*. London: Hurst.

Cornell, S. (1988). *The Return of the Native: American Indian Political Resurgence*. New York: Oxford University Press.

Corntassel, J., and Primeau, T. (1995). Indigenous 'sovereignty' and international law: revised strategies for pursuing 'self-determination'. *Human Rights Quarterly* 17, 343–365.

Corson, D. (1993). *Language, Minority Education and Gender: Linking Social Justice and Power*. Clevedon, England: Multilingual Matters.

Corson, D. (1995). Norway's 'Sámi Language Act': emancipatory implications for the world's indigenous peoples. *Language in Society* 24, 493–514.

Corson, D. (1998). *Changing Education for Diversity*. Buckingham, England: Open University Press.

Corson, D. (1999). Community-based education for indigenous cultures. In S. May (ed.), *Indigenous Community-Based Education* (pp. 8–19). Clevedon, England: Multilingual Matters.

Costa, J., and Wynants, S. (1999). Catalan Linguistic Policy Act: external protection or internal restriction? Paper presented to the Nationalism, Identity and Minority Rights Conference, University of Bristol, September 1999.

Coulmas, F. (1992). *Language and Economy*. Oxford: Blackwell.

Coulmas, F. (1998). Language rights: interests of states, language groups and the individual. *Language Sciences* 20, 63–72.

Coulombe, P. (1995). *Language Rights in French Canada*. New York: Peter Lang.

Coulombe, P. (1999). Citizenship and official bilingualism in Canada. In W. Kymlicka and W. Norman (eds.), *Citizenship in Diverse Societies* (pp. 273–293). Oxford: Oxford University Press.

Cowan, M. (1963). *Humanist without Portfolio: An Anthology of the Writings of Wilhelm von Humboldt*. Detroit, MI: Wayne State University Press.

Crawford, J. (1989). *Bilingual Education: History, Politics, Theory and Practice*. Trenton, NJ: Crane Publishing Co.

Crawford, J. (1992a). *Hold your Tongue: Bilingualism and the Politics of 'English Only'*. Reading, MA: Addison-Wesley.

Crawford, J. (ed.) (1992b). *Language Loyalties: A Source Book on the Official English Controversy*. Chicago, IL: University of Chicago Press.

Crawford, J. (1992c). What's behind Official English? In J. Crawford (ed.), *Language Loyalties: A Source Book on the Official English Controversy* (pp. 171–177). Chicago, IL: University of Chicago Press.

Crawford, J. (1994). Endangered Native American languages: what is to be done and why? *Journal of Navajo Education* 11, 3, 3–11.

Crick, B. (1989). An Englishman considers his passport. In N. Evans (ed.), *National Identity in the British Isles* (pp. 23–34). Harlech, Wales: Coleg Harlech.

Crick, B. (ed.) (1991). *National Identities and the Constitution*. Oxford: Blackwell.

Crick, B. (1995). The sense of identity of the indigenous British. *New Community* 21, 167–182.

Crowley, T. (1996). *Language in History: Theories and Texts*. London: Routledge.

Crozier, G. (1989). Multicultural education: some unintended consequences. In S. Walker and L. Barton (eds.), *Politics and the Processes of Schooling* (pp. 59–81). Milton Keynes, England: Open University Press.

Crystal, D. (1997a). *English as a Global Language*. Cambridge: Cambridge University Press.

Crystal, D. (1997b). *The Cambridge Encyclopedia of Language* (2nd edn). Cambridge: Cambridge University Press.

Crystal, D. (1999a). The death of language. *Prospect* (November 1999), 56–59.

Crystal, D. (1999b). Death sentence. *Guardian* (25 October 1999), G2, 2–3.

Cummins, J. (1986). Empowering minority students: a framework for intervention. *Harvard Educational Review* 56, 18–36.

Cummins, J. (1989). *Empowering Minority Students*. Sacramento, CA: California Association for Bilingual Education.

Cummins, J. (1995). The discourse of disinformation: the debate on bilingual education and language rights in the United States. In T. Skutnabb-Kangas and R. Phillipson (eds.), *Linguistic Human Rights: Overcoming Linguistic Discrimination* (pp. 159–177). Berlin: Mouton de Gruyter.

Cummins, J. (1996). *Negotiating Identities: Education for Empowerment in a Diverse Society*. Toronto: California Association for Bilingual Education.

Cummins, J. (1999a). The ethics of doublethink: language rights and the bilingual education debate. *TESOL Journal* 8, 3, 13–17.

Cummins, J. (1999b). Alternative paradigms in bilingual education research: does theory have a place? *Educational Researcher* 28, 7, 26–32.

Cummins, J., and Swain, M. (1986). *Bilingualism in Education*. London: Longman.

Dale, R., and Ozga, J. (1993). Two hemispheres – both New Right? 1980s education reform in New Zealand and England and Wales. In B. Lingard, J. Knight and P. Porter (eds.), *Schooling Reform in Hard Times* (pp. 63–87). London: Falmer Press.

Daniels, H. (1990). The roots of language protectionism. In H. Daniels (ed.), *Not Only English: Affirming America's Multilingual Heritage* (pp. 3–12). Urbana, IL: National Council of Teachers.

Daniels, R. (1991). *Coming to America: A History of Immigration and Ethnicity in American Life*. New York: Harper Perennial.

Dasgupta, P. (1993). *The Otherness of English: India's Auntie Tongue Syndrome*. London: Sage.

Daugherty, R. (1993). Why policies must be made in Wales. *Times Educational Supplement* (22 October 1993), 18.

Davies, Charlotte. (1989). *Welsh Nationalism in the Twentieth Century: The Ethnic Option and the Modern State*. London: Praeger.

Davies, Christie. (1997). Minority language and social division: linguistic dead-ends, linguistic time bombs and the policies of subversion. In G. Frost (ed.), *Loyalty Misplaced: Misdirected Virtue and Social Disintegration* (pp. 39–47). London: The Social Affairs Unit.

Davies, L., and Nicholl, K. (1993). *Te Māori i roto i ngā Mahi Whakaakoranga. Māori Education: A Statistical Profile of the Position of Māori across the New Zealand Education System*. Wellington, New Zealand: Ministry of Education.

Davis, W. (1999). Vanishing cultures. *National Geographic* (August 1999), 62–89.

Dawkins, J. (1991). *Australia's Language: The Australian Language and Literacy Policy*. Canberra, Australia: Australian Government Publishing Service.

Day, R. (1985). The ultimate inequality: linguistic genocide. In N. Wolfson and J. Manes (eds.), *Language of Inequality* (pp. 163–181). Berlin: Mouton de Gruyter.

de Certeau, M., Julia, D., and Revel, J. (1975). *Une Politique de la Langue. La Révolution Française et les Patois.* Paris: Editions Gallimard.

Dench, G. (1986). *Minorities in the Open Society: Prisoners of Ambivalence.* London: Routledge and Kegan Paul.

Denison, N. (1977). Language death or language suicide? *International Journal of the Sociology of Language* 12, 13–22.

DES (Department of Education and Science). (1985). *Education for All: Report of the Committee of Inquiry into the Education of Children from Ethnic Minority Groups* (The Swann Report). London: HMSO.

de Saussure, F. (1974). *Course in General Linguistics.* W. Baskin (trans.). London: Fontana.

Deutsch, K. (1966). *Nationalism and Social Communication: An Inquiry into the Foundations of Nationality.* Cambridge, MA: MIT Press.

Deutsch, K. (1975). The political significance of linguistic conflicts. In J.-G. Savard and R. Vigneault (eds.), *Les États Multilingues: Problèmes et Solutions* (pp. 7–28). Laval, Québec: Les Presses de l'Université Laval.

de Varennes, F. (1996a). *Language, Minorities and Human Rights.* The Hague: Kluwer Law International.

de Varennes, F. (1996b). Minority aspirations and the revival of indigenous peoples. *International Review of Education* 42, 309–325.

Dicker, S. (1996). *Languages in America.* Clevedon, England: Multilingual Matters.

Dicker, S. (2000). Official English and bilingual education: the controversy over language pluralism in US society. In J. Kelly Hall and W. Eggington (eds.), *The Sociopolitics of English Language Teaching* (pp. 45–66). Clevedon, England: Multilingual Matters.

DiGiacomo, S. (1999). Language ideological debates in an Olympic city: Barcelona 1992–1996. In J. Blommaert (ed.), *Language Ideological Debates* (pp. 105–142). Berlin: Mouton de Gruyter.

di Leonardo, M. (1994). White ethnicities, identity politics, and baby bear's chair. *Social Text* 41, 5–33.

Di Maggio, P. (1979). Review essay on Pierre Bourdieu. *American Journal of Sociology* 84, 1460–1474.

Donahue, T. (1985). 'US English': its life and works. *International Journal of the Sociology of Language* 56, 99–112.

Donahue, T. (1995). American language policy and compensatory opinion. In J. Tollefson (ed.), *Power and Inequality in Language Education* (pp. 112–141). Cambridge: Cambridge University Press.

Donald, J., and Rattansi, A. (eds.) (1992). *'Race', Culture and Difference.* London: Sage.

Dorian, N. (1981). *Language Death.* Philadelphia, PA: University of Pennsylvania Press.

Dorian, N. (1982). Language loss and maintenance in language contact situations. In R. Lambert and B. Freed (eds.), *The Loss of Language Skills* (pp. 44–59). Rowley, MA: Newbury House.

Dorian, N. (1998). Western language ideologies and small-language prospects. In L. Grenoble and L. Whaley (eds.), *Endangered Languages: Language Loss and Community Response* (pp. 3–21). Cambridge: Cambridge University Press.

Drapeau, L., and Corbeil, J.-C. (1996). The Aboriginal languages in the perspective of language planning. In J. Maurais (ed.), *Québec's Aboriginal Languages: History, Planning, Development* (pp. 288–307). Clevedon, England: Multilingual Matters.

D'Souza, D. (1991). *Illiberal Education: The Politics of Race and Sex on Campus.* New York: Free Press.

D'Souza, D. (1995). *The End of Racism: Principles for a Multiracial Society.* New York: Free Press.

Durie, A, (1999). Emancipatory Māori education: speaking from the heart. In S. May (ed.), *Indigenous Community-Based Education* (pp. 67–78). Clevedon, England: Multilingual Matters.

Durie, M. (1998). *Te Mana, Te Kāwanatanga: The Politics of Māori Self-Determination.* Auckland, New Zealand: Oxford University Press.

Durkheim, E. (1956). *Education and Sociology.* New York: The Free Press.

Dworkin, R. (1978). Liberalism. In S. Hampshire (ed.), *Public and Private Morality* (pp. 113–143). Cambridge: Cambridge University Press.

Dworkin, R. (1983). In defence of equality. *Social Philosophy and Policy,* 1, 24–40.

Dwyer, T. (1980). *Eamon de Valera.* Dublin: Gill and Macmillan.

Dyer, R. (1997). *White.* London: Routledge.

Eagleton, T. (1990). *Nationalism, Colonialism and Literature.* Minneapolis, MN: University of Minnesota Press.

Eastman, C. (1984). Language, ethnic identity and change. In J. Edwards (ed.), *Linguistic Minorities, Policies and Pluralism* (pp. 259–276). London: Academic Press.

Eastman, C. (1991). The political and sociolinguistic status of language planning in Africa. In D. Marshall (ed.), *Language Planning: Focusschrift in Honour of Joshua A. Fishman* (pp. 131–151). Amsterdam: John Benjamins.

Edwards, C., and Read, P. (1992). *The Lost Children. Thirteen Australians Taken from their Aboriginal Families Tell of the Struggle to Find their Natural Parents.* London: Doubleday.

Edwards, D. (1993). Education and Welsh language planning. *Language, Culture and Curriculum* 6, 257–273.

Edwards, J. (1984). Language, diversity and identity. In J. Edwards (ed.), *Linguistic Minorities, Policies and Pluralism* (pp. 277–310). London: Academic Press.

Edwards, J. (1985). *Language, Society and Identity.* Oxford: Basil Blackwell.

Edwards, J. (1994). *Multilingualism.* London: Routledge.

Edwards, V. (1991). The Welsh speech community. In S. Alladina and V. Edwards (eds.), *Multilingualism in the British Isles* Vol. 1 (pp. 107–125). London: Longman.

Eller, J., and Coughlan, R. (1993). The poverty of primordialism: the demystification of ethnic attachments. *Ethnic and Racial Studies* 16, 183–201.

Ellison, N. (1997). Towards a new social politics: citizenship and reflexivity in late modernity. *Sociology* 31, 697–717.

Eriksen, T. (1992). *Us and Them in Modern Societies: Ethnicity and Nationalism in Trinidad, Mauritius and Beyond.* Oslo, Norway: Scandinavian University Press.

Eriksen, T. (1993). *Ethnicity and Nationalism: Anthropological Perspectives.* London: Pluto Press.

Eriksen, T. (1998). *Common Denominators: Ethnicity, Nation-Building and Compromise in Mauritius.* Oxford: Berg.

Esteve, J. (1992). Multicultural education in Spain: the autonomous communities face the challenge of European unity. *Education Review* 44, 255–272.

Evans, E. (1978). Welsh (Cymraeg). In C. James (ed.), *The Older Mother Tongues of the United Kingdom* (pp. 5–35). London: Centre for Information on Language Teaching and Research.

Evans, N. (1989). Introduction: identity and integration in the British Isles. In N. Evans (ed.), *National Identity in the British Isles* (pp. 6–22). Harlech, Wales: Coleg Harlech.

Evans, S. (2000). Hong Kong's new English language policy in education. *World Englishes* 19, 185–204.

Fardon, R. (1987). African ethnogenesis: limits to the comparability of ethnic phenomena. In L. Holy (ed.), *Comparative Anthropology* (pp. 168–188). Oxford: Basil Blackwell.

Featherstone, M. (1991). *Consumer Culture and Postmodernism*. London: Sage.

Featherstone, M. (1995). *Undoing Culture: Globalization, Postmodernism and Identity*. London: Sage.

Feinberg, R. (1990). Bilingual education in the United States: a summary of Lau compliance requirements. *Language, Culture and Curriculum* 3, 141–152.

Fenton, S. (1999). *Ethnicity: Racism, Class and Culture*. London: Macmillan.

Ferdman, B. (1990). Literacy and cultural identity. *Harvard Educational Review* 60, 181–204.

Fettes, M. (1999). Indigenous education and the ecology of community. In S. May (ed.), *Indigenous Community-Based Education* (pp. 20–41). Clevedon, England: Multilingual Matters.

Fichte, J. (1968). *Addresses to the German Nation*. New York: Harper and Row (original, 1807).

Figueroa, P. (1991). *Education and the Social Construction of 'Race'*. London: Routledge.

Fishman, J. (1980). Social theory and ethnography: neglected perspectives on language and ethnicity in Eastern Europe. In P. Sugar (ed.), *Ethnic Diversity and Conflict in Eastern Europe* (pp. 69–99). Santa Barbara, CA: ABC-Clio.

Fishman, J. (1989a). Language and ethnicity. In J. Fishman, *Language and Ethnicity in Minority Sociolinguistic Perspective* (pp. 23–65). Clevedon, England: Multilingual Matters (original, 1977).

Fishman, J. (1989b). Language and nationalism: two integrative essays. Part 1. The nature of nationalism. In J. Fishman, *Language and Ethnicity in Minority Sociolinguistic Perspective* (pp. 97–175). Clevedon, England: Multilingual Matters (original, 1972).

Fishman, J. (1989c). Language and nationalism: two integrative essays. Part 2. The impact of nationalism on language planning. In J. Fishman, *Language and Ethnicity in Minority Sociolinguistic Perspective* (pp. 269–367). Clevedon, England: Multilingual Matters (original, 1972).

Fishman, J. (1989d). Whorfianism of the third kind: ethnolinguistic diversity as a worldwide societal asset. In J. Fishman, *Language and Ethnicity in Minority Sociolinguistic Perspective* (pp. 564–579). Clevedon, England: Multilingual Matters (original, 1982).

Fishman, J. (1989e). Language, ethnicity and racism. In J. Fishman, *Language and Ethnicity in Minority Sociolinguistic Perspective* (pp. 9–22). Clevedon, England: Multilingual Matters (original, 1977).

Fishman, J. (1991). *Reversing Language Shift: Theoretical and Empirical Foundations of Assistance to Threatened Languages*. Clevedon, England: Multilingual Matters.

Fishman, J. (1992). The displaced anxieties of Anglo-Americans. In J. Crawford (ed.), *Language Loyalties: A Source Book on the Official English Controversy* (pp. 165–170). Chicago, IL: University of Chicago Press.

Fishman, J. (1995a). Good conferences in a wicked world: on some worrisome problems in the study of language maintenance and language shift. In W. Fase, K. Jaspaert and S. Kroon (eds.), *The State of Minority Languages: International Perspectives on Survival and Decline*. Lisse, Netherlands: Swets and Zeitlinger.

Fishman, J. (1995b). On the limits of ethnolinguistic democracy. In T. Skutnabb-Kangas and R. Phillipson (eds.), *Linguistic Human Rights: Overcoming Linguistic Discrimination* (pp. 49–61). Berlin: Mouton de Gruyter.

Fishman, J. (1997). Language and ethnicity: the view from within. In F. Coulmas (ed.), *The Handbook of Sociolinguistics* (pp. 327–343). London: Blackwell.

Fishman, J. (ed.) (1999). *Handbook of Language and Ethnic Identity*. Oxford: Oxford University Press.

Fishman, J., and Solano, F. (1989). Cross polity perspective on the importance of linguistic heterogeneity as a 'contributing factor' in civil strife. In J. Fishman, *Language and Ethnicity in Minority Sociolinguistic Perspective* (pp. 605–626). Clevedon, England: Multilingual Matters.

Flaitz, J. (1988). *The Ideology of English: French Perceptions of English as a World Language*. Berlin: Mouton de Gruyter.

Fleras, A. (1994). Multiculturalism as society-building. Blending what is workable, necessary and fair. In M. Charleton and P. Baker (eds.), *Cross-Currents: Contemporary Political Issues* (pp. 26–42). Scarborough, Canada: Nelson.

Fleras, A., and Elliot, J. (1991). *Multiculturalism in Canada: The Challenge of Diversity*. Toronto: Nelson.

Fleras, A., and Spoonley, A. (1999). *Recalling Aotearoa: Indigenous Politics and Ethnic Relations in New Zealand*. Auckland, New Zealand: Oxford University Press.

Fletcher, D. (1998). Iris Marion Young: the politics of difference, justice and democracy. In A. Carter and G. Stokes (eds.), *Liberal Democracy and its Critics* (pp. 196–215). Cambridge: Polity Press.

Flude, M., and Hammer, M. (eds.). (1990). *The Education Reform Act, 1988: Its Origins and Implications*. London: Falmer Press.

Forbes, H. (1993). Canada: from bilingualism to multiculturalism. In L. Diamond and M. Plattner (eds.), *Nationalism, Ethnic Conflict and Democracy* (pp. 86–101). Baltimore, MA: Johns Hopkins Press.

Freeman, R. (1998). *Bilingual Education and Social Change*. Clevedon, England: Multilingual Matters.

Friedman, J. (1997). Global crises, the struggle for identity and intellectual porkbarrelling: cosmopolitans versus locals, ethnics and nationals in an era of de-hegemonisation. In P. Werbner and T. Modood (eds.), *Debating Cultural Hybridity: Multicultural Identities and the Politics of Antiracism* (pp. 70–89). London: Zed Books.

Frost, G. (ed.) (1997). *Loyalty Misplaced: Misdirected Virtue and Social Disintegration*. London: The Social Affairs Unit.

Fuchs, E., and Havighurst, R. (1972). *To Live on this Earth: American Indian Education*. Garden City, NJ: Anchor Books.

Furnivall, J. (1948). *Colonial Policy and Practice: A Comparative Study of Burma and Netherlands India*. Cambridge: Cambridge University Press.

Gans, H. (1979). Symbolic ethnicity: the future of ethnic groups and cultures in America. *Ethnic and Racial Studies* 2, 1–20.

Garcia, O. (1995). Spanish language loss as a determinant of income among Latinos in the United States: implications for language policies in schools. In J. Tollefson (ed.), *Power and Inequality in Language Education* (pp. 142–160). Cambridge: Cambridge University Press.

Geertz, C. (1963). The integrative revolution: primordial sentiments and civil politics in new states. In C. Geertz (ed.), *Old Societies and New States: The Quest for Modernity in Asia and Africa* (pp. 105–157). New York: Free Press.

Geertz, C. (1973). *The Interpretation of Cultures*. New York: Basic Books.

Gellner, E. (1964). *Thought and Change*. London: Weidenfeld and Nicholson.

Gellner, E. (1983). *Nations and Nationalism: New Perspectives on the Past*. Oxford: Basil Blackwell.

Gellner, E. (1987). *Culture, Identity and Politics*. Cambridge: Cambridge University Press.

Gellner, E. (1993). Nationalism. In W. Outhwaite and T. Bottomore (eds.), *Blackwell Dictionary of Twentieth-Century Social Thought* (pp. 409–411). Oxford: Basil Blackwell.

Gellner, E. (1994). *Conditions of Liberty: Civil Society and its Rivals*. London: Hamish Hamilton.

Gellner, E. (1996). Reply to my critics. In J. Hall and I. Jarvie (eds.), *The Social Philosophy of Ernest Gellner* (pp. 625–687). Amsterdam: Rodopi.

Gellner, E. (1997). *Nationalism*. London: Weidenfeld and Nicolson.

Genesee, F. (1987). *Learning through Two Languages: Studies of Immersion and Bilingual Education*. Cambridge, MA: Newbury House.

Gibson, M., and Ogbu, J. (eds.) (1991). *Minority Status and Schooling: A Comparative Study of Immigrant and Involuntary Minorities*. New York: Garland Publishing.

Giddens, A. (1984). *The Nation State and Violence*. Berkeley, CA: University of California Press.

Gilbert, R. (1987). The concept of social practice and modes of ideology critique in schools. *Discourse* 7, 37–54.

Giles, H., Bourhis, R., and Taylor, D. (1977). Towards a theory of language in ethnic group relations. In H. Giles (ed.), *Language, Ethnicity and Intergroup Relations* (pp. 307–348). London: Academic Press.

Gillborn, D. (1995). *Racism and Antiracism in Real Schools*. Buckingham, England: Open University Press.

Gilroy, P. (1987). *There Ain't No Black in the Union Jack*. London: Hutchinson.

Gilroy, P. (1990). One nation under a groove: the cultural politics of 'race' and racism in Britain. In D. Goldberg (ed.), *Anatomy of Racism* (pp. 263–282). Minneapolis, MN: University of Minnesota Press.

Gilroy, P. (1993a). *Small Acts: Thoughts on the Politics of Black Cultures*. London: Serpent's Tail.

Gilroy, P. (1993b). *The Black Atlantic: Modernity and Double Consciousness*. London: Verso.

Giner, S. (1984). *Social Structure of Catalonia*. London: Anglo-Catalan Society.

Giroux, H. (1992). *Border Crossings*. London: Routledge.

Giroux, H. (1997). *Pedagogy and the Politics of Hope: Theory, Culture and Schooling*. Boulder, CO: Westview Press.

Glazer, N. (1975). *Affirmative Discrimination: Ethnic Inequality and Public Policy*. New York: Basic Books.

Glazer, N. (1983). *Ethnic Dilemmas: 1964–1982*. Cambridge, MA: Harvard University Press.

Glazer, N. (1997). *We Are All Multiculturalists Now*. Cambridge, MA: Harvard University Press.

Glazer, N., and Moynihan, D. (1975). *Ethnicity: Theory and Experience*. Cambridge, MA: Harvard University Press.

Gleason, P. (1984). Pluralism and assimilation: a conceptual history. In J. Edwards (ed.), *Linguistic Minorities, Policies and Pluralism* (pp. 221–257). London: Academic Press.

Glenny, M. (1996). *The Fall of Yugoslavia: The Third Balkan War* (3rd edn). London: Penguin.

Goldberg, D. (1993). *Racist Culture: Philosophy and the Politics of Meaning*. Cambridge, MA: Blackwell.

Goldberg, D. (1994). Introduction: multicultural conditions. In D. Goldberg (ed.), *Multiculturalism: A Critical Reader* (pp. 1–41). Cambridge, MA: Blackwell.

Gordon, M. (1978). *Human Nature, Class and Ethnicity*. New York: Oxford University Press.

Gordon, M. (1981). Models of pluralism: the new American dilemma. *Annals of the American Academy of Political and Social Science* 454, 178–188.

Gorlach, M. (1986). Comment. *International Journal of the Sociology of Language* 60, 97–103.

Goulbourne, H. (1991a). *Ethnicity and Nationalism in Post-Imperial Britain*. Cambridge: Cambridge University Press.

Goulbourne, H. (1991b). Varieties of pluralism: the notion of a post-imperial Britain. *New Community* 17, 211–227.

Gould, S. (1981). *The Mismeasure of Man*. London: Penguin.

Graddol, D., Leith, D., and Swann, J. (eds.) (1996). *English History, Diversity and Change*. London: Routledge.

Gramsci, A. (1971). *Selections from the Prison Notebooks*. Q. Hoare and G. Nowell-Smith (eds.). London: Lawrence and Wishart.

Grant, N. (1997). Democracy and cultural pluralism: towards the 21st century. In R. Watts and J. Smolicz (eds.), *Cultural Democracy and Ethnic Pluralism: Multicultural and Multilingual Policies in Education* (pp. 25–50). Frankfurt: Peter Lang.

Grau, R. (1992). Le statut juridique des droits linguistiques en France. In H. Giordan (ed.), *Les Minorités en Europe* (pp. 93–112). Paris: Editions Kimé.

Greenfeld, L. (1992). *Nationalism: Five Roads to Modernity*. Cambridge, MA: Harvard University Press.

Greenland, H. (1991). Maori ethnicity as ideology. In P. Spoonley, D. Pearson and C. Macpherson (eds.), *Nga Take: Ethnic Relations and Racism in Aotearoa / New Zealand* (pp. 90–107). Palmerston North, New Zealand: Dunmore Press.

Grenoble, L., and Whaley, L. (1996). Endangered languages: current issues and future prospects. *International Journal of the Sociology of Language* 118, 209–223.

Grenoble, L., and Whaley, L. (eds.) (1998). *Endangered Languages: Language Loss and Community Response*. Cambridge: Cambridge University Press.

Griffith, W. (1950). *The Welsh*. Harmondsworth: Penguin.

Grillo, R. (1989). *Dominant Languages: Language and Hierarchy in Britain and France*. Cambridge: Cambridge University Press.

Grimes, B. (ed.) (1996). *Ethnologue: Languages of the world* (13th edn). Dallas, TX: SIL.

Grin, F. (1995). Combining immigrant and autochthonous language rights: a territorial approach to multilingualism. In T. Skutnabb-Kangas and R. Phillipson (eds.), *Linguistic Human Rights: Overcoming Linguistic Discrimination* (pp. 31–48). Berlin: Mouton de Gruyter.

Grin, F. (1999). *Language Policy in Multilingual Switzerland: Overview and Recent Developments.* Flensburg, Germany: European Centre for Minority Issues.

Grosjean, F. (1982). *Life with Two Languages: An Introduction to Bilingualism.* Cambridge, MA: Harvard University Press.

Grugel, J., and Rees, T. (1997). *Franco's Spain.* London: Arnold.

Guibernau, M. (1996). *Nationalisms: The Nation-State and Nationalism in the Twentieth Century.* Cambridge: Polity Press.

Guibernau, M. (1997). Images of Catalonia. *Nations and Nationalism* 3, 89–111.

Guibernau, M. (1999). *Nations without States.* Cambridge: Polity Press.

Gurr, T. (1993). *Minorities at Risk: A Global View of Ethnopolitical Conflicts.* Washington DC: United States Institute of Peace Press.

Habermas, J. (1994). Struggles for recognition in the democratic constitutional state. In A. Gutmann (ed.), *Multiculturalism: Examining the Politics of Recognition* (pp. 107–148). Princeton, NJ: Princeton University Press.

Hage, G. (1998). *White Nation: Fantasies of White Supremacy in a Multicultural Society.* Annandale, Australia: Pluto Press.

Hall, J. (1993). Nationalisms: classified and explained. *Daedalus* 122, 3, 1–28.

Hall, S. (1992a). The questions of cultural identity. In S. Hall, D. Held and T. McGrew (eds.), *Modernity and its Futures* (pp. 274–325). Cambridge: Polity Press.

Hall, S. (1992b). New ethnicities. In J. Donald and A. Rattansi (eds.), *'Race', Culture and Difference* (pp. 252–259). London: Sage.

Hall, S., Held, D., and McGrew, T. (eds.) (1992). *Modernity and its Futures.* Cambridge: Polity Press.

Halle, L. (1962). *Men and Nations.* Princeton, NJ: Princeton University Press.

Hamel, R. (1997a). Introduction: linguistic human rights in a sociolinguistic perspective. *International Journal of the Sociology of Language* 127, 1–24.

Hamel, R. (1997b). Language conflict and language shift: a sociolinguistic framework for linguistic human rights. *International Journal of the Sociology of Language* 127, 105–134.

Hamel, R. (1997c). (ed.). Special Issue: Linguistic Human Rights in a Sociolinguistic Perspective. *International Journal of the Sociology of Language* 127.

Hamers, J., and Hummel, K. (1998). Language in Québec: aboriginal and heritage varieties. In J. Edwards (ed.), *Language in Canada* (pp. 385–398). Cambridge: Cambridge University Press.

Handelman, D. (1977). The organization of ethnicity. *Ethnic Groups* 1, 187–200.

Handler, R. (1988). *Nationalism and the Politics of Culture in Quebec.* Madison, WI: Wisconsin University Press.

Hannerz, U. (1992). *Cultural Complexity: Studies in the Organisation of Meaning.* New York: Columbia University Press.

Hanson, A. (1989). The making of Maori: culture invention and its logic. *American Anthropologist* 91, 890–902.

Harker, R. (1980). Research on the education of Maori children. In *Research in Education in New Zealand: The State of the Art* (pp. 42–72). Wellington, New Zealand: New Zealand Association for Research in Education / Delta.

Harker, R. (1984). On reproduction, habitus and education. *British Journal of Sociology of Education* 5, 117–127.

Harker, R. (1990). Bourdieu: education and reproduction. In R. Harker, C. Mahar and C. Wilkes (eds.), *An Introduction to the Work of Pierre Bourdieu: The Practice of Theory* (pp. 86–108). London: Macmillan.

Harker, R., Mahar, C., and Wilkes, C. (eds.) (1990). *An Introduction to the Work of Pierre Bourdieu: The Practice of Theory*. London: Macmillan.

Harker, R., and May, S. (1993). Code and habitus: comparing the accounts of Bernstein and Bourdieu. *British Journal of Sociology of Education* 14, 169–178.

Harker, R., and McConnochie, K. (1985). *Education as Cultural Artifact: Studies in Maori and Aboriginal Education*. Palmerston North, New Zealand: Dunmore Press.

Harley, B. (1993). After immersion: maintaining the momentum. *Journal of Multilingual and Multicultural Development* 15, 229–244.

Harmon, D. (1995). The status of the world's languages as reported in the *Ethnologue*. *Southwest Journal of Linguistics* 14, 1–28.

Harris, R. (1981). *The Language Myth*. London: Duckworth.

Harvey, D. (1989). *The Condition of Postmodernity*. Oxford: Basil Blackwell.

Hastings, W. (1988). *The Right to an Education in Maori: The Case from International Law*. Wellington, New Zealand: Victoria University Press.

Haugen, E. (1966). Dialect, language, nation. *American Anthropologist* 68, 922–935.

Heath, S. (1977). Language and politics in the United States. In M. Saville-Troike (ed.), *Linguistics and Anthropology: Georgetown University Round Table on Language and Linguistics* (pp. 267–296). Washington DC: Georgetown University Press.

Heath, S. (1981). English in our language heritage. In C. Ferguson and S. Heath (eds.), *Language in the USA* (pp. 6–20). Cambridge: Cambridge University Press.

Hechter, M. (1975). *Internal Colonialism: The Celtic Fringe in British National Development, 1536–1966*. London: Routledge and Kegan Paul.

Hechter, M. (1986). Rational choice theory and the study of race and ethnic relations. In J. Rex and D. Mason (eds.), *Theories of Race and Race Relations* (pp. 264–279). Cambridge: Cambridge University Press.

Hechter, M. (1987). *Principles of Group Solidarity*. Berkeley, CA: University of California Press.

Hechter, M., Friedman, D., and Appelbaum, M. (1982). A theory of ethnic collective action. *International Migration Review* 16, 412–434.

Held, D. (1995). *Democracy and the Global Order: From the Modern State to Cosmopolitan Governance*. Cambridge: Polity Press.

Heller, M. (1987). The role of language in the formation of ethnic identity. In J. Phinney and M. Rotheram (eds.), *Children's Ethnic Socialisation: Pluralism and Development* (pp. 180–200). Newbury Park, CA: Sage.

Heller, M. (1999). Heated language in a cold climate. In J. Blommaert (ed.), *Language Ideological Debates* (pp. 143–170). Berlin: Mouton de Gruyter.

Henley, J. (1999). Chirac defends pure French tongue against regional Tower of Babel. *The Observer* (27 June 1999), 25.

Henze, R., and Davis, K. (1999). Special Issue: Authenticity and identity: lessons from indigenous language education. *Anthropology and Education Quarterly* 30 (1).

Héran, F. (1993). L'unification linguistique de la France. *Population et Sociétés* 285, 1–4.

Herder, J. (1969). *On Social and Political Culture*. F. Barnard (ed.). Cambridge: Cambridge University Press.

Hernández-Chávez, E. (1995). Language policy in the United States: a history of cultural genocide. In T. Skutnabb-Kangas and R. Phillipson (eds.), *Linguistic Human Rights: Overcoming Linguistic Discrimination* (pp. 141–158). Berlin: Mouton de Gruyter.

Herriman, M. (1996). Language policy in Australia. In M. Herriman and B. Burnaby (eds.), *Language Policies in English-Dominant Countries* (pp. 35–61). Clevedon, England: Multilingual Matters.

Heugh, K. (1997). Disabling and enabling: implications of language policy in South Africa. In R. Watts and J. Smolicz (eds.), *Cultural Democracy and Ethnic Pluralism: Multicultural and Multilingual Policies in Education* (pp. 243–270). Frankfurt: Peter Lang.

Heugh, K. (2000). Giving good weight to multilingualism in South Africa. In R. Phillipson (ed.), *Rights to Language. Equity, Power and Education* (pp. 234–238). Mahwah, NJ: Lawrence Erlbaum.

Heugh, K., Siegrühn, A., and Plüddermann, P. (eds.) (1995). *Multilingual Education for South Africa*. Johannesburg: Heinemann.

Higham, J. (1963). *Strangers in the Land: Patterns of American Nativism, 1860–1925*. New York: Atheneum.

Hill, J. (1978). Language death, language contact, and language evolution. In W. McCormack and S. Wurm (eds.), *Approaches to Language: Anthropological Issues* (pp. 45–78). The Hague: Mouton.

Hill, R. (1995). Blackfellas and whitefellas: Aboriginal land rights, the Mabo Decision, and the meaning of land. *Human Rights Quarterly* 17, 303–322.

Hindley R. (1990). *The Death of the Irish Language: A Qualified Obituary*. London: Routledge.

Hinsley, F. (1986). *Sovereignty*. Cambridge: Cambridge University Press.

Hirsch, E. (1987). *Cultural Literacy: What Every American Needs to Know*. Boston, MA: Houghton Mifflin.

Hirsh, W. (1990). *A Report on Issues and Factors Relating to Maori Achievement in the Education System*. Wellington, New Zealand: Ministry of Education.

Hobhouse, L. (1928). *Social Evolution and Political Theory*. New York: Columbia University Press.

Hobsbawm, E. (1990). *Nations and Nationalism since 1780*. Cambridge: Cambridge University Press.

Hobsbawm, E. (1992). Ethnicity and nationalism in Europe today. *Anthropology Today* 8, 3–8.

Hobsbawm, E., and Ranger, T. (eds.) (1983). *The Invention of Tradition*. Cambridge: Cambridge University Press.

Hoffman, E. (1989). *Lost in Translation: A Life in a New Language*. New York: E. P. Dutton.

Hoffmann, C. (1999). Language autonomy and national identity in Catalonia. In D. Smith and S. Wright (eds.), *Whose Europe? The Turn towards Democracy* (pp. 82–78). Oxford: Blackwell / Sociological Review.

Holborow, M. (1999). *The Politics of English: A Marxist View of Language*. London: Sage.

Hollings, M., Jeffries, R., and McArdell, P. (1992). *Assessment in Kura Kaupapa Māori and Māori Language Immersion Programmes: A Report to the Ministry of Education.* Wellington, New Zealand: Ministry of Education.

Honeyford, R. (1988). *Integration or Disintegration? Towards a Non-Racist Society.* London: The Claridge Press.

Honneth, A. (1995). *The Struggle for Recognition.* Cambridge: Polity Press.

Hornberger, N. (1997). Literacy, language maintenance, and linguistic human rights: three telling cases. *International Journal of the Sociology of Language* 127, 87–103.

Hornberger, N. (1998). Language policy, language education, language rights: indigenous, immigrant, and international perspectives. *Language in Society* 27, 439–458.

Hornberger, N., and King, K. (1999). Authenticity and unification in Quechua language planning. In S. May (ed.), *Indigenous Community-Based Education* (pp. 160–180). Clevedon, England: Multilingual Matters.

Horowitz, D. (1985). *Ethnic Groups in Conflict.* Berkeley, CA: University of California Press.

Howe, K. (1992). Liberal democracy, equal opportunity, and the challenge of multiculturalism. *American Educational Research Journal* 29, 455–470.

Howe, S. (1998). *Afrocentrism: Mythical Pasts and Imagined Homes.* London: Verso.

Hroch, M. (1985). *Social Preconditions of National Revival in Europe.* Cambridge: Cambridge University Press.

Hroch, M. (1993). From national movement to the fully-formed nation: the nation-building process in Europe. *New Left Review* 198, 3–20.

Hroch, M. (1998). Real and constructed: the nature of the nation. In J. Hall (ed.), *The State of the Nation: Ernest Gellner and the Theory of Nationalism* (pp. 91–106). Cambridge: Cambridge University Press.

Huddy, L., and Sears, J. (1990). Qualified public support for bilingual education: some policy implications. *Annals of the American Academy of Political and Social Science* 505 (March), 119–134.

Hughes, R. (1993). *Culture of Complaint: The Fraying of America.* New York: Oxford University Press.

Humboldt, W. von (1988) *On Language: The Diversity of Human Language Structure and its Influence on the Mental Development of Mankind.* P. Heath (trans.). Cambridge: Cambridge University Press (original, 1836).

Hunn, J. (1961). *Report on the Department of Māori Affairs.* Wellington, New Zealand: Government Printer.

Huss, L. (1999). *Reversing Language Shift in the Far North: Linguistic Revitalization in Northern Scandinavia and Finland.* Uppsala, Sweden: Acta Universitatis Upsaliensis.

Hutchinson, J. (1987). *The Dynamics of Cultural Nationalism: The Gaelic Revival and the Creation of the Irish Nation State.* London: Allen and Unwin.

Hutchinson, J. (1994). *Modern Nationalism.* London: Fontana.

Ignace, M., and Ignace, R. (1998). 'The old wolf in sheep's clothing'. Canadian Aboriginal peoples and multiculturalism. In D. Haselbach (ed.), *Multiculturalism in a World of Leaking Boundaries* (pp. 101–132). New Brunswick, NJ: Transaction Publishers.

Imhoff, G. (1987). Partisans of language. *English Today* 11, 37–40.

Imhoff, G. (1990). The position of US English on bilingual education. *Annals of the American Academy of Political and Social Science* 505 (March), 48–61.

Irwin, K. (1989). Multicultural education: the New Zealand response. *New Zealand Journal of Educational Studies* 24, 3–18.

Irwin, K. (1990). The politics of Kōhanga Reo. In S. Middleton, J. Codd and A. Jones (eds.), *New Zealand Education Policy Today: Critical Perspectives* (pp. 110–120). Wellington, New Zealand: Allen and Unwin.

Isaacs, H. (1975). *Idols of the Tribe: Group Identity and Political Change*. New York: Harper and Row.

Isajiw, W. (1980). Definitions of ethnicity. In J. Goldstein and R. Bienvenue (eds.), *Ethnicity and Ethnic Relations in Canada* (pp. 5–17). Toronto: Butterworth.

Jacques, K. (1991). Community contexts of Māori–English bilingual education: a study of six South Island primary school programmes. Unpublished PhD thesis, University of Canterbury.

Jaimes, M., and Churchill, W. (1988). Behind the rhetoric: 'English Only' as counterinsurgency warfare. *Issues in Radical Therapy* 13, 1–2: 42–50.

Jakšić, B. (ed.) (1995). *Interkulturalnost/Interculturality*. Beograd: Savo Bjelajac.

James, P. (1996). *Nation Formation: Towards a Theory of Abstract Community*. London: Sage.

Jamieson, F. (1991). *Postmodernism, or the Cultural Logic of Late Capitalism*. London: Sage.

Janulf, P. (1998). *Kommer Finskan i Sverige att Fortleva?* Stockholm, Sweden: Almqvist and Wiksell.

Jarden, K. (1992). Education: making a Maori underclass. *Race, Gender, Class* 13, 20–25.

Jenkins, P. (1992). *A History of Modern Wales, 1536–1990*. London: Longman.

Jenkins, R. (1986). Social anthropological models of inter-ethnic relations. In J. Rex and D. Mason (eds.), *Theories of Race and Race Relations* (pp. 170–186). Cambridge: Cambridge University Press.

Jenkins, R. (1991). Violence, language and politics: nationalism in Northern Ireland and Wales. *North Atlantic Studies* 3, 31–40.

Jenkins, R. (1992). *Pierre Bourdieu*. London: Routledge.

Jenkins, R. (1994). Rethinking ethnicity: identity, categorization and power. *Ethnic and Racial Studies* 17, 197–223.

Jenkins, R. (1995). Nations and nationalisms: towards more open models. *Nations and Nationalism* 1, 369–390.

Jenkins, R. (1996). 'Us' and 'them': ethnicity, racism and ideology. In R. Barot (ed.), *The Racism Problematic: Contemporary Sociological Debates on Race and Ethnicity* (pp. 69–88). Lampeter, Wales: Edward Mellen Press.

Jenkins, R. (1997). *Rethinking Ethnicity: Arguments and Explorations*. London: Sage.

Jespersen, O. (1968). *Growth and Structure of the English Language*. Toronto: Collier-Macmillan (original, 1938).

Johnson, D. (1993). The making of the French nation. In M. Teich and R. Porter (eds.), *The National Question in Europe in Historical Context* (pp. 35–62). Cambridge: Cambridge University Press.

Jones, B. and Keating, M. (eds.) (1995). *The European Union and the Regions*. Oxford: Clarendon Press.

Jones, G. (1997). *The Education of a Nation*. Cardiff: University of Wales Press.

Joseph, J. (1996). English in Hong Kong: emergence and decline. *Current Issues in Language and Society* 3, 166–179.

Joy, R. (1992). *Canada's Official Languages: The Progress of Bilingualism*. Toronto: University of Toronto Press.

Juteau, D. (1996). Theorising ethnicity and ethnic communalisms at the margins: from Québec to the world system. *Nations and Nationalism* 2, 45–66.

Kā'ai, T. (1990). Te hiranga taketake: mai i te Kōhanga Reo ki te kura. Māori pedagogy: te Kōhanga Reo and the transition to school. Unpublished MPhil thesis, University of Auckland.

Kachru, B. (ed.) (1982). *The Other Tongue: English across Cultures*. Urbana, IL: University of Illinois Press.

Kachru, B. (1986). *The Alchemy of English: The Spread, Functions and Models of Non-Native Englishes*. Oxford: Pergamon Press.

Kachru, B. (1990). World Englishes and applied linguistics. *World Englishes* 9, 3–20.

Kachru, B., and Nelson, C. (1996). World Englishes. In S. McKay and N. Hornberger (eds.), *Sociolinguistics and Language Teaching* (pp. 71–102). Cambridge: Cambridge University Press.

Kalantzis, M., and Cope, B. (1999). Multicultural education: transforming the mainstream. In S. May (ed.), *Critical Multiculturalism: Rethinking Multicultural and Antiracist Education* (pp. 245–276). London and New York: RoutledgeFalmer.

Kamboureli, S. (1998). The technology of ethnicity: Canadian multiculturalism and the language of the law. In D. Bennett (ed.), *Multicultural States: Rethinking Difference and Identity* (pp. 208–222). London: Routledge.

Kane, J. (1997). From ethnic exclusion to ethnic diversity: the Australian path to multiculturalism. In I. Shapiro and W. Kymlicka (eds.), *Ethnicity and Group Rights* (pp. 540–571). New York: New York University Press.

Kanpol, B., and McLaren, P. (1995). *Critical Multiculturalism: Uncommon Voices in a Common Struggle*. Westport, CT: Bergin and Garvey.

Kawharu, I. (ed.) (1989). *Waitangi: Maori and Pakeha Perspectives of the Treaty of Waitangi*. Auckland, New Zealand: Oxford University Press.

Kay, G. (1993). Ethnicity, the cosmos and economic development, with special reference to Central Africa. Mimeo.

Kearney, H. (1989). *The British Isles: A History of Four Nations*. Cambridge: Cambridge University Press.

Keating, M. (1996). *Nations against the State: The New Politics of Nationalism in Québec, Catalonia and Scotland*. London: Macmillan Press.

Keating, M. (1997). Stateless nation-building: Quebec, Catalonia and Scotland in the changing state system. *Nations and Nationalism* 3, 689–717.

Keating, M., and Hooghe, L. (1996). Bypassing the nation-state? Regions and the EU policy process. In J. Richardson (ed.), *European Union: Power and Policy* (pp. 216–229). London: Routledge.

Keating, M., and Jones, B. (1995) Nations, regions, and Europe: the UK experience. In B. Jones and M. Keating (eds.), *The European Union and the Regions* (pp. 89–113). Oxford: Clarendon Press.

Kedourie, E. (1960). *Nationalism*. London: Hutchinson.

Keegan, P. (1996). *The Benefits of Immersion Education: A Review of the New Zealand and Overseas Literature*. Wellington, New Zealand: New Zealand Council for Educational Research.

Kellas, J. (1991). *The Politics of Nationalism and Identity*. London: Macmillan.

Khleif, B. (1979). Insiders, outsiders and renegades: towards a classification of ethnolinguistic labels. In H. Giles and B. Saint-Jacques (eds.), *Language and Ethnic Relations* (pp. 159–172). Oxford: Pergamon Press.

Kincheloe, J., and Steinberg, S. (1997). *Changing Multiculturalism*. Buckingham, England: Open University Press.

Kingsbury, B. (1989). The Treaty of Waitangi: some international law aspects. In I. Kawharu (ed.), *Waitangi: Maori and Pakeha Perspectives of the Treaty of Waitangi* (pp. 121–157). Auckland, New Zealand: Oxford University Press.

Kirisci, K., and Winrow, G. (1997). *The Kurdish Question and Turkey: An Example of a Trans-state Ethnic Conflict*. London: Frank Cass.

Kivosto, P. (ed.) (1989). *The Ethnic Enigma: The Salience of Ethnicity for European-Origin Groups*. Philadelphia, PA: The Balch Institute Press.

Kloss, H. (1971). The language rights of immigrant groups. *International Migration Review* 5, 250–268.

Kloss, H. (1977). *The American Bilingual Tradition*. Rowley, MA: Newbury House.

Kohn, H. (1961). *The Idea of Nationalism: A Study in its Origins and Background*. New York: Macmillan.

Kohn, M. (1995). *The Race Gallery: The Return of Racial Science*. London: Jonathan Cape.

Kontra, M., Skutnabb-Kangas, T., Phillipson, R., and Várady, T. (eds.) (1999). *Language: A Right and a Resource. Approaches to Linguistic Human Rights*. Budapest: Central European University Press.

Kozol, J. (1991). *Savage Inequalities: Children in America's Schools*. New York: Harper Perennial.

Krashen, S. (1996). *Under Attack: The Case against Bilingual Education*. Culver City, CA: Language Education Associates.

Krashen, S. (1999). *Condemned without Trial: Bogus Arguments against Bilingual Education*. Portsmouth, NH: Heinemann.

Krauss, M. (1992). The world's languages in crisis. *Language* 68, 4–10.

Krauss, M. (1995). Language loss in Alaska, the United States and the world. Frame of reference. *Alaska Humanities Forum* 6 (1), 2–5.

Kymlicka, W. (1989). *Liberalism, Community and Culture*. Oxford: Clarendon Press.

Kymlicka, W. (1995a). *Multicultural Citizenship: A Liberal Theory of Minority Rights*. Oxford: Clarendon Press.

Kymlicka, W. (1995b). Introduction. In W. Kymlicka (ed.), *The Rights of Minority Cultures* (pp. 1–27). Oxford: Oxford University Press.

Kymlicka, W. (1998). *Finding Our Way: Rethinking Ethnocultural Relations in Canada*. Toronto: Oxford University Press.

Kymlicka, W. (1999a). Response to Okin. In J. Cohen, M. Howard and M. Nussbaum (eds.), *Is Multiculturalism Bad for Women?* (pp. 31–34). Princeton, NJ: Princeton University Press.

Kymlicka, W. (1999b). Comments on Shachar and Spinner-Halev: an update from the multiculturalism wars. In C. Joppke and S. Lukes (eds.), *Multicultural Questions* (pp. 112–129). Oxford: Oxford University Press.

Kymlicka, W. (1999c). Theorizing indigenous rights. *University of Toronto Law Journal* 49, 281–293.

Labrie, N. (1993). *La Construction de la Communauté Européenne*. Paris: Honoré Champion.

Laitin, D. (1998). Nationalism and language: a post-Soviet perspective. In J. Hall (ed.), *The State of the Nation: Ernest Gellner and the Theory of Nationalism* (pp. 135–157). Cambridge: Cambridge University Press.

Lamy, M.-N. (1996). Franglais. In D. Graddol, D. Leith and J. Swann (eds.), *English History, Diversity and Change* (pp. 32–36). London: Routledge.

Lamy, S. (1986). Policy responses to ethnonationalism: consociational engineering in Belgium. In J. Stack (ed.), *The Primordial Challenge: Ethnicity in the Contemporary World* (pp. 115–137). Westport, CT: Greenwood Press.

Language Plan Task Group (LANGTAG) (1996). *Towards a Language Plan for South Africa*. Pretoria: Ministry of Arts, Culture, Science and Technology.

Lantolf, J. (1996). SLA theory building: 'letting all the flowers bloom!'. *Language Learning* 46, 713–749.

Larner, W. (1996). Gender and ethnicity: theorising 'difference' in Aotearoa / New Zealand. In P. Spoonley, C. Macpherson and D. Pearson (eds.). *Nga Pātai: Racism and Ethnic Relations in Aotearoa / New Zealand*. Palmerston North, New Zealand: Dunmore Press.

Larner, W., and Spoonley, P. (1995). Post-colonial politics in Aotearoa / New Zealand. In D. Stasiulus and N. Yuval-Davis (eds.), *Unsettling Settler Societies* (pp. 39–64). London: Sage.

Leap, W. (1981). American Indian languages. In C. Ferguson and S. Heath (eds.), *Language in the USA* (pp.116–144). Cambridge: Cambridge University Press.

Leibowitz, A. (1969). English literacy: legal sanction and discrimination. *Notre Dame Lawyer* 45, 7–66.

Leith, D., and Graddol, D. (1996). Modernity and English as a national language. In D. Graddol, D. Leith and J. Swann (eds.), *English History, Diversity and Change* (pp. 136–179). London: Routledge.

Lemco, J. (1992). Quebec's 'distinctive character' and the question of minority rights. In J. Crawford (ed.), *Language Loyalties: A Source Book on the Official English Controversy* (pp. 423–433). Chicago, IL: University of Chicago Press.

Levine, H. (1999). Reconstructing ethnicity. *Journal of the Royal Anthropological Institute* 5, 165–180.

Lévi Strauss, C. (1994). Anthropology, race, and politics: a conversation with Didier Eribon. In R. Borofsky (ed.), *Assessing Cultural Anthropology* (pp. 420–429). New York: McGraw Hill.

Lieberson, S. (1985). Unhyphenated whites in the United States. *Ethnic and Racial Studies* 8, 159–180.

Lind, M. (1995). *The Next American Nation*. New York: Free Press.

Lingard, B., Knight, J., and Porter, P. (eds.) (1993). *Schooling Reform for Hard Times*. London: Falmer Press.

Little, D. (1994). *Sri Lanka: The Invention of Enmity*. Washington DC: United States Institute of Peace Press.

Lo Bianco, J. (1987). *National Policy on Languages*. Canberra, Australia: Australian Government Publishing Service.

Lodge, R. (1993). *French: From Dialect to Standard*. London: Routledge.

Louarn, T. (1998). Poignant Report on the regional languages and culture of France delivered to Jospin. *Contact Bulletin* 15, 1, 4–5, November.

Lukes, S. (1996). Humiliation and the politics of identity. *Social Research* 64, 36–51.

Lyon, J., and Ellis, N. (1991). Parental attitudes towards the Welsh language. *Journal of Multilingual and Multicultural Development*, 12, 239–251.

Lyotard, J. (1984). *The Postmodern Condition: A Report on Knowledge*. G. Bennington and B. Massumi (trans.). Manchester: Manchester University Press.

Macedo, D. (1994). *Literacies of Power: What Americans Are not Allowed to Know.* Boulder, CO: Westview Press.

Macías, R. (1979). Language choice and human rights in the United States. In J. Alatis and G. Tucker (eds.), *Language in Public Life: Georgetown University Round Table on Language and Linguistics* (pp. 86–101). Washington, DC: Georgetown University Press.

MacKaye, S. (1990). California Proposition 63: language attitudes reflected in the public debate. *Annals of the American Academy of Political and Social Science* 505 (March), 135–146.

Mackey, W. (1991). Language diversity, language policy and the sovereign state. *History of European Ideas* 13, 51–61.

MacLachlan, C. (1988). *Spain's Empire in the New World: The Role of Ideas in Institutional and Social Change*. Berkeley, CA: University of California Press.

Maffi, L. (ed.) (2000). *Language, Knowledge and the Environment: The Interdependence of Biological and Cultural Diversity*. Washington, DC: Smithsonian Institute Press.

Magga, O. (1995). The Sámi Language Act. In T. Skutnabb-Kangas and R. Phillipson (eds.), *Linguistic Human Rights: Overcoming Linguistic Discrimination* (pp. 219–233). Berlin: Mouton de Gruyter.

Magga, O. (1996). Sámi past and present and the Sámi picture of the world. In E. Helander (ed.), *Awakened Voice: The Return of Sámi knowledge* (pp. 74–80). Kautokeino, Norway: Nordic Sámi Institute.

Magnet, J. (1990). Canadian perspectives on Official English. In K. Adams and D. Brink (eds.), *Perspectives on Official English: The Campaign for English as the Official Language of the USA* (pp. 53–61). Berlin: Mouton de Gruyter.

Magnet, J. (1995). *Official Language of Canada: Perspectives from Law, Policy and the Future*. Cowansville, Québec: Editions Yvon Blais.

Mallea, J. (1989). *Schooling in Plural Canada*. Clevedon, England: Multilingual Matters.

Manatū Māori. (1991). *Māori and Work: The Position of Māori in the New Zealand Labour Market*. Wellington, New Zealand: Economic Development Unit, Manatū Māori.

Mare, G. (1993). *Ethnicity and Politics in South Africa*. London: Zed Books.

Margalit, A., and Raz, J. (1995). National self-determination. In W. Kymlicka (ed.), *The Rights of Minority Cultures* (pp. 79–92). Oxford: Oxford University Press.

Marshall, D. (1986). The question of an official language: language rights and the English Language Amendment. *International Journal of the Sociology of Language* 60, 7–75.

Marshall, D., and Gonzalez, R. (1990). Una lingua, una patria? Is monolingualism beneficial or harmful to a nation's unity? In K. Adams and D. Brink (eds.), *Perspectives on Official English: The Campaign for English as the Official Language of the USA* (pp. 29–51). Berlin: Mouton de Gruyter.

Marx, K., and Engels, F. (1976a). *Marx and Engels Collected Works*. London: Lawrence and Wishart.

Marx, K., and Engels, F. (1976b). *Basic Writings on Politics and Philosophy*. L. Feuer (ed.). Glasgow: Collins.

Maurais, J. (ed.) (1996). *Québec's Aboriginal Languages: History, Planning, Development.* Clevedon, England: Multilingual Matters.

Maurais, J. (1997). Regional majority languages, language planning, and linguistic rights. *International Journal of the Sociology of Language* 127, 135–160.

Maxwell, A. (1998). Ethnicity and education: biculturalism in New Zealand. In D. Bennett (ed.), *Multicultural States: Rethinking Difference and Identity* (pp. 195–207). London: Routledge.

May, S. (1994a). *Making Multicultural Education Work.* Clevedon, England: Multilingual Matters.

May, S. (1994b). The case for antiracist education. *British Journal of the Sociology of Education* 15, 421–428.

May, S. (1995). Deconstructing traditional discourses of schooling: an example of school reform. *Language and Education* 9, 1–29.

May, S. (1997a). Critical ethnography. In N. Hornberger and D. Corson (eds.), *Research Methods and Education. The Encyclopedia of Language and Education* Vol. 8 (pp. 197–206). Dordrecht, Netherlands: Kluwer.

May, S. (1997b). Indigenous language rights and education. In J. Lynch, C. Modgil and S. Modgil (eds.), *Education and Development: Tradition and Innovation* Vol. 1 (pp. 149–171). London: Cassell.

May, S. (1998). Just how safe is Australia's multilingual language policy? In S. Wright and H. Kelly-Holmes (eds.), *Managing Language Diversity* (pp. 54–57). Clevedon, England: Multilingual Matters.

May, S. (1999a). Critical multiculturalism and cultural difference: avoiding essentialism. In S. May (ed.), *Critical Multiculturalism: Rethinking Multicultural and Antiracist Education* (pp. 11–41). London and New York: RoutledgeFalmer.

May, S. (ed.) (1999b). *Critical Multiculturalism: Rethinking Multicultural and Antiracist Education.* London and New York: RoutledgeFalmer.

May, S. (1999c). Language and education rights for indigenous peoples. In S. May (ed.), *Indigenous Community-Based Education* (pp. 42–66). Clevedon, England: Multilingual Matters.

May, S. (ed.) (1999d) *Indigenous Community-Based Education.* Clevedon, England: Multilingual Matters.

May, S. (1999e). Extending ethnolinguistic democracy in Europe: the case of Wales. In D. Smith and S. Wright (eds.), *Whose Europe? The Turn towards Democracy* (pp. 142–167). Oxford: Blackwell / Sociological Review.

May, S. (2000). Accommodating and resisting minority language policy: the case of Wales. *International Journal of Bilingual Education and Bilingualism* 3, 2, 101–128.

May, S. (2001). Multiculturalism. In D. Goldberg and J. Solomos (eds.), *The Blackwell Companion to Racial and Ethnic Studies.* Oxford, and Cambridge, MA: Blackwell (in press).

Mayo, P. (1979). *The Roots of Identity: Three National Movements in Contemporary European Politics.* London: Allen Lane.

Mazrui, A. (1975). *The Political Sociology of the English Language: An African Perspective.* The Hague: Mouton.

McCarty, T., and Watahomigie, L. (1999). Indigenous community-based education in the USA. In S. May (ed.), *Indigenous Community-Based Education* (pp. 79–94). Clevedon, England: Multilingual Matters.

McCarty, T., and Zepeda, O. (eds.) (1995). Special Issue: Indigenous language education and literacy. *Bilingual Research Journal* 19 (1).

McCrone, D. (1992). *Understanding Scotland: The Sociology of a Stateless Nation*. London: Routledge.

McCrone, D. (1998). *The Sociology of Nationalism: Tomorrow's Ancestors*. London: Routledge.

McCrum, R., Cran, W., and MacNeil, R. (1986). *The Story of English*. London: Faber and Faber.

McKay, S., and Wong, S. (1988). *Language Diversity: Problem or Resource?* Boston, MA: Heinle and Heinle.

McLaren, P. (1995). *Critical Pedagogy and Predatory Culture*. New York: Routledge.

McLaren, P. (1997). *Revolutionary Multiculturalism: Pedagogies of Dissent for the New Millennium*. Boulder, CO: Westview Press.

McLaren, P., and Torres, R. (1999). Racism and multicultural education: rethinking 'race' and 'whiteness' in late capitalism. In S. May (ed.), *Critical Multiculturalism: Rethinking Multicultural and Antiracist Education* (pp. 42–76). London and New York: RoutledgeFalmer.

McLoughlin, D. (1993). The Maori Burden. *North and South*, November, 60–71.

McQuillan, J., and Tse, L. (1996). Does research matter? An analysis of media opinion on bilingual education 1984–1994. *Bilingual Research Journal* 20, 1–27.

McRoberts, K. (1988). *Quebec: Social Change and Political Crisis* (3rd edn). Toronto: McClelland and Stewart.

McRoberts, K. (1997). *Misconceiving Canada: The Struggle for National Unity*. Toronto: Oxford University Press.

Melucci, A. (1989). *Nomads in the Present*. London: Hutchinson Radius.

Metge, J. (1990). *Te Kōhao o te Ngira: Culture and Learning*. Wellington, New Zealand: Learning Media, Ministry of Education.

Mey, J. (1985). *Whose Language? A Study in Linguistic Pragmatics*. Amsterdam: John Benjamins.

Michelet, J. (1946). *The People*. C. Cooks (trans.). London: Longman (original, 1846).

Miles, R. (1989). *Racism*. London: Routledge.

Miles, R. (1993). *Racism after 'Race Relations'*. London: Routledge.

Miles, R. (1996). Racism and nationalism in the United Kingdom: a view from the periphery. In R. Barot (ed.), *The Racism Problematic: Contemporary Sociological Debates on Race and Ethnicity* (pp. 231–255). Lampeter, Wales: Edward Mellen Press.

Miles, R., and Spoonley, P. (1985). The political economy of labour migration: an alternative to the sociology of 'race' and 'ethnic relations' in New Zealand. *Australian and New Zealand Journal of Sociology* 21, 3–26.

Mill, J. (1972). *Considerations on Representative Government*. H. Acton (ed.). London: J. M. Dent (original, 1861).

Miller, D. (1995). Reflections on British national identity. *New Community* 21, 153–166.

Miller, H., and Miller, K. (1996). Language policy and identity: the case of Catalonia. *International Studies in Sociology of Education* 6, 113–128.

Milward, A. (1992). *The European Rescue of the Nation-State*. London: Routledge.

Minority Rights Group (1997). *World Directory of Minorities* (2nd edn). London: Longman.

Modood, T. (1992). *Not Easy Being British: Colour, Culture and Citizenship*. Stoke-on-Trent, England: Runnymede Trust and Trentham Books.

Modood, T. (1997). Culture and identity. In T. Modood, R. Berthoud, J. Lakey, J. Nazroo, P. Smith, S. Virdee and S. Beishon, *Ethnic Minorities in Britain: Diversity and Disadvantage* (pp. 290–338). London: Policy Studies Institute.

Modood, T. (1998a). Anti-essentialism, multiculturalism and the 'recognition' of religious groups. *Journal of Political Philosophy* 6, 378–399.

Modood, T. (1998b). Multiculturalism, secularism and the state. *Critical Review of International Social and Political Philosophy* 1, 79–97.

Moerman, M. (1965). Who are the Lue: ethnic identification in a complex civilization. *American Anthropologist* 67, 1215–1229.

Moerman, M. (1974). Accomplishing ethnicity. In R. Turner (ed.), *Ethnomethodology* (pp. 54–68). New York: Penguin Education.

Mohan, R. (1995). Multiculturalism in the nineties: pitfalls and possibilities. In C. Newfield and R. Strickland (eds.), *After Political Correctness: The Humanities and Society in the 1990s* (pp. 372–388). Boulder, CO: Westview Press.

Moodley, K. (1995). Multicultural education in Canada: historical developments and current status. In J. Banks and C. Banks (eds.), *Handbook of Research on Multicultural Education* (pp. 801–820). New York: Macmillan.

Moodley, K. (1999). Antiracist education through political literacy: the case of Canada. In S. May (ed.), *Critical Multiculturalism: Rethinking Multicultural and Antiracist Education* (pp. 138–152). London and New York: RoutledgeFalmer.

Moore, M. (1991). Liberalism and the ideal of the good life. *The Review of Politics* 53, 687–688.

Moran, R. (1990). Language and the law in the classroom: bilingual education and the Official English initiative. In K. Adams and D. Brink (eds.), *Perspectives on Official English: The Campaign for English as the Official Language of the USA* (pp. 285–292). Berlin: Mouton de Gruyter.

Morgan, K. (1981). *Rebirth of a Nation: Wales 1880–1980*. Oxford: Clarendon Press.

Morgan, K. (1995). Welsh nationalism: the historical background. In K. Morgan, *Modern Wales: Politics, Places and People* (pp. 197–213). Cardiff: University of Wales Press.

Moss, S. (1994). Lost for words. *Guardian Weekend* (30 July 1994), 26–30.

Mouffe, C. (1993). *The Return of the Political*. London: Verso.

Mühlhäusler, P. (1996). *Linguistic Ecology: Language Change and Linguistic Imperialism in the Pacific Region*. London: Routledge.

Mulgan, R. (1989). *Maori, Pakeha and Democracy*. Auckland, New Zealand: Oxford University Press.

Myhill, J. (1999). Identity, territoriality, and minority language survival. *Journal of Multilingual and Multicultural Development* 20, 34–50.

Nagel, J. (1994). Constructing ethnicity: creating and recreating ethnic identity and culture. *Social Problems* 41, 152–176.

Nairn, T. (1981). *The Break-Up of Britain: Crisis and Neo-Nationalism* (rev. edn). London: Verso.

Nash, M. (1989). *The Cauldron of Ethnicity in the Modern World*. Chicago, IL: Chicago University Press.

Nash, R. (1990). Bourdieu on education and social and cultural reproduction. *British Journal of Sociology of Education* 11, 431–447.

Nash, R. (1999). Bourdieu, 'habitus' and educational research: is it all worth the candle? *British Journal of the Sociology of Education* 20, 175–188.

National Language Forum (1991). *Language Strategy – 1991–2001*. Caernarfon: National Language Forum.

Naysmith, J. (1987). English as imperialism? *Language Issues* 1, 2, 3–5.

Ndebele, N. (1987). The English language and social change in South Africa. *The English Academy Review* 4, 1–16.

Nelde, P. (1997). Language conflict. In F. Coulmas (ed.), *The Handbook of Sociolinguistics* (pp. 285–300). London: Blackwell.

Nelde, P., Strubell, M., and Williams, G. (1996). *Euromosaic: The Production and Reproduction of the Minority Language Groups in the European Union*. Luxembourg: Office for Official Publications of the European Communities.

Nepe, T. (1991). Te toi huarewa tipuna. Kaupapa Māori: an educational intervention system. Unpublished MA thesis, University of Auckland.

New Zealand Department of Education. (1984a). *Taha Māori: Suggestions for Getting Started*. Wellington, New Zealand: Department of Education.

New Zealand Department of Education. (1984b). *A Review of the Core Curriculum for Schools*. Wellington, New Zealand: Department of Education.

New Zealand Ministerial Advisory Committee (1986). *Pūao-Te-Atatu* (The Report of the Ministerial Advisory Committee on a Māori Perspective for the Department of Social Welfare). Wellington, New Zealand: Government Printer.

New Zealand Ministry of Education (1994). *English in the New Zealand Curriculum*. Wellington, New Zealand: Learning Media, Ministry of Education.

New Zealand Ministry of Education (1996). *The New Zealand Curriculum Framework*. Wellington, New Zealand: Learning Media, Ministry of Education.

New Zealand Ministry of Education (1998). *Nga Haeata Mātauranga. Annual Report on Māori Education 1997/98 and Direction for 1999*. Wellington, New Zealand: Ministry of Education.

Ngũgĩ, wa Thiong'o (1985). The language of African literature. *New Left Review* 150 (March/April), 109–127.

Ngũgĩ, wa Thiong'o (1993). *Moving the Centre: The Struggle for Cultural Freedoms*. London: James Currey.

Nielsson, G. (1985). States and 'nation-groups': a global taxonomy. In E. Tiryakian and R. Rugowski (eds.), *New Nationalisms of the Developed West: Towards Explanations* (pp. 27–56). Boston, MA: Allen and Unwin.

Nieto, S. (1995). From brown heroes and holidays to assimilationist agendas: reconsidering the critiques of multicultural education. In C. Sleeter and P. McLaren (eds.), *Multicultural Education, Critical Pedagogy, and the Politics of Difference* (pp. 191–220). Albany, NY: SUNY Press.

Nieto, S. (2000). *Affirming Diversity: The Sociopolitical Context of Multicultural Education* (3rd edn). New York: Longman.

Nimni, E. (1995). Marx, Engels, and the national question. In W. Kymlicka (ed.), *The Rights of Minority Cultures* (pp. 57–75). Oxford: Oxford University Press.

NOP (1995). *Public Attitudes to the Welsh Language*. London: NOP Social and Political.

Norton, B. (2000). *Identity and Language Learning: Gender, Ethnicity and Educational Change*. London: Longman.

Nunberg, G. (1989). Linguists and the official language movement. *Language* 65, 579–587.

Nunberg, G. (1992). Afterword: the official language movement: reimagining America. In J. Crawford (ed.), *Language Loyalties: A Source Book on the Official English Controversy* (pp. 479–494). Chicago, IL: University of Chicago Press.

O'Brien, J. (1986). Towards a reconstruction of ethnicity. Capitalist expansion and cultural dynamics in Sudan. *American Anthropologist* 88, 898–906.

O'Brien, O. (1993). Good to be French? Conflicts of identity in North Catalonia. In S. Macdonald (ed.), *Inside European Identities: Ethnography in Western Europe* (pp. 98–117). Oxford: Berg.

O'Cinneide, M., Keane, M., and Cawley, M. (1985). Industrialisation and linguistic change among Gaelic-speaking communities in the West of Ireland. *Language Problems and Language Planning* 9, 3–16.

Ó Ciosáin, S. (1988). Language planning and Irish. *Language, Culture and Curriculum* 1, 263–279.

Ó Gadhra, N. (1988). Irish government policy and political development of the Gaeltacht. *Language, Culture and Curriculum* 1, 251–261.

Ogbu, J. (1987). Variability in minority school performance: a problem in search of an explanation. *Anthropology and Education Quarterly* 18, 312–334.

Ohia, M. (1990). The unresolved conflict and debate: an overview of bilingual education in New Zealand secondary schools. *SAME Papers*, 111–132.

Okin, S. (1998). Feminism and multiculturalism: some tensions. *Ethics* 108, 661–684.

Okin, S. (1999). Is multiculturalism bad for women? In J. Cohen, M. Howard and M. Nussbaum (eds.), *Is Multiculturalism Bad for Women?* (pp. 9–24). Princeton, NJ: Princeton University Press.

O'Leary, B. (1998). Ernest Gellner's diagnoses of nationalism: a critical overview, or, what is living and what is dead in Ernest Gellner's philosophy of nationalism. In J. Hall (ed.), *The State of the Nation: Ernest Gellner and the Theory of Nationalism* (pp. 40–90). Cambridge: Cambridge University Press.

Omi, M., and Winant, H. (1986). *Racial Formation in the United States: From the 1960s to the 1980s*. New York: Routledge and Kegan Paul.

Ó Murchú, M. (1988). Diglossia and interlanguage contact in Ireland. *Language, Culture and Curriculum* 1, 243–249.

Oommen, T. (1994). State, nation, and ethnie: the processual linkages. In P. Ratcliffe (ed.), *'Race', Ethnicity and Nation: International Perspectives on Social Conflict* (pp. 26–46). London: UCL Press.

OPCS (1991). *Office of Population Censuses and Statistics*. London: HMSO.

Orange, C. (1987). *The Treaty of Waitangi*. Wellington, New Zealand: Allen and Unwin.

Orellana, M., Ek, L., and Hernández, A. (1999). Bilingual education in an immigrant community: Proposition 227 in California. *International Journal of Bilingual Education and Bilingualism* 2, 114–130.

Ó Riagáin, P. (1988a). Bilingualism in Ireland 1793–1983: an overview of national sociolinguistic surveys. *International Journal of the Sociology of Language* 70, 29–51.

Ó Riagáin, P. (1988b). Introduction. *International Journal of the Sociology of Language* 70, 5–9.

Ó Riagáin, P. (1996). Reviving the Irish language 1893–1993: the first hundred years. In M. Nic Craith (ed.), *Watching One's Tongue: Issues in Language Planning* (pp. 33–56). Liverpool: Liverpool University Press.

Ó Riagáin, P. (1997). *Language Policy and Social Reproduction: Ireland 1893–1993*. Oxford: Clarendon Press.

O'Rourke, M. (1994). Revitalisation of the Māori language. *The New Zealand Education Gazette* 73, 1–3.

Osmond, J. (1988). *The Divided Kingdom*. London: Constable.

Ozolins, U. (1993). *The Politics of Language in Australia*. Cambridge: Cambridge University Press.

Packer, A., and Campbell, C. (1993). The reasons for parental choice of Welsh-medium education. Paper presented to the Fifth International Conference on Minority Languages, University of Wales, Cardiff, July 1993.

Packer, J. (1999). Problems in defining minorities. In D. Fottrell and B. Bowring (eds.), *Minority and Group Rights in the New Millennium* (pp. 223–273). The Hague: Kluwer Law International.

Padilla, A. (1991). English only vs. bilingual education: ensuring a language-competent society. *Journal of Education* 173, 38–51.

Padilla, F. (1985). *Latino Ethnic Consciousness: The Case of Mexican Americans and Puerto Ricans in Chicago*. Notre Dame, IN: Notre Dame Press.

Parekh, B. (1995a). Introduction. *New Community* 21, 147–151.

Parekh. B. (1995b). The concept of national identity. *New Community* 21, 255–268.

Parekh, B. (2000). *Rethinking Multiculturalism: Cultural Diversity and Political Theory*. London: Macmillan.

Pattanayak, D. (1969). *Aspects of Applied Linguistics*. London: Asia Publishing House.

Pattanayak, D. (1985). Diversity in communication and languages; predicament of a multilingual nation state: India, a case study. In N. Wolfson and J. Manes (eds.), *Language of Inequality* (pp. 399–407). Berlin: Mouton de Gruyter.

Pattanayak, D. (1986). Language, politics, region formation, regional planning. In E. Annamalai, B. Jernudd and J. Rubin (eds.), *Language Planning: Proceedings of an Institute* (pp. 18–42). Mysore, India: Central Institute of Indian Languages.

Pattanayak, D. (ed.) (1990). *Multilingualism in India*. Clevedon, England: Multilingual Matters.

Patton, P. (1995). Post-structuralism and the Mabo debate: difference, society and justice. In M. Wilson and A. Yeatman (eds.), *Justice and Identity: Antipodean Practices* (pp. 153–171). Wellington, New Zealand: Bridget Williams Books.

Paulston, C. (1993). Language regenesis: a conceptual overview of language revival, revitalisation and reversal. *Journal of Multilingual and Multicultural Development* 14, 275–286.

Pavkovic, A. (1997). *The Fragmentation of Yugoslavia: Nationalism in a Multinational State*. London: Macmillan.

PDAG (1993a). *Welsh and the Early Years*. Cardiff: PDAG.

PDAG (1993b). *Welsh Language Education*. Cardiff: PDAG.

PDAG (1994). *Development of Welsh Medium Education – 1977–1992*. Cardiff: PDAG.

Pearson, D. (1990). *A Dream Deferred: The Origins of Ethnic Conflict in New Zealand*. Wellington, New Zealand: Allen and Unwin.

Pearson, D. (2000). The ties that unwind: civic and ethnic imaginings in New Zealand. *Nations and Nationalism* 6, 91–110.

Pennycook, A. (1994). *The Cultural Politics of English as an International Language*. London: Longman.

Pennycook, A. (1995). English in the world / the world in English. In J. Tollefson (ed.), *Power and Inequality in Language Education* (pp. 34–58). Cambridge: Cambridge University Press.

Pennycook, A. (1998a). The right to language: towards a situated ethics of language possibilities. *Language Sciences* 20, 73–87.

Pennycook, A. (1998b). *English and the Discourses of Colonialism*. London: Routledge.

Penrose, J. (1995). Essential constructions? The 'cultural bases' of nationalist movements. *Nations and Nationalism* 1, 391–417.

Perera, S., and Pugliese, J. (1998). Wogface, anglo-drag, contested aboriginalities: making and unmaking identities in Australia. *Social Identities* 4, 39–72.

Petschen, S. (1993). *La Europa de las Regiones*. Barcelona, Catalonia: Generalitat de Catalunya.

Peyre, H. (1933). *La Royauté et les Langues Provinciales*. Paris: Les Presses Modernes.

Phillips, A. (1995). Democracy and difference: some problems for feminist theory. In W. Kymlicka (ed.), *The Rights of Minority Cultures* (pp. 288–299). Oxford: Oxford University Press.

Phillips, A. (1997). Why worry about multiculturalism? *Dissent* 44, 57–63.

Phillipson, R. (1992). *Linguistic Imperialism*. Oxford: Oxford University Press.

Phillipson, R. (1997). Realities and myths of linguistic imperialism. *Journal of Multilingual and Multicultural Development* 18, 238–248.

Phillipson, R. (1998). Globalizing English: are linguistic human rights an alternative to linguistic imperialism? *Language Sciences* 20, 101–112.

Phillipson, R. (ed.) (2000). *Rights to Language. Equity, Power and Education*. Mahwah, NJ: Lawrence Erlbaum.

Phillipson, R., and Skutnabb-Kangas, T. (1994). English, panacea or pandemic? *Sociolinguistica* 8, 73–87.

Piatt, B. (1990). *Only English? Law and Language Policy in the United States*. Albuquerque, NM: University of New Mexico Press.

Pilger, J. (1998). Australia, a paradise of blondes and barbecues, shark-infested waters and silver beaches. It has other similarities with South Africa, too. *Observer* (Review Section) (22 March 1998), 5.

Pinker, S. (1995). *The Language Instinct*. London: Penguin.

Porter, J. (1965). *The Vertical Mosaic*. Toronto: Toronto University Press.

Porter, J. (1972). Dilemmas and contradictions of a multi-ethnic society. *Transactions of the Royal Society of Canada* 10, 193–205.

Porter, J. (1975). Ethnic pluralism in Canadian perspective. In N. Glazer and D. Moynihan (eds.), *Ethnicity: Theory and Experience* (pp. 267–304). Cambridge, MA: Harvard University Press.

Porter, R. (1990). *Forked Tongue: The Politics of Bilingual Education*. New York: Basic Books.

Portes, A., and Hao, L. (1998). E pluribis unum: bilingualism and loss of language in the second generation. *Sociology of Education* 71, 269–294.

Preece, J. (1998). *National Minorities and the European Nation-States System*. Oxford: Clarendon Press.

Purvis, A. (1999a). Whose home and native land? *Time Magazine* (Canadian edition) (15 February 1999), 16–23.

Purvis, A. (1999b). Homeland for the Inuit. *Time Magazine* (Canadian edition) (15 February 1999), 34–35.

Quiniou-Tempereau, R. (1988). *The Breton Language in Primary Education in Brittany, France*. Leeuwarden, Netherlands: Fryske Akademy.

Quirk, R. (1981). International communication and the concept of nuclear English. In L. Smith (ed.), *English for Cross-Cultural Communication* (pp. 151–165). London: Macmillan.

Quirk, R. (1985). The English language in a global context. In R. Quirk and H. Widdowson (eds.), *English in the World* (pp. 1–6). Cambridge: Cambridge University Press.

Ramírez, J., Yuen, S., and Ramey, D. (1991). *Final Report: Longitudinal Study of Structured English Immersion Strategy, Early-Exit and Late-Exit Transitional Bilingual Education Programs for Language-Minority Children*. San Mateo, CA: Aguirre International.

Rampton, B. (1995). *Crossing: Language and Ethnicity among Adolescents*. London: Longman.

Rassool, N. (1998). Postmodernity, cultural pluralism and the nation-state: problems of language rights, human rights, identity and power. *Language Sciences* 20, 89–99.

Rassool, N. (1999). *Literacy for Sustainable Development in the Age of Information*. Clevedon, England: Multilingual Matters.

Rassool, N. (2000). Language maintenance as an arena of cultural and political struggles in a changing world. In R. Phillipson (ed.), *Rights to Language. Equity, Power and Education* (pp. 57–61). Mahwah, NJ: Lawrence Erlbaum.

Rattansi, A. (1999). Racism, 'postmodernism' and reflexive multiculturalism. In S. May (ed.), *Critical Multiculturalism: Rethinking Multicultural and Antiracist Education* (pp. 77–112). London and New York: RoutledgeFalmer.

Ravitch, D. (1992). Diversity in education. *Dialogue* 95, 39–47.

Rawkins, P. (1979). *The Implementation of Language Policy in the Schools of Wales*. Glasgow: Centre for the Study of Public Policy, University of Strathclyde.

Rawkins, P. (1987). The politics of benign neglect: education, public policy, and the mediation of linguistic conflict in Wales. *International Journal of the Sociology of Language* 66, 27–48.

Rawls, J. (1971). *A Theory of Justice*. Oxford: Oxford University Press.

Rawls, J. (1985). Justice as fairness: political not metaphysical. *Philosophy and Public Affairs* 14, 223–251.

Réaume, D. (1999). Official language rights: intrinsic value and the protection of difference. In W. Kymlicka and W. Norman (eds.), *Citizenship in Diverse Societies* (pp. 245–272). Oxford: Oxford University Press.

Reay, D. (1995a). 'They employ cleaners to do that': habitus in the primary classroom. *British Journal of Sociology of Education* 16, 353–371.

Reay, D. (1995b). Using habitus to look at 'race' and class in primary school classrooms. In M. Griffiths and B. Troyna (eds.), *Antiracism, Culture and Social Justice in Education* (pp. 115–132). Stoke-on-Trent, England: Trentham Books.

Reedy, T. (1992). *Kura Kaupapa Māori Research and Development Project: Final Report*. Wellington, New Zealand: Ministry of Education.

Renan, E. (1990). What is a nation? In H. Bhabha (ed.), *Nation and Narration* (pp. 8–22). London: Routledge (original, 1882).

Rex, J. (1973). *Race, Colonialism and the City*. Oxford: Oxford University Press.

Rex, J. (1991). *Ethnic Identity and Ethnic Mobilisation in Britain*. Coventry, England: Centre for Research in Ethnic Relations, University of Warwick.

Rex, J., and Mason, D. (eds.) (1986). *Theories of Race and Race Relations*. Cambridge: Cambridge University Press.

Reynolds, D. (1994). Education in Wales 1978–1994: from problems to policies? In W. Bellin, J. Osmond and D. Reynolds (eds.), *Towards an Educational Policy in Wales* (pp. 4–10). Cardiff: The Institute of Welsh Affairs.

Ricento, T. (1996). Language policy in the United States. In M. Herriman and B. Burnaby (eds.), *Language Policies in English-Dominant Countries* (pp. 122–158). Clevedon, England: Multilingual Matters.

Ritzer, G. (1996). *The McDonaldization of Society: An Investigation into the Changing Character of Contemporary Social Life* (rev. edn). London: Pine Forge Press.

Ritzer, G. (1997). *The McDonaldization Thesis: Explorations and Extensions.* London: Sage.

Robertson, R. (1992). *Globalization: Social Theory and Global Culture.* London: Sage.

Robbins, D. (1991). *The Work of Pierre Bourdieu: Recognizing Society.* Milton Keynes, England: Open University Press.

Robbins, D. (2000). *Bourdieu and Culture.* London: Sage.

Robbins, K. (1997). *Great Britain: Identities, Institutions and the Idea of Britishness.* London: Longman.

Rodriguez, R. (1983). *Hunger of Memory.* New York: Bantam.

Rodriguez, R. (1993). *Days of Obligation: An Argument with my Mexican Father.* London: Penguin.

Roediger, D. (1991). *The Wages of Whiteness: Race and the Making of the American Working Class.* London: Verso.

Rogel, C. (1998). *The Breakup of Yugoslavia and the War in Bosnia.* Westport, CO: Greenwood Press.

Rokkan, S., and Urwin, D. (1983). *Economy, Territory, Identity.* London: Sage.

Romaine, S. (1995). *Bilingualism* (2nd edn). Oxford: Blackwell.

Romaine, S. (2000). *Language in Society: An Introduction to Sociolinguistics* (2nd edn). Oxford: Oxford University Press.

Roosens, E. (1989). *Creating Ethnicity: The Process of Ethnogenesis.* London: Sage.

Rorty, R. (1991). *Objectivity, Relativism, and Truth: Philosophical Papers I.* Cambridge: Cambridge University Press.

Rosaldo, R. (1989). *Culture and Truth.* London: Routledge.

Rossell, C., and Baker, K. (1996). The effectiveness of bilingual education. *Research in the Teaching of English* 30, 7–74.

Rossinelli, M. (1989). La question linguistique en Suisse. Bilan critique et nouvelles perspectives juridiques. *Revue de Droit Suisse* 108, 163–193.

Rothschild, J. (1981). *Ethnopolitics: A Conceptual Framework.* New York: Columbia University Press.

Royal Commission on Social Policy (1988). *April Report* Vols. I–IV. Wellington, New Zealand: Government Printer.

Ruiz, R. (1984). Orientations in language planning. *NABE Journal* 8, 2, 15–34.

Ruiz, R. (1990). Official languages and language planning. In K. Adams and D. Brink (eds.), *Perspectives on Official English: The Campaign for English as the Official Language of the USA* (pp. 11–24). Berlin: Mouton de Gruyter.

Ryan, J. (1999a). *Race and Ethnicity in Multi-Ethnic Schools.* Clevedon, England: Multilingual Matters.

Ryan, J. (1999b). Towards a new age for Innu education: Innu resistance and community activism. In S. May (ed.), *Indigenous Community-Based Education* (pp. 109–123). Clevedon, England: Multilingual Matters.

Safran, W. (1992). Language, ideology, and state-building: a comparison of policies in France, Israel, and the Soviet Union. *International Political Science Review* 13, 397–414.

Safran, W. (1999). Nationalism. In J. Fishman (ed.), *Handbook of Language and Ethnic Identity* (pp. 77–93). Oxford: Oxford University Press.

Said, E. (1994). *Culture and Imperialism*. London: Vintage.

Salée, D. (1995). Identities in conflict: the Aboriginal question and the politics of recognition in Quebec. *Ethnic and Racial Studies* 18, 277–314.

Sandel, M. (1982). *Liberalism and the Limits of Justice*. Cambridge: Cambridge University Press.

Sanders, D. (1989). The UN Working Group on Indigenous Populations. *Human Rights Quarterly* 11, 406–429.

San Miguel, G., and Valencia, R. (1998). From the Treaty of Guadalupe Hidalgo to Hopwood: the educational plight and struggle of Mexican Americans in the Southwest. *Harvard Educational Review* 68, 353–412.

Schermerhorn, R. (1970). *Comparative Ethnic Relations*. New York: Random House.

Schiffman, H. (1996). *Linguistic Culture and Language Policy*. London: Routledge.

Schlesinger, A. (1991). The Disuniting of America: what we all stand to lose if multicultural education takes the wrong approach. *American Educator* 15, 14–33.

Schlesinger, A. (1992). *The Disuniting of America: Reflections on a Multicultural Society*. New York: W.W. Norton and Co.

Schmied, J. (1991). *English in Africa: An Introduction*. London: Longman.

Scott, C. (1996). Indigenous self-determination and decolonization of the international imagination: a plea. *Human Rights Quarterly* 18, 814–820.

Seaton, I. (1997). Linguistic non-imperialism. *English Language Teaching Journal* 51, 381–382.

Secada, W., and Lightfoot, T. (1993). Symbols and the political context of bilingual education in the United States. In M. Arias and U. Casanova (eds.), *Bilingual Education: Politics, Practice, and Research* (pp. 36–64). Chicago, IL: The National Society for the Study of Education / University of Chicago Press.

Seton-Watson, H. (1977). *Nations and States*. London: Methuen.

Shannon, S. (1999). The debate on bilingual education in the US: language ideology as reflected in the practice of bilingual teachers. In J. Blommaert (ed.), *Language Ideological Debates* (pp. 171–199). Berlin: Mouton de Gruyter.

Sharp, A. (1990). *Justice and the Maori: Maori Claims in New Zealand Political Argument in the 1980s*. Auckland, New Zealand: Oxford University Press.

Sharples, P. (1988). *Kura Kaupapa Māori: Recommendations for Policy*. Auckland, New Zealand: Te Kura o Hoani Waititi Marae.

Shell, M. (1993). Babel in America: the politics of language diversity in the United States. *Critical Inquiry* 20, 103–127.

Shils, E. (1957). Primordial, personal, sacred and civil ties. *British Journal of Sociology* 8, 130–145.

Shils, E. (1980). *Tradition*. Glencoe, IL: Free Press.

Shore, C., and Black, A. (1994). Citizen's Europe and the construction of European identity. In V. Goddard, J. Llobera and C. Shore (eds.), *The Anthropology of Europe* (pp. 275–298). Oxford: Berg.

Short, G., and Carrington, B. (1999). Children's constructions of their national identity: the implications for critical multiculturalism. In S. May (ed.), *Critical*

Multiculturalism: Rethinking Multicultural and Antiracist Education (pp. 172–190). London and New York: RoutledgeFalmer.

Silber, L., and Little, A. (1995). *The Death of Yugoslavia*. London: Penguin / BBC Books.

Silverstein, M. (1996). Monoglot 'standard' in America: standardization and metaphors of linguistic hegemony. In D. Brenneis and R. Macaulay (eds.), *The Matrix of Language: Contemporary Linguistic Anthropology* (pp. 284–306). Boulder, CO: Westview Press.

Simon, J. (1989). Aspirations and ideology: biculturalism and multiculturalism in New Zealand education. *Sites* 18, 23–34.

Simon, J. (1992). State schooling for Māori: the control of access to knowledge. Paper presented to the AARE/NZARE Joint Conference, Deakin University, Geelong, Australia, November 1992.

Sinclair, K. (ed.) (1993). *The Oxford Illustrated History of New Zealand*. Oxford: Oxford University Press.

Skutnabb-Kangas, T. (1988). Multilingualism and the education of minority children. In T. Skutnabb-Kangas and J. Cummins (eds.), *Minority Education: From Shame to Struggle* (pp. 9–44). Clevedon, England: Multilingual Matters.

Skutnabb-Kangas, T. (1998). Human rights and language wrongs – a future for diversity? *Language Sciences* 20, 5–27.

Skutnabb-Kangas, T. (2000). *Linguistic Genocide in Education – or Worldwide Diversity and Human Rights?* Mahwah, NJ: Lawrence Erlbaum.

Skutnabb-Kangas, T., and Bucak, S. (1995). Killing a mother tongue – how the Kurds are deprived of linguistic human rights. In T. Skutnabb-Kangas and R. Phillipson (eds.), *Linguistic Human Rights: Overcoming Linguistic Discrimination* (pp. 347–370). Berlin: Mouton de Gruyter.

Skutnabb-Kangas, T., and Phillipson, R. (1995). Linguistic human rights, past and present. In T. Skutnabb-Kangas and R. Phillipson (eds.), *Linguistic Human Rights: Overcoming Linguistic Discrimination* (pp. 71–110). Berlin: Mouton de Gruyter.

Sleeter, C. (1996). *Multicultural Education as Social Activism*. Albany, NY: SUNY Press.

Smaje, C. (1997). Not just a social construct: theorising race and ethnicity. *Sociology* 31, 307–327.

Small, S. (1994). *Racialised Barriers: The Black Experience in the United States and England in the 1980s*. London: Routledge.

Smith, A. (1981). *The Ethnic Revival*. Cambridge: Cambridge University Press.

Smith, A. (1983). *Theories of Nationalism* (2nd edn). London: Harper and Row.

Smith, A. (1986). *The Ethnic Origin of Nations*. Oxford: Basil Blackwell.

Smith, A. (1991). *National Identity*. London: Penguin.

Smith, A. (1994). The problem of national identity: ancient, medieval and modern? *Ethnic and Racial Studies* 17, 375–399.

Smith, A. (1995a). *Nations and Nationalism in a Global Era*. London: Polity Press.

Smith, A. (1995b). Gastronomy or geology? The role of nationalism in the construction of nations. *Nations and Nationalism* 1, 3–23.

Smith, A. (1998). *Nationalism and Modernism*. London: Routledge.

Smith, D., and Wright, S. (eds.) (1999). *Whose Europe? The Turn towards Democracy*. Oxford: Blackwell.

Smith, G. (1989). Kura Kaupapa Māori: innovation and policy development in Māori education. *Access* 8, 26–43.

Smith, G. (1990a). The politics of reforming Māori education: the transforming potential of Kura Kaupapa Māori. In H. Lauder and C. Wylie (eds.), *Towards Successful Schooling* (pp. 73–87). London: Falmer Press.

Smith, G. (1990b). Taha Māori: Pākehā capture. In J. Codd, R. Harker and R. Nash (eds.), *Political Issues in New Zealand Education* (2nd edn) (pp. 183–197). Palmerston North, New Zealand: Dunmore Press.

Smith, G. (1992). Tane-Nui-A-Rangi's legacy: propping up the sky. Kaupapa Māori as resistance and intervention. Paper presented to the AARE/NZARE Joint Conference, Deakin University, Geelong, Australia, November 1992.

Smith, G. (1997). Kaupapa Māori as transformative practice. Unpublished PhD thesis, University of Auckland.

Smith, L. (1989). Te reo Māori: Māori language and the struggle to survive. *Access* 8, 3–9.

Smith, L. (1992a). Ko taku ko ta te Māori: the dilemma of a Māori academic. Paper presented to the AARE/NZARE Joint Conference, Deakin University, Geelong, Australia, November 1992.

Smith, L. (1992b). Kura kaupapa and the implications for curriculum. In G. McCulloch (ed.), *The School Curriculum in New Zealand: History, Theory, Policy and Practice* (pp. 219–231). Palmerston North, New Zealand: Dunmore Press.

Smith, M.G. (1965). *The Plural Society of the British West Indies*. London: Sangster's.

Smolicz, J. (1979). *Culture and Education in a Plural Society*. Canberra, Australia: Curriculum Development Centre.

Smolicz, J. (1989). *Who is an Australian? Identity, Core Values and Resilience of Culture*. Adelaide, Australia: Multicultural Education Coordinating Committee.

Smolicz, J. (1993). The monolingual myopia and minority rights: Australia's language policies from an international perspective. *Muslim Education Quarterly* 10, 44–61.

Smolicz, J. (1995). Australia's language policies and minority rights. In T. Skutnabb-Kangas and R. Phillipson (eds.), *Linguistic Human Rights: Overcoming Linguistic Discrimination* (pp. 235–252). Berlin: Mouton de Gruyter.

Smolicz, J., and Secombe, M. (1988). Community languages, core values and cultural maintenance: the Australian experience with special reference to Greek, Latvian and Polish groups. In M. Clyne (ed.), *Australia, Meeting Place of Languages* (pp. 11–38). Canberra, Australia: Australian National University, Pacific Linguistics.

Sollors, W. (ed.) (1989). *The Invention of Ethnicity*. Oxford: Oxford University Press.

Sollors, W. (ed.) (1998). *Multilingual America: Transnationalism, Ethnicity and the Languages of American literature*. New York: New York University Press.

Solomos, J. (1993). *Race and Racism in Contemporary Britain* (2nd edn). London: Macmillan.

Solomos, J., and Back, L. (1996). *Racism and Society*. London: Macmillan.

Sorrenson, M. (1989). Towards a radical reinterpretation of New Zealand history: the role of the Waitangi Tribunal. In I. Kawharu (ed.), *Waitangi: Maori and Pakeha perspectives of the Treaty of Waitangi* (pp. 158–178). Auckland, New Zealand: Oxford University Press.

Soysal, Y. (1994). *Limits of Citizenship: Migrants and Post-National Membership in Europe*. Chicago, IL: University of Chicago Press.

Spinner, J. (1994). *The Boundaries of Citizenship: Race, Ethnicity and Nationality in the Liberal State*. Baltimore, MA: Johns Hopkins Press.

Spinner-Halev, J. (1999). Cultural pluralism and partial citizenship. In C. Joppke and S. Lukes (eds.), *Multicultural Questions* (pp. 65–86). Oxford: Oxford University Press.

Spolsky, B. (1987). *Report of Maori–English Bilingual Education*: Wellington, New Zealand: Department of Education.

Spoonley, P. (1993). *Racism and Ethnicity* (rev. edn). Auckland, New Zealand: Oxford University Press.

Spoonley, P. (1996). Mahi Awatea? The racialisation of work in Aotearoa / New Zealand. In P. Spoonley, C. Macpherson and D. Pearson (eds.), *Nga Pātai: Racism and Ethnic Relations in Aotearoa / New Zealand* (pp. 55–78). Palmerston North, New Zealand: Dunmore Press.

Stack, J. (1986). Ethnic mobilization in world politics: the primordial perspective. In J. Stack (ed.), *The Primordial Challenge: Ethnicity in the Contemporary World* (pp. 1–11). Westport, CT: Greenwood Press.

Stamatopoulou, E. (1994). Indigenous peoples and the United Nations: human rights as a developing dynamic. *Human Rights Quarterly* 16, 58–81.

Stannard, D. (1989). *Before the Horror*. Honolulu: University of Hawai'i Press.

Stavenhagen, R. (1992). Universal human rights and the cultures of indigenous peoples and other ethnic groups: the critical frontier of the 1990s. In A. Eide and B. Hagtvet (eds.), *Human Rights in Perspective* (pp. 135–151). Oxford: Blackwell.

Steinberg, S. (1981). *The Ethnic Myth: Race, Ethnicity and Class in America*. New York: Atheneum.

Stepan, A. (1998). Modern multinational democracies: transcending a Gellnerian oxymoron. In J. Hall (ed.), *The State of the Nation: Ernest Gellner and the Theory of Nationalism* (pp. 219–239). Cambridge: Cambridge University Press.

Stone, M. (1981). *The Education of the Black Child in Britain: The Myth of Multiracial Education*. London: Collins Fontana.

Strubell, M. (1998). Language, democracy and devolution in Catalonia. *Current Issues in Language and Society* 5, 146–180.

Switzerland (1989). *Le Quadrilinguisme en Suisse: Présent et Futur*. Bern, Switzerland: Chancellerie Fédérale.

Szasz, M. (1974). *Education and the American Indian: The Road to Self Determination, 1928–1973*. Albuquerque, NM: University of New Mexico Press.

Tabouret-Keller, A. (1997). Language and identity. In F. Coulmas (ed.), *The Handbook of Sociolinguistics* (pp. 315–326). Oxford: Blackwell.

Tamir, Y. (1993). *Liberal Nationalism*. Princeton, NJ: Princeton University Press.

Tarrow, N. (1992). Language, interculturalism and human rights: three European cases. *Prospects* 22, 489–509.

Tarver, H. (1994). Language and politics in the 1980s. The story of US English. In F. Pincus and H. Ehrlich (eds.), *Race and Ethnic Conflict: Contending Views on Prejudice, Discrimination and Ethnoviolence* (pp. 206–218). Boulder, CO: Westview Press.

Taylor, B., and Thompson, K. (eds.) (1999). *Scotland and Wales: Nations Again?* Cardiff: University of Wales Press.

Taylor, C. (1994). The politics of recognition. In A. Gutmann (ed.), *Multiculturalism: Examining the Politics of Recognition* (pp. 25–73). Princeton, NJ: Princeton University Press.

Taylor, C. (1998). Nationalism and modernity. In J. Hall (ed.), *The State of the Nation: Ernest Gellner and the Theory of Nationalism* (pp. 191–218). Cambridge: Cambridge University Press.

Tennant, C. (1994). Indigenous peoples, international institutions, and the international legal literature from 1945–1993. *Human Rights Quarterly* 16, 1–57.

Te Puni Kōkiri (1994). *Mana Tangata. Draft Declaration on the Rights of Indigenous Peoples, 1993: Background and Discussion on Key Issues.* Wellington, New Zealand: Te Puni Kōkiri (Ministry of Māori Development).

Te Taura Whiri i te Reo Māori, (1995). *He Taonga te Reo.* Wellington, New Zealand: Te Taura Whiri i te Reo Māori (Māori Language Commission).

Thomas, A. (1997). Language policy and nationalism in Wales: a comparative analysis. *Nations and Nationalism* 3, 333–344.

Thomas, N. (1992). *The Welsh Extremist* (2nd edn). Talybont, Wales: Y Lolfa.

Thomas, R. (1992). *Cymru or Wales?* Llandysul, Wales: Gomer Press.

Thompson, J. (1991). Editor's Introduction. In P. Bourdieu, *Language and Symbolic Power* (pp. 1–31). Cambridge: Polity Press.

Thornberry, P. (1991a). *International Law and the Rights of Minorities.* Oxford: Clarendon Press.

Thornberry, P. (1991b). *Minorities and Human Rights Law.* London: Minority Rights Group.

Thornberry, P. (1997). Minority rights. In Academy of European Law (ed.), *Collected Courses of the Academy of European Law* Vol. VI, Book 2 (pp. 307–390). The Hague: Kluwer Law International.

Thornton, R. (1988). Culture: a contemporary definition. In E. Boonzaier and J. Sharp (eds.), *South African Keywords: The Uses and Abuses of Political Concepts* (pp. 17–28). Cape Town: David Philip.

Tickoo, M. (1993). When is language worth teaching? Native languages and English in India. *Language, Culture and Curriculum* 6, 225–239.

Tilly, C. (ed.) (1975). *The Formation of National States in Western Europe.* Princeton, NJ: Princeton University Press.

Tilly, C. (1984). *Big Structures, Large Processes, Huge Comparisons.* New York: Russell Sage.

Todal, J. (1999). Minorities within a minority: language and the school in the Sámi areas of Norway. In S. May (ed.), *Indigenous Community-Based Education* (pp. 124–136). Clevedon, England: Multilingual Matters.

Tollefson, J. (1991). *Planning Language, Planning Inequality: Language Policy in the Community.* London: Longman.

Tollefson, J. (ed.) (1995). *Power and Inequality in Language Education.* Cambridge: Cambridge University Press.

Tollefson, J. (2000). Policy and ideology in the spread of English. In J. Kelly Hall and W. Eggington (eds.), *The Sociopolitics of English Language Teaching* (pp. 7–21). Clevedon, England: Multilingual Matters.

Tomasi, J. (1995). Kymlicka, liberalism and respect for cultural minorities. *Ethics* 105, 580–603.

Torres, J. (1984). Problems of linguistic normalization in the Països Catalans: from the Congress of Catalan Culture to the present day. *International Journal of the Sociology of Language* 47: 59–63.

Tovey, H., Hannan, D., and Abramson, H. (1989). *Why Irish? Irish Identity and the Irish Language.* Dublin: Bord na Gaeilge.

Toynbee, A. (1953). *A Study of History* (Vols. VII–IX). London: Oxford University Press.

Trevor-Roper, H. (1983). The invention of tradition: the highland tradition of Scotland. In E. Hobsbawm and T. Ranger (eds.), *The Invention of Tradition* (pp. 15–42). Cambridge: Cambridge University Press.

Troebst, S. (1998). *The Council of Europe's Framework Convention for the Protection of National Minorities Revisited*. Flensburg, Germany: European Centre for Minority Issues.

Troyna, B. (1993). *Racism and Education*. Buckingham, England: Open University Press.

Truchot, C. (1990). *L'Anglais dans le Monde Contemporaine*. Paris: Robert.

Tully, J. (1995). *Strange Multiplicity: Constitutionalism in an Age of Diversity*. Cambridge: Cambridge University Press.

UNESCO (1953). *The Use of Vernacular Languages in Education*. Paris: UNESCO.

Ussher, A. (1949). *The Face and Mind of Ireland*. London: Gollancz.

Valencia, R. (ed.) (1997). *The Evolution of Deficit Thinking: Educational Thought and Practice*. New York: Falmer Press.

van den Berghe, P. (1979). *The Ethnic Phenomenon*. New York: Elsevier Press.

van den Berghe, P. (1995). Does race matter? *Nations and Nationalism* 1, 357–368.

van Dijk, T. (1993). *Elite Discourse and Racism*. London: Sage.

van Dyke, V. (1977). The individual, the state, and ethnic communities in political theory. *World Politics* 29, 343–369.

van Lier, L. (1994). Forks and hope: pursuing understanding in different ways. *Applied Linguistics* 15, 328–346.

Veltman, C. (1983). *Language Shift in the United States*. Berlin: Mouton de Gruyter.

Veltman, C. (1988). Modelling the language shift process of Hispanic immigrants. *International Migration Review* 22, 545–562.

Verma, G. (ed.) (1989). *Education for All: A Landmark in Pluralism*. Lewes, England: Falmer Press.

Vološinov, V. (1973). *Marxism and the Philosophy of Language*. Cambridge, MA: Harvard University Press (original, 1929).

Vos, L. (1993). Shifting nationalism: Belgians, Flemings and Walloons. In M. Teich and R. Porter (eds.), *The National Question in Europe in Historical Context* (pp. 128–147). Cambridge: Cambridge University Press.

Waitangi Tribunal (1986). *Findings of the Waitangi Tribunal Relating to Te Reo Māori and a Claim Lodged by Huirangi Waikerepuru and Nga Kaiwhakapumau i te Reo Incorporated Society (Wellington Board of Māori Language)*. Wellington, New Zealand: Government Printer.

Waite, J. (1992). *Aotearoa: Speaking for Ourselves. A Discussion on the Development of a New Zealand Languages Policy*. Wellington, New Zealand: Learning Media, Ministry of Education.

Waldron, J. (1993). *Liberal Rights*. Cambridge: Cambridge University Press.

Waldron, J. (1995). Minority cultures and the cosmopolitan alternative. In W. Kymlicka (ed.), *The Rights of Minority Cultures* (pp. 93–119). Oxford: Oxford University Press.

Walker, R. (1990). *Ka Whawhai Tonu Mātou: Struggle Without End*. Auckland, New Zealand: Penguin.

Wallerstein, I. (1979). *The Capitalist World Economy*. Cambridge: Cambridge University Press.

Wallerstein, I. (1983). *Historical Capitalism*. London: New Left Books.

Wallerstein, I. (1991). The construction of peoplehood: racism, nationalism, ethnicity. In E. Balibar and I. Wallerstein (eds.), *Race, Nation, Class: Ambiguous Identities* (pp. 71–85). London: Verso.

Wallman, S. (1978). The boundaries of race: processes of ethnicity in England. *Man* 13, 200–217.

Wallman, S. (1986). Ethnicity and the boundary process in context. In J. Rex and D. Mason (eds.), *Theories of Race and Race Relations* (pp. 226–235). Cambridge: Cambridge University Press.

Walzer, M. (1982). Pluralism in political perspective. In M. Walzer (ed.), *The Politics of Ethnicity* (pp. 1–28). Cambridge, MA: Harvard University Press.

Walzer, M. (1992). *What it Means to be an American.* New York: Marsilio.

Walzer, M. (1994). Comment. In A. Gutmann (ed.), *Multiculturalism: Examining the Politics of Recognition* (pp. 99–103). Princeton, NJ: Princeton University Press.

Ward, A. (1974). *A Show of Justice: Racial 'Amalgamation' in Nineteenth Century New Zealand.* Auckland, New Zealand: Auckland University Press.

Waters, M. (1990). *Ethnic Options: Choosing Identities in America.* Berkeley, CA: University of California Press.

Watson, K. (1999). Language, power, development and geopolitical changes: conflicting pressures facing plurilingual societies. *Compare* 29, 5–22.

Watts, R. (1997). Language policies and education in Switzerland. In R. Watts and J. Smolicz (eds.), *Cultural Democracy and Ethnic Pluralism: Multicultural and Multilingual Policies in Education* (pp. 271–302). Frankfurt: Peter Lang.

Webber, J., and Strubell, M. (1991). *The Catalan Language. Progress Towards Normalisation.* London: Anglo-Catalan Society.

Weber, E. (1976). *Peasants into Frenchmen: The Modernization of Rural France 1870–1914.* Stanford, CA: Stanford University Press.

Weber, M. (1961). *From Max Weber: Essays in Sociology.* London: Routledge and Kegan Paul.

Weinstein, B. (1983). *The Civic Tongue: Political Consequences of Language Choices.* New York: Longman.

Weinstein, B. (1990). *Language Policy and Political Development.* Norwood, NJ: Ablex.

Welsh Language Board (1995). *Draft Guidelines as to the Form and Content of Schemes.* Cardiff: Welsh Language Board.

Welsh Office (1993). *Welsh Social Survey.* Cardiff: Statistics Section, Welsh Office.

Werbner, P. (1997a). Introduction: the dialectics of cultural hybridity. In P. Werbner and T. Modood (eds.), *Debating Cultural Hybridity: Multicultural Identities and the Politics of Antiracism* (pp. 1–26). London: Zed Books.

Werbner, P. (1997b). Essentialising essentialism, essentialising silence: ambivalence and multiplicity in the constructions of racism and ethnicity. In P. Werbner, and T. Modood (eds.), *Debating Cultural Hybridity: Multicultural Identities and the Politics of Antiracism* (pp. 226–254). London: Zed Books.

Werbner, P., and Modood, T. (eds.) (1997). *Debating Cultural Hybridity: Multicultural Identities and the Politics of Antiracism.* London: Zed Books.

Wetherell, M., and Potter, J. (1992). *Mapping the Language of Racism: Discourse and the Legitimation of Exploitation.* London: Harvester Wheatleaf.

Wicker, H.-R. (1997). From complex culture to cultural complexity. In P. Werbner and T. Modood (eds.), *Debating Cultural Hybridity: Multicultural Identities and the Politics of Antiracism* (pp. 29–45). London: Zed Books.

Wildavsky, A. (1992). Finding universalistic solutions to particularistic problems: bilingualism resolved through a second language requirement for elementary schools. *Journal of Policy Analysis and Management* 11, 310–314.

Williams, Charlotte (1995). 'Race' and racism: some reflections on the Welsh context. *Contemporary Wales* 8, 113–132.

Williams, Charlotte (1997). Colour in the pictures. *Planet* 125, 25–30.

Williams, Colin (1982). Separatism and the mobilisation of Welsh national identity. In C. Williams (ed.), *National Separatism* (pp. 145–201). Cardiff: University of Wales Press.

Williams, Colin (1990). The anglicisation of Wales. In N. Coupland (ed.), *English in Wales: Diversity, Conflict and Change* (pp. 19–47). Clevedon, England: Multilingual Matters.

Williams, Colin (1994). *Called unto Liberty: On Language and Nationalism*. Clevedon, England: Multilingual Matters.

Williams, Colin (1995). Questions concerning the development of bilingual Wales. In B. Morris Jones and P. Singh Ghuman (eds.), *Bilingualism, Education and Identity* (pp. 47–78). Cardiff: University of Wales Press.

Williams, Colin (1996). Ethnic identity and language issues in development. In D. Dwyer and D. Drakakis-Smith (eds.), *Ethnicity and Development: Geographical Perspectives* (pp. 45–85). London: John Wiley and Sons.

Williams, Colin, and Raybould, W. (1991). *Welsh Language Planning. Opportunities and Constraints*. Cardiff: PDAG.

Williams, E. (1989). The dynamic of Welsh identity. In N. Evans (ed.), *National Identity in the British Isles* (pp. 46–59). Harlech, Wales: Coleg Harlech.

Williams, Glyn (1987). Bilingualism, class dialect, and social reproduction. *International Journal of the Sociology of Language* 66, 85–98.

Williams, Glyn (1994). Discourses on 'nation' and 'race'. *Contemporary Wales* 6, 87–103.

Williams, Gwyn (1982). *The Welsh in their History*. London, Croom Helm.

Williams, Gwyn (1985). *When was Wales?* London: Penguin.

Williams, J. (1969). *Politics of the New Zealand Maori: Protest and Cooperation*. Auckland, New Zealand: Auckland University Press.

Williams, R. (1976). *Keywords*. London: Flamingo.

Willig, A. (1985). A meta-analysis of selected studies on the effectiveness of bilingual education. *Review of Educational Research* 55, 269–317.

Willig, A. (1987). Examining bilingual education research through meta-analysis and narrative review: a response to Baker. *Review of Educational Research* 57, 363–376.

Wilson, M. and Yeatman, A. (eds.) (1995). *Justice and Identity: Antipodean Practices*. Wellington, New Zealand: Bridget Williams Books.

Wolfrum, R. (1993). The emergence of 'new minorities' as a result of migration. In C. Brölmann, R. Lefeber and M. Zieck (eds.), *Peoples and Minorities in International Law* (pp. 153–166). Dordrecht, Netherlands: Martinus Nijhoff Publishers.

Wood, A. (1997). *Colin McCahon: The Man and the Teacher*. Auckland, New Zealand: David Ling.

Woolard, K. (1985). Catalonia: the dilemma of language rights. In N. Wolfson and J. Manes (eds.), *Language of Inequality* (pp. 91–109). Berlin: Mouton de Gruyter.

Woolard, K. (1986). The politics of language status planning: 'normalization' in Catalonia. In N. Schweda-Nicolson (ed.), *Languages in the International Perspective* (pp. 91–104). Norwood, NJ: Ablex.

Woolard, K. (1989). *Double Talk: Bilingualism and the Politics of Ethnicity in Catalonia*. Stanford, CA: Stanford University Press.

Woolard, K. (1998). Introduction: language ideology as a field of inquiry. In B. Schieffelin, K. Woolard and P. Kroskrity (eds.), *Language Ideologies: Practice and Theory* (pp. 3–47). New York: Oxford University Press.

Worsley, P. (1984). *The Three Worlds: Culture and World Development*. London: Weidenfeld and Nicholson.

Wright, S. (1999). A community that can communicate? The linguistic factor in European integration. In D. Smith and S. Wright (eds.), *Whose Europe? The Turn Towards Democracy* (pp. 79–103). Oxford: Blackwell / Sociological Review.

Wright, S. (2000). *Community and Communication: The Role of Language in Nation State Building and European Integration*. Clevedon, England: Multilingual Matters.

Yates, A. (1998). Language, democracy and devolution in Catalonia: a response to Miquel Strubell. *Current Issues in Language and Society* 5, 204–209.

Yinger, M. (1994). *Ethnicity: Source of Strength? Source of Conflict?* Albany, NY: SUNY Press.

Young, I. (1989). Polity and group difference: a critique of the ideal of universal citizenship. *Ethics* 99, 250–274.

Young, I. (1990). *Justice and the Politics of Difference*. Princeton, NJ: Princeton University Press.

Young, I. (1993). Together in difference: transforming the logic of group political conflict. In J. Squires (ed.), *Principled Positions: Postmodernism and the Rediscovery of Value* (pp. 121–150). London: Lawrence and Wishart.

Young, I. (1997). Difference as a resource for democratic communication. In J. Bohman and W. Rehg (eds.), *Deliberative Democracy: Essays on Reason and Politics* (pp. 383–406). Cambridge, MA: MIT Press.

Young, I. (forthcoming). Two concepts of self-determination. In S. May, T. Modood and J. Squires (eds.), *Ethnicity, Nationalism and Minority Rights*. Cambridge: Cambridge University Press.

Yuval-Davis, N. (1997a). *Gender and the Nation*. London: Sage.

Yuval-Davis, N. (1997b). Ethnicity, gender relations and multiculturalism. In P. Werbner and T. Modood (eds.), *Debating Cultural Hybridity: Multicultural Identities and the Politics of Antiracism* (pp. 193–208). London: Zed Books.

Zentella, A. (1997). The Hispanophobia of the Official English movement in the US. *International Journal of the Sociology of Language* 127, 71–86.

Index